Twentieth-Century Caribbean Literature

This bold study traces the processes by which a 'history' and canon of Caribbean literature and criticism have been constructed, and offers a supplement to that history by suggesting new writers, texts and critical moments that help to reconfigure the Caribbean tradition.

Focusing on Anglophone or Anglocreole writings from across the twentieth century, Alison Donnell asks what it is that we read when we approach 'Caribbean Literature', how it is that we read it, and what critical, ideological and historical pressures may have shaped our choices and approaches. In particular, she:

- addresses the exclusions that have resulted from the construction of a Caribbean canon
- rethinks the dominant paradigms of Caribbean literary criticism, which have foregrounded issues of anti-colonialism and nationalism; migration and diaspora; the 'doubly-colonised' woman; the marginalisation of sexuality and homosexuality
- seeks to put new issues and writings into critical circulation, by reading lesser-known authors and texts, including Indian Caribbean women's writings and Caribbean queer writings.

Identifying alternative critical approaches and alternative critical moments, *Twentieth-Century Caribbean Literature* allows us to re-examine the way in which we read not only Caribbean writings, but also the literary history and criticism that surround them.

Alison Donnell is Reader in Postcolonial Literatures and English at Nottingham Trent University. She is co-editor of *The Routledge Reader in Caribbean Literature* (1996) and has published widely in the field of Caribbean and postcolonial writings. She is also Joint Editor of *Interventions: International Journal of Postcolonial Studies*.

Besides the intelligence and acuity of the readings of individual texts that *Twentieth-Century Caribbean Literature* provides, it amounts to nothing less than a radical challenge to the canon of Caribbean literature and its repressions. It is the only comprehensive sketch of all the major blind spots of Caribbean literary history and criticism, identifying and correcting not only the exclusions of nationalist canons, but also of post-nationalism and feminist ones. It is also the first systematic attempt at tracing representations of homosexuality across Anglophone Caribbean literature. Donnell thus puts into critical circulation a rich, unruly, and diverse body of literature. (Indeed, though I have specialized in Caribbean literature for several years, this book brought to my attention texts I had no idea existed.) One of the particular pleasures of Donnell's work is its delicate intertwining of theoretical and literary insight.'

Shalini Puri, *University of Pittsburgh*

This book will extend the archive of Caribbean texts in challenging and exciting ways and is likely to initiate more generous and promiscuous readings of Caribbean writings, as well as making a valuable contribution to debates about the local and the global which are so central to postcolonial studies.

Denise deCaires Narain, *University of Sussex*

Twentieth-Century Caribbean Literature

Critical moments in anglophone literary history

Alison Donnell

 Routledge
Taylor & Francis Group

LONDON AND NEW YORK

First published 2006
by Routledge
2/4 Park Square, Milton Park, Abingdon, Oxon OX14 4RN

Simultaneously published in the USA and Canada
by Taylor & Francis Inc
270 Madison Ave, New York, NY 10016

Routledge is an imprint of the Taylor & Francis Group

© 2006 Alison Donnell

Typeset in Baskerville by
Florence Production Ltd, Stoodleigh, Devon
Printed and bound in Great Britain by
The Cromwell Press, Trowbridge, Wiltshire

British Library Cataloguing in Publication Data
A catalogue record for this book is available from the British Library

Library of Congress Cataloguing in Publication Data
Donnell, Alison, 1966–.
   Twentieth-century Caribbean literature: critical moments in Anglophone
literary history/Alison Donnell.
       p. cm.
   Includes bibliographical references (p. 000).
   1. Caribbean literature (English) – History and criticism – Theory, etc.
   2. Caribbean literature – 20th century – History and criticism – Theory,
   etc.   3. Caribbean Area – Intellectual life – 20th century.   4. Caribbean
   Area – In literature.   I. Title: 20th century Caribbean literature.
   II. Title.
   PR9205.D66 2006
   820.9′9729′0904–dc22   2005009603

ISBN10: 0–415–26199–6   ISBN13: 9–78–0–415–26199–9 (hbk)
ISBN10: 0–415–26200–3   ISBN13: 9–78–0–415–26200–2 (pbk)

For Jem

Contents

Cover Acknowledgements

Photograph courtesy of Paul Faulkner

Cover of *Small Axe*, Vol 7 reproduced by kind permission of Indiana University Press.

Cover of *Cereus Blooms at Night*, Shanti Mootoo, Granta, London, 1998. By kind permission of the publisher

Cover of *My Jamaican Village*, Erna Brodber, courtesy of the Author.

Cover of *An Island is a World*, Samuel Selvon, Tsar Publications, 1994. By kind permission of the publisher.

Cover of *The Swinging Bridge*. Published by Harper Collins Publishers Ltd. Copyright © 2003 by Rambai Espinet. All rights reserved.

Cover of *Tomorrow is Another Day*, Narmala Shewcharan, Peepal Tree Press, 1994. By kind permission of the publisher.

Cover of *The Routledge Reader in Caribbean Literature*, ed. Alison Donnell, Routledge, London, 1996. Reprinted by kind permission of the publisher.

Cover of *Women Writing the West Indies, 1804–1939: 'A Hot Place Belonging to Us'*, Evelyn O'Callaghan, Routledge, London, 2003. Reprinted by kind permission of the publisher.

Acknowledgements

I am very grateful to the Leverhulme Foundation for a Research Fellowship and funding to visit and to copy vital archives, and to the Department of English and Media Studies at Nottingham Trent University for study leave to complete this book. I also want to extend my thanks to Liz Thompson, my editor at Routledge, as well as Talia Rogers, both of whom have remained endlessly patient, encouraging and cheerful in their communications.

For the opportunity to explore and discuss many of the ideas that are published here I am grateful to the University of the West Indies, the Association of Caribbean Women Writers and Scholars, the Centre for Commonwealth Studies at Stirling University, the University of Oxford Postcolonial Seminar Series, The Open Lecture Series at the University of Gloucestershire and the Black British Canon Conference at University of Dundee.

Small portions from some of the chapters in this book were first published elsewhere: a version of my reading of *Aelred's Sin* in chapter 4 has been published in 'Reading for Reconciliation in Lawrence Scott's *Aelred's Sin*', *Moving Worlds: A Journal of Transcultural Writings* 3.2 (2004), 98–109; a much earlier reading of Olive Senior's poetry appears in 'Here and there in the work of Olive Senior: relocating diaspora discourses in relation to Caribbean women's writing' in *Centre of Remembrance*, Joan Anim-Addo (ed.) (Mango Publishing, 2002), 66–80; my analysis of Una Marson's poetry was given a partial and early hearing in 'Contradictory (W)omens? gender consciousness in the poetry of Una Marson', *Kunapipi*, XVII (1995), 43–58. For permission to use their book covers for my own, I am grateful to Harper Collins Canada, Granta Books, Blackspace, Tsar Publications, Peepal Tree Press and Indiana University Press.

This book has taken a very long time to appear and I have accrued many debts of patience, advice and inspiration along the way. I want to extend my thanks to Helen Taylor and the late (and great) Anna Rutherford who both offered vital encouragement and support at the beginning of my career. I am extremely grateful to Elleke Boehmer, Carolyn Cooper, Denise deCaires Narain, James Procter, Shalini Puri, Katy Stanley and

Greg Woods for their comments and friendly advice on parts of the manuscript at various stages. The many faults and errors that remain are stubbornly my own.

Several of my colleagues deserve special mention: Rajeswari Sunder Rajan and Robert Young, my fellow editors on *Interventions: International Journal of Postcolonial Studies*, who have been a source of constant, if daunting, inspiration and whose shared discussions on postcolonial studies have kept me on my toes; Evelyn O'Callaghan and Denise deCaires Narain who have been generous in their intellectual companionship and friendship; Elleke Boehmer with whom I have shared many positive postcolonial moments over the years and whose energy and commitment remains an inspiration; and Carolyn Cooper, with whom I had the privilege and the pleasure to co-edit a Special Issue of *Interventions*.

I would like to thank all my colleagues for their support and friendship, especially Roberta Davari, Gail Low, Susheila Nasta, Velma Pollard, Sheila Rampersad, Ruvani Ranasinha, Milena Rodella, Lynnette Turner, Patrick Williams, and Nahem Yousaf. Thanks are also due to Natasha Barnes, Leela Gandhi, and Antonia McDonald Smythe, who in brief, enjoyable bursts of companionship have all helped to stretch my thoughts. My gratitude goes to all my students at Nottingham Trent University who, over the last ten years, have often been the first, and most honest, audience for many of my theories and whose comments and questions (and sometimes resistance) have been genuinely instructive.

Despite all the academic support that I have acknowledged, this book would simply not have been possible without my friends and family. Just for keeping me laughing and almost sane, I am immensely thankful to my good friends Paula, Caroline, Carol and Dras. Enormous love and respect is due to my mother who inadvertently turned me into a scholar by insisting that I didn't work too hard during my rebellious years! For simply sustaining the possibilities of my being at all levels, my thanks and love to Jeremy. And to Max and Asher, my sweet boys, for whom my thanks and blessings cannot be measured, more love and, at last, the odd turn in goal!

Introduction

> Properly practiced, one might argue, criticism is a community's mode of *remembering*. It is a form of putting back together (re-membering) aspects of our common life in ways that make visible what has been obscured, what has been forgotten, what has disappeared from view.
>
> (David Scott)

> Sometimes you does have to start thinking all over again when you feel you have things down the right way.
>
> (Sam Selvon)

Perhaps the most important debates with which Caribbean writers have persistently engaged have been those concerning history – both the history of colonialism and the history of English Literature. Yet the history of Caribbean writing is rarely addressed as a subject of such struggle or contestation. This book is, in part, a historiography of Caribbean literary history and criticism and, in part, a supplement to that history which seeks to suggest new writers, texts and critical moments that might help to reconfigure the Caribbean tradition as more movable, divergent and unruly. It asks what it is that we read when we approach Caribbean literature, how it is that we read it, and what critical, ideological and historical pressures may have shaped our choices and approaches. It is concerned to explore how Anglophone or Anglocreole Caribbean literary histories have emerged and been legitimised at particular historical moments, as well as why and how we should read those texts and literary moments that no longer feed into the current set of critical demands?[1]

The book is structured around readings of what I want to argue have been 'critical' moments in the literary history of the Anglocreole Caribbean. Three of the chapters offer strategic re-readings of naturalised critical paradigms and revisit the texts and writers neglected or dismissed by these dominant versions, and the final chapter suggests an alternative moment not yet documented. Throughout, the concern is to encourage new traffic between the present and the received past on offer, to provide new peepholes, supplementary histories and alternative moments that may allow us to re-examine the ways in which twentieth century Anglocreole Caribbean writing, a notably diverse and lively literary archive, may be read and understood from a point at the beginning of the twenty-first century. This book does not claim to offer a coherent or alternative literary history but rather to destabilise and interrogate some of the collisions between literature, cultural politics, theory and history in order to offer a series of provocations to those versions that have emerged to date. It does not have all the answers, but its objective is to look critically at the particular visions and blind spots that characterize the practice of reading Anglocreole Caribbean writing in the present.

Thinking critically about the category 'Caribbean Literature' has been at the heart of my academic research for the last fifteen years. My focus on the 'why?' as well as on the 'what'? and the 'how?' has emerged not least because from almost the very moment that I began my own research career in this field I was constantly asked to identify the reasons for my choice. Why was it that I was studying Caribbean writing when I was not linked to the region by birth, geography or ancestry? And then, often from more knowing interlocutors, why, given that I had chosen to study Caribbean literature, was I researching a group of women poets writing pre-1950 rather than reading what were then the few acknowledged 'greats' such as Lamming, Naipaul, Harris, Walcott or Selvon? Looking back I can see that the answers to these two questions are linked by my intellectual determination to look away from those writers and texts that were already receiving critical attention within the academy and whose value was understood as given and stable. I am aware that my choice to research Caribbean literature was informed by my belief that our connections to others can be based upon a self-critical understanding of difference that need not rely on any essential sameness nor deny the significance of differences. Clearly as a non-Caribbean critic of Caribbean literature my approach is different and, although I shall inevitably be operating with certain blind spots, I hope that I may also have some added insights of an outsider's eye. It is perhaps this sense of being an outsider to the tradition that has made marginal archives, with their inbuilt tensions and ambivalences, particularly productive resources in my work.

In many ways my own critical interests have developed alongside and within the emergent body of postcolonial scholarship that has developed in the UK since the 1980s and they have also been influenced by this critical paradigm. Arguably more than any other branch of literary studies, postcolonial literary criticism has worried away at itself over the last twenty years and transformed itself to emerge almost unrecognisable from the early days of cross-cultural readings and creative anthropology that traded under the banner of Commonwealth Literature. As an interdisciplinary practice drawing on the models and pathways of postcolonial theory, itself a multidisciplinary project which draws on the archives of cultural studies, women's studies, political economics and history among others, it has consistently interrogated the issues and debates concerning domination, equality and liberation that continue to shape the political and literary dynamics of our postcolonial world in the twenty-first century.

As a body of scholarship that seeks to engage with intellectual radicalism and aspires to collaborate with political activism, postcolonial studies is a similar institutional and disciplinary animal to feminism and shares the same uneasy status. Indeed, I would even suggest that in a sense, post-colonial theory has recently walked in the footsteps of feminist criticism in an important way. At its inception feminist criticism was often a term which denoted the study of women's lives, writings and achievements that had previously been marginalised, devalued and misread. This emphasis upon the recuperation, re-evaluation and celebration of women's cultural productions, political interventions and written works has been immensely influential in its many guises and contexts around the world and the issue of gender equality is now better understood and more widely debated as a result. However, many prominent feminist critics have now turned their critical attentions to the subject of masculinity, reframing their interests in terms of a deconstruction of models of dominance that continue to impact negatively on women's and human rights. I would argue that a similar shift has taken place in postcolonial scholarship away from a focus on the unacknowledged talent, agency and identity of the ex-colonised subaltern class and towards the study of globalisation, neo-liberalism and the new 'Empire'. In both cases it is easy to understand that these shifts are informed by the demands for social transformation and an understanding that if we are to effect changes, to bring about justice and equality, then maybe the stumbling blocks to such transformation should be the targets of our intel-lectual energies. However, one consequence of this shift in critical and theoretical agendas has been a downgrading of the 'singularity of litera-ture', to borrow Derek Attridge's term. In the context of a resurgence of American militarism and imperialism, of ethnic violence or of the global AIDS pandemic, it is not unfair to say that close readings of literary texts are often regarded as rather ineffectual, misdirected and even outdated.

In Caribbean studies at present, the celebration of the literary also seems to be waning as many key theorists and critics look to the popular and the oral as the primary sites of cultural invention and resistance (see Scott, Cooper, Gilroy). Others still seem to have reconfigured the Caribbean as a cultural idea rather than an actual region, a dislocated, mobile, hybrid space attractive to the demands of postcolonial theory and its alliances to migrant subjectivities and writings (Boyce-Davies, Clifford). This can be read as a response to the fact that the traditional subjects of history, memory and language find bolder and perhaps more seemingly radical articulation in popular cultural forms and that many writers are writing from outside the region. My focus on Caribbean literature is aimed at

rerouting discussions of representational agency and cultural power back
through a literary tradition which has a very strong history of radical
writing. It is a central objective of this book to demonstrate that, taken as
a whole, writing from the Caribbean across the twentieth century still
holds enormous potential for exploring the issues and debates about cultural
politics, ethnicity, gender and sexuality that continue to be intellectually
urgent in the twenty-first century.

Although my own research has now taken me beyond the 1930s and
an interest in 'women-only' writing, my engagement with the field is still
crucially informed by this interest in what is not commonly attended
to, in the questions that are not being taken up and in the continued
pressures that theoretical and historical imperatives can have on textual
archives. One of the main aims of this book is a critical recomposition
of twentieth century Anglocreole Caribbean writings as a century-long
archive of works by both men and women. It is an interesting feature of
the critical profile of this body of writing that male writers have retained
distinct, individual identities (Walcott, Brathwaite, Naipaul, Selvon), whereas
women writers, although critically well attended to, tend to be designated
as such, under a collective gendered identity. In addition, no book on this
subject has given sustained attention to writing before 1950 as part of the
same body of work as writing produced after Independence. I would argue
that to date, previous scholarship has approached this very diverse tradition of writing in one of three ways. First, through a traditional critical
lens, focusing on the work of a few prominent male writers (Brown, Wilson-
Tagoe, Harney); second, by offering a generally chronological narrative
which examines almost no writing by women except for in an 'annexed'
chapter on 'women's writing' (King, James, Juneja), or third, by examining
only women's writing (O'Callaghan, deCaires Narain) and situating it
within a paradigm of 'black women's writing' (Boyce-Davies, Chancy).
This book is informed throughout by an inclusive understanding of
Anglocreole Caribbean literature from the whole century, incorporating
material from both canonical and neglected writers, consciously challenging
previous gender, ethnic and historical divides and enabling a reading of
different Caribbean literary material, as well as a reading of more familiar
material in different ways.

Given that all histories and traditions are based on acts of selection,
exclusion and preference (my own here included), it is my aim to discuss
the ideological and historical struggles that have informed Caribbean
literary histories to date. To this end, the book is structured around a
series of critical moments. By this I mean to suggest something akin to
David Scott's notion of a 'problem space' which he outlines in his 1999
book *Refashioning Futures: Criticism after Postcoloniality*. For Scott the problem
space is mapped out by the critical demands placed on works to speak
for specific conceptual, political and theoretical positions. It is by addressing
these problem spaces as historically contingent, and by interrogating the

grounds on which the questions which form these problem spaces have emerged, that Scott is able to '[reconfigure] the conceptual terrain in which an object is located' (1999: 9). Although I would align my own methodology with Scott's practice of strategic criticism I am not as concerned with 'determining at any conjecture what conceptual moves among the many available options will have the most purchase, the best yield', as I am with determining at certain specific conjectures how certain yields have come to be valued over others and often to dominate and obscure these others (Scott 1999: 7). Nevertheless, Scott's practice of critical engagement with the problem spaces of the past in order to bring their potential to the light of a new set of questions is extremely useful to my own project.

> A strategic practice of criticism will ask whether the moment of normalization of a paradigm is not also the moment when it is necessary to reconstruct and reinterrogate the ground of questions themselves through which it was brought into being in the first place; to ask whether the critical *yield* of the normal problem space continues to be what it was when it first emerged; and, if not, to ask what set of questions is emerging in the new problem-space that might reconfigure and so expand the conceptual terrain in which an object is located.
>
> (Scott 1999: 8–9)

By examining four critical moments through which I argue the paradigms of Caribbean literary criticism have become normalised around a cluster of issues – anti-colonialism, nationalism; migration and diaspora; the centrality of African Caribbean ethnicity; the concept of women as doubly colonised and the marginalisation of sexuality and homosexuality – this book seeks to revisit crucial problem spaces that have been influential in the emergence of Caribbean literary criticism.

However, it is not only my aim to identify and discuss these critical moments but also to challenge their normalisation and their function in the production of certain textual orthodoxies by reading alternative bodies of texts which bring a new set of demands to these paradigms, sometimes challenging their political-theoretical axes and sometimes revealing the issues and archives they have neglected or suppressed. So while Scott's aim is 'to intervene in – so as to contribute in some way to altering – the existing configuration of the discursive space inhabited by postcolonial criticism', my own more modest objective is to make several interventions in the current configuration of Caribbean literary criticism and history (Scott 1999: 15). My project then is, in part, re-evaluative, as I wish to go back to the questions that have shaped Anglocreole Caribbean literary histories and traditions, and to ask whether they remain relevant and productive now. It is also, in part, a recuperative project that aims to show those writers and texts that the focus on these critical moments has eschewed or eclipsed.

The project is constantly negotiating the possibilities and the pitfalls of tradition. As Scott reminds us:

> Tradition is an active process that . . . depends on a social will, on an active and ongoing labour; that it is not about the past as such but its connection to the present and an anticipated future. On this account, in other words, a tradition is not merely – indeed not at all – about received wisdom or about the mere celebration of what we suppose our forefathers did. For tradition is not merely inheritance, something that you *get*. Tradition is not a passive, absorptive relation between the past and the present. Rather tradition presupposes an active relation in which the present *calls upon* the past . . . In this sense too tradition is not principally about what happened in the past: it is less nostalgia than memory, and memory more as a source and sustenance of *vision*.
>
> (Scott 1999: 115)

It is perhaps not surprising that Scott sees this relation between past and present that tradition offers as enabling, given the fact that his comments are made in the context of his reading of T. S. Eliot's essay 'Tradition and the Individual Talent' in the service of Brathwaite. As Scott argues, for Brathwaite, Eliot's understanding of tradition is read as particularly productive in his own quest to trace and situate the resources of such a tradition in the African cultural presence in the West Indies. Although I would completely endorse Scott's view that tradition is formed by how the present calls upon the past to represent itself, I would want to see this as a more strategic and ideologically invested activity that needs to be opened to scrutiny in order to reveal the possibilities for other, different relations between the past and the present to be represented.

I wish to discuss the ways in which at certain critical moments the 'nationalist', the 'resistant', the 'oppressed' and the 'displaced' have been constructed as bona fide figures of Caribbeanness and how, in these moments, only they have been allowed to occupy the place of the ethical or the redemptive subject. I also want to examine the consequences that these strategic investments have had on the opening up of new critical pathways and the foreclosure of others. It is my argument that by focusing on these critical moments that are both troublesome and illuminating to our current notions of tradition, we can re-locate an engaged and engaging tradition of Caribbean literature by men and women and across the whole of the twentieth century, as well as a literary archive both involved with and animated by questions of social justice, oppositional agency and cultural belonging.

As it is one of the aims of this study to show how every history is based on exclusions, then it is perhaps only fair to announce from the outset what is to be left out of this historical narrative. In the sense that this is a study of the exclusions, eclipses and eschewals embedded in other West Indian literary histories, it is perhaps not surprising that what is omitted in this text is the core body of writers and texts so favoured by general survey works. The base line of Anglocreole Caribbean writing – Walcott, Lamming, Naipaul, Rhys – are not given sustained attention in this study precisely because I am arguing that the profile, prestige and platforms accorded to these literary voices at various stages of literary history have served to drown out the more subtle, strained and sometimes discordant tones of many others, still waiting to be heard. Nevertheless, it is certainly not my aim to marginalize these texts, many of which have nurtured my own understanding of Caribbean Literature and prompted my wider reading in the area.

In the first chapter, I am interested to look back to the early literary histories of the region's writing which appeared in the immediate post-colonial period and to revisit their critical agendas, locating them in the critical moment of cultural nationalism. My aim is also to try to open the archive of pre-1950 writings that the vast majority of literary histories simply do not want to reckon with, in order to revisit those works and cultural positions that the pressures of the critical moment of the 1960s and 1970s served to suppress, especially those which had an investment in European forms and conventions. I want therefore to offer a model for reading material which can be less comfortably read through a history of decolonisation and the dominant critical apparatus which has emerged post-colonisation. In particular I shall focus on Jamaica and the very different but coexistent positions of J. E. C. McFarlane and Roger Mais that help to disturb the idea of a linear progressive tradition. I also want to read poetry by Tropica, Constance Hollar and Thomas MacDermot, as well as works by Una Marson and Vivian Virtue in order to discuss the overlapping and complex registers of affective nationalism and loyalty to Empire that characterise many works in this moment.

The second chapter focuses on the politics of place in Caribbean writing and takes issue with the strong pull that black diasporic criticism has exerted on the reception of Caribbean writings since the early 1990s and the publication of Paul Gilroy's *The Black Atlantic*. It examines the way in which a preference for migration over settlement and dislocation over location has influenced those texts that are being read and discussed. The chapter seeks to resist the wake of Black Atlantic criticism by reconsidering the particular relations between the local and the global, the national and the diasporic that need to be attended to within the Anglocreole Caribbean region. Olive Senior's poetry is read as renegotiating the terms of diaspora both for those who travel and those who are left behind. A reading of two short works by Erna Brodber addresses the idea of place in terms of the spatially bounded and the local in order to reframe the idea of a global village. Issues of cultural belonging and homecoming are also discussed with reference to the poetry of Albinia Mackay (Hutton) and the 'Scottish' poems of her 1912 collection. Although part of a much earlier and white archive, these works also demonstrate an interest in the issues of origin, displacement and belonging. The chapter ends with a discussion of Earl Lovelace's *Salt* alongside Sam Selvon's *An Island Is a World* which helps to enunciate the experience of settlement and an engagement with the conditions of the nation as an alternative redemptive model to that of the Black Atlantic.

The third chapter is concerned to reconsider the gender politics of Caribbean literary history by contesting the term 'double colonisation' that has arguably served to figure women's writing before the 1970s and 1980s as voiceless and invisible. Arguing for a more robust connection between feminist literary criticism and feminist historiography, this chapter offers the figure of the double agent in order to consider how Caribbean women writers can be seen to mobilise gender, as well as ethnicity and cultural identity, as a site of resistance, affirmation and oppositional agency. I begin the chapter by extending my critique of the erasure of the Caribbean with the triangular orbit of the Black Atlantic to a discussion of black diasporic feminist theories and literary critical studies of women's writing published in this powerful moment. I then move on to a discussion of Caribbean feminist historiography that has importantly rebalanced the dynamics between knowledge and power and the possibilities for more informed localised studies such as those of Evelyn O'Callaghan and Carolyn Cooper. Seeking to map out the particular issues that have animated Caribbean feminism and its discontents, I also aim to sketch important directions in indigenous feminist theorising emerging from within the region.

In order to examine what is at stake in both the denial and recovery of a female literary ancestry, given the almost total neglect of women's writing pre-1970, I discuss the various critical moments at and through which Una Marson has been brought to critical visibility and the pressure that these moments have exerted on her literary reputation and archive. I offer readings of Una Marson's early poetry which highlights double agency in its creative feedback to orthodox modes of interpretation, including feminist theory, in order to reconfigure the relationship between literary and theoretical discourses. The final section of this chapter brings scholarship around women's writing into dialogue with the marginalisation of Indian-Caribbean literary works and criticism within the Caribbean canon. Despite the fact that much writing on the subject of feminism in the Caribbean has foregrounded the importance of bringing ethnicity into the orbit of gender politics, very little attention has been paid to Indian-Caribbean women's writing to date. Reading works by Narmala Shewcharan and Ramabai Espinet, I examine the kinds of interventions that Indian-Caribbean women writers and critics have made in recent years in order to stage their own politics and ethics of resistance and liberation. In particular, I outline two new indigenous models through which

Caribbean women's writing is being theorised in the present critical moment. First is Rosanne Kanhai's deployment of the Hindu fertility ritual of *matikor* and its release of erotic energy as a marker of the confident and independent epistemic ground from which Indian-Caribbean women can structure their literary and historical agency. Second is Shalini Puri's concept of dougla poetics that is central to the urgent project of establishing ethical and creative relations between women of different ethnic groups.

The final chapter seeks to situate a critical moment that is emerging in the present through the articulation of sexuality within Caribbean writings, and in particular the articulation of diverse sexualities. During the 1990s when the Buju Banton 'battyman' affair in Jamaica brought the sexual politics of that island to international attention, and the wave of legislation regarding the criminialisation of certain sexual behaviours throughout the region similarly sparked many discussions of sexual politics and sexual rights, Caribbean writers began publishing texts addressing the issues of sexual self-determination and sexual diversity. This chapter will discuss Clem Maharaj's short novel, *The Dispossessed* (1992), as an explicitly sexualised plantation novel. Edwidge Danticat's *Breath, Eyes, Memory* (1994) and Jamaica Kincaid's *Lucy* (1990) are analysed in the context of women's rewriting of Caribbean sexual histories, and particularly the way in which these histories demand the release of historical trauma and pain. Oona Kempadoo's *Buxton Spice* (1998) continues the articulation of sexuality by bringing both the physical tension of adolescence and the political tension of 1970s Guyana to print. Dionne Brand's novel *In Another Place, Not Here* and Shani Mootoo's collection of short stories, *Out on Main Street* are read for their representation of lesbian identity and Lawrence Scott's *Aelred's Sin* as initiating a tradition of male homoerotics for the Caribbean. The representation of AIDS is discussed with reference to Jamaica Kincaid's *My Brother*, Patricia Powell's *A Small Gathering of Bones* and Thom Cross's *The Final Truth*. Finally, Shani Mootoo's novel, *Cereus Blooms at Night*, is read as a text that both represents the troubling consequences of the heterosexual imperatives which operate in the Caribbean, and also offers us the terms of a new social contract through which sexual difference can be mapped onto the identity matrix of Caribbeaness.

Note

1 I use the term Anglocreole in preference to the more usual anglophone throughout in order to indicate that this study looks at works written in the creole languages of the English-speaking region, as well as in Standard English. The term is a transposition of Carolyn Cooper's useful creole/anglophone term that privileges the creole within the Caribbean linguistic spectrum.

1 Difficult subjects
Caribbean writing before the boom

> The New World black had tried to prove that he was as good as his master, when he should have proven not his equality but his difference.
>
> (Derek Walcott, 'What the Twilight Says' 1970)

> Before my eyes a new generation has sprung up which knows very little of the good and great of just a generation ago. This . . . will remind them that not so long ago there lived amongst us men and women inspired and inspiring who have helped to make Jamaica of the present.
>
> (P. W. Gibson, Lord Bishop of Jamaica, 1956)

As I have explained in the introduction to this book, my own Ph.D. thesis was an examination of Jamaican women's poetry 1900–1950. I was very motivated at that time, the late 1980s, to study women's writing as this project connected productively to my interests in feminist theory and gendered forms of knowledge. I found much encouragement among my peers and mentors for this focus on women's writing but far less for my determination to focus on the pre-1950 period. Many colleagues and advisors seemed concerned, even troubled, by my choice to look exclusively at Caribbean writing before the 'boom'. At a time when so many indisputedly wonderful writings were being published by Caribbean women writers such as Erna Brodber, Merle Collins, Jamaica Kincaid, Olive Senior and many others, why did I choose to spend several years of my life reading volumes of poetry and handmade scrapbooks that were notoriously difficult to locate, and once found often uneven and unentertaining at their best? I cannot claim that my choice was goverened by a literary archive that was compelling in its own right. As some of what follows will make clear, it was often a struggle to work productively with many of the volumes that I tracked down and dutifully copied. The point is that what I had really selected through my choice of material and moment were deliberately difficult and awkward subjects, subjects whose work was not only *unknown* to most readers, even within the fairly small specialist field of that time, but whose works were almost *unknowable* to the frameworks and pathways that had then been established for reading Caribbean Literature.

I had been warned that the work I had chosen was juvenile, imitative, politically uncomfortable and aesthetically unworthy. However, this collective writing off of a whole period – a period that I now want to try to re-read as having been disavowed at a particularly crucial critical moment in the development of Caribbean Literature and its reception, the 1960s and 1970s, only made my research more interesting and my conviction stronger. In the decade and a half that has passed since I made my selection of research material for the Ph.D. study, there has been an enormous development in the field of criticism relating to women's writing. It requires something of an imaginative leap to remember that gender was once a marginal category in critical formations or that studying women's writing may have been seen as something of a radical decision. However, attitudes to Caribbean literature from the first half of the twentieth century certainly have not undergone a similar transformation, and the historical moment that was the consciously marginal centre of my study then remains somewhat out of view in the vast majority of studies today.

Indeed, in place of a literary history, Caribbean writing often seems to generate an extraordinary myth of a doubled spontaneous genesis. The first is London in the 1950s with the 'boom' of male writers (Lamming, Naipaul, Selvon) and the second is the 1970s, or even 1980s, usually centred on Jamaica, with a sudden 'explosion' of women's writing. In this chapter my concern is to examine how and why 1950 has remained an enduring genesis moment as well as to consider what came before this new beginning for Caribbean writing. There are still very few critical works that offer a sustained reading of writings from before 1950 and those that do tend to concentrate on a narrow and contained archive, not relating what has gone before to what is there now, or what has not been read before to what is being read now. Some texts from the pre-1950 period have been brought into view but because the claims and narratives that have persistently kept the majority of works out of sight and marginal to configurations of the canon have not been self-reflective about their own exclusions, new conditions for their critical visibility have not yet been established.

In 2002, A. L. McLeod published *Wings of the Evening: Selected Poems of Vivian Virtue* with a substantial critical introduction. McLeod begins this piece by relating the broad contours of Virtue's decline in poetic standing.

> In November 1938 New Dawn Press in Kingston, Jamaica, issued its inaugural publication, *Wings of the Morning*, a volume of poems by Vivian Lancaster Virtue, in an edition of 500 copies (400 bound in hard covers and 100 bound in cloth). By commercial standards anywhere in the English-speaking world at the time, this was a remarkably

ambitious undertaking, for it was Virtue's first book . . . His later poetic enterprises have remained unknown to all but a few, since he led a somewhat reclusive literary retirement . . . As a consequence, over the years his poetry has received decreasing attention in studies of West Indian literature.

(McLeod 2002: 1–2)

I have every admiration for McLeod's dedicated and careful recuperation of Virtue's work which also extends to gifting an archive of his papers to Pennsylvania State University where McLeod is based. However, I cannot be persuaded that it was only Virtue's personal retreat that caused attention to his writings to wane. Beyond the local reviews that McLeod quotes from in his introduction, it is difficult to locate critical studies that pay serious attention to his work even during the years he spent at the heart of Jamaican poetry circles. Given that Virtue was writing rondeaux and villanelles and that, as Professor H. A. Hamilton noted in a personal letter to Virtue in 1939, his verse was marked by 'the absence of the note of protest which appears naturally enough in some Jamaica poetry', it is clear to me that the odds were already stacked against his critical survival. I will discuss the intricacies of Virtue's verse and the problems of critical reception later in this chapter, but it is sufficient to say that given the urgent need to create a distinct cultural identity for Jamaicans at the time when Virtue was first published (1937 had seen the General Strike and 1938 the Moyne Commission) and the continued demands since then for responsive and relevant literary works that somehow connect to the voices, concerns and lives of Jamaican people, it is not surprising that his work has not been central to constructions of the island's or region's poetic tradition. Furthermore, I cannot share McLeod's optimism that as a result of his own edition of Virtue's poems 'it will be difficult to relegate him again to the periphery, known to and appreciated by only the cognoscenti and the historians of literature' (McLeod 2002: 38). Without a significant revision of literary historical paradigms it will be almost impossible to bring Virtue out of the margins, for reasons I shall come to discuss.

Evelyn O'Callaghan's 2003 study *Women Writing the West Indies, 1804–1939* brings to light a fascinating archive of women's narratives that, with the exception of those by Mary Prince and Mary Seacole, are seldom even alluded to in conventional literary histories of the region. O'Callaghan also makes it clear that she regards her contribution in this work as significant to configurations of the wider critical field:

Attention to the early accounts by women adds to the body of literary representations of the region in unforseen and illuminating ways. These narratives form part of the feminist and postcolonial projects of recuperating lost or silenced voices, and comparing their insights and formal strategies with later writing by women of the region, may help to deflect us from categorising Caribbean women's writing in a narrowly prescriptive manner.

(O'Callaghan 2003: 9–10)

However, despite O'Callaghan's convincing account of these narratives as early interventions in the creation of a tradition of West Indian women's writing and her own impressive and extensive scholarship in the area of early women's narratives, there is little evidence to date that other scholars are willing to look back with interest, or to revise the historical or aesthetic boundaries that prop up the received stable, known categories such as Caribbean writing, or Caribbean women's writing, through their encounter with 'early' texts. Although the two publications that I have cited offer some indication that writers from this early period are being reclaimed and recirculated as I write this study, they are only very faint indications and my sense is that this work will not be widely circulated.

To my mind, the rebuttal of writings before the boom by several subsequent generations of Caribbean critics is not solely attributable to the material difficulties of negotiating the libraries, archives and other institutions in order to conduct serious study, although these should not be underestimated in comparison to the relative ease of studying post-1950 writers and their works, especially in the current academic climate when graduate students are all too aware of the demands to publish frequently. What is really at stake here is the way in which and the reasons why critical agendas have remained remarkably set in their chronologies with regard to Caribbean writing. Given that the dismissal of pre-1950 writings has remained a relatively stable trait in Caribbean literary histories since the first wave of critical studies appeared in the 1960s and 1970s, it is important to ask why the judgements of this critical moment have been so powerful and pervasive in subsequent decades. It is the objective of this chapter to try and interrogate this trend as well as to bring writings from this difficult moment to critical attention in such a way as to try to re-establish the complexity of both cultural forms and politics pre-1950, thereby opening this archive up to the present and the future.

Marking the critical moment

As is now well documented, the idea of a West Indian or Caribbean aesthetic, although surfacing in several scattered projects from the beginning of the twentieth century, gained its currency on a wider scale during the 1930s and 1940s. This idea appears as an issue for debate in early 1930s editorials of the *Beacon* in Trinidad and finds expression in Esther Chapman's Jamaican-based venture, *West Indian Review*, that actively sought to publish across linguistic as well as geographical boundaries from 1934. *Bim*, edited in Barbados from 1942, *Focus*, the Jamaican literary and critical periodical edited from 1943 and the federalist journal *Kyk-Over-Al*, which was founded in 1945 in British Guyana, all also contributed to the circulation and publication of writings from different regions and thereby made the idea of a West Indian Literature both more visible and more viable.

As Lamming has pointed out, far from being naive and disconnected voices of an earlier era, many of these ventures and the discussions they aired fed directly into the later debates about cultural relevance and responsibility that became central to the cultural nationalist project as it developed in relation to literature.

> If you look at *Bim* you will find that the composition of the writers in *Bim* changed from about 1947. By 1948 and 1949, there was a Trinidad presence in it and then this presence extended to Guyana and so on. Stage by stage, not by calculation but by – I don't know how to say it – by the gravitational pull of what was happening in the region at the time, *Bim* moved from an island magazine to regional magazine ... It is not by chance that the literary magazines came up around very much the same time, that is the mid-forties. *Kyk-Over-Al* in Guyana was coming out at the same time as *Focus* in Jamaica. It is the time after the War, when the region, that is the English-speaking Caribbean, is being called upon to think in terms of the Federation and the unity of the region ... That regionalizing of politics of the particular islands coincides with the emergence of these various journals and creates a curious marriage, you might say, of politics and culture.
>
> (Lamming in Waters 1999: 193)

Nevertheless, if this marriage did take place then the honeymoon was short-lived. The names of E. L. Cozier and Esther Chapman and perhaps even those of Frank Collymore or A. J. Seymour have little endurance or purchase in terms of our ideas of a Caribbean aesthetic today. How and why has this cleavage in literary history formed between the nascent developments of cultural collectivity and literary indigeneity that we find in the 1930s and 1940s and the bold and often declamatory projects of Brathwaite, Rohlehr, Wynter and Morris in the 1960s and 1970s that establish the grounds for a regional aesthetic and remain our touchstones today?

I would suggest that there are three interconnected reasons why writing and criticism before 1950 have not been granted the same kind of enduring presence within Caribbean literary histories. The first is perhaps the most obvious and also the most troublesome in terms of my project. Many writings from this period simply do not share the same emphasis on estab-lishing a new connection between the Caribbean writer and his or her place, voice and audience. Indeed, as my attention to Vivian Virtue and J. E. C. McFarlane will demonstrate, certain figures during this period were positively opposed to what was then a revolutionary move, and moreover deemed it their obligation as poets to occupy the aesthetic and spiritual high ground, a position which has never been particularly appealing or persuasive within critical models after the 1960s. The second reason is that, despite significant social unrest during the period of the 1930s, there were very few instances of meaningful connection between the mass displays of public discontent and frustration and the intellectual or artistic response to these. This is attributable at least in part to the absence during this period of a higher educational institution (the establishment of the University College of the West Indies came in 1948) and the poor publishing and distribution outlets for journalists and writers. Indeed, the acute isolation that the writers felt across the region at this time is represented by the curious echo of a desert metaphor in their work. Albert Gomes describes the Beacon group in Trinidad as 'the tiny oasis of artistic appreciation I found in the vast philistine desert of Trinidad' (Gomes 1974: 16) and Lamming chooses the very same image for his praise of *Bim*, 'a kind of oasis in that lonely desert of mass indifference and educated middle-class treachery' (1960: 41).[1] Although the inclination towards literary clubs, editorial collectives and reading circles that we find during the 1930s and 1940s points to the desire for a reciprocation between writer and audience, the rather intimate, socially remote and self-congratulatory nature of these arrangements often limited their reach and scope. The third reason is that the first major ventures into literary criticism, literary history and arguably canon-formation grew out of the very ground that had been laid by the critics of the 1960s and 1970s and therefore tended to take the lead from their cultural markers.

I shall discuss each of these reasons during the course of this chapter but it seems important to account first for the factors that helped to create this new critical moment, a moment that made the desert bloom and writers such as Brathwaite, who in the 1950s had felt that 'No writer could live in that stifling atmosphere of middle class materialism and philistinism' (Brathwaite 1970: 37), able to return, and others such as Lamming no longer fear being 'ignored in and by a society about which they have been at once articulate and authentic' (Lamming 1960: 46). This account is especially pertinent given the still tenacious assumption that 'from 1950 until the mid-1960s London was the center for the most visible West Indian accomplishment' (Breiner 1998: 96). The positive publishing statistics; the words of Naipaul in *The Middle Passage* (1962) and Lamming's powerful pronouncement, 'I have lost my place, or my place has deserted me' (Lamming 1960: 50), in the *Pleasures of Exile*, has produced a strong association between writing, the West Indian author and the condition of being elsewhere at this time. Many writers during the 1960s did travel and did make exile their central theme: Jan Carew's *The Last Barbarians* (1961); Andrew Salkey's *Escape to an Autumn Pavement* (1960b); Denis Williams's *Other Leopards* (1963); and Wilson Harris's *The Waiting Room* (1967) come to mind. It is also clear that even for writers who did not make the physical journey to the motherland, the BBC's 'Caribbean Voices' programme, based in London, which began its literary focus from 1945, was a significant centre of literary activity.[2] However, there is equal evidence to suggest that those based in the Caribbean were frustrated by this idea of West Indianness as a form of metropolitan belonging even as it was taking root, and that they viewed being in the region as a positive position that still offered links, dialogues and spaces of articulation in which their work could be read and discussed.

In 'Sir Galahad and the Islands', first published in *Bim* in 1957, Brathwaite possibly initiates the discussion about cultural resources, the exiled writer and the local tradition which remains lively and relevant throughout the following decade. Although not judgemental of the emigrant writer, Brathwaite balances his survey of writings that focus on the need to escape the islands with positive attention to those who have stayed:

> The best poets like Walcott appear to become so socially involved; become that is, so dependent on the situation for the tensions out of which their poetry sings, that they are incapable, if not of accepting the situation, at least of distancing themselves from it.
>
> (Brathwaite 1993: 12, first published 1957)

Brathwaite identifies the problems of the emigrant writer as twofold, 'On one hand, there is the danger, as one commentator harshly put it, of being "infected with foreign isms"; on the other, there is the possibility of losing creative energy and distinctiveness when separated from the islands that were his world' (Brathwaite 1957 (1993): 25–26). As Brathwaite himself demonstrates, for the writers who stayed at home, including the already exceptional Derek Walcott, the awareness of the missing voices of their fellow writers remained a pertinent subject. The Tobagonian Eric Roach's poetry, quoted in Brathwaite's essay, demonstrates an intimate engage-ment with place and his rural home community that is explicitly set in contrast to the loss of the writer in exile in his 'Letter to Lamming in England'.

> Older than you and cooler, more content
> I hold this narrow island in my hand
> While you have thrown yours to the sea
> And jumped for England . . .
>
> Forgive the dream that drags you back to island
> Desiring your genius home again . . .
>
> O man, your roots are tapped into this soil
> Your song is water wizard from these rocks.
>
> (Roach 1952: 36–7)

However, despite being singled out by Brathwaite for his quality and his status as a writer 'of the people', Roach's work has seldom been critically attended to, an absence that is possibly due to his being out of step with the dominant emigrant theme of the 1950s, the decade when his work appeared most regularly in *Bim*.[3]

If Roach's call for return and reconnection evokes a powerful memory of community and the promise of belonging held across water, then Noel Vaz's essay in the 1960 volume of *Focus*, 'Creative Potential at Home,' bears witness to the strain in relations that also existed between those who stayed and worked hard to continue West Indian-based writings and those who left and seemingly received all the critical attention.

> Of course, we look to these writers abroad who in turn look for a foreign market for their novels and plays. One could ask them many pertinent questions, like, why keep on 'flogging' (in the sense of exploiting and selling) the issues of slavery – when the whole world is today living in a nervous tension-ridden state of insecurity. Why then all this fuss and pother [*sic*] about finding an identity when living in the West Indies, good or bad, is full of increasing possibilities and racial and class barriers here are shrinking in spite of (sometimes because of) the seemingly insoluble racial problems elsewhere in the world today. A most pertinent question we should ask our writers abroad – especially those who bleat in exile – is why don't they come home?
>
> (Vaz 1960: 146)

Vaz's essay needs to be read as an intervention in what was clearly an important debate at this time. It is a more pointed exchange with the self-exiled writer but it follows the cues of the editor, Edna Manley's, 'Foreword' to the volume that also points out that 'much has been written and said on the question of West Indian writers who live and work abroad' (Manley 1960). Vaz's comment about Caribbean writers in Britain trading off a history of slavery is interesting in its implication that those who settled in the motherland may have been more confined by its particular 'frozen' notions and preoccupations with West Indian history than those who stayed. A similar point is also raised in 1961, when G. R. Coulthard criticises work by the London-based writers, 'Too much writing based on a West Indies background is becoming stereotyped, repetitious and out of date' (Coulthard 1961: 200).

However, while the value of London-based writing was viewed with suspicion by some, the notion of a remote metropolitan literary capital, disconnected from the Caribbean was often not quite the reality. Some of the developments that took place in Britain fed into the local conception of writing that was to form a common denominator in later critical paradigms. One important example is the BBC radio 'Caribbean Voices' programme that, although based in London, was very clear in its demands for writing that represented the 'local' under the editorship of Henry Swanzy and his Jamaican-based advisor, Gladys Lindo (along with her husband Cedric, whose literature page in *The Gleaner* newspaper had also been an important early outlet for writers). Swanzy was in close contact with Frank Collymore and there was a productive exchange of material between the 'Caribbean Voices' programme and *Bim*. The programme's commitment to Caribbean readers and its literal realisation of broadcasting Caribbean, rather than Standard English, voices also brought it in line with the strong call towards validating the vernacular voice that was taking hold back in the region.

In a different way, the Caribbean Artists Movement which was formed in 1966 by a few radical West Indians, including Kamau Brathwaite and John La Rose who were both disappointed by the lack of political ferment in England, was another venture that successfully bridged the two communities and their own particular demands at this time. CAM and *Savacou*, its ground-breaking publication, became almost a consciously two-part initiative based in the UK (where Andrew Salkey and John La Rose settled) and in the Caribbean, relocated back in Jamaica with Brathwaite from 1968. At odds with accounts of a relocated metropolitan literary centre, *Savacou* represented the possibilities of a transnational, de-centred Caribbeanism that was not at odds or out of step with local agendas. Indeed, not only did this publication become central to the earliest foundations of black British writings and intellectual map-making but also, in its Caribbean arm, it became a touchstone of the new emphasis on vernacular forms and voices within a Caribbean-based tradition.

By the mid-1970s, the tables had turned and new critical foundations and literary flowerings were taking root in the Caribbean region, as the emphasis upon grassroots resources had entirely reshaped critical practice. In the introduction to his anthology *BlueFoot Traveller*, published in 1976, James Berry voices the distinct reversal of fortunes for the West Indian writer in Britain that had occurred during that time-span.

> The Westindian in Britain finds himself in a situation that amounts to a continuation of the old ways of life. Around him white people are still dominant, still in control … Demands are not made on his talents. Society generates no clamour to see him in new dimensions. He cannot unlid himself as his fellow Westindian at home does. He has missed out on the exciting process of rediscovery. He has missed out on the real experience of Independence, of being his own master, and can be part of a new life only by proxy.
>
> (Berry 1976: 8)

Several projects relating to literary and cultural development taking place in the Caribbean may also help us to map out this dramatic turn of affairs in Anglocreole writing that occurred between the 'watershed' of 1948 when SS *Empire Windrush* docked at Tilbury and official Caribbean literary history seems to have relocated to London, and the critical moment of 1971 when tense and contradictory pulls in Anglocreole criticism were to be publicly staged at the ACLALS Conference in Jamaica.

As early as 1963, in his paper 'Roots', Brathwaite begins by ruminating on the dramatically changed scene in terms of West Indian writing and the recent moves towards a literary homecoming.

> *A House for Mr Biswas; In a Green Night,* have been published and acclaimed; *A Season of Adventure* has given us the symbol of Gort, the drummer; Derek Walcott and Errol Hill have been accepted and are working here in the West Indies in their own right as artists; Lamming, Selvon, Naipaul, Hearne, Carew, Sylvia Wynter, Kempadoo have returned home if not to work at least to travel among the islands on assignments or extended stays. All now that is needed to make the story complete is for us to arrange a Conference of Caribbean Writers and begin the publication of our version of something on the scale of *Presence Africaine.*
>
> How then can we account for this change? Was the crack in West Indian sensibility only an apparent defect in the mirror, a passing reflection of the social historical and emotional picture of the time? Or is this move back home only a return to look (for reassurance) before turning away, again, to new adventures abroad?
>
> (Brathwaite 1963 (1993): 29)

Brathwaite goes on to analyse various pieces of writing, most notably singling out Naipaul's writing and his 'remarkable individual talent', but he does not return to answer the question of regional recognition and homecoming. Although many writers have, as we know, moved abroad in the decades since the 1960s, there does seem to be a particularly strong reconnection to the region developing in the Caribbean at this time that merits consideration and that arguably culminated in both the conference and the publication that Brathwaite already had in mind.

The establishment of the University College of the West Indies in 1948 created an enabling space in which intellectual growth could be channelled within the orbit of local knowledge. Several important figures returned to the Caribbean to take up academic positions. Sylvia Wynter, who returned as a lecturer in the Spanish department in 1963, and John Hearne who took up the position of Secretary of the Creative Arts Centre, both at UWI Mona, Jamaica, helped to form a critical mass of intellectuals that became crucial to the 1971 Conference and its foundational debates. Within a regional context, Caribbean people became both the authors and the subjects of research papers on Caribbean phenomenon and the university launched a new journal, *Caribbean Quarterly*, from 1949. With a broad disciplinary remit this journal, which still exists today, sought to bring different perspectives to bear on a regional frame and was pioneering in its publication of material relating to folk traditions. In something of a second wave of periodical publishing in the region, several new publications appeared in the 1960s, these took a place alongside *Bim* which continued to publish many significant essays during this decade. Clifford Sealey edited the literary magazine *Voices* between 1964–66 in Trinidad. Also from Trinidad came *Tapia* (later *The Trinidad and Tobago Review*) an overtly political publication that published critical papers as well as creative work and was the earliest outlet for many of Rohlehr's essays, as well as *Moko Jumbie*. The first issue of *Jamaica Journal*, the highly respected quarterly, was published in 1967 and its passionate commitment to promoting Jamaica's cultural heritage and to recording achievement in the arts and literature, as well as history and science, continues today. *Abeng*, which took its name from the shell used by slaves to communicate with each other, emerged late in the decade from a small leftist group seeking to continue political protest and the radical analysis of history in the wake of Walter Rodney's exile in 1968.

As Jeanette B. Allis argues in her article 'The decade of the critic: West Indian literary criticism in the 1970s', these new journals enabled the dissemination of critical as well as literary voices across the region.

> With the publication of *New World Quarterly*, its successor *Tapia*, *Jamaica Journal*, *New Voices*, *Savacou*, *Kaie*, *Kairi*, and *Revista/Review Interamericana*, all (except *New World Quarterly*) published in the later sixties and early seventies, publishing possibilities for the West Indian critic expanded considerably. In addition, the particular perspective of each journal lent its own dimension to a critical article, so that, for example, an article in *New World Quarterly* might take on a highly political flavour, while one in *Jamaica Journal* might (but not always) seem more in the nature of cultural exposition.
>
> (Allis 1991: 30)

The new political and cultural impetus that informed these publishing ventures was also distilled in many of the pieces they published. Collectively they helped to mark out the foundations of a newly energetic literary nation-building project, and certain individual papers served as particularly monumental foundation stones. While it is beyond the possibilities of this study to attend to each of these, I do want to offer an analysis of a small number of statements that I regard to be critical to both the configuration of West Indian literature as a body of writings post 1971 and, albeit unwittingly, to the disavowal of pre-1950 writings that also marks the literary history of this period.

As I have already documented, Brathwaite was perhaps the most strident and prolific writer in terms of remapping cultural and critical agendas at this time. In a series of essays, including 'Sir Galahad and the Islands'; 'Roots'; 'The New West Indian novelists' (in two parts); and 'Jazz and the West Indian novel' (in three parts), all published during the 1960s, he laid out in fairly straightforward terms a series of arguments concerning the politics of location, attachment to community, social conscience and the representation of Caribbean history that together amounted to a radical epistemic shift enacted through the framing of an alternative cultural resource.[4] Much of this work would be developed further in his 1974 study, *Contradictory Omens* and his 1977–78 three-part work 'The Love Axe'. In these 1960s publications, Brathwaite's careful attention to the literary and linguistic strategies of a series of writers from Walcott and Naipaul to Mais and Patterson, combined with his acute awareness of the complex cultural and political challenges facing West Indian societies in the Independence era, enabled him to provide alert and searching readings that consistently 'return our attention to "West Indian" possibilities' (Brathwaite 1993: 108, first published 1968). His ardent pursuit of 'ground from which we ourselves will see the world, and towards which the world will look to find us . . . a creole culture . . . And a creole way of seeing too' (Brathwaite 1993: 108, first published 1968) became in many ways a reference point towards which other critics either sought to affiliate or differentiate themselves and one that remains core to many contemporary theorisations of Caribbean cultural studies today.

One issue that dominated critical papers of this time was that of language. The connection between linguistic scholarship and the recovery of non-European folk heritage had been made by Frank Collymore in the 1940s with his inclusion in *Bim* of a *Glossary of Words and Phrases of Barbadian Dialect* that was published in book form in 1955. Further linguistic studies that were published in the 1960s also made linguistic–literary–cultural connections more possible as they validated the argument that creoles were languages in their own right.[5] In terms of literary criticism, the emphasis upon finding an appropriate voice or language in which to write was an almost ubiquitous preoccupation. As early as 1960, Lamming had called for attention to 'the peasant tongue' that utters 'the organic music of the earth' (Lamming 1960: 45), but in institutional and publishing contexts the case for vernacular voices was still to be won. Anne Walmsley recalled how her inclusion of Sam Selvon's story 'The Village Washer', in Trinidadian creole, in a proposed anthology of West Indian writing for schools, was 'the main reason for the book's rejection in 1958; the Jamaican Ministry of Education was against texts containing "dialect"' (Walmsley 1995: 76). Indeed, despite the fact that critical reception of Selvon's work had focused in very positive terms on his creative management of lived West Indian language, with Wilson Harris commending Selvon on his use of creole in depicting the consciousness of the narrator as well as the dialogue of the characters, institutional suspicion and western ideas of cultural standards remained rigid, especially with regard to educational resources. As Sylvia Wynter succintly argued, 'The education system was an alphabetic River of Jordan, in which "bad English" was to be washed white' (Wynter 1972: 80).

Although by the mid-1960s the ideological tide had turned somewhat and the anthology was welcomed with two of Selvon's stories among its representations, the way in which nation language was associated with the collocation of race and class shame and the need to challenge the entrenched institutional prejudice on both fronts is evident in Mervyn Morris's important paper, 'On Reading Louise Bennett Seriously', published in the first volume of *Jamaica Journal* in 1967.

> The Jamaican middle-class was slow to acknowledge an interest in dialect which represented for most of them the speech-forms of a lower class from whom they wished to be distinguished ... If one reads Louise Bennett to middle-class school children they are apt to laugh not only at wit and humour but at the language itself. The language which their maids and yard boys use is not yet accepted simply as one of our Jamaican ways of speech.
>
> (Morris 1967a: 69)

Commenting on Bennett's exclusion from several prominent anthologies of West Indian poetry, including *Kyk-Over-Al*'s special issue of 1957 and *Caribbean Quarterly*'s 1958 collection, as well as her annexation under 'Humour' in the *Independence Anthology of Jamaican Literature* (edited by A. L. Hendricks and Cedric Lindo in 1962), Morris calls for serious critical attention to Bennett's work and attempts to initiate this new trend against the grain of previous dismissals. Other relevant articles that followed this path include Kenneth Ramchand's 'Dialect in West Indian Fiction' (1968) and Gordon Rohlehr's 'Sparrow and the language of Calypso' (1970). However, making a more ambitious claim still, in a paper first delivered in 1967, 'Dialect in West Indian Literature', Le Page, a linguist, draws together two of the predominant themes of this moment – the inscription of vernacular voices and the creation of a community of knowledge between the West Indian writer and society – in his projection of a culturally distinctive and authentic language shared between the writer and his community.

> I would look forward to a very healthy period when all West Indian writers interested in developing vernacular usage in literature in depth, for all registers, would be touring around West Indian schools and towns giving readings from their work ... This may be less comfortable than working for the BBC in London and talking only to other West Indian writers in exile, but it would be a way of ploughing back into the soil some of the nourishment which the writer draws from his community ... And it would mean that West Indian

writing had come of age, an indigenous literature in the indigenous language.

(Le Page 1969: 7)

Others were less celebratory. In his essay 'What the Twilight Says' (1970), which looks over the previous twenty years and maps out the shift in consciousness that took place among black West Indian artists during the intervening nationalist period, Derek Walcott is, like Wilson Harris, in certain respects, deliberately distancing himself from the direction of Brathwaite, Rohlehr and others. This is especially clear in his criticism that 'now the intellectuals, courting and fearing the mass, found values in it that they had formerly despised. They apotheosised the folk form, insisting that calypsos were poems' (Walcott 1970: 31).[6] Nevertheless, like Harris, Walcott shares the preoccupation with developing an authentic literary language:

> What would deliver him from servitude was the forging of a language that went beyond mimicry, a dialect which has the forces of revelation as it invented names for things, one which finally settled on its own mode of inflection, and which began to create an oral culture of chants, jokes, folksongs, and fables; this, not merely the debt of history, was his proper claim to the New World.
>
> (Walcott 1970: 15)

While the work of Morris demonstrates the case that needed to be made for the simple acknowledgement, as literature, of works written in creole, and Walcott voices the creative potential located in a language of self-identification, Le Page invests the very future of West Indian literature in an embrace of 'indigenous language'. Staging an ideological reversal, Le Page's proposal that creole writing was the *bona fide* form dovetailed with other new markers of the cultural standards being set down in this critical moment, such as his somewhat utopian vision of a new horizon of contact between writer and society.

The relationship between writer and community was at the heart of debates forming at this time. As I shall go on to discuss, this very subject was at the centre of the political and intellectual controversy provoked by the ACLALS Conference in 1971, but already in the 1960s there were real signs of discontent with establishment views of the writer, literary value and critical practice. In a lesser-known piece from 1968, 'The Arts, The Critics and A New Society', published in the *Express* newspaper in Trinidad, Earl Lovelace, the Trinidadian writer, tackled this question of aesthetic value and cultural relevance in very plain and direct terms.

> The basic principles of artistic criticism are well known to critics. Basically, we ask: What is the artist trying to say? How well has he said it? And, is it worth saying?

However, today, in our condition, we need to look carefully at how we ask these questions. We need to note the context in which we ask them. In fact, we ought to ask: To whom is the artist speaking? Is he speaking to us at all? We need to consider whether the artist is representing us, whether he is speaking to us, and to what extent is he (if he makes the claim), mirroring our hopes, aspirations and attitudes realistically. Or whether he is representing an individual experience that is intimately his own, that does not keep pace with our thinking and our condition. In short, we need, today, to determine the artist's relevance to us.

This question of relevance is of critical importance today because it is only when the artist and the arts are relevant that they fulfil their functions in the society. Most of the intellectuals and artists for a long time now have not really made any strenuous efforts to relate to the community in which they operate or of which they speak.

(Lovelace 1968a: 14)

Lovelace's criticism of detachment and his advocacy of relevance and connection as integral to artistic value was also to be articulated by several others in 1968. Two particularly important pieces were written in response to the publication of Louis James's *The Islands in Between* (1968), the first edited collection of criticism on West Indian writing. Although James himself has recently reflected on the somewhat ironic timing of his book which 'appeared at the moment when radical Caribbean critics were looking for a crusty piece of colonial writing to get their teeth into' (James 2003: 220), one comment that he made in his introduction to the volume indicates his awareness of the strain between his own orientation as an English born and educated critic and that of the cultural products that he was seeking to work with: 'It may be as well here to note the difficulty of writing conventional literary criticism on West Indian culture, or any popular culture (James 1968: 13). It is this attempt to produce conventional literary criticism – for which, following Brathwaite, we may wish to substitute, European, perhaps even colonial criticism, or following Wynter, acquiescent criticism – that so animated both Brathwaite and Wynter, and James's collection of essays provided a useful counterpoint for both in their own projects outlining alternative agendas of West Indian literary criticism.

In her landmark essay, 'We Must Learn to Sit Down Together and Talk About a Little Culture: Reflections on West Indian Writing and Criticism', published in *Jamaican Journal* in 1968, Sylvia Wynter sought to make an intervention that both exposed and undermined James's collection, a work that she also saw as being conducted 'under the guidance and within the perspectives of English criticism' (Wynter 1968: 23). Since returning to Jamaica in 1963, Wynter had published regular pieces on culture and history in *The Daily Gleaner* and in 1965 had premiered her play,

'*1865: Ballad for a Rebellion*', around the events of the Morant Bay Rebellion in Jamaica. Her concern with restoring and rereading West Indian history was already evident. In many ways, Wynter was more rebarbative and unforgiving in her attack on James, and her discussion is characteristically more involved, dense and theoretical than Brathwaite's. Wynter moves with ease from Sartre to James Bond, Adorno to Louis James in order to unlock the deep ideological structures that enable James to offer an overview of West Indian history and a critical perspective on the region's writing that, to her mind, is not only 'in favour of England' (Wynter 1968: 26), but also in denial of the wider historical connections between England's profits and the West Indies' losses – in political, cultural and educational terms.

> He sketches the history of the Caribbean from an Archimedean point outside the historical process. Yet it is a process in which he is as involved as is the West Indian. This pretended objectivity and detachment is the common stance of what I call, for convenience, the 'acquiescent critic.' In attempting to write from outside the process, in pretending detachment, the 'acquiescent critic,' accepts the status quo.
>
> James, as an English teacher teaching in a West Indian university, passing judgement on West Indian writing, is mediated to his bones by the colonial experience, by the colonial myth in which he is involved . . .
>
> (Wynter 1968: 26, 27)

Wynter made the important point that the criticism within the volume was not situated in relation to the historical power dynamic between the West Indies and Britain, a dynamic which she envisaged as being at a critical moment of change.

> Louis James, in spite of the many subsidiary excellencies of his comments, does not see West Indian literature against its necessary background . . . He does not see West Indian literature as the expression of the breaking out of all the Calibans, not only all over the British Empire, but at the heart of Empire itself.
>
> (Wynter 1968: 31)

In his article 'Caribbean Critics' that was published in three different journals in 1969, Brathwaite laid out his objections to the critical practice on offer in James's study. In drawing attention to the

> strange situation where the work of a body of writers, mainly concerned with the communal values of their creole society, is examined in a more or less 'academic' fashion by a body of critics trained to respond

almost exclusively to European influences, and whose main concerns
are with 'the artist', and 'the individual'.

(Brathwaite 1969 (1993): 117)

Brathwaite sketched the radical disjuncture between the preoccupations
of the writers and those of the critics. He saw the grave consequences of
their pull in different directions as leading to a failure to engage with that
which was 'finally important' to him (and, in his view, to the writers themselves): 'their use and transformation of their own local material' (116);
their efforts 'to liberate the consciousness of the submerged "folk"' (117);
'the speech of the folk' (117) and 'Africa, the major constituent element
in Caribbean folk culture' (119).[7]

While two special issues of international journals devoted to West Indian
literature, *Journal of Commonwealth Literature* (1969) and *The Literary Half-
Yearly* (1970), may be regarded as one kind of witness to Wynter's vision
of Caliban's breaking into the institutions of Empire, the sense of imminent
and radical change that Wynter pressages in her statement and that
Brathwaite strongly argued for was also being voiced elsewhere. For Elsa
Goveia, among others, the particular demand of this moment was to
harness the creative and revolutionary energy of the West Indian writer
in a connection with his home society, 'The fact is that unless the writer
throws his weight on the side of the democratisation of West Indian society
he is unlikely ever to be able to find a way of living in his own society'
(Goveia 1970: 13).[8] Also writing from the Jamaican context, Goveia, who
like Brathwaite was based in the History department at Mona, had
witnessed the changes afoot in terms of cultural repossession for and by
the people.

Several important connections between writers, scholars and popular
cultural forms towards the end of the decade also signalled new possibilities for shared ground. In Jamaica, the Yard Theatre movement emerged
and sought to reconnect artistic activity with the folk communities, bringing
performances which often combined poetry, music, drumming and the
work of Bennett and Brathwaite, among others, to small community venues.
When Peter Kempadoo returned to Guyana in the 1960s, he managed a
Folk Arts unit outside Georgetown. In Trinidad, the work of Beryl
McBurnie in establishing the Little Carib Theatre in 1948 and staging
folk dance in the face of middle-class ridicule had been central to a change
in artistic direction and had attracted Walcott, who also wanted to draw
on folk material in his theatre work. Walcott moved to Trinidad in 1959
and was holding weekly workshops thereafter with the first public performance taking place in 1962. Gordon Rohlehr's work on the language of
calypso in Trinidad also provided another connection between popular
cultural forms and academic practice. Indeed, scholarly investigations into
the operations of oppression and resistance in popular cultural forms
had been given excellent example by C. L. R. James's radical and incisive
critique of cricket in his 1963 study, *Beyond a Boundary*.[9]

In more conventional terms the category of West Indian Writing came into being during the 1960s via a number of literary anthologies: Andrew Salkey's *West Indian Stories* (1960a) and *Stories from the Caribbean* (1965); G. R. Coulthard's *Caribbean Literature* (1966); Kenneth Ramchand's *West Indian Narrative* (1966); Barbara Howe's *From the Green Antilles* (1966); O. R. Dathorne's *Caribbean Narrative* (1966) and *Caribbean Verse* (1967); and Anne Walmsley's *The Sun's Eye* (1968). As I shall discuss later, the particular inclusions and exclusions on which these selections were based help us to locate a distinctive trend in terms of the historical and thematic organisation of West Indian literature as a category of writing at this time. Less conventionally, vernacular poetry was also to find a new publishing outlet and profile that would dramatically alter the idea of West Indian poetics. *Savacou*, the journal of the Caribbean Arts Movement (CAM), that emerged from Brathwaite's commitment to invoking and shaping cultural debate on his return to the West Indies, was first published in 1970. The journal's editorial board was initially comprised of Brathwaite; Gordon Rohlehr, a critic whose writing on folk language and musical forms dovetailed nicely with Brathwaite's own cultural concerns; Andrew Salkey, the Jamaican novelist who had joined La Rose and Brathwaite in the London arm of CAM; and Kenneth Ramchand, a young critic from Trinidad whose own views on writing and culture soon became rather separated from the others. *Savacou* is central to any consideration of Caribbean literary history because it published the most radical writings, as well as many of the major critical interventions of the 1970s era.

A 1970 volume of the journal included several significant papers first given at the 1967 CAM conference held at the University of Kent, such as Rholehr's 'Sparrow and the Language of Calpyso' and Else Goveia's 'The Socio-cultural Framework of the Caribbean'. However, possibly its most important contribution to Caribbean literary history came in 1971, when the double-issue poetry collection, *Savacou 3/4*, was published to coincide with the Association for Commonwealth Literature and Language Studies (ACLALS) conference. This was the first substantial publication to showcase poetry coming from the oral, folk nexus that had been given theoretical weight by the critical writings of the decade that preceded it. While the rapso and reggae rhythms, dread talk and vernacular voices of these works may now be regarded as one of the central achievements of this moment, at the time they were greeted with 'deep deep disquiet & anxiety' (Brathwaite 1994: 322) and the establishment was extremely hostile to this shift in (or, as they read it, abandonment of) aesthetics.

Demonstration and debate: the shaping of a critical moment

It cannot go without mention that the period leading up to the 1971 Conference, so central to literary histories, was marked by political unrest and demonstrations of dissatisfaction with the direction of post-Independence governance in many of the islands. As Wynter explains, Independence was something of a disappointment both in terms of its material consequences and its promise of a new politics of identity.

> An experience, inevitably, of intensified frustrations. For the rising expectations are inbuilt and endemic to the kind of economic planning which, whilst c[v]astly [*sic*] improving the opportunities of the society, have reserved the larger share of these opportunities for the upper and middle classes; and a select portion of the working classes. An occasional sprinkle of opportunity falls on the populace as a whole; enough to remind them of the extent of their dispossession from the real areas of growth. The unbridled advertising campaigns of the consumer capitalist superstructure, plus inflation, the increased cost of foodstuffs; and the heightened feeling of powerlessness to affect a society whose increase of power has fallen mainly to the wealthy and middle classes, have all helped to intensify the consciousness of being 'black', and therefore of 'suffering the system.'
>
> (Wynter 1972: 82)

For Brathwaite, who was later to make an important diagnosis of the influence that this frustration and restlessness had in terms of creative and revolutionary outcomes, the 'cultural revolution' that took place in the Caribbean in the 1970s was rooted in the groundswell of intersecting cultural and political interests visibly emerging at that time.

> It started (as it shd) with an awareness among the Youth that although John Brown was dead, his soul, in the Caribbean, was not marching on. Marcus & Martin & Malcolm became heroes, so did Fidel & Che & Samora Machel & Lumumba and Frantz Fanon & the Algerian Revolution & Genet's **The Blacks** and we began to pay some attention to what our artists were saying or rather NOT SAYING. Walter Rodney was a great force even though the University of the West Indies finally betrayed & deserted him and he ended up blown to bits, an alien in his own country & quickly forgotten.
>
> (Brathwaite 1994: 321)

Indeed, key among many events marking these intensified frustrations were the 'Rodney Riots' of October 1968, provoked by the Jamaican Government's refusal to allow Walter Rodney, the Guyanese historian and radical who held a position at the Mona campus of the University of the West Indies, back into the country.[10] The strong support for Rodney signalled an important juncture between grass roots struggles for rights and an intellectual focus on communal black consciousness that was being echoed elsewhere. In 1968 there were protests in Woodford Square in Trinidad's capital against the government's banning of the Black Power leader Stokely

Carmichael, a Trinidadian by birth. The attempted revolution in Trinidad from February to May 1970, that forged a space for coalition between students and working-class people in its urban demonstrations, was further expression of the frustration and anger at a government removed from the people's needs.[11] The fact that this revolution was centrally concerned with issues of self-representation as well as with those of social injustice is made clear by the appearance of revolutionary carnival bands performing pageants of slavery and indenture to the crowd at Independence Square.

In January 1971 the Conference of the Association for Commonwealth Literature and Language Studies was hosted by the University of the West Indies in Jamaica and its central theme was West Indian Literature. This conference, in which the statements and contestations that had begun to emerge around the issue of cultural politics and writing in the region were being debated locally and in a highly charged moment of political and social unrest, brought many issues central to emergent critical agendas to a head.[12] Although clearly a foundational moment in the history of Caribbean criticism, this conference has itself received little critical attention other than in the first chapter of Laurence Breiner's *An Introduction to West Indian Poetry*. Breiner claims that it 'was the first comprehensive presentation of West Indian literature by West Indians that included fully articulated critical positions' (Breiner 1998: 3).

Kamau Brathwaite who had joined the history department, a more radical brother to English, in 1962, and was invited to give the keynote address at the conference. Brathwaite, whose three collections of poems (*Rights of Passage* (1967), *Masks* (1968) and *Islands* (1969) as well as his cultural criticism such as 'Roots' (1963) and 'Jazz and the West Indian novel' (1967b/1969) offered the most radical and dramatic articulation of the ideas of cultural repossession and decolonisation, had recently published works in *Caribbean Quarterly* and therefore his views would have been known within the university community. He had been invited to talk on the issue of 'The Function of the Writer in Society', and used this platform to advance his work 'identifying the matrix of folk culture specifically with the African heritage' and arguing for the recognition of the '"Little Tradition," the culture of ordinary people' (Breiner 1998: 2, 1). In what we can appreciate now as an ironic and even inflammatory move, V. S. Naipaul was the chosen respondent, and his own take on this theme was significantly different. In Brathwaite's account, 'Naipaul wittily sneered his reply – how as a 'Cambridge man' I shd be helping 'the people' I profess to ?love – who in his view are quite beNIGHTed – out of their ignorance, not encouraging them in it w/ talk of folkculture etc.' (Brathwaite 1994: 321).[13]

The exchange that followed Naipaul's paper is now something of a legend in the history of Caribbean criticism and the various debates, snipes and exchanges that the event staged involve, in one capacity or another, most of the 'big' names of that time. The critic Kenneth Ramchand accused Brathwaite of 'folking up' the criticism during the conference itself but even his damning response seemed rather tepid compared to that of Eric Roach (also Trinidadian) who published his eurocentric repost in the *Trinidad Guardian*:

> We have been given the European languages and forms of culture – culture in the traditional, aesethic sense, meaning the best that has been thought, said and done . . . Are we going to tie the drum of Africa to our tails and bay like mad dogs at the Nordic world to which our geography and history tie us?
>
> (Roach 1971)[14]

Accounts even include the absent Walcott who was apparently warned to stay away due to 'CULTURAL GORILLAS' (Brathwaite 1994: 322). As the energetic and vituperative nature of these exchanges makes clear, in this critical moment, the divide between those supporting the establishment and its version of cultural standards and those advocating a radical realignment of cultural values and an urgent re-evaluation of African as well as European cultural legacies opened up in an extreme and defining fashion. In Sylvia Wynter's words 'the conflict and the clash that we have seen reflected here in this conference, [is] on different levels of awareness, between those who justify and defend the system; and those who challenge it' (Wynter 1971: 102).

The kind of bland, imported Leavisite agenda of cultural amelioration that advocated literature as a tool for educational and even moral advancement set itself against the indigenous agenda calling for an impassioned voicing of folk consciousness, vernacular traditions, social conscience and the possibilties for horizontal relations between poet or writer, subject and audience, such as those conceptualised in Rodney's *Groundings With My Brothers* (1969). Although Ramchand had himself dismissed critics who 'have so far failed to serve West Indian literature', his own conception of this task was consciously forged in the shadow of 'the greatest English literary critic', F. R. Leavis, whom he had openly commended for his efforts 'to create a consciousness throughout . . . society that literature matters as literature, not as a substitute for something else; and that literary criticism is a craft calling for maturity, intelligence, and sensitivity to the organisation of words on the page' (Ramchand 1970: 56). Ramchand's insistence on the value of practical criticism over cultural criticism led to a fierce critique of his work by Wynter in her 1972 piece 'Creole Criticism: A Critique'. However, not only did this moment generate significant *ad personam* friction between individual critics but the profound incommensurability of these two agendas became both visible and audible in ways that could no longer be ignored.

Only a few years earlier there had been frequent laments about the lack of local critical interest in West Indian writing:

> That is one trouble. Our novelists, as our cricketers, are recognized abroad for what they are, something new, creative and precious in the organizations and traditions of the West. But what they need is what Heidigger recognized in Holderin – a Homecoming'.
>
> (C. L. R. James: 1967)

> We can improve [conditions for the writer in the West Indies] further ... by offering intelligent critical interest in his work, and by enlarging and improving, through education, the local audience for his work.
>
> (Morris 1967: 129)

> The most meaningful gesture of respect which a society can make towards its writers is to accord their work a careful and rigorous criticism.
>
> (Baugh 1968: 140)

> West Indian literature suffers from a lack of critics ... The place of the University in encouraging West Indian writing, financing the visits of creative writers from abroad, and laying a basis of critical awareness in West Indians, is crucial.
>
> (Louis James 1968: 154, 156)

Suddenly, the University, via the conference, had accelerated the momentum of critical debate greatly and had also defined the shape of intellectual exchange along a divide between the Great Tradition inherited from colonial institutions and, as Brathwaite called it, the Little Tradition, grown from folk traditions, Caribbean languages and the politics of social commitment. Of course, as many made clear at the conference itself, as well as in their work that followed, there was now a sense of shared conviction among a group of key scholars that the Little Tradition carried the future of critical eminence and integrity for the region.

Although not without contention, the emergence of a shared agenda in terms of content, style and form enabled a community of critics to articulate collectively the shape of decolonised narratives, and thereby to set the principles for a regional literary history in motion. The important correspondence between what had been emerging locally as a call for political recognition and rights, and the vigour of intellectual arguments concerning the need to make serious adjustments to ideas of both cultural values and cultural standards, created a very powerful moment of synergy, the energy of which had lasting effects. Perhaps this is not surprising given that the formidable push towards asserting and validating the lives and interests of the majority population, as well as a new ethics of communication, have remained sites of struggle against the continued factors constraining the possibilities of Caribbean self-determination in both the political and the cultural spheres such as structural adjustment, tourism, and satellite television that may be regarded as colonialism by another name. Nevertheless, it is important to recognise that the anti-colonialist bite of these positions that gave them legitimacy at this moment has also secured their continued relevance.

Among the issues that were clearly at stake in this critical moment were the connection of the writer to his society; the demands on the writer to speak both to and from that society that Brathwaite had outlined and Rohlehr had affirmed with his focus on the folk; the need to acknowledge and to affirm popular cultural and oral forms; the need to be mindful of cultural relevance and ownership. In short, the national and transnational identity of the literature and more widely of the culture was at stake.[15] However, as far as I can see what was not discussed in these many exchanges (that must be seen as productive, if not always friendly), and what was not factored in among the stakes of this moment, and has not been factored in subsequently, was the meaning and value of all that had gone before in terms of West Indian writings.

Construction of a literary present and past

Most readers of Anglocreole literature are familiar with the cultural outcomes that this conference may be seen to have consolidated, even if not with the event itself. Rightly so, the interventions of Brathwaite, Walcott, Rholehr, Baugh, Wynter and Harris are seen as the touchstones of Caribbean criticism, even today, but while we use these critics to help us to read writers as far apart historically as Martin Carter and Lillian Allen, or as generically diverse as Louise Bennett and Robert Antoni, they do not help us to read or to remember those writings before the boom in which the agendas of cultural nationalism had a very different resonance. My argument is that in the wake of this powerful moment the demands of criticism were renegotiated and reframed in ways that have continued to have real purchase for readers throughout the twentieth century and that remain both relevant and useful (albeit in more nuanced arguments offered by the latest generation of scholars writing on the region – Cooper, Puri and Scott come to mind) today. It is in no way my aim to contest the value of these works, but rather to question whether so many feet have now followed in these footsteps as to make this epistemic ground seem like the only terrain there ever was?

In a sense the cultural amnesia that the shift of this moment may have enacted is an ironic consequence of the very real need at this point to correct and restore what had been neglected and disavowed by the cultural amnesia of the colonial paradigm with regards to non-European resources during the long moment of acquiescent writing and criticism preceding the 1960s and 1970s. In her 1972 review of *One Love*, a collection of articles and poems edited by Audvil King, Sylvia Wynter acknowledges the significance of idea over form in this moment in which cultural and critical revolutions converge:

> A critique of King's letter goes beyond the considerations of whether or not he has found a new style. Nor are the 'literary' merits of the piece, or the non-merits essentials. The letter is not directed towards this kind of approbation; it does not seek to achieve 'high culture.' Rather it starts to chop away the underbrush; to make that new clearing in the forest, of liberated black and human experience of Being.
>
> (Wynter 1972: 93)

Wynter's strategic privileging of cultural politics, specifically a recognition of African cultural survival, over artistic merit is one instance of the deliberate realigning of critical practice away from the production of a colonial matrix towards the recuperation of Africa forms. As Wynter argues, '*One Love* gains its significance, less from its intrinsic merit, than for its being one of the first texts of an emergent, but as yet confused, conscious apprehension, of a movement that we might label *Afro-Jamaicanism*' (Wynter 1972: 66).

Probably the most vehement and substantive intervention in this debate came in 1974 with the publication of Brathwaite's *Contradictory Omens: Cultural diversity and integration in the Caribbean*. Although more concerned with cultural than literary theory, Brathwaite draws in part upon a literary archive to substantiate his argument. Moreover, I would argue, his radical reconception of Caribbean culture as a process of interaction as opposed to imposition, outlined in this work, has had significant consequences for the organisation of literary histories from the 1970s onwards. Although Brathwaite makes it clear that his analysis is specific both to his time and place, his claim that cultural wholeness can only be restored through 'the acceptance of the culture of this ex-African majority as the paradigm and norm for the entire society' (Brathwaite 1974: 30) encouraged him to focus on the 'vast areas of social and historical formation' that created 'too wide a gulf' between white Creoles 'given the present structure' (Brathwaite 1974: 38) and thereby to suggest separate traditions to which white Creole, Indian and black West Indian cultural forms properly belonged.[16] Certainly the historical contingency of this argument is foregrounded: 'At the moment, it seems to me, it would be impossible to claim that Indians and ex-Africans in the Caribbean, even in Trinidad, share a common culture and that this culture is central to the region and to their own sensibilities' (Brathwaite 1974: 48). Nevertheless, Brathwaite's study firmly positions Jean Rhys' *Wide Sargasso Sea* and Ian McDonald's *The Humming-bird Tree* as markers of 'the ideological barrier' and confidently asserts a dividing line that he had earlier implied in his estimation of Phyllis Shand Allfrey's 1953 work, *The Orchid House* as 'a brilliant but irrelevant novel within the West Indian context' (1993: 51, first published in 1968).

Rohlehr's mapping of a culturally responsible mode of literary critical practice in 1977 also locates the Caribbean critic as a 'man' of this moment.

> The role here is threefold. He must first chronicle the sensibility of his time, locating each poet within the landscape, and against the social background from which his statement emerges. He must next be able, by comparing the statements of different voices, to trace the drift or process of sensibility in his time. This second duty of the critic exceeds the first in that it moves beyond the simple chronicling of events and statements and tries to determine their communal significance.
>
> The critic's third task is that of commenting on the various ways of shaping language revealed by a variety of writers. This requires close reading of individual poems, and a grasp of the principle operating beneath each style of saying.
>
> (Rohlehr 1977: 8)[17]

The nexus between literature and history that Brathwaite sketches in 1974, although not incontrovertible (as the subsequent exchange between Brathwaite and Peter Hulme in the pages of *Wasafiri* has proven), along with the strong sense of the duty of the critic towards social engagement that Rohlehr outlines, had a particular power, relevance and urgency in its own moment and cultural milieu of nationalism and Afrocentrism. Importantly though, this critical moment was also a defining moment in the construction of Caribbean literary canons and literary criticism and what I want to examine now are the ways in which this body of cultural and literary criticism and its anthologising projects have resonated both backwards and forwards, influencing the organisation of literary histories from the beginning of the century to its end.

The new agendas for criticism that were developed in the 1960s and 1970s pioneered many of the most rewarding and challenging studies of Caribbean writing and it would be impossible to consider critical practice without these. As I have already stated, their value is not being debated here. Rather, what I am concerned to raise as a serious issue is whether the impact of this immensely creative and radical moment, premised on the restitution and recovery of a disavowed cultural archive, has now become an exclusionary model in its own right. The emphases upon the folk, black consciousness and cultural nationalism foregrounded during this critical moment are often quite explicitly framed as forms of strategic privileging, a demand of the particular moment in which they emerged.

However, the enduring idea of a literary present with no past, a spontaneous literary genesis, as I referred to it earlier, which this new agenda seemed to demand, has had the effect of obscuring earlier configurations, idioms and traditions.

Early canons

By far the easiest and the most usual route through which early canons constructed a neat trajectory in which cultural independence and political independence were mapped onto each other was simply to ignore the pre-1950 period of Caribbean literature altogether. The explosion of creative writing that occurred in the 1950s created a visible epicentre in terms of the literary history of the region. As Lamming, in 'The Occasion for Speaking', points out:

> The historical fact is that this 'emergence' of a dozen or so novelists in the British Caribbean with some fifty books to their credit or disgrace, and all published between 1948 and 1958, is in the nature of a phenomenon.
>
> (Lamming: 1960: 29)

More significantly, in terms of this study, is the view of Lamming and others at this time that this boom seemingly came from nowhere.

> We have seen in our lifetime an activity called writing, in the form of the novel, come to fruition without any previous native tradition to draw upon . . . Mittelholzer and Reid and Selvon and Roger Mais are . . . the first builders of what will become a tradition in West Indian imaginative writing: a tradition which will be taken for granted or for the purpose of critical analysis by West Indians for a later generation.
>
> (Lamming 1960: 38)

Lamming's representation of full blooms growing from barren ground dovetails with a pervasive sense of a literary beginning without ancestry. In 'Discovering Literature in Trinidad: the 1930s', C. L. R. James comments that he did not 'know much about West Indian Literature in the 1930's – there wasn't much to know' (James 1969: 237). The accounts of West Indian literary histories that were published during this period consolidate a timeline of cultural development and literary activity centred on a 1950 watershed and produce a narrative that persuades us to read twentieth century Caribbean literature as being in harmony with, as shaping and being shaped by, a developmental history of decolonisation and cutural nationalism. If we examine the kind of structure and profile that govern both the first attempts at canon formation through anthologising and the first wave of critical studies that appeared from the mid 1960s through the 1970s, the emergence of a dominant version of Caribbean literature and thereby Caribbean literary history can be traced. Both editors and critics working at this moment construct the pre-1950 period by recourse to a consistent but limited archive.

Andrew Salkey's introduction to his collection of *West Indian Stories*, possibly the first Anglocreole regional anthology, published in 1960, is deliberately non-polemical, but his choice of Mittelholzer, Lamming, Hearne, Selvon, Carew, Harris, Mais and Reid, among others, is clearly motivated by the showcasing of recently published writers. Many of these also dominate his 1965 anthology *Stories from the Caribbean* in which his conviction in a tradition purely of the present is made much more explicit:

> To make the point that our writers from the islands and mainland countries of the Caribbean, with no long-established literary tradition, little or no publishing facilities, and no loyal book-buying public, have none the less in the face of all this produced their 'corporate' work in fifteen years is beguiling to say the least.
>
> (Salkey 1965: 11)

Salkey's genesis moment of 1950 is also present in Kenneth Ramchand's *West Indian Narrative: An Introductory Anthology*, one of several anthologies published in 1966 and probably the most clearly demarcated in terms of its presentation of a West Indian literary tradition. Organised in three parts, Ramchand's 'introductory anthology', moves from writings by non-West Indians before the twentieth century (including Aphra Behn, Matthew Lewis and Maria Nugent), to early West Indian writing (represented by H. G. de Lisser, Claude McKay and C. L. R. James), and then to post-1950s writers (including Mittelholzer, Reid, Lamming, Mais, Naipaul, Selvon, Hearne, Harris). This clear division of writings before and after 1950 clearly points to this as a year that literally, in his work, creates a new chapter in West Indian writing.

G. R. Coulthard's *Caribbean Literature: An Anthology*, also published in 1966, makes a similarly defining separation. He describes writing from the English-speaking region in the early twentieth century as 'provincial, imitative and slip-shod . . . hardly readable today' (Coulthard 1966: 8) and sets this archive against 'writing since the later 1940s . . . its high literary quality' (Coulthard 1966: 9). His selection, which begins with Claude McKay and moves through George Campbell and M. G. Smith, both of whom belonged to the *Focus* groups of 1940s Jamaica that were closely involved with the Independence movement, to the more contemporary voices of Walcott, Selvon, Lamming and Mervyn Morris, implicitly offers a canon of nationalist voices. Barbara Howe's anthology *From the Green Antilles*, yet another 1966 publication, returns to the familiar line-up of literary figures with poems by Walcott, Naipaul, John Hearne, V. S. Reid, Roger Mais, George Lamming, Samuel Selvon, as well as Karl Sealey and Frank Collymore, Austin Clarke, Ismith Khan and the lesser known Trinidadian Daniel Samaroo Joseph and A. N. Forde (Grenadian editor of *Bim*) to represent the English-speaking Caribbean. In his 'Foreword' to the 1966 publication of *Caribbean Voices: An Anthology of West Indian Poetry* selected by John Figueroa, Philip Sherlock confidently states the background of an absent literary history: 'at that time [1948] there were one or two West Indian writers – McKay, C. L. R. James, H. G. De Lisser, but there was no West Indian literature' (Figueroa 1966: vii). The volume, which is selected from fifteen years of scripts for the BBC 'Caribbean Voices' programme, confirms this observation, again signalling 1950 as a genesis year, although its inclusion of a number of women disrupts the usual male profile.

O. R. Dathorne's anthology *Caribbean Narrative* (1966), 'specially chosen for younger readers in their later school and pre-university years', is the only publication to strike out against the confident belief that West Indian writing began in the late 1940s.

> But West Indian literature did not begin when Mittelholzer left Trinidad for England, nor with Lamming and Selvon who followed in 1950, nor with Naipaul's scholarship to Oxford. Indigenous West Indian literature is at least one hundred and fifty years old.
>
> (Dathorne 1966: 3)

His *Caribbean Verse: an anthology* published just a year later in 1967 and presented as a volume 'for the use of students of literature and Caribbean studies', is imaginative in its selections. The introduction is not uncritical in its estimation of the material it selects, indeed it opens with the comment that 'at first sight there seems to be a great deal that is wrong with West Indian poetry' (Dathorne 1967: i). However, Dathorne offers an interesting account that is organised around themes which bring poets into dialogue with each other and his selection is both broad and unorthodox. As well as works by Walcott, Lamming, Mais, Harris, Carter and Campbell, there are also poems by the Jamaicans Vera Bell and Una Marson; Arthur Seymour, the Guyanese editor of *Kyk-Over-Al*; Frank Collymore, the Bajan editor of *Bim*; and lesser known names of C. L. Herbert, Raymond Barrow, E. McG. Keane, among others.

A. J. Seymour's 1972 collection, *New Writing in the Caribbean*, that emerged from the first Carifesta event held in Guyana in 1972, is possibly the most polemical in its introductory framing. Given that the event's theme was 'The Artist in Society, with Special Reference to the Third World', and that it emerged from a conference of writers, musicians, painters and sculptors from across the Caribbean region organised by the radical Guyanese poet Martin Carter shortly before resigning from his post as Minister of Information and Culture in the Forbes Burnham government, it is not surprising that Seymour's introduction addresses agendas of literary nationalism and regionalism in very direct terms. In analysing the works collected in this anthology of deliberately 'new' writing, Seymour notes, 'In the first place, there is a great desire to reject the European influence in thought and language' (Seymour 1972: 15) but he also offers something of a manifesto for regional writing:

> The traditional gap between the elite and folk between the artist and the mass must be bridged and it is contended that the artist must live with and among the people. This is another message of carifesta, that the artist must come home and stay at home for the sake of his integrity and that of the nation and indeed that the process of integration of artist with masses must begin and continue.
>
> (Seymour 1972: 15)

The confident sense of a Caribbean audience allows for a new explanatory narrative that speaks of and for Caribbean writing as a body of known and even cherished work.

It is important to appreciate that for the majority of critics immersed in the process of forging a new literary history cutting loose from a historical narrative coming out of colonialism enabled the writing they valued to be viewed within a context that assumes its own cultural wholenesss. This was an important aspect of the *Savacou* 3/4 collection and the vast majority of anthologies that appeared in and after the 1970s.[18] However, while anthologies of 'new' writing were flourishing in the 1970s, most pre-1950 works appear to have moved out of literary circulation.[19]

In the context of critical studies, G. R. Coulthard's *Race and Colour in Caribbean Literature*, the first book-length critical study of the subject, had been published in 1962. Coulthard, a lecturer in the Spanish Department at UWI, is centrally concerned with mapping both geographical and historical continuities in this study that looks across the Anglophone, Francophone and Hispanic Caribbean. In one sense this makes him much more open to examining writers from the 1930s and 1940s than later critics although, like them, his interest lies in those writers from the early period who fit into the model of insurgent writing and who therefore enable the past to correspond to the demands of the present. He includes writers such as Claude McKay and George Padmore whom, he argues, 'were in the vanguard of the revaluation of African culture long before the nationalist awakening in Africa and before the concept of négritude was developed in the Caribbean' (Coulthard 1962: 117). There is, however, already an awkwardness in terms of the tallying of aesthetic and cultural standards in these earlier works and Coulthard feels it necessary to point out that McKay's 'poetry suffers from an outmoded poetic idiom' (Coulthard 1962: 118).

Even Louis James, whose 1968 edited collection *The Islands in Between* caused much consternation in terms of its affiliations to 'colonial' models of reading, excludes the writings of the first decades of the twentieth century which he identifies as having 'something wrong, something missing. Ultimately it is that their literary sensibility is too English' (James 1968: 25). Like Dathorne's acknowledgement of a 'wrong' poetics and Coulthard's attention to an 'outmoded' idiom, James's comment registers the troublesome relation of the literary past. Already, in the first wave of critical studies, the cadence of these works jars against newly established expectations and their difference, framed in terms of cultural affiliation, necessitates their separation. James also positions a dividing line between writings from 1940 onwards and those earlier works that he acknowledges to be 'pioneers of a literature, writing consciously as West Indians ahead of the national political movements' (James 1968: 25). Like most anthologies and critical studies that will follow, the attention of this collection is focused on a series of individual male writers whose works can be easily accommodated to the agendas of literary indigenisation – Roger Mais, V. S. Reid, George Lamming, Derek Walcott, Andrew Salkey, John Hearne, V. S. Naipaul and Wilson Harris.

In *West Indian Poetry 1900–1970; A Study in Cultural Decolonisation* published in 1971, Edward Baugh also lays down a firm marker of political change and literary redefinition at 1940, declaring that 'The poets of the post-1940 mainstream do not consider themselves to be descendants of these forerunners, who produced a strictly colonial poetry.'[20] As critic, Baugh sees the lack of correspondence between the generations of writers as pretty absolute, asserting that 'such interest as their work can hold now is almost exclusively historical' (Baugh 1971: 5). Speaking as poet, Vivian Virtue's later account of this disavowal confirms his point: 'I have received scant, if any, attention from the younger generation of West Indian critics, most of whom are dismissive of the generation represented in those of us who also formed the Poetry League of Jamaica, now much maligned and sneered at' (Virtue in McLeod (ed.) 2002: 27).

In her 1972 article, 'One love – rhetoric or reality? – aspects of Afro-Jamaicanism', Sylvia Wynter follows Coulthard and Hearne in making strategic connections between the 1930s and the 1960s, constructing something of an anti-colonial literary history in her selection of C. L. R. James, Roger Mais and Vic Reid as pioneers who had 'sought to bring the masses into focus as the principal actors on the . . . historical stage' (Wynter 1972: 70). Kenneth Ramchand's inclusion of McKay, Delisser and MacDermot as the prominent early voices in his 1970 study, *The West Indian Novel and Its Background*, similarly allows for the construction of a progressive narrative based on a very partial archive. The two trends of de-linking the literary past from the present and reclaiming only those writers whose work can be readily apprehended as synonymous with the dominant agendas of cultural nationalism can already be observed.

The second collection of West Indian criticism, *Critics on Caribbean Literature*, edited by Edward Baugh and published in 1978, gathers many of the theoretical interventions that remain landmark to that period now. What is particularly interesting in terms of my project is Baugh's clear demarcation of critical history in his introduction to the volume. Although, like James, Baugh acknowledges the presence of pre-1950 material he describes it as operating within a separate historical dimension, as relating to a past no longer relevant or alive to the present.

> One could begin, say, with a sampling of the random, and usually very slight pieces of criticism from the period prior to 1950, from about which date one marks the significant beginning of the main body of West Indian literature. This could be followed by a look at the criticism by West Indians, followed by the on-going debate among West Indian critics as to what should be the guiding principles of a West Indian criticism of the regional literature . . . These are some of the historical movements, but to have planned the anthology in terms of them would have necessitated the inclusion of too much ephemeral material or material of purely historical interest.
>
> (Baugh 1978: 12)

Baugh's assumption that Caribbean literature and criticism proper began in 1950 not only echoes earlier collections but is also a view consolidated by the two other major survey works that were published at the same time: Bruce King's edited collection *West Indian Literature* (1979) and Lloyd Brown's *West Indian Poetry* (1978).

Anthony Boxhill's chapter on 'The beginnings to 1929', in King's edition, is exceptional in its claim for a unbroken literary lineage: 'All the things for which West Indian literature is known and admired today can be observed evolving over a period of time' (Boxhill 1979: 44), although it cannot be overlooked that the chapter constructs a developmental narrative across the works of H. G. DeLisser, Thomas Henry MacDermot, W. Adolphe Roberts and Claude McKay that is finally presented as a nationalist teleology.

> West Indian writings gradually abandoned their English models, experimented more and more with the language of the West Indian people, and concentrated more and more on trying to present to the people what was distinct and worthwhile in their lives.
>
> (Boxhill 1979: 44)

Reinhard Sander's chapter on 'The thirties and forties' is an extremely detailed and useful survey of literary activity during these decades. His attention is given to the important little magazines which emerged at this time and in particular to the Beacon group whose work was central to the genre of social realism that developed as a result of the determined engagement with 'the people, their problems, customs and beliefs'

(Sander 1979: 53). Sander has comparatively little to say about poetry in the 1930s which he deems to be 'alien, imitative and uninspiring' (Sander 1979: 58) and proposes a dramatic shift in works of the 1940s that 'were fired by the same spirit of nationalism. They shared the new awareness of history, of social and political injustice, and turned to the folk for their material and medium of expression' (Sander 1979: 59). Again though, his final summary of the literary achievement of this era is also implicitly framed within a nationalist trajectory, 'although they recognised the need for change, they had not yet fully succeeded in breaking with the traditions and modes of thinking which they had inherited from their colonial masters' (Sander 1979: 62). While these two chapters document crucial early works and projects clearly associated with the creation and expression of local and regional writings, the presentation of this material as somehow gradually working towards a later goal confirms the view that Sandra Pouchet Paquet articulates plainly in the first line of her chapter on the 1950s: 'It is now commonplace to identify the 1950s as the decade when West Indian literature emerged as a recognisable entity' (Pouchet Paquet 1979: 63). Individual chapters on Mittelholzer, Selvon, Lamming, Walcott, Naipaul, Harris, Rhys and Brathwaite in many ways set out for critical scrutiny the canon that was already forming through the reiteration of various names and works and which mainly remains intact today.[21]

Brown's focus in *West Indian Poetry* is broader in historical terms but equally well-defined in terms of its teleological narrative that 'describe[s] the history of West Indian poetry as a movement from the derivativeness and colonial "conversions" of the earlier years to the more imaginative and complex "transformations" of the contemporary period' (Brown 1978: 11). Setting his study in almost direct opposition to Louis James' work of a decade earlier, Brown declares that West Indian literature and criticism have shunned the European literary experience in favour of 'what they perceive as a distinctive West Indian experience' (Brown 1978: 8). Quoting from Brathwaite, Wynter and Lamming, Brown affiliates his work very clearly with the project of literary nation-buliding and the demands of 'the full emergence of that national consciousness since the last world war, and more recently, since independence' (Brown 1978: 9). It is therefore unsurprising that Brown devotes only twenty pages to the one hundred and eighty years that comprise 'The beginnings' of West Indian poetry up to the 1940s. His estimation of this period as 'uneven at best, and in some respects . . . downright unpromising' (Brown 1978: 19) is characteristic of the way in which he catalogues whole bodies of writing as undifferentiated and unchallenging. Although he makes a significant claim for Una Marson as 'the earliest female poet of significance to emerge in West Indian literature' (Brown 1978: 34) and foregrounds the importance of gender within her work, in nearly two centuries the only poet that he considers to be of real note is Claude McKay. Michael Gilkes' choice of

DeLisser, James, Mais and Mittleholzer as literary pioneers through whose works it is possible to 'view the development of the novel away from a colonial, Europe-orientated condition of "mimicry," toward a self-conscious, "West Indianizing" phase' (Gilkes 1981: 7) in his 1981 study, *The West Indian Novel*, also creates a clear developmental line which is then taken up by his focus on Lamming, Naipaul, St Omer, Reid, Williams and Harris.

As this examination of the anthologies and critical studies that were published during the 1960s and 1970s demonstrates, the scarce attention given to West Indian writing before 1950 is directly related to the need to articulate and narrate an emergent nationalist tradition with West Indian literature at a critical moment of academic and political consolidation. The canonical journey mapped out by the repeated names of H. G. Delisser, C. L. R. James and Claude McKay navigates a fairly smooth if highly selective and all-male crossing from colony to nation. In order to deliver us to 1950 and the 'real' beginning of West Indian writing, these studies cut a narrow pathway through what I want to argue was a complex and densely populated literary scene. They lay bare for us the criteria of ascendent Caribbeaness, so that a text such as C. L. R. James' *Minty Alley* which is set in a barrackyard in Trinidad is adopted as a founding text of the Caribbean tradition and James himself as a *bona fide* Caribbean writer, whereas, on the other hand, Vivian Virtue's *Wings of the Morning*, a collection of sonnets, vilanelles and rondeaux published in 1938, is mentioned only briefly and dismissively, and cannot be accounted for in literary history of the decolonised Caribbean.

The sidelining of pre-1950 material that occurred in the nationalist moment of canon-making has received little sustained critical attention and for the majority of pre-1950 texts there has been no reversal of fortunes to date.[22] Shalini Puri has commented very recently on the silencing still effected by 'the critical strategy that makes revolutionary consciousness a precondition for gaining entry into the canon' (Puri 2003a: 38). The general attitude towards Caribbean literature in the first half of the twentieth century is that it is merely the sawdust remaining on the floor once the robust literary figures of Walcott, Lamming and Naipaul had been carved out – an embarrassing and undesirable reminder of imitative writings dependent on colonial forms and ideologies. The possibilities of connections or continuities between writers pre- and post-1950 has not been acknowledged or explored. As A. L. McLeod points out, the need to force an interruption between past and present, which was clearly driven by the historical imperatives of this era, had a very detrimental effect both on those writers whose work was neglected and on the conception of literary development emerging at that time.

> By the 1960's there were undeniable signs that a new poetic had replaced the old . . . in the Caribbean . . . the older generation of writers

was speedily consigned to the historical record rather than being
respected as the founders of what was then a dynamic development
of experimentation in expression.

(McLeod 2002: 26)

Although the exact historical markers of literary redefinition may shift
between 1940 and 1950 in these works, what is clear is that the body of
early writings became a necessary archive against which the newness
of the 'revindication of blackness', to borrow Sylvia Wynters' term, could
be viewed. In other words, the historical point at which the crucial separation between a literary past and a literary present is figured is less
important than the trend towards the disavowal of particular kinds of
writing and the construction of a teleology of cultural progression that has
flattened out many interesting texts and moments.

Cultural contexts

I want now to restore something of the context that I believe is enabling
to an understanding of pre-1950 works and their extraordinary aesthetic
and political range. The cultural politics and the cultural forms which
need to be discussed with reference to Caribbean literature in the first half
of the twentieth century are far more complex than the representation
they found in the 1960s and 1970s indicates. There was no single nationalist
ideology and the expressions of the need and desire for a distinctly Caribbean (or island-centred) culture did not cohere in any easily definable
manner during this period. Rather than the neat ethnic and ideological
divides proposed by the early anthologies and critical studies, Caribbean
writers during this period were positioned along a broad continuum of
cultural involvement and allegiance and, at moments, spoke in a context
as politically highly charged and unstable as the 1960s and 1970s. The
Beacon group's fierce rebuttal of Victorian codes, idioms and values; Roger
Mais' recasting of a culturally relevant modernist manifesto; the relocation of representational agency within a Caribbean landscape which is
achieved through the writings of Vivian Virtue's 'Cassia Tree' or Tropica's
'Busha's Song' on the one hand and C. L. R. James' *Minty Alley* with its
inscription of urban barrackyard life on the other; and the publication
of works in creole by Louise Bennett and Una Marson, all signal the
kinds of literary innovation and cultural nationalism that is most readily
associated with the 1960s.

Having attempted to represent the strength and confidence with which
the dominant critical moment of the 1960s and 1970s came into being
and how this shaped the earliest attempts at literary history and canon-
building, I now wish to open this 'difficult' archive of pre-1950s writings
up to the present. The collective writing off of the earlier period, enacted
in part by the condemnatory conclusions of the first wave of critics, in

part by the drive to attend to a new body of writing that was very clearly experimental and engaged in ways that were politically enabling, and in part by the institutional momentum away from time-consuming archival work, has seemingly sealed the wax on the archives before 1950 and (with a few exceptions such as Claude McKay and C. L. R. James) most remain literally untouched. It is my strong sense that a more sustained engagement with these archives will enlarge our understanding of the Caribbean literary tradition across the twentieth century. On the one hand it will allow for the retrieval of connected struggles and aligned, although not identitical, projects regarding the politics of self-representation. In this respect, I want to draw attention to the many debates, manifestos and other such endeavours that sought to address the demand for local inscription that became so clear in the 1960s. On the other hand, material that does not conform to the demands of a retrospective agenda allows us to interrogate what it is about writing of this period that not only fails to be accommodated in the heuristic label 'Caribbean' but that almost needs to be masked in order not to threaten its integrity. Probably the most contentious aspect of this project is to read the most unpopular, even unreadable, texts of a Caribbean tradition in order to bring them into the literary history of twentieth century Anglocreole writings and initiate some discussion about their value to us as twenty-first century readers.

The very involved and discordant literary context of Jamaica during the pre-1950 period offers a useful portal through which to trace that which has been incorporated into literary histories and that which has been disavowed. The various disputes, crises and even imprisonment which afflicted the central participants in the struggles over Jamaican literature and cultural identity pre-1950 are testimony to the highly charged nature of this activity. The serious differences in orientation between J. E. C. McFarlane and Roger Mais, and the organizations and publications with which they were associated, offer a useful organising lens through which to consider the different debates and influences that were crucial at this time, as does their curious intersection.

J. E. C. McFarlane has left a careful record of his offerings to Jamaican writing and in particular poetry. Through collections of lectures which he delivered at the Institute of Jamaica during the 1930s and 1940s and documents detailing his involvement with the Poetry League of Jamaica it is clear that he was a prominent poetic critic of the time. The confidence and authority of McFarlane's essays are suggestive of a dominant as well as a prolific presence within the Jamaican literary scene. Although his prose attacks on civil and Christian institutions and Jamaica's 1934 crisis reveal him to be politically forward thinking in terms of economic analysis, as Financial Secretary he held a lofty position in the Colonial Office, his attitude to poetry was far more conventional. He was irreverently known as 'the black Englishman'.[23] McFarlane was the founding and arguably the most active member of the Poetry League of Jamaica, a branch of the

Empire Poetry League that was formally initiated on 19 September 1923. With its public meetings, lectures, prizes and Year Books (from 1939), the League undoubtedly served to raise the profile of poetic activity in Jamaica. Many of the poets who were published during this period and whose works were broadcast on the 'Caribbean Voices' programme were associated with the League in some way, including Mais himself.

Several documents pertaining to the League's events, found in the West India Reference Library in Kingston, point to the particular involvement and recognition of certain individuals. There are pamphlets recording the 'Formal recognition of Thomas Redcam as poet Laureate of Jamaica at tenth annual meeting of the Jamaican branch of the Poetry League, Ward Theatre 26 October 1933' as well as a 'Memorial Address in honour of Constance Hollar and Astley Clerk' given by J. E. C. McFarlane in 1945. It is also possible to find several figures involved in the West Indian literary scene who give credit to the League. In a 1948 article celebrating twenty-five years of the Jamaica Poetry League, Archie Lindo reflects on

> years of pioneer work, of high endeavour and of struggle in the face of public indifference and sometimes of lack of interest from their own members.
>
> The League which was founded by Mr. J. E. Clare McFarlane has accomplished a great deal. It has helped to keep the writing fraternity together. It has been responsible for the encouragement of the young writer, for the publication in print of the work of our poets and for a kindling of interest in our literature by means of public lectures and radio broadcasts.
>
> (Lindo 1948: 19)

This view of the League as a key forum for literary activity with a clear ability to promote and publish material, as well as to generate an audience for poetry written by Jamaicans is also echoed by A. J. Seymour in 1950, who comments on how 'The Poetry League seems to have provided a framework for encouraging a poetic literature in Jamaica, by lectures and discussions and by encouraging and fostering the teaching of poetry in schools' (Seymour 1950: 20).

The League's function as a designated place in which poetry could be shared and discussed clearly had a significant impact, not least in the debates and challenges concerning Jamaican poetry which they provoked but, like the reading circles of this time, the League was middle-class in social orientation and functioned as a means for the educated minority to assert their knowledge and appreciation of what they supposed to be high culture. As Honorary Secretary Wycliffe Bennett proudly asserts in 1948, 'The Poetry League of Jamaica is not a political organisation. We consider that our work transcends politics. Nor is it a clique. Our perspective derives from our vertical relationship with God and our horizontal relationship with one another' (Bennett W. 1948: 6). Moreover, McFarlane's didacticism and his insistent opinions on the special status of poetry removed from social context must also be acknowledged. In his annual Presidential Address, 'On the nature of poetry', delivered before the Jamaica Poetry League on 30 October 1924. McFarlane advocated that 'poetry can be of greatest service to humanity: in restoring the lost outline, in raising it from the maze of sensuous things into the clear atmosphere of the spirit' (1945: 107).

Just over ten years later, during a period of acute economic deprivation and social unrest and after a decade that had been marked by the return of Marcus Garvey to Jamaica in 1927 and his purposeful focus on black intellectual recovery work, as well as by the empowerment of the working class through labour struggles, McFarlane's address, 'The Challenge of Our Time', delivered at the Institute of Jamaica on 31 January 1935, again framed the relation between poetry and society through the rhetoric of redemption and within the context of Jamaica as colony.

> Therefore as representatives of a great tradition we offer you Poetry, upon which we feel certain the true foundation of this Empire rests and by which it will be preserved throughout the storm that hangs above the horizon of civilization . . . The Poetry League is proposing to you that you begin the change of your environment and the improvement of the quality of your public men by changing and improving the pattern and quality of your individual thought . . . We offer you the inexhaustible riches of poetry with which to do this.
>
> (McFarlane 1945: 34 and 29)

As an imperial preservative, McFarlane's recipe for poetry openly declares its cultural orientation towards Empire and sets the permanence of poetry against the changing weather of political climes. The tenacity of his views is striking. Even in 1953, when tremendous political and aesthetic transformations had taken place, McFarlane adheres vehemently to the belief that poetry should transcend the concerns of quotidian reality in order to offer 'the gold amidst much dross; the eternal and imperishable amidst the topical and ephemeral' (McFarlane 1953: 126). This sense of adulation is bizarrely embodied by his own garlanding as Jamaica's second poet laureate in 1952, a ceremony that V. S. Reid describes as 'late in the day of the revolution to be holding coronations; but the tenacity of poets, especially when strengthened by an Empire Poetry League, is legendary' (Reid 1978: 6). McFarlane's high profile within Jamaican literary circles for such an extended period almost certainly resulted in his vision of Jamaican poetry being powerfully communicated to many of the island's poets. Nevertheless, his defiant resistance to historical change and to the increasingly clamorous demands for relevance and the reshaping of literary language and form, as well as content, position him as an almost antithetical voice to Roger Mais.

Although Mais was in no way the same self-styled authority on aesthetic matters as McFarlane, an analysis of his works and opinions help us to map out the other narrative around writing and social engagement that emerged in Jamaica during the first half of the century. Mais began his journalism career as a reporter on the *Daily Gleaner* in the 1930s and, as Brathwaite explains, he became 'caught up in [the age of West Indian nationalism] . . . Mais became a "socialist", that is, an intellectual committed to the cause of social justice' (Brathwaite 1993: 172). Mais took a job as a staff writer with *Public Opinion*, the weekly paper of the People's National Party (PNP) led by Norman Manley, and was closely associated with its successor in the 1940s, *Focus*, the literary journal of the PNP. Both publications were edited by Manley's wife, Edna, and were crucially concerned with the intervention that literature could make in terms of imagining cultural and social transformation. In her Foreword to the first issue of *Focus* in 1943, Edna Manley affirmed that 'Great and irrevocable changes have swept this land of ours in the last few years, and out of these changes a new art is springing . . . art gives a picture of contemporary life . . . it contains within in the germs of the future' (Manley 1943). Mais published stories in both the 1943 and 1948 issues of *Focus* and wrote in all genres, although he is probably best remembered for his novels *The Hills Were Joyful Together* (1953), *Brother Man* (1954) and *Black Lightning* (1955) which interestingly allow his work to be co-opted for the post 1950 moment of nationalism.

In many ways Mais' novels do epitomise the commitment to social realism and social justice that had also been articulated in *And Most of All Man Stories* (1942) and *Face and Other Stories* (1946). In an interview after the publication of *The Hills Were Joyful Together*, Mais declared that his intention was 'to give the world a true picture of the real Jamaica and the dreadful conditions of the working class' (Dakers 1953). While his engaged representation of the urban dispossessed and his sympathetic rendering of a Rastafarian hero were regarded as transgressive and even shocking works when they were published, especially from the pen of a light-skinned, middle-class writer, Mais' political conviction had been sharper still in the 1940s. In 1944, the year that the British Colonial Office announced the policy leading towards self-government, Mais went to St Catherine's prison for six months on a charge of sedition relating to his article 'Now We Know'. Striking out against the very preservation of Empire that McFarlane advocated, Mais railed against Churchill's pronouncement of continuing imperial rule:

> Now we know why the draft of the New Constitution has not been published before . . . The man of brave speeches has told the world again and again that he does not intend the old order to change; that he does not mean to yield an inch in concessions to any one, least of all to people in the colonies.
>
> (Mais 1944)

While Mais' disloyalty to Empire was equal in strength to McFarlane's loyalty, and his calls for social engagement equally weighted to McFarlane's demands for transcendence and disengagement, Mais also argued forcefully on the matter of poetic register and the implied relation between poet and audience.

> We are Jamaicans writing for Jamaicans. Let us for the sake of illustration turn this proper noun into a commonplace adjective. Let us say instead 'We are Jamaicans writing for a Jamaican Public'. This is what you get, – we, from the heights of Parnassus are writing down to you fellows below there! ... Nothing is intrinsically wrong with our reading public ... I resent this implication of mediocrity, therefore I refuse to read your poems, because they teem with little simpering clichés.
>
> (Mais 1940: 12)

His objections to the kind of work that McFarlane produced, promoted and published was also concerned with the misunderstanding of historical value that a colonial education had encouraged.

> Your minds grew until they caught up with Chaucer, Milton, Shakespeare ... and then they stopped growing. In a word they stopped growing with the school syllabus ... If only you would wake up for long enough to give the matter some thought you would realise that these men in their day were the last syllable in modernity! Chaucer broke new ground and a lot of traditions, so did Milton, so did Shakespeare.
>
> (Mais 1940: 12)

Echoing the fierce guidelines of Ezra Pound in 'A Few Don'ts by an Imagiste', Roger Mais attacks the practice of merely appropriating all the aesthetic markers of poetry, as mediated through colonial institutions, without any consideration of their relevance.

> One of the troubles with people who write poetry is that they have picked that medium. It is not a medium that lends itself to practising nothing more than the modicum of mediocrity ... Why go to all that pains to say in rhymed lines, what you would be ashamed to say in indifferent prose? Do you think you can hide superficiality behind assonance or alliteration, or successfully camouflage the trite between a sequence of rhymes?
>
> (Mais 1940: 12)

In opposition to McFarlane, Mais advocates a recognition of the present in terms of contemporary aesthetic developments and Jamaica's lived reality. In his characteristically ebullient style, Mais declares his unwillingness to conform to the prevalent version of Victorianism, enmeshed in both the cultural and aesthetic values of certain Jamaicans.

> As to your dogged refusal to accept the more modern form; that in itself constitutes an insult to my mentality. I refuse to be hurled back into the dark ages, or to be dragged there supinely on the back of a sure-footed, nimble quadruped.[25]

Mais's provocative style is clearly part of his attempt to engender a reconstruction of Jamaican poetics and often represents his own less polite and more politicised demand for a growth in consciousness.

Both McFarlane and Mais were clearly conscious of the particular, if divided, expectations that governed the relationship between the Jamaican writer and their society. Both were also committed to the development of a local literature – albeit in contesting forms. It is perhaps still surprising though that these two figures, whose views seem antithetical, moved in each other's cultural orbit. For example, J. E. C. McFarlane's survey of Jamaican literature during the 1920s and 1930s, *A Literature in the Making*, included Mais among its literary line-up.[26] Mais also published several of his poems in the Jamaica Poetry League's 1940 Year Book. The career of Una Marson also seems to suggest that what look like two opposing cultural realms were actually connected. Marson, the first secretary of the League, was included in *A Literature in the Making* and published in the anthologies edited by McFarlane. She also, like Mais, wrote for the radical weekly *Public Opinion* and in 1928 had founded the monthly journal *The Cosmopolitan: A Monthly Magazine for the Business Youth of Jamaica and the Official Organ of the Stenographers Association*. This journal often featured McFarlane on its local poets page and yet is was emphatically modern and cosmo-politan in orientation, and pioneering in its strong commitment to women's rights. As even this brief snapshot shows, to reduce Mais and McFarlane to the positions of anti- and pro-Empire is to overlook the intricate politics of ideological attachment operating in this time and place.

I want to argue that we need to enlarge our understanding of these positions and their intimacy with each other in order to appreciate the very complex pulls of homeland and motherland; the authority of the past and the demands of the present; the value of English Literature and the need for local writing that operated as peculiarly connected paradigms in the first half of the twentieth century. Moreover, this overlapping involve-ment in very different kinds of cultural projects is an important context through which to read the multiple attachment to both orthodox and 'modern' forms, rhetorics and ideas of belonging that makes the standing of many works published before 1950 difficult to fix in terms of cultural authenticity.

In our own historical moment which is less charged with the urgency of claiming representation for a devalued majority and more aware of the pressures that historical narratives place on unruly moments in time, opening up an archive of uneven and unpredictable writings will yield a sense of an unstable past that may be less directly useful to a teleology of literary nationalism, but more honest to the cultural transitions and transactions from which Caribbean literature took its first soundings and made its first voicings. My aim is not to propose that we skilfully recuperate all of this past as a positive precursor to the creative emergence of writings post-1950 or to claim that all of it is equally worthy of detailed critical attention, but rather to suggest that critics of Caribbean literature could make more acknowledgement of the significant, fragmented and often unmanageable archive of writings that does represent a literary past that made the present possible through both its failures and its successes.

Cultural ambivalence and the crime of mimicry

Although the majority of writings from this period do not explicitly address the social and political upheavals of the time and cannot be easily read as fulfilling an agenda of cultural decolonisation, this does not mean that they are simply mouthpieces of Empire. Indeed, the first real occasion of Jamaican literary nationalism appears in 1899 from a Creole: Tom Redcam's (Thomas MacDermot's) All Jamaica Library (1904 to 1909) was sponsored by *The Jamaica Times*, the leading literary newspaper which MacDermot edited from 1900–1920.[27] This project became a valuable outlet for cheap editions of local writers, with the specific aim 'to present to a Jamaican public at a price so small as to make each publication generally purchasable, a literary embodiment of Jamaican subjects' (Cobham-Sander 1981: 72). A level of commitment to Jamaican cultural and literary matters was also shown by the group of writers responsible for *Singers Quarterly* that began in 1932. This scrapbook poetry collection, into which both popular and original poems were pasted, was edited by Albinia Hutton and distributed around fourteen individuals, including McFarlane, many of whom lived rather detached lives in the hills.[28] Although it could hardly be calibrated on a scale of West Indianness as conceived from the 1960s onwards, this journal is significant in the nascent West Indian aesthetic which it fostered by its focus on 'excerpts concerning the West Indies or by West Indians'.

In the crucial crossing between Empire and nation that marks the political narrative of this era, it is clear that some writers had made an early landing and these are the figures whom we are encouraged to remember through anthologies and critical studies (Claude McKay, C. L. R. James, George Campbell and Roger Mais). Many more writers though remained somewhere between colony and nation in their formal and linguistic structures, and often in their subject matter too, and it is clear that this was increasingly read as a failing that threatened their place in literary history. Several reviews of McFarlane's edited collection, *A Treasury of Jamaican*

Poetry, published in 1949 just on the cusp of that watershed year, focus on the seeming absence of nation and the presence of colony. Omar St John's piece in *The West Indian Review* registers his difficulty with reconciling the works of the volume with their place and time:

> Such a volume should be a landmark in the development of the island's culture but ... this is no articulation of a new culture in birth, no voice crying in the wilderness; if it is the voice of Jamaica it is a small and rather refined voice.
>
> (Omar St John 1950: 17)

In his harshly titled review, 'Barren Treasury', published in the same year in *Public Opinion,* John Hearne also accuses the poets included of being out of step with both the events and the voice of the island.

> Primarily the fault of our poets is in their lack of awareness. They have not caught the spirit and have realised little of the substance of the age in which they live ... They are in the worst sense middle-class, artificial and agonisingly self-conscious.
>
> (Hearne 1950: 6)

George Cumper, in his 1957 review 'Literary Period Piece' that discusses those writers included by McFarlane in his critical survey, *A Literature in the Making,* sees the dependence upon culturally inappropriate models as the primary artistic limitation: 'There is, first of all, a complete lack of technical inventiveness. It is the fashionable verse-forms of nineteenth century England which appear'.[29] In a much later piece Arthur D. Drayton also draws attention to this quality in *A Treasury of Jamaican Verse,* where he identifies 'the triteness, the "second-hand" mentality' (Drayton 1970a: 86). To most, the basic criteria for cultural reorientation was to leave behind any stylistic or content-based striving towards pseudo-Britishness. Discussing works from this period more generally, G. R. Coulthard, in his 1961 survey 'The literature of the West Indies' for *The Commonwealth Pen,* commented that, 'The impatience felt by the young writers of today with this literature is largely due to its old-fashioned, hackneyed poetic idiom and basic unoriginality' (Coulthard 1961: 187). In a different piece, Drayton asserts that this derivative format was so totemic of the poetry being written that the criteria of evaluation came to be based on how authentic an imitation was provided.

> The reader came to measure the validity of literature by its capacity to remind him of the long English twilight, its capacity to affect the various moods and interests of the Romantics, to find equivalents for daffodils and lilies and lakes, to reproduce familiar English situations, and above all to achieve this within metropolitan varieties and

manipulations of the English language that alone, in the eyes of the reader, were permissible.

(Drayton 1970b: 75)

Certainly, the commonest criticism of Anglocreole Caribbean poetry during the period from 1900 to 1945 was its reliance upon British models and its lack of experimentation. Aesthetic critics challenged the worth of the poetry on the basis that it relied too heavily upon received colonial poetic models to offer any exciting or innovative insights into language, imagery or form. Cultural critics disputed the poetry's worth on the basis that it was too dependent upon the experiences and ideas of the colonial predecessor to merit the label Jamaican. Both charges reveal that imitation was seen as the principal stumbling block to real achievement and bring us to the crime of 'colonial' mimicry. The cultural politics embedded in this charge become clearer when we consider that Marson's blues poems, in which, as Lloyd Brown points out, 'she attempts to combine Jamaica's rural folk language with the black American's blues tradition' (Brown 1978: 37), have not been read as a sign of mimicry but rather of innovation and authenticity.

There might be some value in understanding that imitative forms were often an attempt to seize all that went with a centrality of discourse – recognition, publication and even money. As Edward Baugh suggests, 'it is as if one of their chief aims was to show that the natives of the colonies could write verse like that which poets of the "mother country" had written' (Baugh 1971: 5). However, complicating this view of mimicry as a rite of passage, some critics have argued that imitation should not be viewed in a purely pejorative light, as the single most shameful failing on the part of the individual writer, but rather as an inevitable consequence of a historically and culturally specific situation.

> A Victorian sitting-room in a contemporary West Indian country house; a West Indian, with no professional interest in literature, correcting an English expatriate teacher who has misquoted Wordsworth; a 'Letter to the Editor', attacking English colonialism in classical English style, all to some extent indicate the way English and European ways of life and attitudes have been absorbed into the living tissue of West Indian society. These are not a continuing outside influence; in many cases they now no longer correspond to the contemporary English scene.

(James 1968: 23)

James here makes a crucial point that is seldom to be found in the evaluations of West Indian writing which retains classical English style, diction and form. These choices of style cannot be taken merely as the vestiges of colonialism, or as a guarantee of the preference for Europe over the Caribbean. In many instances the issue that James describes is very clearly located in the social fabric of the Caribbean and the attachment to western forms and cultural residues that were no longer valued in the motherland created something of a colonial time-warp through which Jamaica may have been more 'properly' British in its literary taste than Britain.

However, if these readings help to explain the signs of mimicry, others may help us to decode them. More recent theoretical interventions concerning mimicry and the politics of speaking via the other's language may help us to clear a space in our own time for the kinds of subtle coding that the demands of nationalist criticism in the 1960s and 1970s could not allow for. Postcolonial critics familiar with Homi Bhabha's influential theory that 'Mimicry marks those moments of civil disobedience within the discipline of civility: signs of spectacular resistance. When the words of the master become the site of hybridity' (Bhabha 1994: 121), may not be at all surprised to find the marked presence of mimicry in these works that are situated so precariously at the historical cusp between assent and dissent, speaking with and speaking against. They may be more surprised to see that Brathwaite had made a similar observation and acknowledgement of the complex matrix of inheritance and innovation twenty years earlier: 'I would say that our real/apparent imitation involves at the same time a significant element of creativity, while our creativity in turn involves a significant element of imitation (Brathwaite 1974: 16), pre-empting Henry Louis Gates, Jr's point, in his discussion of African-American writers' engagement with canonical texts as a mode of protest, 'ours is repetition, but repetition with a difference, a signifying black difference'.[30] As I hope to show, the line between a mere imitation of a European literary model and a rewriting of it is difficult to draw and in many cases is as reliant upon a politics of reading as of writing. To my mind, therefore, the use of stylised English language and the conscious adoption of British literary models should be viewed suspiciously by the critic searching for an imitative lineage in order to substantiate claims of unbroken colonial domination.

Nevertheless, it is perhaps unsurprising that it is Mais and not McFarlane that we find being taken up in critical studies and anthologies of the 1960s. The issues of cultural relevance, the relation between writer and his society, the demands of political independence and the adoption of literary forms and language better able to register the distinctiveness of West Indian experience that lie at the core of Mais' journalistic and literary achievements are closely matched to the central concerns that informed debates in the 1960s and early 1970s. However, if Mais has had an enduring, although increasingly marginal, presence within Caribbean literary histories since the 1960s, it is all too possible to imagine why McFarlane's works and those of the vast majority of the poets he represented in his collections could not be sustained in these accounts. By 1970, these 'acquiescent' writers had been relegated not only to an earlier phase of literary development but a regressive one. In an aptly entitled article, published in *Jamaica Journal* in 1970, 'Ideas of patriotism and national dignity in some Jamaican writings', Leo Oakley marks the late 1930s as a moment of change when there emerged

> a different brand of writers ... who did not hesitate to assert their Jamaicanness, their nationalism. They could not identify with England and English ways. They were for things Jamaican, and they gave voice to the nationalist movement of the time.
>
> (Oakley 1970: 19)

Neither Oakley, nor any other critic that I have found, accounts for the significant historical overlap between Mais and McFarlane or Marson and Reid that would complicate this presentation of a revolutionary history that had now become the grand narrative of literary development.

Dividing loyalities: colonial nationalism, local longings

As my attention to McFarlane and Mais has shown, the lack of consensus over what properly constituted culture in Jamaica, or more contentiously Jamaican culture, is an important context for an understanding of many works which sought to represent the island. However, if, as Bill Ashcroft states:

> The most contentious problems in postcolonial theory continue to be those hinging on the capacity of the colonized subject to intervene in colonial discourse to contest it, change it, or generally make the voice of the colonized heard.
>
> (Ashcroft 2001: 45)

then I would argue that for Caribbean literary scholars these questions find their most vexing and perhaps most productive archive in writing pre-1950, much of which displays an unsteady and often intricate cultural code-switching. In his work on C. L. R. James, Stuart Hall has drawn attention to something of the complexity of the European influence within Caribbean cultures, pointing out that James had 'a very profound and complicated feeling towards Europe which needs much more exploration' (Hall in Schwarz 1998: 24). Most significant for this study is Hall's point that this 'feeling' cannot be understood by the crude response of 'contemporary intellectuals towards Europe ... we must either ditch it or kill it, love it or mimic it' (Hall in Schwarz 1998: 24). As Hall is keen to emphasise, the over-simplistic assumption of a binary, 'either/or', identification in relation to Europe is inadequate to describe the complex register of overlapping affiliation and double consciousness (to use duBois' term) that finds repeated articulation in works written before 1950. I would argue that the marked presence of a persistent unresolved and affective discourse in relation to Europe and Empire is one of the central reasons why these works have been collectively dismissed as being outside the interest of Caribbean cultural critics.

The presence of colonial discourse cannot be ignored within this poetry and in his introduction to *Voices From The Summerland* (1929), the first published anthology of Anglocreole verse, David M. Mitchell proudly declares that

> Once more our restless sea-bourne race has explored the wine-dark ocean and founded new homes for its children over not one but many seas. And of its ever loyal cherishing of our English poetic tradition this volume is proof.
>
> (Mitchell 1929)

The confident assertion concerning the achievements of 'our race' which Mitchell makes here suggests an almost supremacist attitude and a clear relation between the cultural form of this poetry and the cultural politics of Empire. Furthermore, his argument based on 'our race' shows no recognition of the ethnic diversity of the writers whose work is published within this volume (poems by both Claude McKay and J. E. C. McFarlane, the volume's editor, appear). The clear eurocentrism of this introductory comment is further corroborated by the title of this volume: it is only when defined within a European conceptual framework that Jamaica is a 'summerland'. However, this particular representation of Jamaica within the cultural reference system of Europe is not an isolated means of codification. In several poems ostensibly 'about' Jamaica it is possible to trace the way in which European myths are relocated within the Caribbean. In much of the poetry written by Creole women poets that is published in volumes across the first half of the century, Jamaica is exoticised and transformed into a jewel, a glittering vision of the 'Isle of beauty', 'God's hills' and 'this island a fairy dream'.[31]

Possibly the most persistent eurocentric myth to be inscribed onto Jamaica is that of Eden, the prelapsarian paradise. The historical significance of this as a myth of conquest is discussed by Lowenthal.

> The West Indies share the reputation of tropical islands everywhere for beauty and physical comfort. Images of Eden kept alive in medieval gardens and embellished by travellers from the Orient aroused expectations for the Caribbean that Columbus and his followers were happy to confirm. And the islands did conform to preconceptions of paradise ... Ignored or forgotten are less attractive aspects of West Indian nature.
>
> (Lowenthal 1972: 14)

Certainly the status of this representation as a projection of European fantasy makes its cultural politics fairly straightforward, as does its constant reiteration, even in the twenty-first century, by tourist companies, alcohol advertisements and popular romance narratives.

The enduring life of this myth as an explanatory narrative for the extreme natural beauty of the islands appears to have naturalised the reference to Eden as a shorthand for expressing the magnificence of the islands' landscape, even in the work of those whose decolonizing strategies are well-known. In the poetry of Una Marson, the allusion to an Edenic vision first appears in *Tropic Reveries* (1930) in 'Jamaica' which situates the Jamaican landscape as a positive inversion of the English scene: 'No fields and streams are covered o'er with snow,|But one grand summer all the year through' (Marson 1930: 60–1). The difficult negotiation of cultural frames necessary to the task of representing Jamaica in comparison to England can be traced in this phrase. Marson's opening poetic gesture which celebrates the absence of snow can certainly be read as a positive representation given Brathwaite's observation that 'in terms of what we write, we are more conscious of the falling snow ... than the force of the hurricane' (Brathwaite 1984: 8). However, the fashioning of the Jamaican climate as 'one long summer' in which 'earth seems a Paradise' again returns the island to an Anglocentric gaze. The fact that the representations of both the English and the Jamaican landscapes resort to a 'picture postcard' vocabulary seems to suggest the established rhetorical frames through which a stylised landscape comes to figure an evaluative rather than merely descriptive scene. The ready-made rhetorical structures create a natural world seemingly abstracted from any actual place as the representations are highly dependent on cultural forms and the historically embedded narratives of cultural difference that they service. Given the imperative for 'authentic' representations that govern critical agendas from the 1960s onwards, it is not surprising that this poem (and the many others that share its theme and form) have not been discussed. Yet, while this representation of Jamaica does not conform to later standards of authenticity, what it does usefully force is a questioning of how notions of an 'authentic Jamaica' may have been conceived given the constant recourse to culture (often European) even for representations of nature.

In Marson's second volume, *Heights And Depths* (1931), 'Jamaica', although more formally adventurous in its acrostic style, again balances on the very edge of stereotype with Jamaica styled as a conventional, even twee, tropical retreat: 'Just a lovely little jewel floating on fair Carib's breast' (Marson 1931: 19). However, 'In Jamaica', in the same volume, offers a shift in perspective with a very self-conscious deployment of the prelapsarian view as a structure of privilege. The poem is emotionally complex, as it mingles bitterness towards the reductive and misguided myth created by tourists, 'They call it a garden of Eden', with a genuine affection for the island's beauty. The ambivalence of the first stanza: 'It's a lazy life that we live here, Tho' we carry a fair share of work'; develops into a clearly defined picture of a society racially and economically divided.

> O, it's a wonderful life in Jamaica
> For the tourists who visit this shore,
> ... But it's a dreary life for the beggars,
> And the large slums are all pretty rough.
> ...
> It's a gay life for the children
> ... whose skin is light,
> But the darker set are striving
> And facing a very tough fight.
> (Marson 1931: 82)

This poem makes a far more significant gesture of comparison than the earlier 'Jamaica', as Marson reveals the scene of an island home onto which the frame of island paradise is overlaid. In this version, which addresses the politics of cultural positioning, the familiar rhetorical representations of Jamaica are de-naturalised and de-familiarised through the inscription of the socially real.

The problem of voicing the exploitation of the landscape and its inhabitants whilst also seeking a language in which to celebrate its intense and affirming natural beauty remains evident in recent works. Olive Senior's 'Meditation on Yellow' offers a clear criticism of the continuous stream of Europeans who 'consumed the Caribbean' (to borrow Mimi Sheller's term) from the conquistadors in search of El Dorado to the tourist laying 'bare-assed in the sun' (Senior 1994: 15). It also expresses the need to clear a space in which she too can enjoy the beauty of her island. Again it is the landscape that is evoked and invested with cultural agency:

> I want to feel
> You cannot stop
> Yellow Macca bursting through
> The soil reminding us
> Of what's buried there
>
> You cannot stop
> Those street gals
> Those stregghs
> Allamanda
> Cassia
> Poui
> Golden Shower
> Flaunting themselves everywhere.
> (Senior 1994: 16–17)

This same pull towards the recognition of past and present destructive forces and the acknowledgement of sustaining beauty is sketched by Derek Walcott who explicitly draws on the imagery of Eden: 'No metaphor is too ugly for the hatred and cruelty the West Indies endured; yet their light is paradisal, their harbours and shielding hills, their flowering trees and windy savannas Edenic' (Walcott 2000: 61).[32] As these examples demonstrate, the project of literary decolonisation has been very much involved with developing a language through which to name, affirm and cherish the beauty and sustenance that is found in a Caribbean landscape, yet even today this is quite hard to achieve without seeming to accrue those rhetorical structures that romanticise or sentimentalise the Caribbean within a eurocentric frame.

Perhaps now in the twenty-first century it seems almost too obvious to note, but the naming, or more significantly re-naming, of the landscape was a hugely important phenomenon in the poetry of the 1930s and 1940s. Sonnets to the hibiscus rather than the rose, odes to the market woman rather than the muse, were early markers of the possible congruity between writing and the Caribbean locale. While the substitution of Caribbean subjects alone may not have guaranteed the kind of cultural transformation that we associate with later agendas of indigeneity, these landscape poems were clearly registering a strong sense of local awareness and value. Although often uneven and strained, the works of several early-twentieth-century writers demonstrate a poetic seeking to accommodate the beauty and specificity of a Caribbean world.

The tentative inscription of the Jamaican landscape overwhelmed by gestures to classical poetry can be found in some of Vivian Virtue's poems published in his 1938 collection, *Wings of the Morning*. 'Coffee Blossoms' figures the Caribbean landscape through Europe's eyes, as the plant's blossom is imaged as snow falling on the branches, 'Snow on my summer trees this glad March morn!', almost fulfilling Brathwaite's observation of an externalised consciousness to the letter (in McLeod 2002: 64). In 'Cassia Glory', the native tree plays host to the western myth.

> See where in fretted folds of gold brocade –
> Or is it moth-filled samite which long years
> Lay yellowing in casket old, with tears
> Of Dierdre's sorrow stained? – the cassia maid,
> Queen of our summer trees, reigns, half afraid
> Of her own loveliness, which has no peers;
> More royal in this broidery she wears
> Proud balkis never rode out on parade!
>
> Now I remember olden myths which tell
> How, ofte, some mortal maiden rivalling
> A fair immortal, would transfigured be.

> Perhaps, beneath an immemorial spell,
> Here stands a nymph Arcadian sorrowing,
> Lending her glory to a tropic tree.
>
> (McLeod 2002: 50)

Rather than validating the intrinsic beauty of the tree, the implication of this poem is that the beauty or 'glory' of the cassia is actually rooted not in the Caribbean itself but in the myth of an Arcadian nymph who has been transfigured into the tree.

Constance Hollar's 'Cassia', also deploys the image of the Jamaican tree as an imaginative trigger for a whole string of mythic associations (including the Golden Gates and Sheba's Queen) that bear no relevance to a Caribbean location.

> Laburnum gold shining 'neath Tropic skies
> Or Jason's fleece in Colcis' leafy halls.
> This weeping gold from dazzling azure eyes
> Cascades of primrose charmed before they fall.
>
> (Hollar 1941: 93)

However, 'Mangoes', in the same volume, a still-life in verse, offers a focus on the aesthetic and sensual qualities of the native fruit.

> A dish of mangoes dripping light. It serves
> To charm my fancy, light this sombre room:
> So rich in colour and deep powdered bloom,
> All bashful beauty and seductive curves.
>
> (Hollar 1941: 73)

Similarly, Nellie Olson's four-page poem, 'The West Indian Hurricane', published posthumously in a 1956 collection spanning 1924 to 1941, articulates a stylised version of the landscape in which the tensions between received poetic diction and form, and a desire to render the dreadful power of the hurricane can be heard. The strong stresses on the voicing of both disaster and alarm are compromised by the strangely restrained and received 'Hark!'

> Doomed, we know, are all bananas!
> Doomed our coconuts again!
> Hark! The cries of wind-blown people –
> Screaming homeless through the rain!
>
> (Olson 1956: 62)

In Tropica's (Mary Adella Wollcott's) *The Island of Sunshine* (1904), the earliest volume to be studied here, there is a sustained interest in the geography, history and peoples of Jamaica which is unrivalled, to my mind, by any other volume written, or anthology composed, by a Creole writer. This thin but carefully presented volume also includes photographs of black workers and of Jamaican scenes printed alongside the poems. In 'The Heart of the Island', nature is not abstracted but rather becomes a social environment and the poem clearly situates contact with black working-class Jamaicans as necessary for an appreciation of its qualities.

> He has never known the island who never has truly known
> And felt the simple people, as if they were his own;
> Who has never talked with the woman bearing her market load,
> And heard yam-diggers singing at night on a lonely road.
> (Tropica 1904: 6)

Nevertheless, even this recognition of the intrinsic and crucial presence of Jamaica's black population to any understanding of its cultural environment does not make this work accessible to a post-1960s version of literary nationalism. It is not simply the issue of Standard English language and orthodox poetic form. The poem does not escape a voyeuristic aesthetic through which the subjects of the poet's gaze become 'simplified' and romanticised as it transforms black labour, the historical foundations of Caribbean societies, into an archive of living knowledge to be acquired by a subject outside of its history.

Several of Tropica's later poems also take the working-class as their subject. In 'Busha's Song' (1929), the figure of the plantation overseer is excessively romanticised.

> Give me the lunch snatched gaily
> Down by the wayside hut;
> The roasted yam, the water
> Fresh from the great green nut;
>
> . . .
>
> These are the simple pleasures
> That are life to the busha's soul!
> (in McFarlane 1929: 293)

The implied message of this poem is that the busha has taken the job simply because he is a lover of nature. All questions of economics or of the hierarchical structuring of a plantation society are notably absent and there is no insight into the often invidious position of the busha figure within these. Through Tropica's poetic frame the busha becomes a pastor, but the fact that plantation life is not an innocent, simple, care-free existence is never addressed. Even in her poem, 'The Workers', published in the *Year Book of the Poetry League of Jamaica*, her representation remains severely limited by a persistently aestheticised collocation of rural labour and the pastoral frame. Given the huge wave of workers' protests that had swept through the Caribbean in the late 1930s, the characterisation of the worker as privileged and contented demonstrates an almost wilful blindness to social reality – a clear stumbling block to its later recognition.

> I have a picnic seldom –
>> Trice yearly, let us say;
> But the workmen of Jamaica
>> Have a picnic every day!
> . . .
> Envy no one, happy workmen;
>> Just be glad that you were born![33]

A similar reassuring and condescending representation can be found in Eva Nicholas' 'A Country Idyll'.

> Fragrant loads of green pimento
> On the barbecue,
> Crushed green leaves among the berries
> Giving perfume too;
> Voices mellowed by the distance,
> Sounding sweet and low;
> Gay pimento pickers moving
> Briskly to and fro.
>> (in McFarlane 1929: 217)

As McFarlane comments in his *A Literature in the Making*, 'To her [Nicholas's] sensibilities the world has lost none of its charm, or mystery' (McFarlane 1957: 25). It is precisely her poetic charm offensive that styles rural labour as pastoral indulgence that makes these works so challenging to read. They do not meet the demands of the 1960s and 1970s critical moment and they are wilfully disengaged from the demands of their own. Although these representations draw attention to cultural difference (often in corporeal terms) they do not show any engagement with the cultural values or lived realities of the population they represent or attempt to give subjectivity to the Jamaican folk.

Tropica's 1940 poem 'Jamaica (After Walt Whitman)' is possibly the most ardent endeavour found in the creole archive in terms of a desired connection to Jamaica, specifically figured through the worker.

> I love thee Jamaica. There is nothing about the
>> place I do not love.
> . . .
> I follow the motion of women's arms breaking
>> stones by the roadside;

I am those women; I feel the shock as the stone
    shatters –
I grow tired with them – I talk and laugh with them.

I see the workmen digging yams on the hillside;
I feel the sweat on my brow as the hoe sinks into
    the ground.
I hear the men singing weird songs after the
    digging is over;
I sing with them; I feel how good it is to have
    the work done.

                   (in Lindo 1940: 33)

While the poem clearly seeks to voice a communion with the folk at some level, what speaks most loudly to our ears is the distance and difference between poet and subjects. This is registered most consistently through the restrained language that describes but does not perform an empathetic engagement, and through the markers of cultural exoticism – their 'weird songs'.

In seeking to differentiate between those works which need to be recovered as part of an archival project, mapping the diversity of a disavowed literary past, and those which merit detailed attention as literary works, Tropica's verse might usefully be read alongside Vera Bell's better-known work, 'Ancestor on the auction block' of 1948, which is also structured around empathetic engagement, this time with a slave woman.

Across the years your eyes seek mine
Compelling me to look
Is this mean creature that I see
Myself?
Ashamed to look
Because of myself ashamed
Shackled by my own ignorance
I stand
A slave.
                  (Bell 1948: 187)

Not only is Bell's poem far more self-conscious in its collapsing of the self/other divide, but the involved pattern of recognition, denial and empathy that the poem marks is crucially a recognition of historical positioning. In Bell's work the 'sweating, toiling, suffering' of the working body is given historical depth and the jarring dissonance between poet and subject that marks the pastoral identification is replaced by the recognition of shared ancestry and the bond of history.[34]

Another possibility for creating representational agency for the Jamaican subject informs Marson's 'Canefield Blues' published in 1937, in which a worker whose partner dies in the fields laments her death.

> Bury me Mandy,
> By de garden gate,
> Bury me Mandy,
> By de garden gate,
> Now dere's nothing lef' for me,
> What a cruel fate.
> (Marson 1937: 94)

While this work is immediately more readable in its choice of Jamaican speech rhythms and African-American 'blues' form, it is the shift from a downward to a horizontal gaze, as well as that from a highly framed vision to an unmediated voicing that registers its difference in terms of cultural politics.[35] 'The stone breakers', from the same volume, also offers direct access to Jamaican women's voices and similarly communicates the sense of mortal pain and futility that constitutes their lives as a white man's work machine.

> Me han hat me,
> Me back hat me,
> Me foot hat me
> . . . dough de work is hard
> I will has to work fe pittance
> Till the good Lard call me.
> (Marson 1937: 70)

The workers' capacity for resilience and endurance is not emotionally indulged in this poem, as the women's words reveal work to be more than a spiritual bargain: 'But whey fe do, . . . | Me haf fe buy frack fo de pickney dem'. The everyday pain and practical necessities of sustaining their children not only implicates the exploitation of the poor by the wealthy, and the black population by the white, but also the self-indulgence of men: 'Dem wotless pupa tan roun' de bar | A trow dice all de day-'. The poem makes it clear that the cultural oppression which dictates their misery is only made more intolerable by the sexual oppression of their own partners. The absence of a narrator who might act as a cultural mediator, or softener, produces a very different representation of the labouring body and a powerful expression of both real suffering and social problems.

These early works certainly make their status as poems written in the Caribbean more visible, but to what extent can they be either included in or dismissed from a Caribbean canon on these grounds? While they register varying degrees of cultural attachment to Jamaica, the way in which they nearly all conflate the seemingly opposing demands of a connection to the local and allegiance to the colonial – in terms of language, form and a superior perspective – remains problematic to their recovery according to available critical models. Michael Gilkes offers a conventional viewpoint on these 'emergent' texts.

> Caribbean culture began by looking outward towards the 'Mother Country'. And even though our early writers saw the emotional necessity for the expression of a local life, a local landscape, it was often a life, a landscape copied from Europe but with local names substituted . . . The flora and fauna became local, but the imagery and diction remained obdurately foreign.
>
> (Gilkes 1986: 4)

Gilkes' description is accurate. Many early attempts to represent the indigenous landscape as well as the thoughts, voices and bodies of those Jamaicans previously unrepresented in texts are charged by the politics of Empire and strained by the poetic (and educational) residues of another time and place. In his view (echoed in the studies I have already quoted), the persistence of European poetic frames and diction confirms the status of works as 'looking outward'. My argument is that by placing more value on the incorporation of distinctly Caribbean subjects, and giving a more solid weighting to the politics of affect, there is perhaps equal value in reading these works as looking inward, as gradually placing sufficient strain on the foreign model to bring it to new possibilities of representation. As Walcott's Shabine suggests: 'we, | if we live like the names our masters please, | by careful mimicry might become men' (Walcott 1977: 12).

Mulattos of style and sentiment

Although loyalty to the West Indies and loyalty to Empire are assumed to be contradictory pulls from the 1960s onwards, in the period before 1950 there appears to have been little conflict of interests between these allegiances and it is not uncommon for works to offer complex representations of nationalist sentiment that look in both directions. Employing an interesting vocabulary of hybridisation, J. E. C. McFarlane draws attention to the cultural bifocation that informs notions of the homeland in Tom Redcam's (Thomas MacDermot's) poetry.

> The ruling passion of his verse [is] loyalty to Britain and love for Jamaica. In the pattern of his soul and of his poetry these two affections so blend into a harmony of sound and colour as to be incapable of a separate existence.
>
> (McFarlane 1957: 8)

Indeed, Redcam's 'O, Little Green Island Far Over the Sea', written when the poet was ill in London, expresses exactly this designation of England as the site for 'loyalty' (political belonging) and Jamaica for 'love' (emotional belonging).

> For England is England, brave, patient and true.

> But my little Green Island, far over the sea,
> At eve-tide, Jamaica, my heart turns to thee.
> (in Hollar 1932: 30)

This version of nationalism with the blending (or blurring) of the sentiments of loyalty and love offers a curious conflation of ideologies suggested by formulations such as 'colonial nationalism' and 'colonial freedom' and also foregrounds the complicated and involved pattern of nationalist thought amongst the 'cultural elite' at this time, reminiscent of Hall's 'very profound and complicated feeling'. However, just as Hall points to the lack of scholarly attention to this 'feeling today', it is easy to see why these works, that operate so clearly in the register of affect, rather than of politics or of intellect, have not been read as a viable form of Caribbean rhetoric by nationalist critics. In a sense they are doubly disavowed as their vocabularies are both affective and colonial.

It is also by looking across the volumes of poetry that this crossover of national and imperial loyalties can be mapped. *Pondered Poems* (1956) by Mrs Nellie France Ackerman Olson represents the poet's life's work and was published by her husband in the year of her death. However, I do not believe that it is due to a wide timespan alone that 'Salute to the Queen', a sincere homage, appears in the same volume as 'Diving Boy' that celebrates the black male body in classical terms:

> Ebon brown, with nymph like grace,
> Lithe of limb, each sculptured line
> Is a curve of classic beauty;
> With your skin like bronzed silk,
> Nude you stand above the pool.
> (Olson 1956: 50)

Despite the unequal balance of power which existed between the authority of British colonial culture and Jamaican culture (whether defined within or against the cultural parameters of the motherland) a curious union of allegiance to these two was not uncommon. This seemingly paradoxical attitude, expressing nationalistic pride in Jamaica alongside adulation and respect for Britain, is present in much of the Creole women's poetry which focuses on the concept of a homeland. There are several works that endorse the concept of Jamaica as an emotional home within the politically imperial framework of the globe, as Leo Oakley observes in 1970:

> Constance Hollar too loved Jamaica, but, like so many at that time,
> she seemed bound up by the historical situation within which she
> found herself . . . and she seemed quite sincere about her 'Songs of
> Empire' publication in 1932. There was nothing denoting 'pure'
> Jamaican patriotism in the writings of Albinia Catherine Hutton. In
> 'The Empire's Flag', the Union Jack, she could see a 'gallant symbol',
> or what she regarded as 'the Flag of Freedom'.
>
> (Oakley 1970: 17)

As Oakley's estimation clarifies, the complexity of these works is generally
ironed out by the pressures of the historically driven imperative of this
moment to align 'purely' with colony or nation. In a critical moment
governed by this imperative, it is not difficult to understand why these
works that fail to comply with and cannot be negotiated by a dominant
nationalist frame have been simply overlooked or reduced to their crudest
cultural possibilities.

Revisiting these works in a less highly-charged moment of nationalist
politics and with the benefits of postcolonial theory's attention to the ethical
possibilities of both mimicry and hybridity, the poetry of this period can
be read as testifying to a complex and overlapping cultural matrix in which
Jamaican and imperial allegiances cannot be clearly separated. As a body
of work, I would argue that writings before 1950 provide a substantial
challenge to the history of Caribbean aesthetics as drawn by Arthur D.
Drayton in 1970:

> The first writers were Europeans and whether migrant or Creoles
> of local birth, saw themselves as nothing else . . . In literature this
> produced an attempt to recreate in the English-speaking islands the
> literary scene of London.
>
> (Drayton 1970b: 86)

While these works have nothing of the sophistication, luminosity or linguistic
creativity of Walcott's self-defined 'mulatto of style', that has so enraptured
critics and readers alike, they do perhaps share something of that structure of feeling and offer a portal on a genuine, if not politically radical,
'local longing' that remains seldom acknowledged.

Staging an escape from history

In addition to the difficult presence of Empire, I would argue that one of
the major factors that has led to these writers being exiled from literary
history is their apparent attempt to escape from their own historical
moment. As my discussion of Tropica's poetry above demonstrates, the
disengagement from history which leads to her refusal to see the Jamaican

folk, in whom she clearly has an affectionate interest, as historical subjects has paralysed her poetics. Frozen and abstracted in an aesthetic frame, her poetic subjects seem increasingly out of step with other models of representation and subjectivity that began to gain purchase during the era of popular nationalism. It is important to acknowledge that, like much of the literature selected for dissemination in colonial schools, these poems that refuse to speak to history are ideologically invested at the very moment of seeming to be devoid of ideology.

Work of this kind – of which there is a great deal – brings us to one of the central questions provoked by an engagement with the majority of writing before the boom. How do we read a piece of writing in which content and context refuse to speak to each other, especially when we have been so encouraged by constant recourse to the exceptional few (McKay, C. L. R. James, Roger Mais) to read Caribbean writings as characterised by social engagement? In a sense this issue becomes even more acute when we consider that it was not that these poets looked away from the events of their time altogether – indeed, many of their works are situated poems, marking occasions and events but rather that the events that inspired their works remained outside of what we now regard as the history of this period. While many of the poets in Jamaica at this time wrote occasional poems and (despite the obvious denigration of these as trivial and transient aesthetic statements) therefore do indicate some level of engagement with social and historical events, they are not locally referential in a way that can be welcomed by the ideological embrace of the 1960s and beyond. Indeed, the majority commemorate visits by monarchs and other 'esteemed' European visitors.

Constance Hollar's *Songs of Empire* (1932) which was published to mark the visit of the Prince of Wales and Prince George in 1931 is a clear example. As Drayton observes, the title of this volume indicates an unproblematic allegiance to Empire, confirmed by the sweeping declaration of Sir William Morrison's Foreword.

> The songs themselves although pitched in various keys and from different outlooks all express unbounded loyalty and devotion of the People of Jamaica to Their Majesties the King and Queen and to the Members of the Royal family and the intense love which all the inhabitants of this ancient and loyal Colony bear to the Motherland.
> (Morrison 1932)

Hollar's three 'Welcome' poems that open the volume are transparently devotional to the Royal visitors, and McFarlane's 'The Fleet of The Empire (Reflections on the visit of the Special Service Squadron, July 1924)' echoes the muscularity and masculinity of imperial conquest narratives in its own tribute to the military might of Empire.

> For dauntless, undismayed as they,
> Forward, whatever tempests sweep,
> Our Empire plunges thro' the deep
> Into the dawn of greater day.
>   (Hollar 1932: 11–12)

Like Albinia Hutton's 'On sighting the Oropesa from the mountains, February 3rd, 1931', this poem make a gestures towards recorded history but on both occasions it is a history of colonial intervention that makes no appearance on nationalist chronologies.

However, some of the poems collected under this colonial banner are again less straightforward in their cultural politics. The refrain of Tom Redcam's 'Jamaica's Coronation Ode', like his 'O, Little Green Island Far Over the Sea', published in the same volume, stages the oxymoronic harmony of colonial freedom and the carefully balanced allegiance to King and Country (here Jamaica).

> We are marching to conquer the Future,
> We are sons of Jamaica the free,
> We are true to our King and Country
> We are heirs of the ages to be.
>   (Hollar 1932: 13)

William Morrison's 'The Flag and Jamaica' also navigates the same tightrope between loyalty to Jamaica and to England and figures this union as a marriage in which the 'Antilles Queen' is loyal to her 'Lord Supreme'. Pushing her allegiance closer to Jamaica, Tropica's 'The Green, Blue and Gold' makes Jamaica 'queen of the islands' and although similarly burdened by the weight of archaic poetic language as her other works, the poem focuses solely on Jamaica with no reference to royalty or Empire. Eileen Cooper's 'Jamaica, the isle of springs' also offers unconditional loyalty to the island:

> I cannot think that greater beauty lies
> Elsewhere on earth . . .
>
> And all my dreams
> Would be of home within these circling sands.
>   (Hollar 1932: 33)

Framed by Hollar's own adulation of 'England, soft, great mother of the west' (1932: 43), which both opens and concludes the volume, this collection gives significance to both colonial history (marked by the royal visit) and loyalty, but a confident and proud loyalty to Jamaica is also strongly articulated.

In his introduction to Vivian Virtue's 1938 volume, *Wings of the Morning*, J. E. Clare McFarlane singled out Virtue's 'Ode to the Coronation of Their Majesties, King George VI and Queen Elizabeth, May 12, 1937' as being worthy of 'a permanent place in the poetic literature of Jamaica' (McLeod 2002: 8). Interestingly, McLeod's own critique of this poem in 2002 is based on how out of touch it was with the realities of British life in 1937:

> Unfortunately, this poem to the 'chosen, beloved' is in archaic, fustian diction and ignores the political realities of the occasion: Edward's abdication, the line of succession, the Depression, and the imminent European conflagration . . . unemployment, hunger, and bad housing (all concerns of Edward VIII).
>
> (McLeod 2002: 11)

While it is true that the poetic world of this poem fails to register the kinds of problems that faced the newly crowned monarch of England, what is perhaps more striking still is the context to which McLeod, as well as Virtue, fail to refer, that of Jamaica in 1937. This was the year in which workers' strikes spread across the Anglocreole region, the year in which *Public Opinion* started its weekly political analysis, and in which the Garveyite Jamaica Women's Liberal Club was founded.

It was also the year that Una Marson published her third volume of poems, *The Moth and the Star*, and her rather different version of an occasional poem, 'At the Prison Gates'. Against the chronicle of colonial history, this piece provides an instance of counter-memory in its focus on the desperate urban poverty experienced amongst the working classes in Jamaica during the Depression and more particularly the actual incident when men pleaded to be 'imprisoned' in order to be fed.

> They marched
> To the prison walls and knocked at the gates,
> And when he who was director came forth
> They spoke and said unto him
> 'We are hungry, we need food for our bodies,
> We would join your band of prisoners
> And work, so be that we are fed.'
>
> (Marson 1937: 85)

Marson's poetic account, and in particular its stilted diction, does not easily resonate with contemporary versions of 'history from below' but the historical conviction and engagement of this poem, along with others in this volume including one on the murder of two Abyssinians by Italians, confirms that language and form alone are not reliable markers of cultural orientation or politics.

Stewart Brown's recent review of *Wings of the Evening*, McLeod's collection of Virtue's work, concludes that

> the best you can say of these poems is that they are 'worthy' and interesting to the extent that they demonstrate the forces of that colonial ideology which so powerfully informed his – and most of his literary generation's – cultural values.
>
> (Brown 2003: 62)

Holding on to the idea of a clear division in literary history, Brown positions Virtue as one of the last poets to stay the 'other' side of

> the line you could draw between the last of the colonial versifiers and the first generation of 'West Indian poets' proper. It was essentially a matter of attitudes; towards language, towards the roles and functions of the poet in Jamaican society and – more or less explicitly – towards England.
>
> (Brown 2003: 61)

Of course, there is nothing improper about Virtue's work and this, I would argue, is partly its failing. Its language, range of classical reference, deployment of complex European forms and spiritual subject matter are all too 'proper' in a moment when those voices and experiences that had been denigrated and denied literary expression were literally clamouring to be heard. But can the line be comfortably held when we read Marson and assess her attitude to language, her conventional Romantic view of the poet and set this alongside her explicitly anti-colonial politics? The varying cultural politics of elements within single works often threatens their position on either side of the line and makes them difficult to decode.

In contrast to Brown's model of a dividing line, which has been confirmed as a new horizon in most critical studies to date, I want to suggest that many of this generation's works actually map out a complex, overlapping and mobile continuum along which content, form and language continually shift. If, as Stuart Hall argues,

> Cultural identities are the points of identification, the unstable points of identification or suture, which are made, within the discourses of history and culture. Not an essence but a *positioning*.
>
> (Hall 1990: 395)

then these poems testify to the particular historical and cultural forces which created a destabilised series of identifications made within different, but not always separate, cultural registers and histories at this time. The absence of clear attempts to differentiate the Jamaican nation from the imperial motherland and to authenticate a language and experience of its people cannot be dismissed as a clear denial of place or nationalist sentiment. In order to be open to the works of this uneven and unsteady Caribbean literary past, perhaps we need to develop a more incremental and plastic scale of cultural standards that does not trade so confidently in the divisions between right and wrong, home and foreign, inside and outside and that therefore erodes the defining historical and ideological barriers of pre- and post-1950 to allow a more nuanced exploration.

As the works of McFarlane, Tropica, Virtue and others force us to consider, there is a serious problem of critical discourse in relation to many writings of the pre-1950 period. These works cannot be folded neatly into the pages of a nationalist teleology and yet that which exceeds the margins of the nationalist page is not a supplement, difference or ambivalence that we have been encouraged to value. On one level it may seem perfectly logical and reasonable to write off those poems that make no connection whatsoever to a Caribbean context – not by subject, or language, or reference to time or place. However, if we do not acknowledge these works as being part of that tradition, then we are creating a different agenda and horizon of expectation than would be acceptable today. We would be horrified if poems by Caribbean authors had to speak their cultural allegiance in such crude terms today, and yet how would we judge most of Lorna Goodison's work, or a significant number of poems by Walcott, or Fred D'Aguiar, or Ramabai Espinet by the rubric of relevance that has governed critical judgements on these earlier works?

My particular interest here has been to focus on those works that have previously only been seen out of the corners of this tradition's eyes and to examine what pressures they exert on our dominant ideas concerning national consciousness. As I hope to have shown, while some of the material written during the first half the twentieth century may well have fallen into neglect simply because of a lack of access, others became unreadable and therefore unread. It should be said though that there are many neglected publications that could usefully be written into the dominant narrative. The collection *14 Jamaican Short Stories* published by the Pioneer Press in 1950 has several wonderful pieces that render the quotidian reality of Jamaican life without strain or excessive rhetoric. From Ulric Simmonds' 'Granny Bell' which links to an alternative archive of history through the slave ancestor, through W. G. Oglivie's 'Half a Fork' that offers a poignant but humorous narrative of a small community thrown into internal conflict by the promise of a colonial inheritance, to R. L. C. Aaron's 'Late Flowering' that described the blossoming of a relationship late in life, the portraits of Jamaican people, both middle and working class, are tender but not sentimental. Many stories do focus on the lives of the poor or disempowered, such as the child in Vera Bell's 'The Bamboo Pipe' or the old lady in Ethel Rovere's 'The Mongoose', but the attention to both their vulnerability to manipulation and their strength is measured and unadorned. The collection ran to a second edition in its first year and yet has subsequently disappeared from literary histories.

I should also point out that despite the constant recourse to 1950 as a turning point in Anglocreole literary histories, the fairly extreme ideological and aesthetic range of material persisted past this marker of creative change and explosion. For example two very different poetry collections were published by Jamaican women in 1956 and 1957. Louise Bennett's *Anancy Stories and Dialect Verse* (1957) probably needs the least description. This volume, published by the Pioneer Press, was Bennett's fourth publication, and in both form and content it clearly marks the growing profile of nation (language) poetry at this time. *Poems* by Vivian Hazel, published in Devon by Arthur H. Stockwell (1956), has a short note to the reader which informs us that: 'Perhaps I should mention that I was born in the West Indies of African ancestry and that my only language is English, in the use of which I try my best.' It is just as well that Hazel gives us this information as there is nothing in the 'The ballad of the White Wife' or the love poems 'To – ' and 'Song' that would suggest her birthplace or her ancestry. Even the solitary poem that does make any connection to Jamaica, 'A Negro's Prayer', is so highly sentimentalised and so clumsily rendered in the vernacular as to make its cultural credentials highly questionable to the backward glance of critics from the 1960s onwards.

> Of t'ings dis earth adorn,
> For ever make me bless
> De day dat I was born.
> (Hazel 1956: 27)

It is my hope that one of the effects of opening up the archive of these difficult subjects will be to clear a space in which such incongruities can be read and questions about historical value discussed. Even if these works cannot be read as being generative of the majority of Anglocreole writings after the boom, indeed, even if they can only be recovered as an archive of forgotten failure for most critics, they do very powerfully remind us that the linear progressive narrative constructed in the 1960s and 1970s to accommodate works published from 1950 onwards was a powerful and sustaining myth of origin but, like other myths of origin, it held other stories and other claims in suspicion and abeyance. In our critical moment of the twenty-first century, the Little Tradition of the early 1970s has become the Great Tradition; the minor writers of that age are now the major writers of ours. While Caribbean critics and writers of the 1970s struggled to resist being defined within the stories of Europe and of Empire within their own critical moment, I am advocating that the writers of the period before the 1950s might now need to be released from the stories that they became caught up in as a result of the cultural and political revolution of the 1970s.

Notes

1 Brathwaite also makes huge acknowledgement to the role that *Bim* played in his own development as a writer and critic: 'For me, it was the only outlet at the time. All my stuff is in *Bim* – short stories, literary criticism, poetry. The only newspaper that ever published any literature consistently was Cedric Lindo's section in *The Gleaner*. When I came to Jamaica in 1968, Lindo took me up and he published a lot of my stuff, but most had already been published in *Bim*, and I had already been published by Oxford, so that was a different situation then. It was *Bim* when I was a struggling writer and people were not supporting what I was doing and I couldn't get support from friends, family, critics or writers' (Smilowitz 1991).

2 For detailed accounts of the 'Caribbean Voices' programme see Glyne Griffiths (2003) and Philip Nanton (2004).

3 It is also significant that Roach never published a volume of his works during his lifetime (1915–74). *The Flowering Rock: Collected Poems 1938–74*, edited by Kenneth Ramchand was published in 1992.

4 Brathwaite's insistence on the role of Africa in Caribbean history was particularly radical in the context of a Jamaica in which, as Anthony Bogues (2002) argues, 'Manley established a pattern in which Creole nationalism would pay attention only to one historical component of Jamaican society – colonialism'.

5 See Bailey (1996), Cassidy (1961) and Le Page (1960, 1967) for significant linguistic studies published in the 1960s.

6 In his address, 'Tradition and the West Indian Novel', first given as a lecture at the London West Indian Students' Union in 1964, Wilson Harris made the point that writers were beginning to be too driven by easy political agendas. 'It seems to me vital – in a time when it is easy to succumb to fashionable tyrannies or optimisms – to break away from the conception so many people entertain that literature is an extension of a social order or a political platform. In fact it is one of the ironic things with West Indians of my generation that they may conceive of themselves in the most radical political light but their approach to art and literatures is one which consolidates the most conventional and documentary techniques in the novel' (Harris 1967: 45). Although Harris' own challenge to orthodox literary conventions was equally motivated by his project to remap conceptions of history and cultural organisation within a West Indian framework, his methodology differed significantly from that of literary realism. His work remains respected within a Caribbean intellectual tradition but has not been central to critical agendas.

7 Although much of the fault lies in cultural blindness rather than stubborn vision, James' question, 'Is popular culture therefore the real basis for the evolving national life of the islands, and Creole the only natural basis for literature?' Louis James (1968: 22), does possibly suggest an inbuilt critical resistance to the new agendas being championed by Brathwaite, Rohlehr and others.

8 This quotation first came to my attention in Louis James (2003: 221).

9 See also Orlando Patterson, "The ritual of cricket," *Jamaica Journal* 3 (March 1969): 23–25.

10 Rodney returned to Guyana and was assassinated by a bomb in the middle of Georgetown on 13 June, 1980.

11 For a detailed narrative and analysis of the attempted revolution see Meeks, (1996: 9–36). The Black Power movement and the attempted revolution in Trinidad also had an effect elsewhere in the Caribbean during the 1970s. As well as the People's Revolution led by Maurice Bishop and his Marxist New Jewel Movement in Grenada in 1979, in that same year political contestations

and uprisings of sorts also took place in Union Island (a St Vincent ward), Dominica and St Lucia.

12 Some of these issues, particularly the relationship between the poet and their audience, had been debated at an earlier Symposium at the Mona Campus of the University of the West Indies in 1965. Participants included Brathwaite, Walcott and Morris.

13 I am very grateful to Professor Edward Baugh for pointing me to this footnote in Brathwaite's collection and for his brilliant outlining of the event and period in his Plenary Address to the 23rd Annual Conference on West Indian Literature.

14 It is ironic that this response came from Eric Roach whose work Brathwaite had championed in 'Sir Galahad and the Islands' and whom he had identified as a poet 'of the people'.

15 Gordon Rohlehr's highly influential work 'Literature and the folk' was first delivered as a paper at the conference.

16 His first note points out that a study of Guyana or Trinidad, 'less simply black/ white cultures' (Brathwaite 1974: 66), would have arrived at different conclusions.

17 This quotation first came to my attention in Allis (1990).

18 For an excellent discussion of the terms and consequences of the '*Savacou* debate' see Breiner 1993.

19 It is not insignificant that the 1980 revised edition of Ramchand's *West Indian Narrative: An Introductory Anthology* had a contracted first part and lost de Lisser's 1929 *The White Witch of Rosehall* from its second. Ramchand expresses his hope that 'the essential points about the development of West Indian writing are still being made' (Ramchand 1980: x). His developmental narrative from Equiano to McKay is now even stronger and more obviously in line with the conception of a tradition based upon anti- and non-colonial works and writers. The 1978 collection *From Trinidad: An Anthology of Early West Indian Writing*, edited by Reinhard Sander with the assistance of Peter Ayres, does represent work by twenty-seven writers before 1950 but is also concerned to represent those texts associated with the birth of literary independence and nationalism.

20 As a home-grown critic, it is interesting that Baugh cites 1940, the beginning of political and cultural redefinitions of West Indian relations to Britain (rather than 1950, the metropolitan watershed) as his historical marker.

21 See for example Glyne A. Griffiths' *Deconstruction, Imperialism and the West Indian Novel*, published in 1996.

22 Most major critical studies of Caribbean writing have not attended to writings from the first half of the twentieth century, except those of C. L. R. James. See for example Griffith, Wilson-Tagoe, Doring and Gikandi. Published in 2001, *The Caribbean Novel in English* by M. Keith Booker and Dubravka Juraga offers an almost identical male-centred model of the literary tradition in which MacDermot handed the baton on to Herbert DeLisser and then Claude McKay in Jamaica, with a shift in the 1930s to the Beacon Group in Trinidad and its core members C. L. R. James and Alfred Mendes, to the affiliated de Boissiere and into the 'second renaissance' of the 1950s with Mittelholzer, Vic Reid, Roger Mais and then John Hearne and Andrew Salkey in Jamaica and Jan Carew in Guyana. The trinity of Selvon, Lamming and Naipaul mark out the 'boom' of the 1950s located in London.

23 Letter from Cedric Lindo, 10 June 1991.

24 Mais' advice is similar in register and reason to Pound's in 'A Few Don'ts by an Imagiste', *Poetry* March 1913, 'Do not re-tell in mediocre verse what has already been done in good prose. Don't think any intelligent person is going to be deceived when you try to shirk all the difficulties of the unspeakably diffi-cult art of good prose by chopping your composition into line lengths', in

Imagist Poetry edited by Peter Jones (Harmondsworth, Middlesex: Penguin 1972), pp. 130–31.

25 Mais' frustrations finally drove him to London, as he explains in his 1952 piece, 'Why I love and leave Jamaica'. However, he returned in 1954 and died in 1955 of cancer.

26 *A Literature in the Making* was first published in serial form in *West Indian Critic and Review* from 1929 to 1931, republished in 1939 in the political magazine for which Mais worked, *Public Opinion*, and finally by the Pioneer Press as a single volume in 1957. As this example indicates, one major problem to be faced when sketching the literary history of Jamaica during the period 1900 to 1945 is that it is virtually impossible to be certain of when much of the material was produced. Articles and poems often appeared in various places at very different times. Also many poems were only published in collected works which often spanned more than a decade of writing, with rarely any indication of the year they were written in. Lena Kent's *The Hills of St Andrew* published in 1931 presents some poems written before the turn of the century and in the foreword to Constance Hollar's *Flaming June*, she points out that the volume has been delayed some twenty-five years. Constance Hollar's volume of poetry, *Flaming June* (Kingston, Jamaica: New Dawn Press 1941) was published shortly before her death. As the poetry in this volume represents her life's work it is extremely difficult to date individual poems. This is also the case with certain anthologies. 'Caribbean Voices' selected by John Figueroa and published in 1966 contains many poems written decades before. In a private letter, 14 November 1990, Cedric Lindo wrote that Vivette Hendriks' poems were 'written when she was a school girl or shortly afterwards, appeared only in the BBC's "Caribbean Voices" and two in *Focus* of 1960 (those two having been broadcast on Caribbean Voices many, many years before)'.

27 Henry Swanzy has taken Redcam's achievements, along with those of H. G. de Lisser and Claude Mckay, to be 'the first positive break in West Indian silence' in 'The literary situation in the Caribbean', *Books Abroad*, 30, 266–74. For further information see Mervyn Morris, 'The all Jamaica library', *Jamaica Journal*, 6, (1972), 47–49.

28 The scrapbook was circulated among: Miss Wolcott [Tropica], Miss King [Lena Kent], Astley Clerk, Vivian Virtue, Miss M. M. Ormsby, Mr Clare MacFarlane, Mrs R. Hutton, Miss Moulton Barrett, Miss C. Hollar, Miss Nicholas, Miss Owen, Mrs F. F. Brown, Miss Plummer, Mrs J. W. Hutton. Now very dusty, fading and frail, its hand corrected, pasted and gaudy pages reveal an amazing range of materials from biblical postcards, snapshots, biographies of relatives, and letters from friends, to a pets' page with poems about and to animals. The extreme eclecticism of the journal can be illustrated with reference to one edition from Spring 1943, which presents poems by Edna St Vincent Millay, Kipling, Christina Rossetti and Walter de la Mare, alongside those by Lena Kent, Elsie Hutton, Constance Hollar, Clara Maude Garrett, Pennib, and Archie Lindo. In addition there is an extract from *Time* magazine and a letter from Clara Maude Garrett in Canada with the address of a Canadian book-binder willing to take on volumes of poetry.

29 George Cumper, 1957.

30 'Criticism in the jungle' in Henry Louis Gates, Jr (ed.) *Black Literature and Literary Theory* (London: Routledge 1984) p. 3.

31 Lena Kent, 'Isle of beauty', *The Hills of St Andrew* (Kingston, 1931), p. 43, Albinia Hutton, 'God's Hills', *Hill Songs and Wayside Verses* (Kingston, Jamaica: Gleaner 1932), p. 13 and Tropica, 'Blinkeys', *The Island of Sunshine* (New York: Knickerbocker Press 1904), p. 47 respectively.

32 This quotation first came to my attention in Sheller (2003: 69).
33 'The workers', *Year Book of the Poetry League of Jamaica, 1942* (Kingston, Jamaica: New Dawn Press 1942), p. 8.
34 Bell is possibly best known for her work *Soliday and the Wicked Bird*, the first Jamaican pantomime performed at The Little Theatre in 1943.
35 Denise deCaires Narain has argued persuasively that the assumption that 'West Indian poetry comes into its own when Creole language is inscribed' is itself another 'dominant genealogy' (2003: 13). See also 'The lure of the folk: Louise Bennett and the politics of Creole' in deCaires Narain (2002a).

2 Global villages and watery graves:

Recrossing the Black Atlantic

Will exile never
End?

(Kamau Brathwaite)

The voice belongs to the family group dead and alive. We walk by their leave, for planted in the soil, we must walk over them to get where we are going.

(Erna Brodber)

This chapter is concerned to continue the discussion of neglected texts and the mapping of literary history around certain 'critical moments' in which the demands of one particular methodology or ideology have dominated critical interests and clearly privileged one construction of a Caribbean literary archive over others. My particular focus here is on the strong purchase that a black diasporic critical framework has held within studies of Caribbean writings since the early 1990s and the dramatic reversal of fortune for nation-based texts since the 1960s and the then dominant agendas of cultural and literary nationalism. The Black Atlantic model, most clearly articulated by Paul Gilroy's 1993 landmark study *The Black Atlantic*, offered a powerful redress to the claims of nationalism but, to my mind, created an equally forceful critical sway, diverting attention away from increasingly marginal texts focused on the located and the local. Just as I have sought to challenge the normalisation of nationalist claims in the 1960s and 1970s, so too I wish to resist the theoretical orthodoxies of this later critical moment and their implied claims that interest in the nation is both outdated and regressive. My perception is that in the present moment what seems to receive less attention, certainly outside the Caribbean, are those writers who have stayed and whose works have embedded themselves in their island and region.

Clearly many Caribbean peoples and writers have travelled to and settled in the West and it is therefore entirely appropriate to develop critical attention to diasporic writing. Moreover, the operations of neocolonial globalisation on a cultural, as well as an economic front, demand that we do look across national boundaries. Indeed, these acts of looking across have generated some very interesting and productive work. However, given that the Caribbean is seen to epitomise the hybrid, syncretic, mobile, deterritorialised cultural space so favoured by postcolonial theorists emerging from the critical moment of the Black Atlantic in 1990s, there seems to be a need to argue for the value of reading Caribbean writers who have stayed, as well as those such as Naipaul, Alvarez and Brand whose work fits more neatly into theoretical models proposed by Benitez-Rojo (1992), Gilroy (1993), Robbins (1998), Brennan (1997) and others which focus on the cosmopolitan rather than rooted, the traveller rather than the dweller.

I have already examined the propensity within literary histories to relocate to London in the 1950s and some of the frustrations and consequences that writers 'at home' expressed concerning the shift in critical discourses away from the Caribbean to metropolitan centres. Now, just a half century later, ideas of location no longer have the same purchase. On a global matrix of twenty-first century belongings, the claims of national identity and those of place of habitation have multiple permutations and postcolonial intellectual sway has tended to favour those points at which the two are most distant from each other. In part, this may be taken as an understandable response to a new phase of mass migration which has emerged since the 1980s.

> There has been a rapid increase in migration across the globe since the 1980s. These mass movements are taking place in all directions, the volume of migration has increased to Australia, North America and Western Europe. Similarly, large-scale population movements have taken place within and between countries of the 'South'. More recently events in Eastern Europe and the former Soviet Union have provided impetus for mass movements of people. Some regions previously thought of as areas of emigration are now considered as areas of immigration. Economic inequalities within and between regions, expanding mobility of capital, people's desire to pursue opportunities that might improve their life chances, political strife, wars, and famine are some of the factors that remain at the heart of the impetus behind these migrations.
>
> (Avtar Brah 1996: 178)

As Brah herself makes clear, the social conditions under which people move remain diverse and often involuntary, and it is crucial to account for the trauma, loss and risk involved in many of these movements. Moreover, as Puri has pointed out, we may be persuaded by the rhetorics of migration – both the defensive rhetorics that are mobilised by nationalist interests against the 'swamping' effects of 'foreigners', and the celebratory rhetorics that fashion migration as dissolving the always politically regressive nation state – into believing that migration is more disruptive of world orders than it actually is.

> Despite the increasing mobility of people across national borders, it is worth remembering that only about 2.5% of the world's population migrates across national boundaries. Contrary to those who invoke the appearance of "the Third World in the belly of the First" as a sign of the demise of nation-state, center, and periphery, I suggest that those migrations to the First World testify to the continuation, and possibly the intensification, of national inequalities – inequalities which only a tiny fraction of the world's population can attempt to mitigate by migration. To declare these migrations evidence, therefore, of the transcendence of the nation-state risks abandoning the urgent task of social and economic reconstruction of peripheral nations.
>
> (Puri 2004: 7–8)

It is precisely the way in which attention has been diverted away from the possibilities as well as the problems of Caribbean states and towards the migrant's condition that I want to address in this chapter. Although I am interested to work at the level of literary history in this study, it is crucial to recognise where the political and intellectual force of this paradigm has come from, what the tensions between these two levels of engagement may be, and how, given that both the statistics and the material realities of migration tell a different story, a disproportionate and almost utopian focus on the migrant has emerged in our critical moment. The focus in this chapter is on the way in which these Caribbean writers may be seen to renegotiate and re-present the concerns around locality, cultural belonging and an emancipatory relation to other cultures. My aim is to go against the 'flow' of Black Atlantic studies by focusing on writings that contest the seemingly naturalised version of Caribbean identity as always elsewhere, works that are clearly located and concerned with dwelling, as well as with the cultural crossings and oceanic journeys to be negotiated at home. It is important to acknowledge the Caribbeanness of many diasporic communities which extend globally, as well as the fact that the model of creolised subjectivity which has emerged from a Caribbean intellectual context and from Caribbean historical experience, is an alluring model for postcolonial cultural identity in wider terms. Nevertheless, the existence of significant under-researched archives, and the continued emergence of new writers and new critical journals within the Caribbean region, all suggest that attention to geographical location remains important and worthwhile.

In order to root the proliferation of diaspora discourses in metropolitan postcolonial theory in the 1990s, I am interested to examine the particular purchase of Paul Gilroy's highly influential 1993 study, *The Black Atlantic: Modernity and Double Consciousness*, within readings of postcolonial and Caribbean writing. The conception and consolidation of the Black Atlantic paradigm has become one of the most important critical moments of postcolonial studies in recent years and one that I would argue has impacted seriously on the kinds of critical reception afforded to Caribbean writings.[1] Gilroy's effort to bring black peoples back into the conceptualisation of modernity and his discussions of the concepts of 'double-consciousness' and 'double-vision' (from Du Bois (1903) and Wright (1953) respectively) clearly demonstrate both a political force and an intellectual ambition directed at the recognition and continuation of black struggle. Much of his work in these respects is very useful to a reading of Caribbean writing, but what has perhaps been less enabling is that these concepts and struggles tend to consistently position black peoples as being 'between nations' (in his later work 'between camps').

Although Gilroy's own study is grounded in historical specificities, to my mind, the discourses of migrancy, transnationalism and transatlanticism, at least as they have proliferated in postcolonial studies in the 1990s, have often suggested a dubious equivalence between the historically and politically scripted movements of populations and the cultural flows and fluid subjectivities in which postcolonial criticism has heavily invested. Postcolonial conceptualisations of postnationalism, transnationalism and transatlanticism have become associated with a liberatory poetics that releases culture from the assumed confines of the nation state and have seemingly had huge success in turning the heads of readers and researchers away from the settler in favour of the migrant.

As Laura Chrisman points out in her critique of the Black Atlantic, Gilroy's theory dovetailed nicely with the intellectual milieu of that moment.

> Gilroy's formulations mesh neatly with the 1990s metropolitan academic climate, which saw the rise in popularity of concepts of fusion, hybridity and syncretism as explanatory tools for the analysis of cultural formation. The 1990s was also a decade in which postmodernist intellectual concerns with language and subjectivity infused both academia and 'new left' politics to create a dominant paradigm of 'culturalism' for the analysis of social relations.
>
> (Chrisman 2003: 73)

Certainly Gilroy's publication has been central to the Black Atlantic agenda of the 1990s. Nevertheless, it is important to note the significance of another major work of postcolonial scholarship published in 1993, Edward Said's *Culture and Imperialism*. I would argue that Said's book, as well as Gilroy's, was instrumental in making the shift towards 'culturalism' that Chrisman describes.

In his study, Said works astutely and elegantly through the towering texts of a Western canon in order to reveal their involvement in imperial culture. Reading the 'classics' contrapuntally against the texts of Third World intellectuals, including the West Indians Frantz Fanon and C. L. R. James, Said traces the roots and routes of imperialism in the discursive continuities of literature and other forms of cultural representation. He is quite explicit in marking the historical and political moment in which he makes his intervention.

> There is no question that in the past decade the extraordinarily intense reversion to tribal and religious sentiments all over the world has accompanied and deepened many of the discrepancies among polities that have continued since . . . the period of high European imperialism.
>
> (Said 1993: 40)

Through his remarkable intellectual energies, by the end of the book Said has moved to a very different conception of the relation between national and cultural identity, as well as between the politics of identification and those of location. His new configuration is clearly set against the ideological sway of a resurgence of nationalism that he identified at the beginning of his work.

> It's no exaggeration to say that liberation as an intellectual mission, born in the resistance and opposition to the confinements and ravages of empire, has now shifted from the settled, established and domesticated dynamics of culture to its unhoused, decentered and exilic energies, whose incarnation today is the migrant and whose consciousness is that of the intellectual and artist in exile, the political figure between domains, between forms, between homes, and between languages.
>
> (Said 1993: 403)

It is not difficult to appreciate why the models of plural, hyphenated identities that Said delivers and those of transatlantic cultural flows put forward by the Black Atlantic model that Gilroy's work initiated have been attractive to scholars seeking to theorise diasporic postcolonial writings. Yet, there is a political consequence to this mode of intellectual engagement, a consequence registered not in the metropolitan academy but in the postcolonial nation. It is important, just over a decade on from the publication of this work, to reconsider the conditions of possibility under which such freedom as the Black Atlantic identifies has come into being. While these works had a very strong purchase in their own critical moment, characterised by moves towards postnationalism in the political sphere and culturalism in the intellectual sphere, from our critical moment we are more able to track the consequences of this shift and possibly more suspicious of the disregard shown to national paradigms considering what has developed in their wake. Stephen Shapiro's account of the political consequences of postnationalism seems particularly important given the Caribbean's proximate relations to US political and cultural hegemony.

> The recent call for postnationalism responds to three key post-1989 developments: the impact of new information technologies, like the internet, as devices that further erode time-space distinctions; the end of the first Cold War, which problematizes organic notions of the West, as the Soviet Union's break-up unleashed a wave of 'white nation' decolonization; and the increased awareness about corporate techniques of globalization and their use of meta-state institutions, like the IMF or WTO, to privatize national social welfare schemes, while relying on local police to safeguard private property and suppress democratic protest. Given that all three trends have worked to reinstall US global authority, to what degree does postnationalist criticism reinforce the current reconfiguration of American hegemony under the different conditions of the inter-millennial phase?
>
> (Shapiro 2001)

The way in which the flows of people, capital, profits and information are directed by an increasingly militarised US superpower is clearly important to take into account, as it signals an important rupture between the intellectual and political momentum of the postnational project as it was envisaged in the early 1990s. What is more visible in our own, post-September 11 moment, are the renewed attempts to, in Said's words, 'rule others', 'classify them or put them in hierarchies' as well as 'the reiteration that Western (US/British) is number one' (Said 1993: 408). This is not only visible in the crude military operations of imperialism but also in the new demands for cultural representation that often find articulation in the very acts of crossings that Gilroy and Said read as empowering – such as fingerprinting on entry to the US. I make this distinction between these two moments, not to reduce the possibilities of cultural counterflow and the numerous and significant sites of resistance to this powerful overcurrent that continue to exist today, but rather to offer up some suspicion of the Black Atlantic as a liberatory discourse and to draw attention back to the local and the dweller as figures worthy of intellectual attention.[2]

Although Said's metonym of the voyage in and Gilroy's chronotype of the ship have been very valuable and useful to an analysis of the cultural movements and transformations, there is still a sense in which they privilege certain versions and histories of marginality over others and what remains forgotten and suppressed are the differential realities of these journeys and the many histories of non-metropolitan engagement. The skeleton of Gilroy's critical agenda may seem particularly appropriate and even appealing to an analysis of Caribbean cultural formations in that it proposes sustained attention to 'the Atlantic as one single, complex unit of analysis' (Gilroy 1993: 15). However, the flesh that Gilroy offers to these bones is very clearly based on a Northern triangular figuration of Africa, America and Europe (Britain), and thereby a cultural geometry that essentially bypasses the Caribbean (he chooses to discuss African-Americans Toni Morrison, Charles Johnson, W. E. duBois, Richard Wright, James Brown and others). As Shalini Puri has commented 'When critical cultural theory speaking in the name of the Black Atlantic repeats the subordination of the Caribbean, it must surely give us pause (Puri 2003b: 36).[3]

Moreover, as Robin Cohen has argued, the Black Atlantic model cannot account for the cultural complexity and overlayering of different flows and returns that characterise the Caribbean diaspora.

> Whatever the sophistication and complexity of the black Atlantic argument, at root it is a historical simplification, which cannot fully explain the process of indigenisation and creolization in the Caribbean, despite the lack of indigenees. Nor can it account for the complexities arising from the large Asian presence in the Caribbean and *its* subsequent diasporization.
>
> (Cohen 1998: 33, italics original)

It is through attention to the many and complex acts of crossing, settling and crossing again that comprise the diasporic flows of Caribbean peoples across four centuries that a different kind of diasporic criticism can emerge. However, if the excess of ethnic difference that is contained under the sign of the Caribbean raises one important question concerning the applicability of the Black Atlantic paradigm, then its suppression of gender difference raises another. It cannot be ignored that Gilroy privileges male experience and that his Black Atlantic is the scene of a wonderful black *male* intellectual odyssey.

While Black Atlanticism has opened up new and enabling critical pathways, my concern is that it has perhaps, albeit unwittingly, closed down others.[4] Diaspora discourses, both theoretical and literary, have been important to the construction of postcolonial studies and in particular, to the attempts within this discipline to articulate a politics of identity which takes account of the mobility of peoples and cultures across a postcolonial world. However, the anti-foundationalist politics of postcolonialism appear to have generated a preference for dislocation over location, rupture over continuity, and elsewhereness over hereness. The idea that migrancy is a condition of being that somehow describes the identity issues of the twenty-first century for postcolonialists may be suggested by the number of critical works that emerged in that moment and that focus on the migrant or migrancy as the central figure and trope (Chambers 1994, Boehmer 1995, Boyce Davies 1995 – as well as Gilroy 1993). As Ian Chambers states in his study, *Migrancy, Culture, Identity*:

The migrant's sense of being rootless, of living between worlds, between a lost past and a non-integrated present, is perhaps the most fitting metaphor of this (post)modern condition.

(Chambers 1994: 27)

Although Chambers does insert the substantial caveat,

This seemingly common grid, offering simultaneous connection and distinction, cannot obliterate the real differences between the forced movement and exiles of individuals and peoples induced by war, economic deprivation, political repression, poverty, racist slavery, and that diffuse sense of mobility that characterises metropolitan life, charted in the privileged channels of movement represented by the media, information technology, advertising, tourism and a generalised consumerism.

(Chambers 1994: 28)

taken as a whole his study is far less interested in these 'real differences' than in the 'diffuse sense of mobility'.

This emphasis on migratory subjectivities within postcolonial studies has come from many theoretical directions – Gilroy 1993; Said 1993; Appadurai 1996; Bhabha 1994; Cohen 1995; Clifford 1988, 1992, 1994, 1997; Kaplan 1996; Robbins 1998 – and their convergence has created a critical practice in which diaspora narratives take centre stage in many postcolonial literary discussions.[5] Moreover, given that the Caribbean can be constructed as the archetypal 'migrant' space in which multiple diasporas intersect – African, South Asian, Irish, Scottish, Chinese – it is perhaps not surprising that in his 1988 study, *The Predicament of Culture*, James Clifford overlaid the cultural diversity of the Caribbean with the metropolitan axis of cultural theory to declare that 'We are all Caribbeans now . . . in our urban archipelagos' (1988: 173). The way in which the Caribbean person is given an emblematic status as the metropolitan migrant is clear here but Clifford's pronouncement is loaded in other ways. In this enunciation of being the politics of location and of identity are centred on the 'we' and not the 'Caribbeans'. Does the fact that the western 'we' have become 'Caribbeans' in the urban archipelago, imply that 'they', the 'real' Caribbeans, achieve their Caribbeanness in the actual archipelago of islands – a necessary reflection for the constitution of the metropolitan travelling subject? Or, perhaps, Caribbeanness has become an identity reconstructed in the moment of 'culturalism' without historical or geographical bearings?

At the level of description Clifford seems to be suggesting that Caribbean people are symptomatic of the contemporary human condition of displacement and metropolitan migration, but at another level he is also invoking a new form of postcolonial humanism – a levelling out of the West and the Rest by the experience of dislocation – a concept understandably alluring for postcolonial metropolitan critics, both western and non-western, who have been plagued by the painful awareness of their own privilege and their inability to respond productively to their freedom and power in the face of the oppression and restrictions which govern the lives of their indirect subjects of study. However, I would argue that this claim to a shared position is a rather troubling short-circuit to the real task of understanding and negotiating not only cultural diversity but also social inequality.

Indeed, Clifford's declaration may be a useful way to rethink the cultural consequences of globalisation and mass migration in positive terms, but does this mean that the words of Walcott's Shabine in 'The Schooner Flight', 'Either I'm nobody or I'm a nation', are now a pathetically modest claim that should be translated into 'Either I'm nobody or I'm the world'. Or, does it mean that Shabine is really nobody after all because the processes that created him have been disembodied and reassembled in urban, metropolitan archipelagos? What might be at stake for the Caribbean given that creolisation is no longer a theoretical concept particular to the region has been fully and intelligently explored by Mimi Sheller in her chapter 'Theoretical Piracy on the High Seas of Global Culture'. As Sheller argues:

> Earlier generations of Caribbean intellectuals invented theoretical terms such as 'transculturation' (Ortiz 1947 [1940]); cf. Spitta 1997), 'creolization' (Brathwaite 1971; cf. Nettleford 1978), and 'transversality' (Glissant 1981) to craft powerful tools for intellectual critique of West colonialism and imperialism, tools appropriate to a specific context and grounded in Caribbean realities.
>
> (Sheller 2003: 188)

However in the work of Gilroy and Benitez-Rojo,

> The explosive, politically engaged, and conflictual mode of conceptualising creolisation in the nationalist period of the 1970s has been met with a later usage, from a different (metropolitan) location, in which creolization refers to *any* encounter and mixing of dislocated cultures. This dislocation has enabled non-Caribbean metropolitan theorists to pirate the terminology of creolization for their own projects of de-centring and 'global' mobility.
>
> (Sheller 2003: 191)

Sheller's work demonstrates the way in which the more general and flattened enunciations of Caribbeanness and creolisation which are being circulated at a theoretical level by postcolonial cultural theorists have obscured Caribbean people as historical agents and discusses how returning to the Caribbean roots of the concept of creolization, regrounding it in its specific social and cultural itineries ... might recover the political meanings and subaltern agency that have been barred entry by the free-floating gatekeepers of 'global' theory.

(Sheller 2003: 196)

Just as the work of Benedict Anderson (1983) has taught us to appreciate the ways in which 'the nation' is an imaginary construction, in as much as it is created by the investments that national subjects have in its production, then so too we may argue that the migrant is a fantasy, the product of people's desire to identify outside and beyond nation-states, the product of a willed collective identity that can bring together the rich and the poor, the Western and the non-western; the university professor and the slum dweller in a utopian postcolonial self-identification. In the same vein though, just as we know that nation-states are real and that their realities impinge upon the political and economic welfare of their subjects, so too we know that migrants, exiles and refugees are real too and that their experiences of crossing spatial boundaries vary greatly depending on their economic, national and often phenotypical status. As Avtah Brah reminds us, 'The question is not simply who travels, but when, how, and under what circumstances?' (Brah 1996: 182).

If the first crossings by boat to England that provided the narrative substance of Lamming's *The Emigrants* and Selvon's *Lonely Londoners* in some ways led to the neglect of writers writing back in the Caribbean during the 1950s and into the 1960s, as I argued in Chapter One, then it may be possible to argue that the Black Atlantic moment of the early 1990s led to something of a second phase of neglect in which writers such as Brodber, Hodge, Senior and Lovelace, who retained an island base in terms of the focus of their work, were (and remain) far less discussed and critically attended to than Kincaid, Danticat and Phillips among others whose work spoke to the critical demands of diaspora criticism more loudly and clearly. The distinction between writers who have stayed and those who have left is not always straightforward and many writers have dual (at least) residency (Goodison, Senior and Walcott come to mind). The privileging of the metropolis, small populations and the weak infrastructure left behind by the colonial powers means that travel, to some extent, is a necessity.[6] Nevertheless, the Black Atlantic moment seems to have created a pronounced interest in diasporic Caribbean writers whose writings bear the signature of their travelling lives.

At the most basic level this can be detected by the preference for certain authors over others. It explains why far more critical attention has been paid to Naipaul's *A Way in the World: A Sequence* (1994) than to Earl Lovelace's *Salt* (1996), both of which engage with the task of understanding and representing the place and history into which you are born, in both cases that of colonial Trinidad (see Burnett 1999, Gourevitch 1994, Jones

2000, Phillips 1994, Pouchet Paquet 1997). Naipaul returns to Trinidad in order to reconnect with a place whose history can only be known to him through the 'the bird's eye view' and through Walter Raleigh, Francisco Miranda, Foster Morris and C. L. R. James. Naipaul left the island in 1949 and has not been 'on the ground'. Moreover, his reconnection as a diasporic, exilic subject allows him to be at home in Trinidad, as anywhere else in the world. His text can be read productively, even affectionately, within the Black Atlantic moment. As I shall discuss later, Lovelace's text is far more interested in 'roots' than 'routes' and in a commitment to an understanding of the complex political, psychological and cultural struggles that have weighed into the history of Trinidad. Although Lovelace's novel radically deconstructs the idea of the nation as ethnically or culturally homogenous, his geographically bounded narrative does not fit well with the oceanic model.

My request here for a recognition of place, the local and the situated, deliberately goes against the grain of Black Atlantic studies as it has developed since the early 1990s that almost takes for granted the fact that in a moment of accelerated globalisation the most interesting debates and issues arise from the study of movements and flows. However, I do not mean to argue in favour of cultural interiority or confinement. As I aim to show, within a Caribbean context being in one location by no means implies cultural homogeneity or statis. If Black Atlantic studies suggest, by implication, that the dweller is to the nation what the migrant is to the postnational, then I would argue that Caribbean writing that is not only grounded in but also committed to the local undoes this equivalence by demonstrating that the constant interplay of 'roots' and 'routes' is not just the experience at sea, but also that on land. I want to argue that the kinds of transcultural and intercultural work that Gilroy locates as somehow exceeding and even deconstructing the nation can actually be located within the Caribbean nation, city or even village.

Nationalism without absolutism

Given the implied suspicion of the nation within the Black Atlantic paradigm, it is perhaps important to remember that the particular style in which Caribbean nationalism imagined itself into being was often not narrow but already inclusive and plural, and significantly often voiced within the context of global anti-colonialism. A few literary examples may indicate the way in which national consciousness was often internationally, as well as intranationally, inflected within the region's writings. An editorial in *The Beacon*, published in Trinidad in 1932, reported on India's struggle for freedom and in the same year, Beatrice Greig (1932) wrote on article on 'Mahatma Gandhi' and his attempts to promote Muslim and Hindu Unity. Greig also reports on the fact that a deputation of Indian women to the Viceroy in 1917 marked the first step to repeal the

Indenture system in Trinidad, confirming the reciprocated flow of oceanic anti-colonial transnationalism.

In Sam Selvon's second novel, a wonderful but much neglected text, *An Island is a World*, published in 1955, Foster, the contemplative Ulysses, discusses the absence of any absolutist version of nationalism within Trinidad in very direct and positive terms. For Foster, the condition of interested detachment that emerges from 'mixing with so many other nationalities' in his island home, was initially prized as enabling a humanistic philosophy to flourish.

> I used to think that . . . we'd be able to fit in anywhere, with anybody, that we wouldn't have prejudices or narrow feelings of loyalty to contract our minds . . . I used to think of this philosophy as being the broadest, the most universal, that if it ever came to making a deci-sion on an issue involving humanity itself, that we'd be able to see the way clearer, unbounded by any ties to a country or even a race or a creed.
>
> (Selvon 1993: 106, first published in 1955)

However, having crossed the Black Atlantic, in London, Foster confronts the consequences of coming from the non-nationalist nation. The special claim of unbelonging is no longer philosophically or politically enabling as he comes to recognise that 'You can't belong to the world, because the world won't have you. The world is made up of different nations, and you've got to belong to one of them, and to hell with the others' (Selvon 1993: 107). In one sense Selvon situates Trinidad as transnational and transcultural – Black Atlantic even – *avant la lettre*. Foster's perspec-tive may be read as betraying the metropolitan provenance of the Black Atlantic paradigm which may provide a redemptive philosophy for those subjects within such absolutist nation states, but appears as merely descrip-tive to many Caribbean nations whose national constitutions developed very differently and whose imagined communities were always already translocal.

This history of coexistence, of overlapping and shared struggles that refuse ethnic boundaries and absolutes that Selvon represents in 1955, continues to be a powerful and enabling paradigm for national construc-tion based on transversality. In 'They Came in Ships', the Guyanese poet Mahadia Das connects the historical experience of Indian indentured labourers to that of earlier subjected groups echoing an oral archive of rooted memories.

> At the horizon's edge, I hear
> Voices crying in the wind. Cuffy shouting:
> 'Remember 1763!' – John Smith – 'If I am
> a man of God, let me join with suffering'.

Akkarra – 'I too had a vision.'

Des Voeux cried,
>   (Das 1987: 288–9)

Das's poem seems to confirm the dominant view among cultural commentators that historically Caribbean populations have always already been informed by the transactions and interactions of a series of (forced) migrations. Stuart Hall's observation, 'African-Caribbean people are already a people of a diaspora', extends to Caribbean people in general (Hall 1990: 235). In a sense, what these different utterances show is that the kind of 'cultural insiderism' that Gilroy in his Black Atlantic paradigm implies as endemic to nation states possibly never took hold in the Caribbean where an 'ethnically homogeneous object' (Gilroy 1993: 3) may have been the dream of certain groups but the achievement of none.

Gendering diaspora discourses

What is also noticeable in Das's poem is the grounding of women's experience of labour: 'My grandmother worked in the field . . . tears among the paddy leaves.' Indeed, as Clifford argues in his 1994 essay, 'Diasporas', 'Diasporic experiences are always gendered' (1994: 313), an observation that is followed by his stronger statement in 1997 that 'when diasporic experience is viewed in terms of displacement rather than placement, travelling rather than dwelling . . . then the experiences of men will tend to dominate' (Clifford 1994: 258–9). However, as Barbara Kirshenblatt-Gimblett points out in a response article in the same journal as Clifford's 1994 piece, it is precisely this 'male' version of diasporic experience that is consistently foregrounded in contemporary studies.

> Diasporic discourse . . . is strong on displacement, detachment, uprooting, and dispersion – on disarticulation. It is appealing precisely because it lends itself to a strategic disaggregation of territory, people, race, language, culture, religion, history, and sovereignty. Rearticulation – how the local is produced and what forms it takes in the space of dispersal – is trickier because of the risk of closure, essentialism, or premature pluralism.
>
>   (Kirshenblatt-Gimblett 1994: 339)

While historically it is true that Caribbean women have migrated and this should not be played down, particularly in the post-1970 period with more women than men migrating at present, the migration patterns of women are different from those of men and, as Olive Senior establishes in her study *Working Miracles: Women's Lives in the English Speaking Caribbean* (1991), the mass migration of men that has been a distinctive feature of Caribbean social history throughout the twentieth century has also impacted on the conditions of empowerment and subjectivity for the women who stayed at home.

> From the latter part of the nineteenth century to the mid-1920s, the menfolk of these territories left their homelands for the big construction and agricultural projects then under way. The size of this emigration was substantial – Jamaica experienced a net loss of some 146,000 persons between 1881 and 1921 and Barbados 104,000 persons between 1860 and 1920 . . .
> The sex-selective nature of this emigration is remarkable. For instance, in Jamaica, three years of emigration, 1881–4 (when the French made the first attempt to build the Panama Canal), attracted one-fifth of the male population of reproductive age, and a similarly high outflow continued to the end of the decade. In Barbados, fully 70 per cent of the total net emigration over the period 1861–1921 was of males . . . The emigration of the 1960s and 1970s consisted mainly of able-bodied males . . . Female independence in this period was reinforced by the fact that it was on the women left at home that the burden of maintaining the household and caring for the children fell.
>
> (Senior 1991: 108–9)

In the light of this context, Walcott's now memorable words, 'The sea is history', begin to look like a male script, to which we might counterpoise Senior's words, as poet rather than sociologist, 'Gardening in the Tropics, you never know|what you'll turn up' (1994: 83). Before I come to analyse what is 'turned up' in Senior's poetry, I wish to discuss the particular ways in which the emphasis on disaggregation within discussions of diaspora has influenced frameworks for theorising Caribbean women's writing in the wake of the Black Atlantic moment. I want to argue that in this field too some attention needs to be given to the 'trickier' inscription of location and the local, not only as diasporic community, but also as home community.

Two studies that examine Caribbean women's writing in the Black Atlantic moment, Carole Boyce Davies' *Black Women, Writing and Identity: Migrations of the Subject* (1994) and Myriam J. A. Chancy's *Searching for Safe Spaces: Afro-Caribbean Women Writers in Exile* (1997), employ migrant writing as a defining paradigm for their readings of selected Caribbean women's writing. Given that only a handful of critical studies on Caribbean women's writing were published during the whole decade, the influence as well as the confluence of these books is important to note. Both books work towards: 'centralizing the Black woman's experience across the diaspora in ways that remove her from the place of marginalization in a variety of cultures' (Chancy 1997: 14). Boyce Davies' work deliberately casts its net across a vast sea, broader and deeper than Gilroy's oceanic crossing, and it does not seek to offer a way of reading particular to Caribbean women's writing. Nevertheless, Caribbean women writers are a substantial part of her 'catch' and the heavily front-loaded theoretical apparatus assembled to read their 'migrations of the subject' does bid for interrogation as it brings the critical moment of black diasporic criticism firmly within the orbit of Caribbean (women's) writing.

By working across a range of cultural contexts, both Boyce Davies and Chancy are able to draw our attention to the ways in which black women writers and their work intersect with each other across the Black Atlantic. This centripetal model of criticism provides a valuable alternative over-arching framework to that offered by the dominant critical paradigm of postcolonial theory or the reading pathways prescribed by national literary (sub)traditions (such as African-American or Black British). Nevertheless, I think that we need to be aware of what might be lost, as well as gained, by the privileging of the migrant black woman as the subject of enquiry. To my mind, both the figure of the migrant and the exclusive attention to African-Caribbean women are limited horizons which bring into view the favoured subjectivities of their own moment but do not represent Caribbean women's writing as a historically or ethnically diverse tradition.

The critical paradigm through which Caribbean women's writing is read and constructed in Boyce Davies' work is clearly informed by careful research and scholarly expertise in the field. The book's first chapter establishes the five central concepts of its theoretical framework and is interspersed with five auto/biographical 'Migration horror stories'; stories which ground the experiences of migration in the social frame of legal, national and cultural imperatives that disrupt the 'free flow' between locations. However, the fact that the story of an absent Costa Rican mother whose children followed their father to Barbados and then the US only to find that they literally could reside nowhere because of immigration laws appears alongside Boyce Davies' own experience of having to endure a colleague's wife's story of her Caribbean cruise, as well as her nightmare of having been silenced by bishops, is indicative of the way in which the condition of migration is conceptualised as an almost all-encompassing frame within which differences in terms of social relations almost evaporate. Indeed, against the cautionary tales of loss, fear and silencing, this book's theoretical apparatus powerfully invokes an almost ideal intellectual, diasporic space to which writing by black women can come 'home'. Echoing something of the utopianism that Gilroy also invests in, Boyce Davies comments that:

> Black women's writing ... should be read as a series of boundary crossings and not as a fixed, geographical, ethnically or nationally

> bound category of writing. In cross-cultural, transnational, translocal,
> diasporic perspectives, this reworking of the grounds of 'Black Women's
> Writing' redefines identity away from exclusion and marginality. Black
> women's writing/existence, marginalized in the terms of majority–
> minority discourses, within the Euro-American male or female canon
> or Black male canon ... redefines its identity as it re-connects and
> re-members, brings together black women dis-located by space
> and time.
>
> (Boyce Davies 1994: 4)

The way in which her own model is defined against that which is
'ethnically or nationally bound' clearly signals an affinity to a Black Atlantic
aesthetics, and the 'cross-cultural, transnational, translocal, diasporic' space
that the book offers could be read as a harbour for the black African
female Ulysses – a differently gendered but similarly travelled subject
to Gilroy's figure.

Despite attention to the 'complicating locations of these multiple and
variable subject positions' in later chapters, the complex pathways established by black women's diasporic lives and writings, as well as the sense
of mobility, difference and mediation feed ultimately into a stable, albeit
problematised, collective identity of 'black women' (Boyce Davies 1994:
8). The emphasis upon acts of crossing within the theoretical underpin-
nings of the book, rather than the specific locations from which crossings
begin and end, serves to foreground the conceptual sameness rather than
the geographical or cultural or gendered distinctiveness of these crossings.
Deployed in this way, there is a sense that 'the routing of diaspora discourses
in specific maps/histories', which James Clifford views as so crucial to
theorizations of diasporic movements, is lost and, as Clifford warns, the
concept 'slips easily into theoretical discourses informed by poststruc-
turalism and notions of the multiply-positioned subject ... [as] a master
trope or "figure" for modern, complex, or positional identities, crosscut
and displaced by race, sex, gender, class and culture' (Clifford 1994: 319).
Furthermore, this tendency to stabilize diasporic identity (even though it
is stabilised as radical, deterritorialised and transformative) seems to have
important consequences for dominant constructions of Caribbean women's
writing, as does the model of black female subjectivity that Boyce Davies
proposes through her theorising of these migrating subjects:

> Black female subjectivity then can be conceived not primarily in terms
> of domination, subordination or 'subalternization,' but in terms of
> slipperiness, elsewhereness ... Black female subjectivity asserts agency
> as it crosses the borders, journeys, migrates and so re-claims as it
> re-asserts.
>
> (Boyce Davies 1994: 36–7)

In Chancy's 1997 book too, acts of crossing and the achievement of a positive female subjectivity are linked with the condition of exile now functioning almost as a prerequisite to self-determination:

> Women within the Caribbean are also speaking out, but their voices are often lost to the cause of nationalism (more or less male-defined) or coopted to service male versions of women's identity. In exile, Caribbean women can ironically politicize their discourse . . . resist assimilation.
>
> (Chancy 1997: 5)

It is my argument that this emphasis on empowerment becomes troubling when it is presented as the dominant function of exile or migration, and when journeying becomes an assumed route to agency. For Chancy, the enabling effects of exile are similarly to be seen in the literature, which she describes as 'a tapestry of sounds and perspectives on what it has meant for Afro-Caribbean women to take control of their bodies, their lives, and, in order to do so, to have removed themselves from their roots' (Chancy 1997: 6–7). The irony is that this theorising of Caribbean women's writing as somehow fully or properly expressive only when in exile or diaspora has actually contributed to the 'lost voices' of women writing within and about the Caribbean. I want to show that situated writing is not circumscribed by male versions of female subjectivity or nationalism but rather that it engages with the conditions of being in the Caribbean in a range of creative and positive ways that do structure agency as a possibility from within the region.

The emphasis on migration and exile as the most rewarding areas of enquiry becomes particularly problematic at the point at which it defines itself against a homeland which is both undifferentiated and undervalued. While the freedom to travel and to settle elsewhere has doubtless been enabling to many Caribbean women, writers and academics included, there is an increasing body of work documenting a long history of women's agency, activism and writing *within* the Caribbean which cannot be written off (Shepherd *et al.* 1995, Shepherd 1999, Momsen 1993). The focus on migrant subjects that I would characterise as a major feature of the Black Atlantic moment is of particular concern given that increasingly little attention is being given to the Caribbean region as site of possibility. In Boyce Davies' account, the Caribbean reality and people so epitomise the theories of creolisation that Clifford expounds that the region almost slips off the world map as culturalism offers the new way of mapping the globe.

> Caribbean identities then are products of numerous processes of migration. As a result, many conclude that the Caribbean is not so much a geographical location but a cultural construction based on a series of mixtures, languages, communities of people.
>
> (Boyce Davies 1994: 13)

Despite the fact that we must acknowledge the extraordinary cultural admixture that constitutes the Caribbean region and its long history of creolisation, as well as the many Caribbean diasporic communities that extend globally, the erasure of territory in favour of cultural forms seems extreme. The displacement of 'geographical location' by 'cultural construction' further shifts debates away from the demands of hereness and of Caribbean place. Although the greater power and profile exerted by publishing houses, the media and academic institutions in Western metropolitan centres may well mean that many of the struggles and debates associated with Caribbean identities and societies are taking place outside the region, it would be both misleading and unfortunate if we allowed the discourse of diaspora to move us away from the Caribbean as a real location. I wish to argue that looking at the Caribbean, in all its regional complexity and diversity, might help us to re-think ways of theorising diasporic identities and the writings which engage with these.

With a national narrative very much involved with the African and South Asian diasporas, as well as with European colonial migration, the Caribbean is a particularly interesting location for discussions about 'here' and 'there'. In a region repopulated by absentee landlords, African slaves and Indian indentured labourers ideas of homeland have always held the trace of other places and the idea of return. Claims to belonging were and are not based on a common point of origin and although the Amerindian population in Guyana is gaining political and social profile, diasporic identifications do not generally take place against autochthonous claims. Instead, identifications with 'here' and 'there' remain more mobile and provisional even within a fixed place and time. An individual may, in different contexts and for different purposes, identify themselves as Trinidadian, as Indo-Caribbean, as Muslim, as female, as Caribbean. Although the identities function as a series of roll-calls, the multiple calls of Caribbean identities are often more pronounced. The hyphenated identities which we have come to associate with diasporic metropolitan communities (African-American, Black-British) are also important to Caribbean peoples who wish to retain their connections to a historical homeland and a contemporary community which survives, at least partially, through cultural, religious and domestic practices, as well as through narrative.

From ship to craft, sea to land

In *The Black Atlantic*, Gilroy deploys the image of the sailing ship as a Bakhtinian chronotope that signifies the spatial crossings across oceans, as well as the foundational, historical crossing of the Middle Passage (from Africa to the Caribbean), in order to locate a time and space in which the black subject exists in the history of modernity. I want to argue that the more modest 'craft' that becomes one motif in Olive Senior's poetry collection, *Gardening in the Tropics*, indicates a rather different connection between history, travel and the dynamics of intercultural exchange. As the work of both Senior and Erna Brodber demonstrates, in the Caribbean model of the Black Atlantic, the nation is not the opposite of the transnational, just as the sea is not the antithesis to the land, nor the ship to the shore, nor the oar to the spade.

Many of the short stories in Senior's three collections to date – *Summer Lightning* (1986), *Arrival of the Snake Woman* (1989) and *Discerner of Hearts* (1995) – address the issues of migration and relocation which are so much part of the Caribbean reality. Nevertheless, her texts do not tread the familiar literary footsteps to harbours or airports with their protagonists' journeys to a metropolitan centre, but rather retain a close and interested focus on rural Jamaica. Senior's heroines (and heroes) are not exceptionally gifted in the 'canonical' way – bright beyond their community with a compulsion to learn and to leave – indeed this is often a path which they reject or from which the narrator chooses to divert our attention. While many of her stories, like the major cultural and historical narratives of the Caribbean region itself, depend on arrivals and exiles, they do not trace the pilgrimage to the metropolitan centres but rather concentrate on those journeys which take place within the island and on those individuals who travel (see 'Arrival of the Snake-Woman' and 'The Two Grandmothers' in *Arrival of the Snake-Woman*). Her work is also interested in the complex ramifications of return. The stories 'Ascot' in *Summer Lightning* and 'The case against the Queen' in *Discerner of Hearts* engage with the emotional and psychic consequences of Stuart Hall's statement that 'Migration is a one-way trip. There is no "home" to go back to' (Hall 1996: 115) by exploring what the experience of returning home means both for those who have left and those who have stayed, thereby addressing an often neglected dimension of the migration story.

Both in her short fiction and her poetry, Senior elects a tight locational frame in which to recuperate the lives of those who remain excluded, unknown and significantly unknowable by the metropolitan narratives and metanarratives. As one of the few creative writers who remained in the Caribbean even after her work received critical acclaim, Olive Senior has acknowledged her commitment to 'a literature that is being written from the inside out instead of the outside looking in' (Rowell 1988: 486). Although she now divides her time between Jamaica and Canada, Senior's work is always located in the Caribbean, more specifically in rural Jamaica, and I want to argue that paradoxically it is the locatedness of her work that enables us to think about the diaspora paradigm in new and interesting ways.

Nevertheless, it is significant to note that her 1994 collection, *Gardening in the Tropics*, published right in the Black Atlantic moment, cannot escape being pulled into the wake of the grand ship of black diasporic criticism that was making such powerful sailings at this time. This publication is described by its Canadian publisher, McClelland and Stewart, as Senior's 'first Canadian publication', and yet, as their own back-cover description suggests, the case for this volume as a Canadian publication is not easily made.

> *Gardening in the Tropics* contains a rich Caribbean world in poems offered to readers everywhere, but with an especial nod to Canadian readers. This Caribbean world thrives in a Canada that is felt only briefly in the volume (as an image of colourful shoes against snow), just enough to suggest a potential meeting between northern and tropical climates and ways.
>
> (Back cover, *Gardening in the Tropics* 1994)

The claim for *Gardening in the Tropics* as a bi-locale volume is very tenuous and speaks strongly about the need to yoke Senior's poetry back to Canada and to a Canadian readership via a dominant critical model of trans-nationalism. This need is symptomatic of the desire for so-called 'diasporic' writings to display their multipositionality. Unlike the more prominent Caribbean-Canadian women writers, such as Dionne Brand and Nourbese Philip, Olive Senior has not critically engaged with Canada's national rhetoric of inclusivity or its hidden history of racist oppression and exploitation, but rather maintains Jamaica as the centre of emotional energy and interrogation in all her work. Although Senior has herself become a diasporic subject, she refuses to see this literal movement as necessitating a de-centring of her work. In a recent interview with Dolace McLean and Jacqueline Bishop, Senior was asked about the 'large issue on our agenda which has to do with living in North America but writing about the Caribbean. Why is it that you live in Canada and write about Jamaica from that place?' (McClean and Bishop 2003: 6). Refusing to see it as 'the large issue', Senior simply replied, 'It's accidental that I left. I didn't leave to leave. I'm still very much engaged with Jamaica and what's going on there' (McClean and Bishop 2003: 6). Refusing to be redefined as a diasporic writer, Senior dismisses the associations of elsewhereness and unbelonging, of displacement and detachment. Senior may work and reside in Canada but her recently published extensive *The Encyclopedia of Jamaican Heritage* (2004), that took over twenty years to complete, in many ways confirms her commitment to the recovery and recognition of indigenous knowledge, history and culture and proves that location does not set the limits of commitment or belonging to a place.

Indeed, the single image of the rainbow shoes against the snow, in the poem 'My Father's Blue Plantation', which is taken by the publishers to confirm the Canadianness of the volume, actually signifies a failed attempt to reconnect to a Caribbean landscape of primary colours and of emotional belonging, more than it confirms a multicultural presence in a new home. Having reflected on the small world of the childhood home and the careful balancing of economic and moral values in the selling of bananas and the buying of shoes for church, the second part of this poem crosses into a description of contemporary adult life in the western metropolis.

> But this was ages ago
> We children fled the blue for northern
> light where we buy up all the shoes
> in sight. My closet filled – finally –
> with a rainbow of shoes in Hot Tropical
> Colours (which look marvellous against
> the snow.) My father's house (I'm told)
> is visible from all directions now . . .
> Alone fanning sand and stoning breeze,
> my father lets in all that air, lets that
> Hot Tropical Sun pour down to fill his
> blue lungs and warm his old and vegetating
> bones.
> (Senior 1994: 84)

Although the image of the rainbow shoes is one of agency, as the poetic persona asserts her right to buy the bright colours shunned by her father, there is a strong sense that the act of crossing entails loss as well as gain. The distancing of the two parts across the space of the page (with left and then right margin alignment) further illustrates the difficulty of bridging a stretch of water which also marks a threshold between generations, lifestyles and values. While she connects to her siblings as other migrants she has disconnected from her father whose life, although the off-centre focus of the poem, is now only a reported image. If her journey to the shoe shops of Canada is one which asserts agency it is perhaps an uncomfortable reminder of how empowerment too can be slippery, taking us elsewhere than we had intended, and of how individual journeys take place across a global political terrain with full closets and barren plantations.

In *Gardening in the Tropics* the process of navigating this space between the point of residence and the point of attachment is achieved through craft – that is both the literal vessel in which crossing can be made but also the imaginative vessel of writing. In 'My Father's Blue Plantation', Senior makes the journey across the page, and her vision of her father's plantation is deliberately poetic, a crafted place of familial memory. As a vessel, a craft implies something more domestic, low-key and precarious than a ship and it is no coincidence that Senior's work tends to focus on the desperate journeys of the poor and the powerless – there is no Ulysses here. The sea is not charged with cross-cultural flows or tides of intellectual exchange, but with the fears and hopes of the 'Illegal Immigrant' and the 'Stowaway' whose identities are lost at sea with no certainty of landing.

If I never make this uncharted
    passage
one way or another, never tell
    my children
        (Senior 1994: 42)

There's this much space between me and
    discovery
a hairline fracture getting wider with
    each wave.
I feel it, though I cannot see to
    hold
My thoughts together – they're
    running loose
All over; someone's bound
    to trip
        (Senior 1994: 43)

The figure of the migrant as lost or erased works almost directly against the tide of the Black Atlantic as it is reframed in Boyce Davies' and Chancy's work to express exile and migration as a site of agency. In these poems, the journey is made in a 'dugout' and a 'grave', the craft less stable and purposeful, the oceanic passage connecting to the Middle Passage in a different hermeneutics of memory to that which Gilroy restores.

'Caribbean Basin Initiative', also in this volume, takes its title from the exact phrase used to describe the Regan Administration's US – Caribbean Trade Partnership Act of 1983 that was designed to reverse the possibility of communist expansion in the region (exemplified by the New Jewel movement in Grenada and the Soviet–Cuban pact). Enforcing the model of the market-place as the basis for democracy, it is now accepted that the CBI was a failure in economic terms and led to the collapse of the Jamaican economy in the 1980s. In her re-scripting, Senior takes the desperate attempts by Haitians to cross the water to the US as a different initiative that is equally bound up with the politics of US–Caribbean relations and their role in disempowering the region. The illegal flow towards US shores becomes a tragic mimicry of the one-way free flow of the legal trade agreement. The sea is invested with dreams but as the broken craft begins to sink, it is hopes as well as bodies that are bailed out.

Like limpets we cling
on craft that ply
in these waters
where our dreams lie . . .

No sailor am I.
I was farming

till my seed
failed to yield
fell on stony
ground. I cried:

What is harder
than stone?
Never knew
at the time
the answer is:

Water.
     (Senior 1994: 30–33)

Far from being the liberated from the hard, barren ground of the nation, the Haitans are entrapped by the cycle of failed crossings, unable to find redemption on land or in water, they 'thirst|till we die|surrounded|by water' (Senior 1994: 33).

As in Danticat's short story, 'The Children of the Sea', that also describes the trauma of the attempted crossing from Haiti to the US, the Black Altantic is a place where dreams become hauntings and not realities: 'I dream that the winds come out of the sky and claim us for the sea. We go under and no one hears from us again (Danticat 1991: 6). While Senior's craft makes the crossing only to be 'spared|to navigate again|some other dry season' (Senior 1994: 33), in Danticat's narrative the craft does not hold and the young man takes his fatal baptism. In one sense, both Senior and Danticat offer their craft, writing, as the vessel in which to make the crossing – as Senior herself has stated, '"the writer's country is writing", and that seems to apply to me' (McClean and Bishop 2003: 6). The poem deploys poetic craft to represent the human traffic that flows in the wake of the trade agreement and, as in her other works, to offer ideology critique at the level of personal loss. In Senior's collection, the sea is a place of watery graves but the tides that claim these victims are very clearly driven by political currents and we can usefully read this poem as 'uncover[ing] . . . an ethics of freedom to set alongside modernity's ethics of law' (Gilroy 1993: 108).

While the ontology of the Black Atlantic speaks over the epistemology in these poems, detailing the perilous crossings of the dispossessed, the craft of writing does figure as a secure vessel in which to travel in Senior's poem for Jean Rhys, 'Meditation on Red'. A reflection on a visit to Rhys' English grave, this poem is in part an act of restitution or reparation that brings Rhys (exiled by Brathwaite) back into the literary Atlantic triangle. Acknowledging Rhys' own insecurities about her writing:

   . . . never quite
believing

your craft
to be
worthy.
      (Senior 1994: 45)

Senior figures Rhys' craft as a safe vessel in which she too can traverse
the Sargasso Sea. Senior's own craft then both reinstates Rhys' writing
as a safe passage back home and marks her own work as more interested
in the 'voyage out' than in Said's metropolitan 'voyage in'.

But I'll
Be able to
Find my way
Home again

For that craft
you launched
is so seaworthy
tighter
than you'd ever been.
      (Senior 1994: 51)

As poet, Senior is able to rescue Rhys, 'marooned | in the grey', but the
motif of the maroon and maroonage is also vital to her reconfiguration
of Black Atlantic history. Although the volume title suggests the rootedness and interiority of the garden, in fact this volume explores the
experiences of migration and diaspora across 500 years of Caribbean
history. In one sense Senior's choice of the maroon motif has everything
to do with her own location, as she grew up near Cockpit Country in
Jamaica which was home to the Maroons (the runaway slaves who escaped
colonisation and were eventually granted their own land). However, the
fact that the Maroon is the leitmotif of this volume seems important for
two other reasons. First, because it signals a rooting of discourse in a
specific place and history and second, because it allows Senior, somewhat
typically, to leapfrog the plethora of ready-made discourses that describe
cultural movements that Clifford has described as:

An unruly crowd of descriptive/interpretive terms now jostle and
converse in an effort to characterize the contact zones of nations,
cultures and regions: terms such as *border, travel, creolization, transculturation,*
hybridity, and diaspora (as well as the looser *diasporic*).
      (Clifford 1994: 303)

By side-stepping this crowd, Senior is able to look afresh at the issue of
diaspora and displacement in a specifically Caribbean context. Crucially,

she draws attention via this particular motif to the tension between agency and hegemony, between gain and loss, and between strength and vulnerability which each crossing involves. It is also significant that within this lexicon maroon stands out as a figure of resistance and survival. I want to argue that part of what this maroon figure resists, as it appears here, is interpellation into the agendas of 1990s black diasporic criticism.

In 'Gardening on the Run', which chronicles the life of the first runaway in Hispanola in 1502, the emphasis is again bifurcated with the courage and empowerment of the Maroons acknowledged alongside the recognition that the inability to settle, to cultivate and to nurture had a real cost:

> The brave ones abandoned plantation
> for hinterland, including women
> with children and others waiting
> to be born right there in the
> forest (many mixed with Indian),
> born to know nothing but warfare
> and gardening on the run.
> (Senior 1994: 105–106)

In 'Hurricane Story 1951', the imperatives of economic migration drive a mother to maroon herself in a cold England for a nursing career designed to support the son she eventually abandons by default. Ostensibly the most conventional representation of migration within this volume, the scattering of a family across the US, the Caribbean and Britain is a recognisable Black Atlantic tale. It is a tale in which parents seek out a better life in the colonial and neo-colonial motherlands, a tale in which political mother(land)s also abandon their children, and ultimately a tale in which disconnection and dispossession are the markers of crossing. Here also, the dating of the poem (at the beginning of the era of mass migration to Britain initiated by the recruitment of workers into the service industries) offers a specific location in time and place and helps to anchor the distinctiveness of the crossing. The poem opens with a close constellation of promise:

> Margaret and her man Delbert
> such a fine young couple
> everybody said
> so full of ambition
> so striving
> their little boy so bright
> so handsome
> so thriving
> (Senior 1994: 34)

This image of familial strength and cohesion breaks down after the hurricane as Margaret travels to England to nurse, and Delbert moves to America to farm, and the unnamed boy passes from father, to grandmother, to stepmother. The accustomed tale of migrating subjects is defamiliarised here by the focus on the abandoned son and his withdrawal from language. Throwing 'sounds across the ocean', he finally communicates with his mother whose ocean is now reduced to the pail of dirty water she cleans with, but their connection is an act of simultaneous drowning at distant shores – an ambivalent connection in which the evocation of an amniotic ocean and the entanglement of emotions and memories sits rather power-fully, if soberly, alongside a familiar narrative of diaspora. The absence of a language that flows between them is also the absence of a craft in which this ocean can be navigated.

This collection also restores the often obscured and gendered dimension of diaspora that Senior has drawn attention to in her sociological study – the fact that it was often the women who were left behind. In 'All Clear 1928', set during a period of severe economic decline when a large number of men left the Caribbean to work in Central America, the female narrator rememories how:

> All, all the men went with our dreams,
> our hopes, our prayers. And he
> with a guinea from Mass Dolphy
> the schoolteacher who said that boy
> had so much ambition he was bound
>
> to go far. And he had. Gathering
> to himself worlds of experience
>
> which allowed him to ride over us
> with a clear conscience. I never
>
> told anyone. For I would have had
> to tell his children why he hadn't
>
> sent money for bread, why his fine
> leather boots, why his saddle,
>
> his grey mare, his three-piece suit,
> his bowler hat, his diamond tie-pin . . .
>   (Senior 1994: 56–57)

Again the empowerment of self and the expression of agency associated with migration that we find foregrounded from Gilroy to Boyce Davies is a male success story, achieved at the cost of detachment not just from place, but from a community, a family. The poem describes how the male traveller becomes an independent centre of gravity, gathering experiences and possessions, but what Senior allows us to perceive is that the tale of diaspora cannot be owned by the traveller alone, it also belongs to those left behind, and just as each place is home to many different histories, so is each journey.

If the motifs of craft and maroonage signal the 'routes' of Caribbean history then the motif of gardening brings attention to the roots that both transverse across a landscape but also burrow down into the soil. As with her migration tales, Senior's gardener digs up deliberately untold, secret histories, that link the workings of agriculture to political culture, of cultivation to redemption. In a sense agriculture is the foundational culture of the Caribbean as the peoples who now populate the island were brought forcibly to labour on the plantations, growing cash crops for the west's profits. The delinking of peoples and their ancestral land was a major consequence of colonialism, but in a region where the land, as well as the sea, is the cemetery of genocide and slavery, and where mono-crop agriculture and US policy continue to govern the possibilities of production, gardening is not a simple, innocent task of reconnection. The domestic, interiorised pursuit of gardening turns up skeletons, seeds and roots that can only be accounted for by a recourse to history.

The politicisation of the pastoral that Senior both quietly and modestly effects here is important to note given the fact that the pastoral, like the nation, has been configured as regressive and nostalgic in the wake of the Black Altantic moment. As Sarah Phillips Casteel points out:

> J. Michael Dash's *The Other America* (1998) and Chris Bongie's *Islands and Exiles* (1998), are both profoundly suspicious of pastoral motifs which they see as promoting a mystifying narrative of the recovery of a lost essence and therefore as obstructing a more direct engagement with the actual conditions of Caribbean life. Illeana Rodriguez (1994) and Antonio Benitez-Rojo (1992) also tend to associate pastoral with a regressive politics, and in general, scholars of Caribbean literature celebrate a turn away from pastoral settings in favour of more urban ones.
>
> (Phillips Casteel 2003: 16)

In Senior's work the focus on the garden is in part a claim to the land denied by colonialism in a region where 'There was enough | in the jungle to provide gardens for everyone'. Yet it is also about acknowledgement of a lost connection between the land and the people, both in terms of the preservation of non-metropolitan traditions and the possibility of a home-grown poetics. The 'Nature studies' section of the volume addresses the issue of multipositionality in a very rooted way, as lost plants and an abandoned cosmology are restored to a contemporary Caribbean which is too often unaware of what was saved in the cultural crucible of colonisation. 'Anatto and Guinep', one of series of poems centred on Caribbean fruits and flora, opens with the observation that:

> No one today regards anatto and guinep
> as anything special
>
> No one puts them on stamps or
> chooses them
>
> for praise-songs or any kind
> of festival
>
> (Senior 1994: 74)

Yet while these poems do restore what is lost within a cultural landscape, the garden that emerges across the volume as a whole is not a tranquil retreat or a template for authenticity. As Denise deCaires Narain has commented, Senior's 'strategically coy tone enlivens poems in which garden soil is excavated to provide an archaeology of History' (deCaires Narain 2003: 15). *Gardening in the Tropics* ploughs through land that must accommodate many different histories, peoples and traditions and Senior's poetic spade turns over the layering of lives and deaths from the pre-Columbian peoples, the slaves and the maroons, to the drug barons of the present.

In a critical moment in which the states of in-betweenness, migration and exile have accrued value through postcolonial theorisations to the point where dislocation is regarded almost as a virtue in itself, Senior's writing helps us to explore what it means for those people who have to stay, who choose to stay, or for whom moving on is not moving up. Her poetry also helps us to appreciate how these questions are particularly pertinent to those in the Caribbean whose very identities have been redefined on the international cultural circuit by the discourses of the Black Atlantic moment and to acknowledge that Caribbean gardens, as well as metropolitan centres, are places where acts of journeying, of dwelling and of craft take place.

My village, the world

Two fairly recent pieces of writing by the Jamaican woman writer Erna Brodber also enact a reterritorialisation of the Black Atlantic model. These pieces have not received the critical attention of Brodber's three novels, but I want to argue that they help us to think about her ideas in relation to location and locution that also find articulation in these fictional works.[7] The first piece is a pamphlet entitled *The People of My Jamaican Village, 1817–1948* (1999) that is very clearly concerned with local history. Published in 1999, this work has the look of a hand-made publication and was indeed first published in Brodber's village, Woodside, by Blackspace, an imprint linked to the Centre for the Study of Africa and the Diaspora which Brodber runs quite literally from her own backyard, in her birthplace, Woodside. The second piece is an essay entitled 'Where are all the others?' in the book *Caribbean Creolization* edited by Kathleen Balutansky and Marie-Agnes Sourieau and published jointly in 1998 by the University Press of Florida and the University of the West Indies. This is a collection in which many of the major, if not towering, figures of a Caribbean intellectual tradition write on creolisation – including Wilson Harris, Antonio Benitez-Rojo and Raphael Confiant. Given that Brodber is not mentioned in Paget Henry's study *Caliban's Reason: Introducing Afro-Caribbean Philosophy* (2000), and neither is she is interviewed in either Daryl Cumber Dance's 1992 collection or Frank Birbalsingh's 1996 work, her inclusion here is clearly strategic. Indeed, Brodber's inclusion may be traced to the editors' declared motivation in producing this volume which was closely connected to their own awareness of geographical bias in previous works.

> We noted that much of the critical and theoretical writing on the subject [of creolization] is produced by scholars from North American and other universities . . . our increasing interest in providing a truly cross-Caribbean assortment of opinions that could fully disclose the intricate nature of creolization as a cross-cultural and transnational phenomenon led to this anthology.
>
> (Balutansky and Sourieau 1998: vii)

It was perhaps Brodber's Caribbean location that went in her favour – for once!

As one might expect from two such very different contexts, these are very different pieces of writing and yet both help us to position Brodber's ideas on the relationship between place and consciousness which is so crucial to all her literary works. They also, I would argue, help us, through Brodber, to reposition some of the dominant theoretical configurations through which issues of place and identity are currently constructed. In particular I think that Brodber's intricate historically and geographically embedded narratives offer an important counterpoise to the proliferation and celebration of migrant tales. Her reterritorialisation of the Black Atlantic experience, rooted in the village archives and oral histories, as well as in the contemporary configuration of the village itself, both brings Gilroy's ship ashore and also forces us to witness the realities of its historical dockings.[8]

Brodber's *The People of My Jamaican Village, 1817–1948* has a clearly stated audience and purpose:

> The present work . . . is specially written for the people who live in Woodside and whose responses provided the base data . . . It is my

hope that linking the present inhabitants of Woodside with their enslaved ancestors who lived and worked on the Neilson's Woodside coffee plantation in the early nineteenth century, as this work does, will give us, the new generation, a sense that we are part of a process from slavery to freedom and will lend us a greater measure of responsibility.

There is the hope too, that others in Jamaica and the rest of the African diaspora will read and feel the process with us in Woodside.

(Brodber 1999: 22)

In this work Brodber recovers what she can of the lives of the slaves who were brought to work on the 1000-acre Woodside coffee plantation from the earliest 'slave returns' of 1817 and later government records and tax returns, as well as from testimonies of ancestors still living.[9] She traces their children, their relationships and the nature of their working lives on the plantation.

Although Brodber's method is documentary, and in no way resembles the saga or scandal narrative, she researches the village's foundational myths and seeks to restore the conditions of possibility under which they may be understood.

According to the Ferguson family history, Billy [probably the mistress's first slave] had a daughter with this, the master's daughter. The married name of this child is Margaret Green. The Neilson daughter . . . appears to be Mary Ann, the last daughter of the Neilsons. Billy at 10 or 12 . . . would have been about the same age as Mary Ann . . . It is easy to understand how friendship could have developed between the master's daughter and Billy and how they could eventually have made a child.

(Brodber 1999: 22)

As I shall come to discuss later, this particular family story and that of the relationship between the stipendary magistrate, Alexander Gordon Fyfe, and Mother Lindsay, his non-white housekeeper, have interesting implications for Brodber's conceptualisation of the Black Atlantic community.

The story of Woodside is a very centred narrative and has a very rooted character list, and yet its telling involves the crossing of at least three continents and the invocation of massive movements of populations through the foundational historical experiences of the Caribbean – slavery, colonisation and indenture. While Brodber looks consciously to the rest of the African diaspora in her foreword, she does also discuss the East Indians of her Jamaican village. Although East Indians settled in relatively small numbers in Jamaica (unlike Trinidad and Tobago and Guyana),

Brodber is keen to sketch the fullest picture of village folk. The kinds of intimate exchanges that have taken place as a result of the brutal, capitalist transactions of slavery and the indenture system become evident in her description of a complex pattern of creolisation. Describing the lineage that can be traced back to George Brown (an Indian), Brodber explains:

> What is certain, is that his five acres extended itself through marriage into a [*sic*] area of Woodside called Aitkin Town. Aitkin Town abuts Dryland. Here George Brown and his wife, the mulatto daughter of a Scottishman who had established a compound of kin there, settled to swell the small store of brown faces and long silky hair in Woodside. The store further increased with the advent of and connection with the mulatto Colemans and the Paynes who had moved into the district.
>
> (Brodber 1999: 29)

Brodber also, interestingly, moves towards restoring the reputation of Mrs Neilson, the white plantation mistress, who is generally acknowledged by the village to have been proud and whose demise is seen as her just 'come-uppance'. By foregrounding Mrs Neilson's gifts of her great house for an Anglican school and a piece of her land with a spring as a common ground, Brodber brings the white mistress into the narrative of the village community and demonstrates that she also played a part in its transformation.

On one level, this pamphlet is very much a specific, locally invested piece of writing, yet on a different level we might read this local history as an intervention in theoretical debates over the interaction of local and global, and the relationship between place and identity. In this reading we might argue that what Brodber does is to take the most localised world she knows, her village, and use this location to return our gaze to both the global imperial forces and the local struggles and triumphs that have shaped the lives of Jamaican people now and in the past. The village's collective biography anchors Caribbean creolisation – both ancestral and contemporary – to the historical processes that created the Caribbean and in this way Brodber's work details that although creolised identities may be newly fashionable they are not new. By tracing the local contours and small crossings set in motion by the huge passages and tramlines of tricontinentalism, Brodber writes in the people who have stayed and thereby restores what might be otherwise lost in theoretical metanarratives which consistently reinterpret the local through the global.

The individual genealogies, as well as the cultural and ethnic interactions between people that Brodber documents, testify to the fact that actually belonging somewhere specific – in this case the village of Woodside in Jamaica – does not mean that you cannot belong to other places as well, both spiritually and emotionally. By focusing on this small community,

Brodber is able to work against the flattening out of difference that often occurs when home or dweller are evoked in discourses of migration or diaspora and set against the mobility of the traveller. The history of Woodside demonstrates that home in this case is not that which is static, originary, and regressive against which the fluid, multiple and liberatory condition of migration or disapora can define itself. Woodside, like Jamaica and the Caribbean more widely, is shown through Brodber's work to be simultaneously 'rooted' and 'routed' (to borrow Gilroy's dichotomy), to be informed by a perspective and identity that is both 'here' and 'else-where'. In a sense Woodside is a very localised and yet profoundly diasporised place. It may be said to offer a radical reconfiguration of the global village to that which circulates in contemporary cosmopolitics as a false indicator of the effective collapse of space between nations via migration, the information highway and the marketplace and that is used as a brand name to sell data communication products, public access tele-vision, package holidays and even English language schools. As Puri has already argued, in this model, 'space is not being collapsed; it is being reorganized' (2004: 9).

Brodber's focus on the local strikes me as particularly important given the strong theoretical interpellations of postcolonial and Black Atlantic studies towards particular kinds of mobility and cultural complexity located in diasporic subjects. Her work re-territorialises Caribbean subjects in an important act of restitution that has impact for both the local community of the village and global intellectual community beyond that. In this way her work confirms the importance of thinking about place that Bill Ashcroft outlines.

> Place is never simply location, nor is it static, a cultural memory which colonization buries. For, like culture itself, place is in a continual and dynamic state of formation, a process intimately bound up with the culture and the identity of its inhabitants. Above all place is a *result* of habitation, a consequence of the ways in which people inhabit space.
>
> (Ashcroft 2001: 156)

This refiguring of the relationship between consciousness and place is also important to the second piece, 'Where are all the others?'. Although the main narrative focus of this piece is on the two Miss Mandas, before I discuss these two village women, I want strategically to foreground one section of the narrative that appears almost as an aside in the work itself. Reflecting on the poverty with which she associated Joe Chiss, Miss Manda's husband, Brodber concludes:

> Joe Chiss stands out in my mind as poor because (so the story went, and I believed it) he sold his land by the banana roots, two shilling

and six pence per piece, when in need ... No one – but no one – sells his land. Weeds may grow on it; the grass may die; you may plant nothing viable on it; but you do not sell your land. It is the evidence that your forebears lived; to sell it is to sell not just yourself but your dead.

(Brodber 1998: 69)

This conceptualisation of land as an ancestral claim, even an archive in the absence of written records, makes a very clear connection between this piece and Brodber's local history project based at Woodside. Both affirm that the connection to place is not only about being able to locate oneself in relation to geography but also in relation to history. The idea of land as heritage clearly lays out the importance of roots within a historical narrative so determined by routes and, as in Senior's work, that the claim to a local, settled identity requires something to hold on to.

However, it is the entangled cultural and linguistic heritage that Miss Manda has held on to that forms the main interest of this piece. This article begins as an almost straightforwardly auto/biographical narrative that tells a story of two village women, their social standing and linguistic prowess. The story of two Miss Mandas is short and very compressed. It swiftly but affectionately describes the fate of the first Miss Manda, 'Mrs. Manda Bean and her husband were poor, illiterate, hard-working, begging people. They were *normal*' (Brodber 1998: 69, italics mine). The piece then moves on to focus on the 'real Miss Manda' who sang and stole and fought and spoke in Standard English – and who was therefore marked out as not being normal.

Whoever heard of a fighter saying, 'Let me go'? What was required at a time such as this was huffing and puffing, no words at all. Much railing. Body language only. And when the words finally came, they should be in the local language.

(Brodber 1998: 71)

As Brodber's other voice – that of sociologist, researcher and intellectual worker – registers, of all her transgressions this linguistic trespass was the worst in the eyes of the village. 'The trouble with Miss Manda was that she knew another language', but more than this she used another language, a language identified as belonging to her social 'other'. To quote Brodber: 'Miss Manda sinned twice: she got the match between form and occasion wrong, and she spoke in a tone and language that were not befitting her class. Miss Manda did not know her place' (Brodber 1998: 72).

Miss Manda's predicament of being out of place in her own village is an important one for two reasons. First, because it demonstrates that just as the diverse experiences, histories, voices, and bodies that have landed in the Caribbean may have collectively formed new whole communities, such as Woodside, so too differences of class or gender may not be entirely harmonised within the whole and can still enunciate variations that are received as troubling echoes of past privileges and social exclusions. Second, for Brodber, Miss Manda's discordant code-switching identifies an absence in the kind of intellectual work crucial to a reconstruction of Caribbean wholeness.

> So much work, 'scientific work' has been done on the lower class in the Caribbean, on the concept of plurality, on the notion of class, on creolization, but we don't know Miss Manda's pain. She is suffering from incomplete creolization. How many others are there??
>
> (Brodber 1998: 73)

This declared interest in the 'others', here the educated, middle-class creole woman, is picked up later on in this piece when Brodber reflects on the transfer of cultural properties manifest in language, and specifically a linguistic texture and body of songs which links Barbados, African America and Australia via the Irish. Brodber's search, as with Miss Manda, is for the connections that scholarship has yet to attend to. Thinking back to the Irish she asks

> Which of those secondary whites, living so close to slave, ex-slave, and peasant-class African Jamaicans passed on those ribald songs to Miss Manda? Which of them gave us those children's games which survive in indisputable English? I want to know what the Irish, the Scottish, the Welsh gave to the Creole mix as much as I want to know: 'Is it Ibo, Fulani, what particular part of Africa is my heritage?' I have no doubt that with this kind of work being done by Kamau Brathwaite and Maureen Lewis-Warner – to mention those whom I know best – I will solve the African riddle, but who will tell me about the others? Where are the others?
>
> (Brodber 1998: 75)

This question which directs us back to these 'others' of the Caribbean is not about privileging Europe or the west again, it is about complicating and scrutinising our notions of Europe and the west and their connections to the Caribbean in order to understand that all identities are interrelational and intersubjective, and that wholeness cannot be achieved whilst parts are still missing or disavowed. This emphasis upon the recognition of all cultural elements is echoed, at a more personal level, by the Jamaican writer Lorna Goodison.

> My great grandfather was a man called Aberdeen, who obviously came from Scotland. And my great grandmother came from Guinea, and because they had a mating and produced my grandmother, who looked

like an American Indian – I have relatives who look like Egyptians
and my son is an African prince – all of it belongs to me. If somebody tells you, take some and leave some, that is his or her problem.
I am not going to do that. All of it belongs to me!

(Goodison in Binder 1991)[10]

We know that access to the ear and pen of history is not equal for all at
all moments, but it is interesting and provocative that the history that
Brodber sees as being obscured in her piece is that of the 'secondary
whites' and subalterns of the West – the Irish.

The idea of coming to know one's place through others and being able
to enunciate one's self through others is arguably part of the theory of
creolisation itself and yet what Brodber draws attention to in this collection of essays, all of which are concerned with creolisation, is that perhaps
there are others still who need to be traced and connected before anyone's
idea of place and voice can be fully realised. This process of accom-
modating untold stories, particularly those that have been disavowed
because of the defining binarism of race, may be observed in Brodber's
novels through the incorporation of White Hen into the healing community of *Myal* and the marriage of William Alexander Whiting, born to
white tobacco planters, to Tia, his nanny's black god-daughter in *Jane and
Louisa Will Soon Come Home*. Indeed, as Tia's name may suggest to readers
of Jean Rhys' *Wide Sargasso Sea*, Brodber appears to write in the very
possibility of a self-conscious relationship between blacks and white in
the Caribbean that Brathwaite had seemingly written off in the 1970s
in his *Contradictory Omens*. While Brathwaite dismisses the possibility of any
sustaining friendship between Antoinette, the daughter of the plantation
owner, and Tia, a local black girl, Brodber not only allows a marriage to
take place in her fictional study but she also affirms the possibility, within
her local history, of the union between a slave and the mistress' daughter
that results in a child. Indeed, Brodber's choice of words in an interview with Nadia Ellis Russell in 2001 could be read as an almost direct
response to Brathwaite's 1974 declaration that

> White Creoles in the English and French West Indies have separated
> themselves by too wide a gulf . . . to give credence to the notion that
> they can . . . identify or be identified with the spiritual world on this
> side of the Sargasso Sea.
>
> (Brathwaite 1974: 38)

Brodber speaks against this separation of interests.

> So, we have to accept that the other side has something to give us as
> well . . . So there's always the possibility of the meeting. But the meeting
> has to be a real one in which we understand ourselves.
>
> (Brodber in Ellis Russell 2001)

Brodber's representation of this meeting is not only to be found in her novels that reach international academic audiences but also in her community work within her village. As part of the annual Emancipation Day March, held on 1 August at Woodside, the villagers take part in a historical socio-drama that is partly scripted by Brodber.

> Then comes the recreation, which starts with a reading of Queen Victoria's Emancipation Proclamation of 1834. Various villagers step forward, portraying the responses of their ancestors. At one point, a light-skinned village woman is the subject of mistrust, as another villager worries whether she will be entitled to greater freedoms because of her planter heritage. In steps the narrator: 'We all suffer. It no matter the skin, we all suffer.'[11]

In this sense Brodber may be seen almost to have returned the tide of Gilroy's *Black Atlantic* that is concerned to trace how 'the history of blacks in the West and the social movements that have affirmed and rewritten that history can provide a lesson which is not restricted to blacks' (Gilroy 1993: 223). Brodber's writing and her theorising of a space in which all members of the Caribbean community can come to an understanding of themselves alongside and through others, as well as her creation of a literal place within her village in which the restitution of a tricontinental history can be made, offers a challenge to the Black Atlantic model that is more open in its geographical and historical indices to both the flows and returns of peoples and that moreover allows for an acknowledgement of the way in which these flows have been rooted, as well as routed.

My argument is that by drawing on both roots and routes, the African self and the European other, Brodber is not in any way flattening out the field of history on which these two groups have taken very different paths at very different inclines. Her primary interest in all her works remains the recovery of the black experience, its connections across the African diaspora and untold stories of that experience. However, Brodber works at the level of community and nation, as well as of race, and acknowledges that each part of the whole must be restored if both the parts and the whole are to develop fully. In this respect, her writing seems to confirm Lovelace's observation that

> The biggest gift to be made in the issue of reparation is to yourself, to ourselves. We must give back what we have taken from ourselves, we must give back to ourselves the love and appreciation of the world, of beauty, of diversity, of the wonder of people . . .
>
> (Lovelace in Aiyejina 2003: 183)

This in itself becomes a more grounded and politically directed version of Walcott's now familiar image of the Antilles:

Break a vase, and the love that reassembles the fragments is stronger than that love which took its symmetry for granted when it was whole ... Antilliean art is this restoration of our shattered histories, our shards of vocabulary, our archipelago becoming a synonym for pieces broken off the original continent.

(Walcott 1992: 2)

Yet while Walcott witnesses the existing beauty it would seem that both Brodber (and Lovelace) see this assemblage as process rather than result. Their writings are most crucially efforts to continue to work and write towards a vision of wholeness that has the promise to deliver both social justice and emotional and spiritual transformation at the level of race, community and nation.

Although very different, I would want to argue that both of Brodber's pieces are allied by the idea of restitution and by their encoding of complexity, diversity and possibility in the local and the located. In both, bounded and spatially-defined communities are not static or monolithic because they are not positioned as oppositional to the cosmopolitan margins of metropolitan diasporas. Indeed, if we take the cosmopolitan to be one who enjoys membership of a global community, we might argue that Brodber shows us that the villagers of Woodside, like Foster and his fellow Trinidadians is Selvon's *An Island Is a World,* are founders of a particular kind of located cosmopolitism. In the current intellectual milieu in which rootedness is not seen as liberatory in the same way as border crossing or migrancy, Brodber's writings are very important because they allow us to see history as a form of agency and they also bestow agency and identity on those subjects for whom global mobility is not an option.

Incomplete creolisation – Albinia MacKay and a voice out of place

Ostensibly, Albinia MacKay, a Jamaican Creole writer of the first half of the century, whose writings are both orthodox in form and language and conservative in terms of cultural politics, may seem to be working from an almost opposing cultural script to Erna Brodber, whose works have always been profoundly sourced by her connection to folk traditions and her commitment to the recovery of hidden (hi)stories of the African diaspora. However, I want to suggest that in reconsidering the poetics and the politics of disapora from another perspective we may read MacKay as a Miss Manda figure, or at least read her poetry as articulating a subjectivity suffering from incomplete creolisation.

Albinia Catherine MacKay was born in Kingston, Jamaica in 1894, of Scottish parents with a Scottish poet for a grandfather – William Shand Daniel of Dumbarton. She also published under two married names – Albinia Hutton and later Hutton-Davis. Given that I want to engage in a discussion of the politics of place in MacKay's work it may be important to indicate her own home location. In his essay on her work in *A Literature in the Making*, J. E. C. McFarlane takes some time to describe both Hutton's residence and her vista.

> About a mile from Spanish Town the road to Montpelier turns northward; a steady climb of ten miles from that point, through country dear to the heart of the forest lover, brings us to what appears the very top of the Island; to the east and west and north are hills, peers of the peak on which Montpelier stands, with intervening valleys thick with vegetation; southward lies the grand panorama of sea and plain, stretching from beyond Kingston and Port Royal, past Port Henderson and Spanish Town to Bog Walk and Old Harbour Bay, certainly one of the sublimest spectacles this country affords. Such is the prospect that was for many years our poet's daily companion, and to which her spirit is attuned, perhaps finding there reminders of its ancestral home.
>
> (McFarlane 1956: 29)

In one sense, this location may help us to construct MacKay as a remote figure, disconnected from the realities of urban life in Jamaica. In her own 1930 work, *Life in Jamaica*, a curiously fond but condescending portrait of village life, Hutton (née MacKay) sketches 'A Day in Jamaica' of a woman, such as herself, engaged in household duties. This work is insistently located in the village, which she constantly refers to as 'our' village, and attempts to record the speech and lifestyles of the 'country people', as well as the vegetation and the animal life.

At one level this text demonstrates a commitment to the local and very much figures Hutton herself as at the heart of village life – tending to the sick, conversing with the schoolteacher and buying food at the market. Yet, while Hutton seeks to inscribe her intimacy with her village community in this piece, it is her difference from the village folk that is clearly marked to our view. Her descriptive vocabulary is heavily weighed by colonial cultural values, the people around her are described as 'smiling peasants' and 'street urchin'. Moreover, there is a transparent acceptance of the social order that keeps mistress over servant, and "proper" English over vernacular speech. It may be useful to connect the core ambivalence of Hutton's attachment to the village and its folk to the complex but unresolved affective register of colonial nationalism found in the work of creole writers at this moment that I discussed in Chapter One. Never-theless, despite its naïvety and ineptitude, Hutton's attempt at recording Jamaican speech does acknowledge the crucial connection between voice and the rendering of subjectivity. Most of the speech is represented as part of a conversational exchange or, perhaps more interestingly, an effort to record how she is regarded by others: 'Poor Buckra Pickney! A how him a go get home tonight? An it not even moonlight self. Den watch how de gallinpper (mosquitoes) a bite him!' (Hutton 1930: 5).

If both McFarlane's words and Hutton's own self-representation seem to confirm a remote attachment to the village or the hills, rather than an allegiance to the island and its urban centre, it is important to remember that Hutton was also the founder and editor of *Singers Quarterly*, a circulating scrap book of poetry with a West Indian focus, and that she was on the board of Una Marson's radical magazine, *The Cosmopolitan*, founded in 1928. In different ways, this ambivalence between the remote and the engaged presence, the acknowledgement of an alternative cultural world but also the pull towards a privileged place of beauty informs all of Hutton's work and is perhaps the register through which we can hear her incomplete creolisation.

If Hutton is remembered at all then it is probably for her loudly patriotic poem, 'The Empire's Flag', in which the Union Jack is given space to voice its achievements. However, I wish to discuss a small number of poems from her 1912 collection (published under the name MacKay) that are dedicated to Scottish history and in particular the struggle between Englishmen and Scots for the rule of Scotland and cultural self-determination, some of which are written in Scottish idiom. Although initially these two poetic directions may seem antithetical, the particular context of Scottish nationalism and also the historical conditions which inform the connections between Scotland and Jamaica may help us to read the seeming incommensurability of location and locution in these works.

After the act of Union in 1701 Scotland had to remake its patriotism within the frame of Britishness and therefore there is less of a contradiction than there may initially seem to be between these 'Scottish' poems and Hutton's verse in praise of the British Empire. In many ways her poems may be read as part of the movement known as Sentimental Jacobitism in which the heroic Scottish spirit is romanticised. MacKay's 'The Prayer Before The Battle Of Bannockburn', looks back 600 years to 1314 and a decisive battle in Scottish history when Robert the Bruce defeated the English under Edward II and claimed back Scotland. In the poem, the poetic voice implores God to empower the Scottish people in their fight for liberation.

> Help us to set this our dear country free,
> The land that to our sires was given by Thee.
> Lay the usurper low, and let the right
> Again arise triumphant over might.
>
> (MacKay 1912: 19)

In a similar vein, 'Caledonia' praises Scotland and the bravery and loyalty of the Scottish people.

> Like the wild storms that on thy mountains rave,
> Thy children's feelings boil within their breasts,
> The race who ever loyal, tru and brave,
> Will sooner die than be by thrall oppressed.
>   (MacKay 1912: 14)

These impassioned representations of the injustice done to the Scots, and their ability and right to resist the claims and force of England are clearly historically and culturally specific. Although both involve a direct engagement with the issues of violent encounter, political usurpation and cultural domination so pertinent to the colonisation of Jamaica, as well as of Scotland, there is no suggestion of any parallels to the colonial condition of Jamaica and no reference to Jamaica's unfree. This absence – or refusal – of a shared history is both engaging and perplexing and seems again to locate her work on this strange matrix of attachment and displacement, allegiance and aloofness.

'The Jacobite Exile's Lament', written in a Scottish idiom, tells of a man who must leave Scotland after the defeated rebellion of 1745 when the Highlanders gave support to the exiled Stuart King James and his descendant Bonnie Prince Charlie but were defeated by the English King William III.

> Now I maun leave the land I l'oe best,
>   To wander in distant lands
> Wi ma father's banes mine canna rest,
>   But be buried by strangers' hands.
>
> But I shall l'oe my country still
>   (MacKay 1912: 12)

The inscription of a vernacular voice, here Scottish nation language, is an implicit acknowledgement of the significance of language in the formation of cultural identities. Furthermore, the position of being bodily absent from but culturally connected to an ancestral homeland is a situation analogous to that of many Caribbean peoples, not only those who arrived as part of the African and Asian diasporas, but also those born Creoles. However, despite such glaring points of common interest, a recognition of the possible relevance in terms of the cultural politics of this poem written in the Caribbean is notably absent. The most urgent and relevant transcultural identification is simply missing from this cross-cultural lyric. In order to tease out the politics of location within these works I want to draw on two contexts in which I believe the works can speak in more interesting ways than is apparent at a first reading. First, that of the immigration of Scottish people to Jamaica and second, that of literary experiments with the vernacular voice in Jamaica around 1912.

The (missing) link between Scotland and Jamaica via the Jacobite Rebellion is not purely one of fictive nostalgia. Hutton's inscription of the Highlander's voice and claim is perhaps more interesting when we consider that it not only fits into a wider picture of anti-English nationalism but also connects to a low-profile dimension of Jamaican history. One of the largest influxes of Scots into Jamaica came after the failure of the Jacobite Rebellion in 1745 when the Highlanders were forced to give their family lands and properties to King William III. For those who remained in the Highlands the process of colonisation was enforced by the English education system and the prohibition of Gaelic – speaking this language was marked as a hanging offence, as was the wearing of tartan. Many of those that left joined the exodus of Scots to Jamaica where they built up new estates and businesses, becoming not the colonised but the coloniser. It has been ventured that by the middle of the eighteenth century one third of the white population in Jamaica were of Scottish origin. Many arrived as penniless exiles but were soon slave owners taking advantage of the huge profits to be made from the coffee, cotton and spice trades. Scots arriving in the Caribbean (mainly to Jamaica) entered into a society in which social relations were most clearly marked by race and thus they were able to use this to their own advantage, their whiteness masking their ethnic and class difference and enabling them to thrive as planters and slave-owners.

As Avtar Brah argues, 'The British diasporas in the colonies were internally differentiated by class, gender, ethnicity (English, Scottish, Irish, Welsh) and so on, but the discourses of Britishness subsumed these differences as the term "British" assumed a positionality of superiority' (Brah 1996: 190). The Scottish clearly used this positionality to advance themselves in economic terms but there was still a residue of cultural difference. Those who made their fortunes and homes in the mountains of Jamaica have left a legacy of their success. The place names Culloden, Craigie and Aberdeen, as well as St Andrews demonstrate the impact that they had on the organisation of the island. Others have perhaps left no trace, there is evidence that some dispossessed Highlanders worked on lands in the Southern States of America and one account even tells of how, in Barbados, a shipload of Highlanders was traded for ten tons of sugar. This context may help to reveal Hutton's individual ambivalence as a strained relation to place that is embedded in the Scottish history of Jamaica, informed both by the experience of dispossession and acute repression leading to exile on the one hand, and by the practice of crude exploitation through participation in the plantation system on the other.

However, an appreciation of the moment in which these poems appear may also help to position their entangled attachments. I want to argue that works on this subject, in a nation language, at this time and place, Jamaica 1912, makes this small archive a more provocative resource for considering the politics of location. The year was something of an early literary high-point in Jamaica. H. G. deLisser published his *Twentieth Century*

Jamaica in 1913 and *Jane's Career* in 1914. Even the Governor at this time, Sydney Olivier, had a personal interest in creative writing and literary pursuits. Claude McKay's 1912 *Songs of Jamaica* are dedicated to Olivier, although he was no radical. This moment was also a period of interest in nation language, with Claude McKay's *Songs of Jamaica* and *Constab Ballads*, both being published in 1912, and Thomas MacDermot also experimenting with Jamaican language.[12] In the context of this small but significant literary experimentation with nation language and a more general emergent focus on the local, MacKay's verses written in 'Scotch', as she names it, and on the subject of Scottish history take on a curious status as not quite right, not quite black (to misquote Bhabha's 'not quite right, not quite white'). Her own 'nation language', being not Jamaican, but Scottish, although not comfortably aligned to a regionally specific cultural nationalist project, still importantly represents an anti-English (and implicitly) anti-imperialist stance. Furthermore, her inscriptions of the Scottish landscape are clearly nostalgic reconstructions of her localised vista in the hills of Jamaica. There is then an enticing coexistence or collocation between Hutton's work during this period and the cultural nationalists' emphasis upon inscribing the local, but still her voice remains strangely out of place. The strain of being incompletely creolised is articulated in her disconnection from her actual location and the displacement of Scotland onto Jamaica which enables her to voice the issues of belonging, the claims of ancestral identity and the rights to self-determination but only as an ancient cause, a male battle and a remote echo.

While MacKay's verses perhaps represent one of the 'trickiest' inscriptions of location and the local to be found within a Caribbean literary archive, they do enable us to see how notions of hereness and elsewhereness, of location and dislocation are played out in a range of cultural fields. MacKay's experience of the psychic multilocationality of the diasporic subject offers a different genealogy and a different place of imagined belonging but testifies to the same emotional current as those identifications towards Africa and India that find legitimation in the black diaspora paradigm. Her textual utterances may be seen, via Gilroy's Bakhtinian frame, as an example of cultural heteroglossia in which different voices speak the possibilities of being that are open to, but not fully controlled by, MacKay in that moment. As Brodber makes clear, and MacKay seemingly exemplifies, incomplete creolisation is a serious side-effect of the different discursive claims made on Caribbean identities from the colonial era onwards.[13] Although I have argued that the recovery of these 'difficult' texts has a value to our conceptions of literary history, in her ethic of restitution Brodber goes further in asserting the necessity of restoring the history of each voice and ethnicity in order for any people or culture to be whole: 'Until they have written their thing and thought through their thing they still keep a piece of me which I don't know, because I am related to them' (Ellis Russell 2001).

A new ethics of belonging

The idea of a new ethics of relationality and connection is also central to
Earl Lovelace's 1996 novel *Salt* that, despite winning the 1997 Commonwealth Writers Prize, has received very little critical attention to date. *Salt*
may be seen in some ways as a national epic, a *New Day* for Trinidad, in
as much as it covers the historical sweep of centuries from the days of
slavery when Bango's ancestor Guinea John flew back to Africa to the
present day.[14] As in his other works, Lovelace represents Trinidadian
(Caribbean) people as agents involved in struggles for survival, for love,
for meaning and for reparation. However, rather than reading *Salt*
alongside Vic Reid's *New Day* (1949), I wish to read it alongside Selvon's
An Island Is a World (1955), another critically neglected work that is also
crucially concerned with the claims for (and against) national belonging.
In his critical piece, 'Rhythm and Meaning' (in Aiyejina 1983), Lovelace
singles Selvon out as being

> a very important novelist in terms of language as it relates to expressing
> the being of the people. If we look at *The Lonely Londoners* . . . through
> that medium he gives a sense of the sensibility of the people. Of course,
> he identifies very closely with them.
>
> (Aiyejina 2003: 93)

It is interesting that Lovelace takes Selvon's *The Lonely Londoners* as his
example here. Even as a fellow Trinidadian, Lovelace seems to confirm
that Selvon's achievement is both the rendering of a Trinidadian vernacular and the representation of the experience of the migrant – two skills
that arguably peak in his 1956 classic text. While I would not contest the
classic status of this text, I would contest the way in which *The Lonely
Londoners* has come to characterise Selvon's writing, to stand as the text
through which we recognise his voice and by implication his identification with the migrant. This is a recognition conditioned no doubt by the
preference for narratives of metropolitan engagement in its own critical
moment and for those of exile and migration in ours. To my mind it can
be argued that Selvon demonstrates his identification with the people more
strongly in *A Brighter Sun* (1952), *An Island Is a World* (1955) and *Turn Again
Tiger* (1958) that examine the experience of the dweller, as well as the
migrant. For the purposes of this chapter, I want to suggest that *An Island
Is a World* provides an interesting intertext to Lovelace's *Salt* with its focus
on the lure of the bigger world, the problems of local politics and the
possibilities for emotional belonging within the nation.

Selvon's *An Island Is a World* follows the fortunes of five male characters,
the migrant brothers Foster and Rufus, Johnny the ineffectual patriarch,
Father Hope the rooted rural preacher and Andrews the artist-teacher-
politician. Set in the 1940s and early 1950s, Selvon's novel can be read
as a dense, almost compressed, representation of its own recent historical

moment in which the pulls and tugs of migration were reshaping the contours of Trinidadian history, and literary history, in a profound way. In this era when the process of decolonisation and the promise of Federation charged the hopes and ambitions of Trinidadians in different directions – Johnny returns to the newly independent India, Rufus makes his way as an illegal to live in the US and Andrews and Foster marry and settle in Trinidad – Selvon devotes one third of his narrative to the contrasting migrant tales of Rufus and Foster. The first, enamoured with the US and longing to be free from his ties to Trinidad, is entirely caught up in the metropolitan sway of the Black Atlantic, so much so that when he returns to Trinidad to secure his divorce 'it was as if the ship were travelling back- wards all the way to Trinidad, the way he kept his mind on America and the life he was leaving behind' (Selvon 1993: 151, first published 1955). The second though is estranged by the narrowness of the motherland and the lack of direction he finds there, 'Everything looks aimless to me, a general movement to nowhere' (Selvon 1993: 154).

However, the novel is not simply a reference book of possible routes for the virtually postcolonial Trinidadian. In its discussions of the different cultural and political currents that flow across the Black Atlantic and their impact on the prospective project of nation building, Selvon's text speaks very clearly of and for its own cultural moment in which people are journeying *beyond* the nation *before* the nation even comes into being, to the imagined communities of India, America, as well as a West Indies Federation. It also registers the commitment to the nation that is found in the figures of Andrews, the solid and dedicated teacher and councillor; Father Hope, the preacher and community worker who has returned to Veronica, the 'small place' where he was born; and finally in Foster, the disillusioned migrant, whose experience of the motherland brings him to an understanding of the national cause, 'We have a task to build up a national feeling' (Selvon 1993: 106).

An Island Is a World is very much a book of ideas as well as of characters, as Ramchand comments in his introduction to the 1993 reprint, 'the philo- sophical substance dominates the character of the characters' (Ramchand 1993: vii). One important idea in the novel, published during the moment of the boom when the metropolitan motherland was being recast as the new literary centre of West Indian fiction, is the reversal of metropolitan and parochial values. I want to argue that this reversal is central to the book's discussion of cultural flows and blockages. Resident in the mother- land, Foster feels both indignation and injustice that the tidal wave of English colonial culture that had engulfed the West Indies had not resulted in even a ripple returning in the other direction.

> He wasn't going to educate a pack of ignorant Englishmen who believed cannibals lurked in the hills. 'Yes, we have lions,' he told another viciously some other time . . . it didn't seem fair that West

Indians had to know all about England in the schools, and on the other hand Englishmen didn't know anything about the West Indies.
(Selvon 1993: 50)

It is his experience of racism and of narrow nationalism, the profound lack of global vision at the supposed hub of the world that ironically returns him to his own island home: 'No one thinks of the world. I am an Englishman. I am an American. I am a white man. I am a black man. No one thinks: "I am a human being, and you are another"' (Selvon 1993: 155).

By the end of the novel two of the men have departed, two have remained and one is dead. Selvon seems neither to write in favour of, nor against, migration. Rather, what he explores in this work is the impact of the various imagined communities on the possibilities of the coming nation and what bonds and affiliations will structure its political and emotional architecture. Interestingly, the novel is not preoccupied with the divides of race within Trinidad. It is not until towards the end of the text when the 'Back to India' movement takes off in the wake of Indian Independence, that the ethnicity of Foster and Rufus is marked as Indian-Caribbean. Andrew's African Trinidadian ethnicity is only commented on in terms of his surprising empathy with those returning to India. In many ways the characters stand as Trinidadians and as men more than as people of Indian and African descent.[15] As I have already discussed, Foster's sense of himself as a global citizen by nature of being a Trinidadian is central to the book's investigation of identity politics within the post-war Black Atlantic zone, 'He had been brought up a Trinidadian – a member of a cosmopolitan community who recognised no creed or race, a creature born of all the races in the world' (Selvon 1993: 211). The enduring friendship between Foster and Andrews is one based on exchange and debate but race is never on their agenda. What they discuss most are the ideas of commitment to the people and the nation, as if that will be the deciding factor in their lives.

From the restless Foster to the rooted Father Hope, the characters must all work out their connection to the world and their island home. Indeed, while the majority of the characters themselves seem to be preoccupied with the possibilities of being elsewhere, the narrative structure of the work brings them back to Trinidad in its final part. Furthermore, the denouement takes place in Father Hope's idealised rural community of Veronica in the Caura Valley, in the company of Foster and Andrews, the artist and the writer, who have decided to settle at home. Although Foster declines to take Father Hope's place in Veronica, there is a sense in which he is finally reconciled to his place in the world. A contemplative Ulysses, he finally concurs with Father Hope's view that 'an island is a world' (73), not a perfect world, but as good a place to philosophise and agonise as any other.

Despite the tendency to read Selvon's writings through the lens of *The Lonely Londoners*, as migrant tales, I would argue that *An Island Is a World* insists on drawing our attention to the project of building a Trinidadian nation, even as it acknowledges the pressures and strains that limit the possibilities of that project. This is not to argue that Selvon's text is a nationalist piece of writing, as it shifts the discursive ground away from a unitary framework from which the nation can emerge. It is rather to acknowledge that this work is interested in the possibility of Trinidad as a place of intellectual, emotional and cultural exchanges in which the essential recognition – 'I am a human being, and you are another' – can take place. Published eight years before Independence and the breakdown of Federation, Selvon's text can only imagine the kinds of affiliations, accommodations and disjunctures that may condition the shape of national and regional unity. It is in his narration of this national tale that I see Lovelace's *Salt* as a productive intertext with *An Island Is a World*. However, if Lovelace's tale takes us forward through the collapse of Federation and the achievement of political independence to contemporary Trinidad, it also takes us back, way back, to slavery. In order to deliver us to the present, *Salt* is far more explicitly interested in how the past must instruct us to read, interpret and respond to our own critical moment.

In Selvon's novel, politics is a degraded business orchestrated in London and more about divisions between peoples than the possibilities of mutual empowerment. Despite his commitment to the ideal of Federation, 'I have faith in Trinidad, and in the destiny of the West Indies', Andrews, the politician figure, decides to marry Marleen and put his own happiness above the nation's.

> I have my ideals and ambitions, but I'm very human too. I want the simple pleasures of life as much as the next man. I want a wife and a home and children, and a piece of land to raise corn. Why should I sacrifice that for a worthless cause? Do you think Trinidadians care very much whether the island progresses or continues to rot? Do you think I care?
>
> Yes. You care. And that's the difference. When someone like you comes along, it's a great pity to see you go by the way of all the others. This island needs men like you to pull it out of this stagnation it's been in all these years. It needs selfless, honest men.
>
> (Selvon 1993 (1955): 136)

Whereas Andrews falls away from the centre of Selvon's narrative, as both Rufus and Foster return to the island, in *Salt*, the politician figure remains central, as does the ethic of engagement. Unlike Selvon's narrative, Lovelace pursues the questions of leadership and the potential for social unity. In its sustained exploration of Alford George and Bango, his narrative may be seen to be concerned with how to produce such a leader.

Initially Alford George is a Foster figure, contemptuous of the smallness of his 'dot' on the globe, with his thoughts directed towards migration and 'the world' beyond. Yet, although Alford is Naipaul's mimic man in a way that Foster never is, Alford does not migrate and Lovelace's novel is not an account of the damage and trauma that has been enacted on the colonial subject by the epistemic violence of the colonial motherland. On one level, what is notable about Lovelace's text is that despite the great pull towards migration, both as a social and a literary phenomenon, he manages to write a convincing account of Trinidadians who do not leave but who are engaged in 'making a home of one's place' (Rahim 1999: 153). Indeed, in his status as dweller, Alford moves from a Foster figure to an Andrews. Like Andrews, he is a teacher who finds himself recast as a politician after his hunger strike in protest at the élitism of the school system. Alford's realisation that the implied lesson of all his twenty years of dedicated service as a teacher was self-loathing and estrangement brings him to resist the system.

> To fail to escape was defeat; defeat even before you began. And that was why you could accept the secondclassness of the place. Secondclassness was the punishment for the defeated, the failures. What redeemed this system? How many did escape? How many did in fact win a College Exhibition? In all the years the school had been preparing students for the examination, three of them had won College Exhibitions. Those left behind were the failures, the dregs. He realized that saving the two or three, if you could call it saving, was not enough for his life's vocation. If he was to go on, he would have to begin afresh to prepare the children for living in the island.
>
> (Lovelace 1996: 76)

During his thirty-two day hunger strike, Alford meets all manner of people who identify and sympathise with his cause, and he is fashioned by them as the people's leader. When Alford takes a formal political position his motto is 'Seeing Ourselves Afresh' and this is exactly what his encounter with Bango offers him.

Bango is clearly marked as an ancestor figure by his connection to Guinea John and thereby to African folklore, as well as to his great-grandfather JoJo who called his slave master to account. He is, at the same time, equally recognisable as the archetypal Trinidadian success – captain of both the steel band and the cricket team. Bango is Father Hope's selfless, honest man, dedicated to the people of his community, 'the weakness of others demanded from him greater strength. The extravagance of others required from him greater sacrifice'. It is Bango, nominated to request the land he lives on as reparation, who brings Alford to an awareness of the larger historical and cultural narrative that had been subject to political amnesia, and of the necessity of finally answering JoJo's request for emancipation to made meaningful by reparation. JoJo's request for 'a beginning . . . a new start . . . for both of us' (Lovelace 1996: 182), both echoes and roots Alford's call to see ourselves afresh. In telling Alford the story of his ancestor who requested compensation for 'the mashing up of our lives' (Lovelace 1996: 182), Bango offers Alford a way of investing the rhetoric of change with meaning, of matching ethical commitments to political ones.

By going back to the foundational history of the Caribbean – that of slavery – and to both JoJo's and Bango's refusal to forget the wrongs of this history, Lovelace actually enables a different scripting of both the present and the future. It is a version in which people are not frozen in the moment of conquest, a moment represented by Columbus with his lance and cross as an originary Caribbean moment in the mural that adorns the prime minister's office. Neither are they delivered into the flat horizon of a faked pluralistic present, also represented 'in the foreground, a tall white child and next to him a shorter Black girl and an Indian boy and a Chinese girl, so comfortable, so easy' (126). I would like to agree with Rahim's observation that 'the mural's stereotypical, hodgepodge panorama of the history and culture of the island inadvertently consolidates the old dichotomies of conquest and its scale and mode of representation merely glorify the colonial presence, and patronize the native' (Rahim 1999: 159). This mural demonstrates that Lovelace is very aware of the way in which 'cultural hybridity has offered the ruling classes a means of stabilizing the *status quo* through various strategies of displacing a politics of equality' (Puri 2004: 50). In *Salt*, this process is summed up in Ethelbert B. Tannis' estimation of the prime minister's speech (a direct reference to Eric William's 1960 'Massa Day Done' address), 'But then he end up giving slogans . . . He end up saying Massa Day done without taking action that would bring Blackpeople liberation' (Lovelace 1996: 192).

It is not incidental therefore that Bango stands against this mural when he offers his own oral account of history. Alford recognises Bango's story as a contemporary narrative that speaks to the requirements for full emancipation in his own moment as much as in the historical one, 'He had invoked JoJo; but I suspected that what he had just told us could have been his very own story. Things had not changed all that much' (Lovelace 1996: 187). Reparation is the model through which Lovelace proposes a new connection between then and now, 'Look at us, we have the treasury of the world right here, of skill and language, but we can't get nowhere until we settle accounts with history' (Lovelace 1996: 192). As Rahim asserts, Alford's recognition of this identity, history and community, enables him to move against the lure of Western assimilation and come to a new sense of belonging. As she phrases it, the epiphany of *Salt* is, albeit unwittingly, almost an exact echo of Selvon's title, 'Obviously, from Alford's renewed/redeemed perspective, his world is no longer the margin but it is the centre. *The island is the world and therefore, finally home*' (Rahim 1999: 160, italics mine).

However, the ending of the novel does not move us beyond reparation or stage the unity it may achieve. By refusing the faked representations of pluralism, Lovelace does confront the issue that Selvon side-steps – that of racial inequality and hostility. Sonan Lochan (the Indian-Caribbean) and Adolphe Carabon (the white Creole) do not join the final march. Crucially though, Lovelace does not rehearse the racialised versions of the past, but rather calls for a recognition of shared history that makes a strong echo across to Brodber's writings. If, as Bango's nephew declares at the end of the narrative, 'The tragedy of our time is to have lost the ability to feel loss' then the triumph of *Salt* is that it restores the affective dimension to Trinidadian characters. Its liberatory discourse is located most simply and profoundly in its ability to make people across the racial spectrum recognise both themselves and their others as heroic, complex, sentient, flawed, vulnerable – essentially to recognise them as equal and human.

Redemption and reparation: the energetics of commitment

As Shalini Puri points out, in many ways the political, economic and social conditions that have shaped the Caribbean region since Independence have drastically limited the possibilities of imagining 'the people'.

> The Caribbean offers an instance where imagining 'the people' has been a project fraught with particular difficulty. The region included what are surely some of the world's most fragile nation-states, often marked by repressive, if weak, governments, neo-colonial dependency, cyclical and mass migrations of population, environmental degradation, saturation by an international tourist culture, and economies that concentrate wealth in the hands of a tiny elite. Its history of colonial subjection and post-colonial dependency has made national sovereignty and regional self-determination hard to sustain. Nonetheless, against the deconstructions of 'the people' as a fabricated identity, I place the idea of imagining 'the people' in democratic and egalitarian ways as a political achievement worth struggling for.
>
> (Puri 2004: 12)

I want to suggest that the kind of imaginings that we find in Brodber's, Lovelace's, Selvon's and Senior's writings, while making full acknowledgement of the problems of the past and the present, are also testimony to the value and the potential of this project. To my mind, what distinguishes the work of these writers in particular is what I would like to call their energetics of compassion and commitment, or as Jennifer Rahim describes it, the 'ethical forthrightness' of their writing (Rahim 1999: 151).

These writers are not engaged in the detached and remote version of postcolonial humanism that enables Clifford to occupy the same position as a Caribbean subject at a theoretical level and yet remain immune to the duress of their political position. Indeed, their call for a postcolonial humanism is a way of expressing a shared horizon of expectation and hope that nonetheless requires a serious involvement with the inequalities of the past and the present. The call for reparation, which they each figure in different ways, evolves from a continued involvement in their societies and the urgent need to transform the alterity and hostility that conditioned interaction between different groups under the colonial mode of relations and that lingers still today. Reparation locates the ethical and political principles that guide these works.

> We need to release sections of our population from guilt, from shame, from the feeling of injustice and victimhood. Tolerance is not good enough. We need something more affirmative to overcome the ideas of slave and slave master and nigger and coolie.
>
> (Lovelace 2003: 100, first published in 1992)

Given my emphasis on a reading of wholeness and unity, it is perhaps important to address how we reconcile the emphasis on the experience and identity of the African that characterises both Brodber's and Lovelace's work within this inclusive vision. The response to this question can be found in both the historical and contemporary imbalance in terms of cultural recognition and self-value that is accorded the African presence in the Caribbean. Writing in 1968 Lovelace drew attention to this situation in Trinidad:

> We cannot be surprised at Syria House, or at the Chinese Association, or the Portuguese Association, or the Indian clubs . . . What we need to be surprised at is that there is no Africa House, that there is no African Association, that there is, indeed, no creative African community in Trinidad and Tobago, or for that matter in the West Indies.
>
> (Lovelace 2003: 112, first published in 1968)

Nearly forty years later Carolyn Cooper describes a similar social condition in relation to Jamaica.

> [It is] the racial identity of the African majority who have been elided from the 'out of many, one' inscription of elitist 'Jamaican' nationality and remain unnamed. Whereas Europeans, Chinese, Syrians and

Indians, for example, are all raced and placed in their very naming, it is only people of African descent in Jamaica who do *not* usually define their racial identity in terms that denote ancestral homelands. They are unhyphenatedly 'black'. Or worse, unnamed . . . 'Africa' has been so dehumanized in the colonial imaginary that relatively few Jamaicans – even today – want to identify themselves as African . . . Even in cases where some racial admixture is evident, the African element in the mix is always the half that has never been told. Mixed-race (African) Jamaicans define themselves as half-Indian, half-Chinese, half-Syrian, half-white. But never half-African. I would concede that this unnaming of the black half may signify that 'African' is grudgingly recognized to be the unacknowledged norm. But, much more likely, this silence speaks eloquently of the unresolved question of race and the contested status of African people in Jamaican society.

(Cooper 2004: 3)

In order to achieve an inclusive vision, the African experience and identity must still be made visible. Its naming must be made with commitment, integrity and force as an act of balancing the grounds of history in order to make the rhetoric of equality and inclusivity meaningful.

It is certainly true that many of the ethical moves that I have identified in the work of these settled writers have also been played out in the works of migrant writers. Wilson Harris and Caryl Phillips come to mind in their stretching, both historically and geographically, of the boundaries of connected communities. However, I want to offer these particular texts as an alternative to the proliferation of migrant tales that paradoxically appear more authentically Caribbean to readers now because the Caribbean has been reconfigured theoretically in the metropolis as a diasporic space and identity. My argument is that the preference for metropolitan diasporic writings that has emerged in tandem with the Black Atlantic, diasporic critical model has trumpeted the Caribbean as a theoretical utopia in which creolisation, hybridity, syncrenicity and deterritorialisation find their models of articulation but not their archives. The idea of the Caribbean as a cultural space, mobile, syncretic, and almost free-floating, has not served to direct attention back to the region as a site of possibility. In this model, the Caribbean nation, place and region becomes the dispossessed centre from which literal and intellectual trajectories take their point of departure but make no return. My argument is that by returning the critical gaze to the local and the dweller we can recover the literary connection to forms of resistance and agency that seek to secure the pathways between social justice, cultural recognition and the writings/rightings of history.

I have chosen to read the texts discussed in this chapter as consciously investing in the possibility of a shared national space, in the energetics of commitment and the rewards of self-scrutiny. Nevertheless, it is possible to see the geographically specific call for reparation and for account, enunciated most clearly in Brodber and Lovelace's work, as part of

> a proliferation of demands by various peoples and national govern-
> ments that acts of aggression committed against them in the near and
> distant past be recognized and acknowledged as historical wrongs;
> and that the aggressors offer apology, compensation and restitution
> for their wrongdoing.
>
> (Sunder Rajan 2000: 160)

Framing these located texts within a global movement demanding a 'righting of wrongs' may seem to work against the intellectual momentum of this chapter, which has sought to affirm the continued relevance of place and of the local in the face of globalising discourses that tend to flatten out the distinctive histories of 'small places'. However, this particular demand to attend to the politics of the past opens up a radically different route between postcolonial nation and western metropolis to that offered by the theoretical discourses of diasporic criticism that are generally less interested in the historical residues of injustice, violence and loss than in the 'new' identity categories and cultural flows that these historical processes have set in motion. More importantly, bringing the work of these Carib-bean writers within the orbit of this movement re-politicizes the channels and connections between postcolonial nations and western super-states, it 'both reveals and impels new stakes in the construction of collective subject positions and identities – and therefore new takes on historicity' (Trouillot 2000: 173).

Notes

1 James Procter's study *Dwelling Places: Postwar Black British Writing* (2003) is an important project that has earlier sought 'to intervene in, and interrupt, the logic of diaspora thinking: reintroducing and supplementing its "travelling theories" with an investigation into the cultural politics of "dwelling"' (12).

2 Jamil Khader's work on Puerto Rican women's rewriting of home asserts a similar suspicion in relation to the emancipatory claims of the Black Atlantic: 'Because of the material histories of exclusion and repression that Puerto Rican feminists experience in both insular and metropolitan terrains, I am sceptical of idealized readings of such disembodied mobility. By having free access to the metropolitan United States, moreover, these mobile subjectivities and their root-less cosmopolitan trajectories serve as an alibi for US global hegemony. Such a location of extraterritorality and rootlessness celebrated by circular migrancy theorists is simply untenable for subaltern cosmopolitans' (2003: 71).

3 For a detailed and searching analysis of the relationship between cultural hybridity and social equality which accounts for both the possibility of the pull of transnationalism and the imagining of the nation see Puri (2004).

4 Several monographs have employed this conceptualisation, such as Marcus Wood's *Blind Memory: Visual Representations of Slavery in England and America* (2000)

and Alan Rice's *Radical Narratives of the Black Atlantic* (2003) which repeats the North Atlantic model of Gilroy's study and gives sustained exploration to the interrelationship between black Atlantic cultures in the context of African-American works. Brent Hayes Edwards' *The Practice of Diaspora: Literature, Translation and the Rise of Black Internationalism* (2003) examines black transnational culture in the 1920s and 1930s, and the connections between intellectuals in New York and Paris. There is also a Black Atlantic Studies Centre at Rutgers University, Cultures of the Lusophone Black Atlantic project at Kings College London, special issues of various journals, e.g. *Journal of African Literatures* (1996) and, in some regards, the journal *Diaspora*.

5 Some of these studies are more suspicious of the way in which diasporic identities are importantly interpellated by the politics of globalisation. Important critiques of the move away from nation states and national stakes include Lazarus (1999) and Dirlik (1997).

6 I would like to thank Denise deCaires Narain for her suggestions on this point.

7 Even Brodber's remarkable novels have received markedly less international attention than they deserve. 'From Kumblas to Blackspace: A Symposium on Erna Brodber' organised in April 2002 by the Department of Literatures in English at the University of the West Indies, Mona (Jamaica) in Woodside, St. Mary, Jamaica did give serious recognition of Erna Brodber within the Caribbean intellectual community.

8 Edmondson offers an important alternative to the direction of my own scholarship in her work that argues that 'the writing of immigrant women is literally "making" the West Indian nation from another direction' (Edmondson 1999: 10).

9 Whilst working at the Institute for Social and Economic Research (ISER) in Mona, Jamaica, Brodber collected the oral histories of elders in rural Jamaica and this work later informed her third novel, *Louisiana* (1994).

10 This quotation first came to my attention in Denise deCaires Narain's book, *Making Style: Contemporary Caribbean Women's Poetry* (2002b: 167).

11 http://inthefray.com/200105/imagine/brodber2/brodber2.html#.

12 In her important unpublished Ph.D. study, 'The Creative Writer and West Indian Society, Jamaica 1900–1950', Rhonda Cobham-Sander draws attention to this flash point and also suggests the political index of this experimentation in creole: 'At a literary level it is perhaps not accidental that the two periods of greatest interest in dialect as a literary medium, between 1900 and 1914 and again in the 1940s, coincide with periods of heightened discontent within the upper middle classes with colonial rule' (1981: 125).

13 Before we write off Hutton's memories that cross the ocean and the centuries as simply eccentric, it is interesting to note that these Celtic connections are also foregrounded in John La Rose's 1974 piece, 'A West Indian in Wales' published in *Savacou*. 'So much of the volcanic land reminded me of the Caribbean islands' (1974: 109). 'Roads crisscrossed the land everywhere, as in Barbados ... This was a Costa Brava, a coast, beautiful, rugged, wild like Trinidad's North East coast. Memory crossed the seas and returned' (La Rose 1974: 111).

14 This is a reference to Vic Reid's 1949 landmark national epic for Jamaica, *New Day*.

15 It has to be said that women remain subsidiary figures (both Penelopes and Calypsoes) in Selvon's work and even Lovelace's text does not structure agency for women. This is clearly problematic in terms of gendering the communities of equals.

3 Double agents

Gender, ethnicity and the absent women

> The coupling of postcolonial with woman . . . inevitably leads to the simplicities that underlie unthinking celebrations of oppression, elevating the racially female voice into a metaphor for 'the good'.
>
> (Sara Suleri)

> For women and men in the Caribbean the twentieth century draws to a close in a manner radically different from the way (in which) it began . . . There has . . . been a rupturing of traditional relations of gender inherited from the post-slavery, 'emancipated' nineteenth century.
>
> (Eudine Barriteau)

> The biggest failure of the feminist movement in the Caribbean has been its inability to advocate for, and support Indian women.
>
> (Nesha Haniff)

As I have argued in the previous chapter, the attractions and persuasions of a Black Atlantic paradigm exerted considerable pressure on the critical approaches to Caribbean Literature that developed in the early 1990s, promoting a persistent focus on the figure of the migrant as both writer and character that seemingly obscured attention to the dweller and the local. In this chapter part of my concern is to argue that this pressure was also registered within the narratives of Caribbean feminism emerging during this period. A respected body of work that critiques the Black Atlantic for its erasure of the Caribbean from its triangular configuration already exists, but there has been no argument to date concerning the specific tailoring of feminist theories and literary studies around this model. I wish to examine how the demands of black diasporic criticism have shaped feminist scholarship on Caribbean women's writing and draw attention to what has been eclipsed as a result of this dominant methodology and its concentration on contemporary, diasporic, African Caribbean women writers.

In line with my practice in previous chapters, I wish to balance my examination of the particular demands placed on women's writing within this critical moment alongside readings of texts that are arguably equally important to a consideration of this tradition but that have so far received scant scholarly attention by comparison – writing by women before 1970 and writing by Indian-Caribbean women. My attention to women's writing before 1970 is also motivated by my desire to contest the trope of invisibility that has been ascribed to Caribbean women writers before the second boom under the sign of 'double colonisation'. The continued marginalisation of Indian-Caribbean women's writing has generated more recent and more combative critical attention and I wish to draw attention to two particular indigenous feminist positions, *matikor* and *dougla poetics*, that offer radical possibilities for a transformation of the rubrics of Caribbean feminism and women's writing.

As I argued in Chapter One, there has been surprisingly little scholarship interested in the constructions of Caribbean literary history and what emerges in the place of an historical perspective is this extraordinary myth of a doubled spontaneous genesis. I have already situated the first assumed genesis in London in the 1950s. The second literary creation story, this time for women writers, often begins in Trinidad in 1970 with the publication of Merle Hodge's *Crick, Crack, Monkey* and takes off in the 1980s, usually centred on Jamaica, with the publication of works by Erna Brodber, Olive Senior, Lorna Goodison, Jean Binta Breeze and Sistren. However, the critical moment in which this second genesis narrative is consolidated and circulated is the early 1990s, when critical studies of Caribbean women's writing as a distinct body of work in its own right began to emerge. It is not incidental, though, that the critical paradigms of black diasporic and postcolonial feminist criticism were also prominent at this same moment, and I wish to examine how the collocation of these theoretical agendas has shaped the ways in which Caribbean women's writing has come to critical attention.

Feminist criticism in the wake of the Black Atlantic

The most explicit acknowledgement of the way in which black diasporic criticism has been mobilised in the epistemological consolidation of Caribbean feminist literary theory in the 1990s can be found in Carole Boyce Davies' 1994 study, *Black Women, Writing and Identity*. Although not specifically a study of Caribbean women's writing, it discusses many works by contemporary Caribbean women's writers and Boyce Davies' declared methodology of reading black women's writing and subjectivity as transnational and migratory is traced directly to the historical experience of her Caribbean mother and female relations whose 'annual migrations, between the Caribbean and the United States, are persistent re-membering and re-connection' (Boyce Davies 1994: 1). Indeed, the concept of re-membering is central to this work, but it is the consequences of the way in which Boyce Davies shifts the epistemology of re-membering away from the more established historical perspective towards a diasporic critical intervention, offering a re-assemblage of black women's writing across national and ethnic boundaries, that I am interested in here.

> Because we were/are products of separations and dis-locations and dis-memberings, people of African descent in the Americas historically have sought reconnection. From the 'flying back' stories which originated in slavery to the 'Back to Africa' movements of Garvey and those before him, to the Pan-Africanist activity of people like Dubois and C. L. R. James, this need to re-connect and re-member, as [Toni] Morrison would term it, has been a central impulse in the structuring of Black thought . . . Remembering or the function of memory means re-membering or bringing back all the parts together . . . The process of re-membering is therefore one of boundary crossing.
>
> (Boyce Davies 1994: 17)

As I discussed in the previous chapter, Boyce Davies' work is very clearly situated in the critical moment of Black Atlantic studies in which theoretical sights are guided by acts of looking across rather than those of looking back. However, it is unfortunate that what is lost in the theoretical shift from a historical perspective that focuses on a male intellectual tradition to a diasporic model that focuses on contemporary women's writings is the substance of Caribbean (black) women's literary and intellectual history. In her study, which is infused with the valuable insights of postcolonial feminist and black diasporic critiques, what is not remembered or re-membered is writing by Indian-Caribbean and Creole writers, and Caribbean women's writing before its acknowledged 'boom'.

Although Boyce Davies' work enunciates its affiliations to black diasporic criticism most clearly, her work can be read alongside a cluster of books and chapters devoted to the study of Caribbean women's writing that were published in the 1990s. A closer examination of the strategies for contextualisation employed in these works reveals similar, although often less self-conscious, acts of looking across the Black Atlantic for a meaningful past. My argument here is that even when they do not situate themselves as working within a black disaporic framework, many of the critics who published on Caribbean's women's writing in the 1990s were inevitably drawn in its wake. Most significantly, the absence of critical narratives looking back to the Caribbean past can be seen to put the idea of Caribbean women's history and their long tradition of writing under question, if not under threat.

In *Caribbean Transactions: West Indian Culture in West Literature*, Renu Juneja opens her survey chapter of women's writing by looking to the foundational historical experience of the Black Atlantic – slavery. Importantly though, the history that Juneja chooses to recover is that of Celia, a slave woman in Missouri in 1855 who attempted to liberate herself from the sexual abuse of her 'owner', Robert Newsom, and who was eventually executed for his murder. Juneja invokes Celia 'as a fitting muse in this chapter where I will isolate some distinctive features of fiction by contemporary women writers from the West Indies' (Juneja 1996: 22). However, as it emerges, Celia functions not so much as a muse than as a mute.

> Never having told her story, Celia herself remains voiceless and gains visibility only through the creative efforts of a writer . . . The voice-lessness of women during slavery and much after is even more endemic in the Caribbean than in the United States because in the Caribbean there are few counterparts to Sojourner Truth, Harriet Tubman or Harriet Jacobs. If the cultural reconstruction taking place in the Caribbean today is propelled by the need of the people to inscribe their history in their own voice, then such a need for self-expression is an even more urgent concern with women writers today.
>
> (Juneja 1996: 23)

Although Celia's story is given voice, her presence as a Black Atlantic ancestor figure serves to block the recovery of other women and their voices. There are two major problems with Juneja's routing of Caribbean women's literary history through the figure of Celia. First is that it implies that the history of Caribbean women's experiences of slavery and later forms of oppression (which are acknowledged here as being different from those of African-Americans) are not known and have not been recovered (despite the now famous narratives of Mary Prince and the later Mary Seacole). Second, while it is certainly true that much contemporary Anglo-creole women's writing has sought to give literary agency to female histor-ical subjects whose own voices were muted by the forces of brute and subtle forms of oppression alike, it is also true that there are literary voices, as well as voicelessness, upon which our understanding of contemporary women's writing might be contingent. What is entirely eclipsed in Juneja's critical manoeuvre from Missouri 1855 to Trinidad 1970, and the publi-cation of Hodge's *Crick, Crack, Monkey*, is the existence of Caribbean women's writing before 1970 and feminist historiography from within the region – both of which could have offered a Caribbean past leading to a Caribbean present.

In *Searching for Safe Spaces* (1997), Miriam Chancy clearly establishes Black feminist criticism as her theoretical paradigm. Working through the theories put forward by Barbara Smith, Deborah E. McDowell, Hazel Carby and Audre Lorde, Chancy explains that she 'utilize[s] a modified form of Black feminist criticism which I term "Afro-Caribbean diasporic feminism"' (Chancy 1997: 13). She argues persuasively that 'Black feminism

. . . has become a critical method serving the needs of Black women scholars cross-culturally and cross-nationally' (Chancy 1997: 17), and the frameworks that she uses do indeed make these crossings freely, so that American slavery can provide a context for reading Caribbean black British works by Beryl Gilroy and Joan Riley. However, it should be noted that the 'Black feminism' that Chancy takes as her core model is not so much a transverse, horizontal relational model that navigates between Caribbean, African, black British and African-American feminist theories as it is a nuclear model with African-American theory at the centre and only peripheral interest in other black feminisms. The book does give a very brief overview of the British and African contexts in which western feminist scholarship has been challenged and redefined, but the only mention made of Caribbean feminism is to the position that emerges from the introduction to *Out of The Kumbla* (1990) in which Carole Boyce Davies and Elaine Savory Fido discuss the particular purchase of the terms feminism and womanism in relation to their own positions and a Caribbean context. Apart from the reading of Michelle Cliff and Marie Chauvet which is staged by reference to the shared history of *marronage* in both Haiti and Jamaica, the diasporic context is given weight in terms of contextualising the writings and the issues that Caribbean writers tackle. The book reads both British-Caribbean and American-Caribbean works and its emphasis in terms of history and theory is mainly to the western side of the hyphen – the links back to the Caribbean are not strongly made, particularly in relation to theory or history. In this study then, African-American feminist theory becomes reframed as 'Afro-Caribbean' under the powerful sign of the 'diasporic' rather than through any attention to the specificities of gender operations in the Caribbean.

The boldest displacement of a Caribbean historical and theoretical archive can be found in Belinda Edmondson's 1999 book, *Making Men: Gender, Literary Authority, and Women's Writing in Caribbean Narrative*. In her chapter 'Theorizing Caribbean Feminist Aesthetics', which examines the issue of what 'constitutes a Caribbean female subjectivity', Edmondson focuses on the work of Jamaica Kincaid and that of Marlene Nourbese Philip. In Edmondson's view, both of these writers are crucially writing within the diaspora because they are unable to find writing models in the Caribbean. Indeed, her framework seemingly conflates issues of residency with those of literary and cultural tradition as evidenced in her observation that 'so many of the current spate of Caribbean women writers reside in North America and indeed write within an African American tradition' (Edmondson 1999: 83). Deftly grafting African-American theory and history onto the model of Caribbean women's writing, Edmondson effectively writes *over* rather than writing *about* Caribbean feminist aesthetics. As she plainly states, 'I will lay a theoretical groundwork for Caribbean women's writing that finds its authority in the experience of being black and female in North America' (Edmondson 1999: 83).

In her particular manoeuvre from a discussion of Caribbean to African-American feminist aesthetics, Edmondson privileges a few auto-biographical statements made by Nourbese Phillip and Jamaica Kincaid in which they claim that they did not consider the possibility of being a writer within a Caribbean context and uses this as a basis for claiming their empowerment as black American women. This is not only an argument that Kincaid has explicitly denied on occasion, but also one that overlooks the many aspects of both of their writings that connect directly to a Caribbean cultural tradition and context. More crucially though, to my mind, it fails to address the 'misses' as well as the 'matches' that result from an attempt to map African-American theory onto a Caribbean context, and therefore does not speak adequately to the diverse ethnic groups within the Caribbean who do not share an African past and whose Indian, Chinese or European histories and traditions are given no discussion. Furthermore, it is her replacement of an assumed absence in terms of a Caribbean literary past with an African-American presence that confirms the idea of Caribbean women's literary silence before 1970 and the necessity of a theoretical substitution.

> Many Caribbean female-authored texts and readings of those texts are inevitably refracted through the prism of African American feminist theory and narrative, which jointly have provided *the only theoretical framework* for the engenderment of the black and female subject.
>
> (Edmondson 1999: 102, italics mine)

Edmondson works through a very similar line-up of African-American feminist theorists to that proposed by Chancy – Barbara Smith, Hazel Carby, Angela Davies, Hortense Spillers – with barely a mention of any feminist critic working from within the Caribbean or working specifically on Caribbean material. Despite the title of her chapter, there is no discussion of the very important and sometimes conflicted theorising of Caribbean feminism and feminist aesthetics that has been produced by scholars working within or specifically on the region since the late 1980s.

Given that the 1990s was the first moment in which book-length studies began to attend to Caribbean women's writing as a discrete field, the strong purchase of Black Atlantic criticism in a high proportion of works has arguably shaped both a normative archive and methodology on which discussions of women's writing and feminist theorising have taken place. Nevertheless, the kind of consensus and mutual endorsement of an African-American historical and theoretical perspective that is generated by this cluster of publications is implicitly challenged by two important studies by Caribbean women scholars also published in the Black Atlantic moment of 1993: Evelyn O'Callaghan's *Woman Version: Theoretical Approaches to West Indian Fiction by Women*, the first monograph study of women's writing in the region, and Carolyn Cooper's landmark contribution to the study of popular cultural and oral forms, *Noises in the Blood: Orality and the 'Vulgar' Body of Jamaican Popular Culture* (1993).

O'Callaghan's book is the first sustained attempt to place the project of establishing a theoretical framework for a reading of Anglocreole Caribbean women's writing at its intellectual centre. However, as she wishes to emphasise, her quest is defiantly not for any mono-theory through which to read the very diverse writings by West Indian women that she discusses in this study.

> I do not attempt to construct a single theoretical model for West Indian women's writing but, rather, to suggest the need for plural and syncretic theoretical approaches which can take account of the multiplicity, complexity, the intersection of apparently conflicting orientations which we find in the writing: approaches which can combine heterogeneity and commonality while refusing to be ultimately formalized under any one 'ism'.
>
> (O'Callaghan, 1993: 15)

Rather she remains alert to the fact that

> in most of the texts discussed in this book, a continuum of political directions operates, and exploration of ideological currents in literature, feminist or otherwise, needs to be sensitively aware of intersecting agendas within the specifics of the text's cultural matrix.
>
> (O'Callaghan, 1993: 101)

By conducting readings that are sensitive and searching in this way, O'Callaghan may be seen to be performing a very localised model of feminist literary criticism that refuses any homogenisation of women's experiences and writings within the region. Working against the deflection of Caribbean works away from their local historical and intellectual bearings, and therefore against the intellectual sway of the Black Atlantic moment that is about to take shape, O'Callaghan argues that 'Caribbean women writers, perhaps more than most, inevitably interact with "power-structures" in their societies ... and this interaction implicitly shapes what they say in their art' (O'Callaghan 1993: 98). Her chapter on 'Early versions: outsiders' voices/silenced voices' which examines narratives by Eliza Fenwick, Mariah Nugent, Mrs Carmichael and Mrs Henry Lynch in the nineteenth century, as well as later work by Jean Rhys, Phyllis Shand Allfrey and Eliot Bliss, offers an important model of white women's literary history in the region that challenges the limitations of the black diasporic studies that will follow, both its historical range and its attention to ethnic diversity.

Although Carolyn Cooper's *Noises in the Blood* does not examine women's texts exclusively, its attention to Louise Bennett, Jean Binta Breeze and

Sistren made a significant contribution to feminist literary scholarship within the region at this moment. In particular, I would argue that Cooper's reading of Louise Bennett's poetry has been pivotal to a recognition of oral and folk expression as an indigenous form of feminist discourse and offered an important model for the reading of creative and vernacular feminist voices. What is also important and distinctive about Cooper's work is the way in which it sets Bennett's poetry and the feminist politics of the 'cunny Jamma oman' (cunning Jamaican woman) in the context of the historical operations governing gender politics in twentieth-century Jamaica, thereby restoring the social dimensions of women's creativity in the region. Moreover, attending to Bennett's own historical references to Caribbean women as both empowered and resistant, Cooper argues that Bennett's 'allusion to [Maroon] Nanny situates contemporary Jamaica "oman lib" within a long-established heritage of consolidated male/female defence of cultural and political sovereignty' (Cooper 1993: 49).

Like O'Callaghan, Cooper makes confident reference to a long historical tradition of both women's writing and various forms of theorising around issues of gender with the Caribbean itself. Both studies locate writing as an important site for the structuring of oppositional agency and they also begin the recovery of a woman's, if not an unproblematically feminist, literary history. Yet, as these localised agendas began to develop in the works by women scholars within the region – and the work of Honor Ford Smith and Rhonda Cobham also needs to be credited in this respect – the critical momentum of the Black Atlantic and the popular claims of black diasporic criticism were already pulling a large number of literary critical works in a very different direction.

Invisible women and the demands of double colonisation

While the success of black diasporic studies of women's writing published in the 1990s may be measured by the level of critical attention now afforded to writers such as Jamaica Kincaid, Marlene Nourbese Philip, Edwidge Danticat and others, the splicing of African-American history and theory into the narrative of Caribbean women's writing has seemingly licensed the denial of a literary past and the invocation of the resonant trope of the invisible, voiceless ancestor.

In the single chapter devoted to 'Contemporary women writers' in the revised 1995 edition of Bruce King's edited collection, *West Indian Literature*, Renu Juneja reads the work of contemporary Caribbean women writers as emerging 'in response to the historic voicelessness of their condition' (Juneja 1995: 89). This is a critical platform that she further develops in her 1996 book, *Caribbean Transactions: West Indian Culture in West Literature*. Again, there is a single chapter dedicated to women's writing, and the repeated insistence on women's writing as emerging from a literary vacuum: 'Indeed, our understanding of women's creativity is contingent on our appreciation of this voicelessness' (Juneja 1995: 23). Juneja's refrain finds a more recent echo in Tobias Döring's *Caribbean-English Passages: Intertextuality in a Postcolonial Tradition* in which he argues that 'for female Caribbean writers . . . the premise of literary production lies in "the absence of writing"' (Döring 2002:10).

In general terms it might well be significant to note that Caribbean women's writing, like many other literary traditions outside of western metropolitan male interest, has been subjected to a whole range of material obstacles and critical biases which have affected the quality of literary production and reception. However, such an observation should not suggest that being silenced is synonymous with being voiceless, or that neglect is somehow the same as absence. Just as I have argued that the early survey texts of Caribbean writing published in the 1960s have imprinted a 'master copy' of the bona fide Caribbean writer and writing that remains strenuous in its hold even today, I would similarly argue that these works published during the 1990s have established the dominant tramlines for readings of Caribbean women's writings. Moreover, as I have tried to illustrate in relation to the construction of a nationalist teleology, fixed points of origin and lines of attachment are as much about neglect and disavowal as they are about affiliation and affirmation.

Clearly many of the arguments that I have made in Chapter One concerning the awkward cultural politics of so-called early writings and the way in which these works appeared to put the hard-won ideological gains of the 1960s under threat remain relevant to the neglect and denial of women's writing from before 1970 and its possible threat to the reputation and status of Caribbean women's writing as it seemingly arrived into its own critical moment. However, I also want to propose that the particular overlap of Black Atlantic and postcolonial feminist agendas in the early 1990s created a critical milieu in which the broad descriptor of double colonisation shifted from postcolonial studies, where it served as useful a trope that spoke powerfully to the shared oppression of women's lives and the marginalisation of women's narratives across diverse cultural contexts, to a more localised context in which it confirms the dismissal of literary history through the figure of the invisible woman.

In one sense my choice of the alternative descriptor, 'double agent' is a direct challenge to the term 'double colonisation' that has served as a powerful shorthand description of the very complex position of black women within the colonial and patriarchal social order imposed by colonialism and its after-effects. Rather than seeing postcolonial women (writers) as always inevitably doubly disempowered, I want to consider how Caribbean women writers can be seen to mobilise gender, as well as ethnicity and cultural identity, as a site of resistance and affirmation. Signalling both the realm of espionage, disguise and subterfuge, as well as the capacity for agency that has passed unacknowledged, the term 'double agent' will, I hope, enable an opening up of the possibilities for Caribbean women and their literary works to be read as resistant, rebellious texts that demand a more specific and differentiated understanding of 'Caribbean woman' as both subject position and positioned subject.

A 1986 collection of essays on women's writing edited by Kirsten Holst Petersen and Anna Rutherford took the term double colonisation for its title. In their foreword to the collection, the editors unpack the genealogy of the term as it appears to them.

> The African and Caribbean women suffered from a reflection of this [colonial] ethos. Regardless of what role or status they had in their own traditional society, inclusion into the expanding Western sphere in their countries usually meant loss of status, as this inclusion took place mainly through the medium of education which was given primarily to boys. African and Caribbean women writers therefore exist as writers against enormous odds and under pressure of a double set of myths which seek to deny their creative existence. They are literally fighting for visibility.
>
> (Holst Petersen and Rutherford 1986: 9)

The rather broad strokes of historical and cultural reference that paint this picture of double colonisation have continued to resonate across a range of critical contexts. As the authors of the revised edition of *The Empire Writes Back* claim, as recently as 2002, double colonisation 'has proven to be a durable description of the status of women in colonialism' (Ashcroft, Griffiths and Tiffin 2002: 206). My particular concern here is with its resonance within Caribbean literary histories. This term did offer an ideological identity tag to African-Caribbean contemporary Caribbean women's writing that enabled its incorporation into the wider study of black women's writing that emerged in the late 1980s and early 1990s and was reflected in collections such as *A Double Colonisation, Unheard Words: Women and Literature in Africa, the Arab World, Asia, the Caribbean and Latin America* (Holst Petersen and Rutherford 1986) and *Motherlands: Black Women's Writing from Africa, the Caribbean and South Asia* (Nasta 1991). However, it also seems to have created a critical discourse around the tropes of invisibility and silence that has not been useful in terms of situating Caribbean women's writing as part of a long-standing regional literary tradition or history.

In their 1990 study *Out of the Kumbla*, Carole Boyce Davies and Elaine Savory Fido comment that, 'The double marginalization or dual colonization of the Third World woman (writer) has already been demonstrated by a number of scholars in a variety of fields' (Boyce Davies and Savory Fido 1990: 1–2). Nearly a decade later, Renu Juneja reiterates this accepted status of the term, 'Women of color, and this is a repeated refrain in the evolving critical discourse on women's literature, suffer from a dual marginalization, a dual colonization' (Juneja 1996: 24). While this term has accrued value by its citation and application in a range of feminist postcolonial scholarship, its usefulness and appropriateness has not been tested against the particular Caribbean archive under discussion in these works. It is not a term that these scholars offer as a conclusion to their analyses and investigations but rather a way of compressing the entanglements of history into a phrase, almost a sound bite. It functions as an opener to discussions of postcolonial women's conditions of possibility and in these cases, those of the Caribbean woman writer, but what it does not signify is the particularity of the Caribbean woman's experience.

I want to argue that in relation to a Caribbean archive the idea that women writers are 'literally fighting for visibility', a notion that is intimately connected to the concept of their double-colonisation, has actually served, in itself, as a silencing device as well as a platform. In critical studies of Caribbean literature in which women's writing is often a marginal category, annexed in a single chapter, the myth of a spontaneous genesis is rarely challenged. In Gikandi (1992) and Juneja (1995), 1970 and the publication of Hodge's novella is inscribed as an unproblematic point of origin for women's writing. In Louis James' account, the period of the 1970s and 1980s is explicitly framed as a second boom, this time for women.

> These changes partly reflect the impact, since the 1970s, of Caribbean women's writing. This development is striking. Out of the sixty West Indian novelists listed in Kenneth Ramchand's 1903–67 bibliography, only six were women ... By contrast, in 1988 an international Conference at Wellesley brought together some fifty women Caribbean writers and critics. This explosion of women's writing in some ways parallels the male-dominated 'phenomenon' of West Indian writing in the 1960s.
>
> (James 1999: 199)

Importantly, just as the boom of the 1950s and 1960s is seen to bloom from the desert, so this second explosion is often described as having no roots. Clearly this version of a second spontaneous genesis, like its earlier counterpart, is based upon the lack of critical attention given to writings that were published before that moment. As late as 1989, Pamela Mordecai and Betty Wilson lamented the lack of scholarly interest in their introduction to *Her True-True Name: An Anthology of Women's Writing from the Caribbean*. 'If Caribbean writers have been generally neglected it is no exaggeration to say that Caribbean women writers have been virtually abandoned' (Mordecai and Wilson 1989: x). They also pointed to the obstacles facing the reconstruction of women's literary history in the region, 'poor documentation and archival work that seems at its best biased' (Mordecai and Wilson 1989: x).

Even those critical studies devoted to Caribbean women's writing that began to be published in the early 1990s and thereby to undertake this much needed work did not always problematise this rather narrow view or correct the tropes of invisibility and voicelessness. *Out of the Kumbla: Caribbean Women and Literature* (1990), edited by Carole Boyce Davies and Elaine Savory Fido, introduces its volume of scholarship with the bold declaration that 'Out of this voicelessness and absence, contemporary Caribbean women writers are beginning some bold steps to creative expression' (Boyce Davies and Savory Fido 1990: 2). Yet, in the same introductory essay, the editors do point out that 'There has been a long history of women writing in the Caribbean' claiming that 'it is only through feminist re-visioning that these invisible writers are being seen' (1990: 2). This perception does not, however, inform the selection of their own collection which discusses, almost exclusively, women's writings published after 1970. Rhonda Cobham's chapter 'Women in Jamaican Literature 1900–1950', although stretching the chronology of the volume, is primarily interested in representations *of* women rather than *by* women and discusses male writers and works more than those by women.

In the same year, in the introduction to his edited volume, *Caribbean Women Writers: Essays from the First International Conference*, Selwyn Cudjoe makes the more spectacular claim that the 1988 conference of Caribbean women writers, from which the papers are collected, was 'the founding event of Caribbean women's writing' (Cudjoe 1990: 5). At the same time, Cudjoe discusses the work of Una Marson (writing during the 1930s and 1940s) in some detail in his introduction. Is there then a suggestion that such writing does not really count, or that Marson is an eccentric presence as a pre-1980s woman writer? Miriam Chancy also makes only a customary nod in the direction of a women's literary tradition in the prologue to her study, *Searching for Safe Spaces: Afro-Caribbean Women Writers in Exile*:

> In fact, women writers from the Caribbean have a long history. Early twentieth-century writers include Jean Rhys (Dominica) and Una Marson (Jamaica) . . . The writing that is now appearing from the feminine Caribbean has a history, but that history is still largely obscured and ignored.
>
> (Chancy 1997: xix)

While the studies that I have discussed above have undertaken significant and valuable work in their efforts to bring Anglocreole women's writing from the 1970s to more considered and careful critical attention, it would appear that the critical 'new beginning' for women's writing heralded by these Black Atlantic-inflected studies of the 1990s operates a form of double speak in which the awareness and tentative articulation of earlier works by women is drowned out by the need to enunciate a clear line marking the success and achievement of women's writing in the 1970s, 1980s and onwards. The fascinating works of writers such as Phyllis Allfrey, Elma Napier, Vera Bell, Una Marson and Raj Kumari Singh, among others, remain outside of critical interest.

Unheard interlocutors and missed conversations: feminist historiography and theory

The collective impact of this critical moment in which the demands of a Black Atlantic agenda seemingly fused with those of a postcolonial women's writing agenda has been to consolidate the view that Caribbean women's writing is a body of work by black (African-Caribbean) women emerging from, or even exploding out of, voicelessness in the 1970s and 1980s. The absence of Caribbean women as historical subjects, as feminist theorists and as early writers remains a serious deficiency.

It seems absolutely crucial to an appreciation of Caribbean women's writing that women are restored not only as writers but in all their historical dimensions – as slaves, as rebels, as mothers, as workers. The absence of an open conversation between feminist historiographers and literary critics until very recently seems to underwrite the neglect of Caribbean women in the accounts of history that these studies present in their turn to the US or Britain for an historical context. As with the denial of literary and intellectual foremothers, the question is not, in fact, one of absence but simply one of disconnection. Although George Lamming has argued that 'this treatment of the female as an invisible presence – that is, made absent when she is most present – is a continuing factor in the political and intellectual backwardness of our institutions' (Lamming 1995: 38), it is important to acknowledge that feminist historiography is a very active mode of scholarship in the Caribbean and that as O'Callaghan's and Cooper's works had already illustrated, Caribbean women had a past that mattered to an understanding of their present.

Juneja could have turned to Barbara Bush's 1990 study, *Slave Women in Caribbean Society 1650–1838* in order to recover the life of a Caribbean women slave, a figure whom Bush describes rather prophetically as 'the invisible black woman in Caribbean history'. As Bush argues in her study, 'to focus on her specific identity in the slave context is to come to a closer understanding of the unique nature of Afro-Caribbean society both past and present, for the very identity of West Indians is rooted in the historical experience' (Bush 1990: 10). In this work the distinctiveness of Caribbean slavery is made visible alongside the importance of recovering a past owned by ancestry and place, 'In the Caribbean . . . it is impossible to evaluate properly the black woman's present position if her slave predecessors are not taken into account. The study of slavery points towards the future' (Castañeda 1995: 141). This sense of the past as a vital resource for an understanding of the present and a productive engagement with the conditions of the future has been pivotal to many interventions in Caribbean feminist historiography.

In the introduction to their jointly edited 1995 volume, *Engendering History: Caribbean Women in Historical Perspective*, Verene Shepherd, Bridget Brereton and Barbara Bailey foreground the importance of historical work within feminist agendas.

> The women's movement played a critical role in raising key questions such as what accounts for women's situation as 'other' and what perpetuates it historically. In answering these questions, academic feminists and other scholars used an explicitly historical approach as this could enable feminist theory to fulfil its potential for radically changing the existing epistemologies. Therefore women's history became regarded as central – not tangential – to feminism.
>
> (Shepherd *et al.* 1995: xi)

The intellectual drive towards history as an energetic resource to the projects of feminist epistemology and its efforts to analyse the conditions of possibility that have structured Caribbean women's lives in the past, also finds expression in Verene Shepherd's 1999 edited text book, *Women in Caribbean History*. As a study designed to make 'information on the history of women in the Caribbean territories which came under the political control of England available for history teaching in the schools' (Shepherd 1999: xv), this book quite clearly offers accounts of women's history within the region – their economic, social and political activities – not only as a model of heritage but also as a model of inspiration.

Yet, despite the shared chronology of publications relating to Caribbean women's writing and Caribbean women's history, the evidence of productive exchange between these two methodologies and archives has been limited to date.[1] It is important however to acknowledge the work of Verene Shepherd, particularly her 2002 work *Maharani's Misery: Narratives of a Passage from India to the Caribbean* that reconstructs the fate of an Indian woman who was raped and subsequently died on the ocean crossing to the Caribbean. Equally Honor Ford-Smith's long-standing contributions on women's history and writing should be mentioned. Her recent piece that documents how the pioneering feminists and anticolonialists Una Marson and Amy Bailey mobilised the skills they had acquired in Garvey's Universal Negro Improvement Association in order 'to fight for their own political rights, for access to professions and clerical work, and for representation in government' (Ford-Smith 2004: 29), directly contests Edmondson's (1999) claim that African-American feminist theory offers '*the only theoretical framework* for the engenderment of the black and female subject'.

It is not my concern here to explore the subject of Caribbean feminist historiography in any detail, but merely to point out that there is a very significant historical archive to which critics of Caribbean writings can turn in their search for contextual material. Against the myth of absence and silence, these works have enunciated both a methodology and an epistemology that challenges at every level (author, subject, methodology, archive) the need to turn towards the US for a re-membering of Caribbean women's experience. While the Black Atlantic model invoked by the recovery of black history in the US or Britain may speak to the common experiences of black women within a comparative framework, the cutting and pasting of one historical experience into the place of another has been performed at the cost of specific, localised knowledge that also offers a valid theoretical framework.

Caribbean feminism and its discontents

The contributions of feminist historiography have clearly helped to rebalance the dynamics between knowledge and power in favour of Caribbean women and in this sense can be read as integral to the movement towards 'more meaningful feminist theoretical constructs' (Barriteau 2003: 4) that Eudine Barriteau calls for in the introduction to her major edited study *Confronting Power, Theorizing Gender: Interdisciplinary Perspectives in the Caribbean*. As Patricia Mohammed argues in her essay within this collection, 'A symbiotic visiting relationship: Caribbean feminist historiography and Caribbean feminist theory'.

> The first contribution of historiography was to recover the visibility of women from obscurity. By consciously recognizing woman as a sex that had contributed to past history while making history, women's history also brought to the drawing-board the problem of gender in history. In identifying the presence of categories of women whose femininity may be differently shaped and between whom there are power imbalances, feminist theory also enters a dynamic frame, not simply the opposition or difference between masculinity and femininity, but situating as well variations by race, ethnicity, class. This is the basis in which feminist theorizing in the region must be grounded, as contemporary explanations of gender in each society can be safely measured only against past constructions of gender.
>
> (Mohammed 2003: 117–118)

Although Mohammed is centrally concerned with the way in which feminist historiography has informed and shaped feminist theory, her argument that 'there is a seeming eclecticism of the feminist movement and feminist theory in the Caribbean because women have responded at the same time to issues of class, race/ethnicity and (to other concerns with sexual and) gender identity' (2003: 124), applies equally to feminist literary theory, which is my main concern in this work.

One of the persistent intellectual challenges within Caribbean feminism that is reflected in literary criticism has been how to positively address the need for constant redefinition and renegotiation of the demands of gender politics alongside those of ethnicity, class, nationality and sexuality. In their introduction to *Out of the Kumbla: Caribbean Women and Literature*, the first collection of critical essays published on Caribbean women's writing, Carole Boyce Davies and Elaine Savory Fido acknowledge the global impact of the mass women's movement and developments in feminist theory on the consolidation of critical discourses relating to Caribbean women's writing.

> A sustained critical response to the growing number of women writers and the representation of women in Caribbean literature began to emerge only in the seventies. This we must concede, could only exist within an international feminist climate and the growing body of feminist literary criticism.
>
> (Boyce Davies and Savory Fido 1990: 12)

However, although 'feminism' is named unproblematically as an international epistemology, its specific availability and relevance to the editors needs to be addressed in terms of its inbuilt assumption of an 'outside' cultural context. Carole Boyce Davies declares that as an African-Caribbean woman she finds herself 'using "womanist" in a few contexts and "feminist" in most', although 'womanism is a strong term for me, but only as an important redefinition of the term feminism for other experiences than those of Western and white women' (xii–xiii). Elaine Savory Fido, who identifies herself as 'being white and foreign' makes the claim that

> womanism for me is a softer, more flexible option than feminism. Feminism is necessary as protection, as groundbreaking work, as our best route to a new landscape of gender relations ... Feminism/ womanism is for me then a way towards better, more honest and complex relations between men and women in the region.
>
> (Savory Fido 1990: xv–xvi)

In a later chapter Savory Fido proposes the 'image of the crossroads' as a useful position from which to envisage both Caribbean woman writer and critic. Again this model, along with their attachment to more than one frame through which to address the politics of gender, endorses a preference for multiple, and possibly intersecting intellectual and political possibilities over allegiance to any single position (Savory Fido 1990: 30). What emerges most clearly from their exchange on this subject is that while their commitment to making meaningful connections between feminist theory and Caribbean women's writing is evident, their own relations to the genealogy and epistemology of feminism as an imported product remain tense and unresolved.

As Rhoda Reddock has commented, 'possibly no other word in modern times has been so vilified for its European origins as feminism' (Reddock 1990: 61). Patricia Mohammed has also observed that

> the word 'feminism' has itself been part of the problem of feminism and writing on gender in the region ... Where the word is used, as it must be, for a thing has to be named, it has to be constantly defined in context.
>
> (Mohammed 1998a: 23).

Some of the most fraught and productive debates within feminist theory in recent years have been centred on finding adequate definitions that do not privilege gender over issues of race or class or sexuality, because as Wilkinson and Kitzinger point out:

> This assumption that Otherness is constructed only in terms of gender, that Otherness is conferred by femaleness alone, takes for granted the primacy of gender in women's lives, and obscures other dimensions of power and powerlessness.
>
> (Wilkinson and Kitzinger, 1996: 4)

In a Caribbean context, Sylvia Wynter's provocative essay 'Beyond Miranda's meanings: un/silencing the "demonic ground" of Caliban's "woman"' that gave the afterword to *Out of the Kumbla* (Boyce Davies and Savory Fido 1990) refused the very possibility of brokering an agreement between feminism and the politics of black identity. In this densely argued piece, Wynter traces how Western Europe's post-sixteenth century colonisation of the New World not only offered a new form and rationale for oppression, but also instigated a crucial shift from anatomy (sex) to physiognomy (race) in the construction of essential otherness. Using Shakespeare's *The Tempest* as a textual locale in which to play out the implications of this shift, Wynter points out that 'the most significant absence of all, [is] that of Caliban's Woman, of Caliban's physiognomic-ally complementary mate'. However, Wynter resists the argument that 'native' women are doubly colonised in relation to the single colonisation of European women to argue instead that the silencing of this new category of inferior other 'enables the partial liberation of Miranda's hitherto stifled speech' (Wynter 1990: 363). For Wynter, it is this model of white women's enfranchisement of voice being acquired at the expense of black women's silencing which makes the possibility of a black feminist position too difficult to negotiate within the Caribbean context.

In her careful but combative analysis of this piece, 'Reluctant Matriarch: Sylvia Wynter and the Problematic of Caribbean Feminism', Natasha Barnes explores the particular ideological matrix between nationalism and feminism that informs Wynter's 'repudiation of feminism as a site of emancipatory imagining' (Barnes 1999: 41).

> The implications of her refusal to be labelled as feminist are instructive, in that they excavate common pitfalls that plague our efforts to construct a Caribbean feminist genealogy: the slippages that punctuate our scholarship when we make synonyms of the categories 'woman' and 'feminist', and the ease with which a tradition of feminist activism is constructed from ideologically uninterrogated designations such as 'strong/rebel woman' and binary analytical terms such as 'double colonization' that do little to describe the nuanced ways in which the subjectivity of women is contradictorily experienced.
>
> (Barnes 1999: 36)

As Barnes elucidates, some of Wynter's objections to the label feminist may be useful in their demands to reconsider the terms (both linguistic and political) through which consideration is given to gender relations in the Caribbean. However, Wynter's afterword insists on race as the primary governing site of oppression in what Natasha Barnes refers to as the '"race-first" principle' (Barnes 1999: 42). Wynter therefore denies the model of multiple and overlapping ideological demands that Caribbean feminism, in both literary and other disciplinary contexts, has sought to foreground, and that Barnes has usefully identified as a 'layered and unruly process' (Barnes 1999: 38).

Although the seemingly competing demands signalled by the term feminism have animated scholars in recent years, they may have obscured the fact that for Caribbean women as historical subjects the struggles of nationalism were always gendered and the struggles of women's rights were always informed by the politics of race and colonialism. It is notable that at present Caribbean feminist scholarship announces itself more directly in the disciplines of history, education and sociology than in literary criticism, a methodology that remains attached to a black diasporic paradigm, as I have outlined above.

Feminist historians have had an important involvement in the unearthing of women's involvement in anti-colonial insurgency as well as their contribution to nationalist struggles. Thanks to the work of feminist historians and sociologists such as Patricia Mohammed, Verene Shepard and Rhoda Reddock, we know that there were groups of women resisting and campaigning for liberation on both fronts and that by the early twentieth century, women were trying to organise and promote the empowerment of other women. In her ambitiously titled essay 'Indigenous feminist theorizing in the Caribbean' Patricia Mohammed argues that

To speak of a feminist movement in the Caribbean which predates the contemporary second wave movement is to bring alive on paper the individuals who would not be silent, those who spoke or wrote on behalf of others.

(Mohammed 1998a: 16)

Una Marson and Amy Bailey are two key figures whose resistance was directed at both race and gender oppression. They were both involved in many practical projects in the 1930s in Jamaica that were directed at improving the conditions of working class, black women's lives. In February 1939 Amy Bailey chaired the first Jamaican Women's Conference, held at Collegiate Hall, Kingston, and a report in the *Daily Gleaner* describes the demands for equal rights which were made: 'Ridiculing the age-old institution of women's inequality to men, proclaiming the world-wide dawn of a new feminine era, and declaring that women of Jamaica are ready, willing and able to march side by side with men' (Bailey 1939). Bailey contributed several very polemical pieces to the pages of *Public Opinion*, and in her article 'Women and Politics?', she argues forcefully that women should not accept differentiated roles but equip themselves as intellectual equals and as leaders.

Another requisite for the women who would enter politics is that of leadership. If she is to go in, and do something besides making up the numbers, then she must train herself in that direction. She needs to have independent thought as well as the ability to see the other man's point of view, courage, quickness of perception and broad views.

(Bailey 1937: 10)

Like Bailey, Marson published quite strident articles in local publications concerning women's roles and responsibilities. Indeed, she actually uses the term feminism as the title to her 1937 article that clearly sees the need to explain what models of liberation might be available to women.

The idea of feminism is not to make a woman more conscious of her sex but to develop that within her which will make for a live, active mental and physical personality ... There may be men who are satisfied with women for wives who will merely mother their children ... I have discovered that in some parts of Africa the men depend solely on the advice and help of their women who are equal in any emergency.

(Marson 1937c: 10)

While there has been far less recovery research on Indian women's participation in similar ventures to date, the recently recovered voice of Thora Mahabir, writing in Trinidad in 1944, indicates that there were also Indian women who saw journalism as a positive forum through which to address ideas of female liberation.[2] Like Amy Bailey, Thora Mahabir saw the issue of female education as absolutely central at this time.

> Indian women suffer most, they are not given a fair opportunity for educational advancement and the privilege of making themselves more useful in the world . . . They are forced to marry at an immature age . . . Motherhood, especially among Indians, has been a great dis-advantage to women . . . The cry today is educate, educate. This must equally apply to men and women.
>
> (Mahabir 1944: 10)

Yet, despite the common agendas of African- and Indian-Caribbean women campaigning for women's rights since at least the 1940s, in very recent years, several Indian-Caribbean women scholars have spoken about the marginalisation of their voices, histories and views within constructions of Caribbean feminism.

Rosanne Kanhai expresses the situation very simply in the introduction to her pioneering collection of essays, *Matikor: The Politics of Identity for Indo-Caribbean Women*, 'Indo-caribbean women remain a token presence in the predominantly Afro-Caribbean feminist discourse' (Kanhai 1999: xii.) This view is confirmed by Rawwida Baksh-Soodeen, who argues that

> Feminist organising has also been largely viewed as the domain of African women, rather than as a space in which women of differ-ent racial/cultural identities and experiences interact. Women who have been 'left out' in this process include the remaining indigenous inhabitants, Indian, Chinese, and other groups such as the Indonesians. The experience of the white woman has also been left out.
>
> (Baksh-Soodeen 1998: 79)

Baksh-Sooden's point about a whole series of exclusions is important but given that Indian women form a majority in Guyana and Trinidad, their continued exclusion from feminist discourse is particularly troubling. It is clear that some excellent scholarship is emerging on Indian-Caribbean women as historical subjects (Shepherd, Angrosino), and on the issues of relating ethnic difference to ideas of both dominant feminist and nationalist discourses (Espinet 1991; Mohammed 1998b; Reddock 1998b). I shall discuss these in more detail later.

It is significant, however, that most of the scholarship on Indian-Caribbean women's lives in the Anglocreole Caribbean has centred on Trinidad to date. Basmat Shiw Parsad offers some explanation of this in her sketching of a Guyanese context.

> East Indian communities and East Indian women, in particular, have strongly resisted the ideological wave of women's rights that has been spreading from the industrialized west . . . The problem is that while

women's issues has been articulated and pursued largely by Afro-
Guyanese women, the majority of East Indian women have either
ignored or tacitly resisted a confrontation of these issues.

(Shiw Parsad 1999: 58)

It is also true that comparatively little creative writing by women has come
from an Indian Guyanese context since the poetry of two foundational
figures, Rajkumari Singh and Mahadai Das. Das's work in particular
demonstrates a clear struggle to match her own voice and vision of an
independent nation with that which emerges during the Forbes Burnham
era. Her radical shift from energetic nationalist poet in her 1977 collection to its bitter critic and elegist in her 1982 volume speaks in a powerful
and immediate register to the issues of race, gender and the politics of
liberation that are also central to the more recent Guyanese novels by
Narmala Shewcharan and the mixed ancestry writer, Oona Kempadoo,
that I shall also discuss.

In the introduction to her substantial 2003 edited volume, *Confronting
Power, Theorizing Gender: Interdisciplinary Perspectives in the Caribbean*, Eudine
Barriteau acknowledges that 'there is still much work to be done in
Caribbean feminist theorizing around the complications of power in – and
of – gender' (Barriteau 2003: 4). As I have already shown, Barriteau is
not alone is drawing attention to the gaps, absences and concerns that
still need to be addressed in terms of Caribbean feminist scholarship. In
its constant foregrounding of strategies of negotiation and renegotiation
that must address the demands placed upon analyses of gender in order
to account properly for the relations of class, ethnicity and sexuality,
Caribbean feminism may appear more tentative and even vulnerable
than Anglo-American, French or African-American feminisms. However,
I would want to argue there is a sense in which this continued awareness
and an increasingly open conversation about multiple and competing
claims of difference may actually be strengthening to Caribbean feminist
thought. Readings and debates that return feminist theory to the questions
raised by the lived realities of Caribbean women and their historically
embedded identities arguably enable Caribbean feminism to thrive as a
politics as well as an epistemology.

The politics of recovery

A fuller appreciation of the works and ideas of Caribbean intellectuals
such as Amy Ashwood Garvey and Amy Bailey, activists such as Elma
François and Aggie Bernard, and literary ancestors such as Agnes
Ramcharam and Mary D. Kallo would bring to light an historically
embedded perspective on the intersecting freedom fights (of race, class and
gender) that all of these figures were involved in, and which have been
so central to the model of contemporary feminist and woman-centred

thought and writing in the region. I wish to focus on Una Marson's writing and critical reception as a strategic entry point into the issues involved in reading for recovery and the management of this abandoned archive. Although Marson and her writings have now received more recognition and discussion than many early Caribbean women writers, my aim is to show how her recovery has been structured through the political-cultural agendas of various critical moments, including that of the high-point of feminist criticism in the mid-1980s.

Marson is now well recognised as an important literary role model and there is no shortage of tributes to her. In their introduction to *Watchers and Seekers* (1987), Rhonda Cobham and Merle Collins remind us that 'in the search for foremothers to the writers presented in this anthology, the figure and work of the poet and playwright, Una Marson, cannot be over-looked' (Cobham and Collin 1987: 3). While such gestures are significant in sentiment, the brief biography and scattered quotations from her poems that this introduction offers do not effect any real unearthing or recognition of Marson as either writer or intellectual. Similarly, E. A. Markham's introductory comments to the anthology *Hinterland: Caribbean Poetry from the West Indies and Britain* (1989) only revive interest in Marson in line with the renewed interest in vernacular voices, and a hesitant sense of gender politics, that marks this critical moment.

> We note with some satisfaction, the general revival of interest in pioneering figures like Claude McKay (Jamaica/USA, 1889–1948) and Una Marson. McKay's somewhat visionary quality and his early use of nation-language and Marson's near feminist perspectives and wide social sympathies appeal to the present time.
>
> (Markham 1989: 22)

None of Marson's work is included in the collection.

Other acts of recovery have also only allowed a partial version of Marson's literary profile to be brought into view. A more detailed analysis of how the dominant criteria of different critical moments affects the possible recuperation of literary foremothers is provided by a brief history of the critical reception of Marson's work from its publication to date. Given the urgent struggles for the rights to self-definition and self-representation that informed both nationalism and feminism, it is perhaps no surprise and no shame that critical readings of her work endorse Trinh T. Minh-Ha's observation that

> she who 'happens to be' a (non-white) Third World member, a woman, and a writer is bound to go through the ordeal of exposing her work to the abuse of praises and criticisms that either ignore, dispense with, or overemphasize her racial and sexual attributes.
>
> (Minh-Ha 1989: 6)

The particular pressures of these critical moments have conditioned the terms on which Marson's work has been brought back into circulation. My argument here is not only that each moment seeks to fold writers into their own scripts and thereby to fold over vital aspects that remain unreadable and unread, but also to point out what is excluded in all accounts. While feminist criticism has enabled a more astute and searching analysis of gender politics, it has not displaced the dominant agendas relating to cultural politics and therefore what remains difficult, almost unspeakable, in Marson's work, even for feminists, is the residue of colonial forms, high poetic diction and the ethic of devotion.

Although the number of critics who have written on Marson remains small, there are significant traits to be observed. The only indications of the critical response to Una Marson's poetry contemporary to its publication in the 1930s and 1940s are those opinions expressed by male academics in the introductions to three of her four volumes. Introducing Marson's third volume of poetry, *The Moth and The Star*, in 1937, Philip Sherlock identifies the nationalistic feeling with which her poems are imbued and interprets her sentiments of cultural belonging as an extension of her emotional generosity: 'how strong is Miss Marson's love of her homeland and its people' (Sherlock 1937: xiii). Although he condones the expression of her 'love' in this respect, Sherlock seems to believe that her emotional utterance tends towards the excessive in certain other poems, displaying 'more of sentimentality than of sentiment' (Sherlock 1937: xiii). It is interesting that sentimentality is employed here as a disparaging term, denoting Marson's inability to restrain emotional expression, as this signals an implicitly gendered evaluation in which the 'feminine' quality of her verse is seen to jeopardise its literary merit.

Sherlock's comments are also curious in what they neglect to register, as well as in their choice of register. It is in this 1937 volume that Marson presents her most stridently gendered poems that synthesise the politics of feminism and the politics of anti-colonialism (such as 'Cinema Eyes', 'Black Burden' and 'Kinky Hair Blues'). Moreover, it was in 1937 that Marson published a series of clearly feminist articles in the radical Jamaican weekly, *Public Opinion*, including her piece entitled 'Feminism'.[3] In response to recent attacks on women that had been published in the Jamaican press, Marson asks 'Are there no feminists amongst us who can rise up and flay the male of the species?' (Marson 1937c: 10). She also reproaches women for that fact that

> At present here in our island, our women are not keeping pace with our men . . . It is not lack of brains, nor lack of ability – it is lack of courage and confidence; lack of realisation of the value and importance of individual mental development.
>
> (Marson 1937c: 10)

Given that Marson herself had demonstrated such courage and confidence and had claimed a very public profile in relation to the debates around gender politics in Jamaica at this time, Sherlock's total neglect of this aspect of her work may appear bizarre, even vexing. However, as Jarrett-Macauley points out in her 1998 biography of Marson, her intellectual interventions on women rights were not necessarily appreciated, or even acknowledged. In fact, her insistence on the issue of gender politics led to her being seen as out of step with the 'positive ideas' of the day.

> She was the one always pushing 'the woman question' but who 'never had any constructive ideas other than the assertion that women must speak up ... I used to think her speeches a bit empty of content, I don't think she was very much in tune with the positive ideas that were coming up, the idea that we should rule our own country and that sort of thing, the idea of promotion of culture'.
>
> (Hart in Jarrett-Macauley 1998: 115)

What Hart's estimation reflects is how irrelevant, distracting and even unwelcome Marson's focus on the 'woman question' was seen to be in Jamaica of the late 1930s to a young male activist and also how, like Wynter, he sees feminism as usurping the nationalist cause. In seeking to expand and refine the narrow nationalist agendas of this time, Marson was seen only as missing the point and therefore, it would seem, her point was simply missed out by critics of her work. Marson's attention to the way in which the politics of race and gender were often complex and entwined is either unseen or unacknowledged and Sherlock's critical response chimes quite comfortably with that of Sir William Morrison, in his introduction to *Heights and Depths* in 1931, and his emphasis on the feminine sensibility of her verse. Furthermore, the inscription of her verse as 'strongly indicative of the poetic temperament of its Author' seems to establish a transparently gendered and curiously tenacious version of Marson's poetics as somehow releasing or compensating for personal truths, even as Morrison names it 'women's problems' (Morrison 1931: x).

Marson does figure in the broad survey works of Caribbean Literature published in the 1970s that established the contours of a nationalist literary history. However, Anthony Boxhill's chapter devoted to 'The beginnings to 1929' in Bruce King's edited book, *West Indian Literature* (1979), only alludes to Marson's poetry under a group identity along with that of many of her contemporaries as 'sentimental, imitative of Romantic and Victorian nature poetry, and strives too hard to seem elevated'.[4] Both the charge of mimicry and the stress on anachronistic literary registers are common accusations in this critical moment informed by the demands for a clear nationalisation of literature that I have already discussed in Chapter One. Boxhill's inability or unwillingness to attend to individual figures rather than to characterise a tepid literary past against which the brilliant present can be set demonstrates how the search for foremothers (and fathers) was simply not part of the construction of a literary tradition at this moment.

However, in *West Indian Poetry* (1978), Lloyd Brown devotes more attention to Marson, providing a fuller analysis of her verse. Indeed, he makes a significant claim for her as 'the earliest female poet of significance to emerge in West Indian literature' and foregrounds the importance of gender within her work (Brown 1984: 34). Nevertheless, Brown remains unable to offer any sustained evaluation of Marson's early poetry and simply dismisses *Tropic Reveries*, her first collection published in 1930, as 'extremely immature . . . adolescent love lyrics' suggesting that her poetry is, in these romantic and devotional poems, unsuccessfully a woman's verse (Brown 1984: 32). It is interesting that even though Brown is the first critic to identify the significance of gender within Marson's work, he perceives the clearly gendered poetry of *Tropic Reveries* as threatening her status as a serious poet. In his desire to discuss gender only in terms of an awareness of oppression and an oppositional politics, a position clearly motivated by the political claims beginning to be made for women's literature as well as for national writing during the 1970s, he dismisses a very visible, if difficult, aspect of Marson's poetic archive and consequently fails to negotiate the complex representation of gendered consciousness which her poetry as a whole offers.

Indeed, it was not until the 1980s, almost half a century after the publication of Marson's four volumes of poetry, that any critical essays devoted solely to her poetry appeared. Erika Smilowitz's biographical article 'Una Marson – A woman before her time', in 1983, and her critical reading, '"Weary of life and all my heart's full pain": the poetry of Una Marson', in 1984, redressed this absence. Smilowitz's biographical essay was of central importance to the act of unearthing Marson as a significant figure and reassessing her creative achievements alongside those of her male contemporaries. Until the publication of Delia Jarrett-Macauley's *The Life of Una Marson, 1905–1965* in 1998, it remained the main source of biographical information. Smilowitz catalogues Marson's diverse interests and achievements in journalism, social work and broadcasting, as well as her steadfast and vehement commitment to cultural expression as a crucial source of national pride and development. Smilowitz does not deny the significance of gender within Marson's poetry, but rather declares that she 'wrote as a woman. Her poems tell of passion, of desire, of frustrated love and above all, of loneliness' (Smilowitz 1983: 63). This construction of 'woman' is not only limited, but more importantly selective. Smilowitz moves swiftly (and rather transparently) from Marson's personal crises to her poems in order to fix an arresting and powerful image. In a sense Smilowitz's literary-biographical line of enquiry, although no doubt influenced by powerful works of feminist scholarship of the late 1970s and early 1980s that validated the personal as political, does not position itself too distantly from Sir William Morrison's first critical pronouncement in 1931.[5]

In the 1984 critical essay, Smilowitz does pay close attention to the poetry and identifies many of its subtleties and ironies. Nevertheless, to Smilowitz, Marson's first volume, *Tropic Reveries*, strikes a note of honesty: 'The emotions are straightforward, distressingly sincere and depressing' (Smilowitz 1984: 22). She advocates that there is 'no escape for women in Marson's poetry' and that 'Marson leaves no doubt in her reader's mind as to her perception of the plight of women, and it is a convincingly despondent picture' (Smilowitz 1984: 24). Even when Smilowitz does discuss the balance between resignation and rage which Marson sets up in *Tropic Reveries*, through her inclusion of poems which both celebrate and ridicule self-sacrificial love, she cannot reconcile the two images as coexisting and so turns to the classic feminist model of consciousness raising.

> On the one hand, she writes that she wishes to be a 'slave' to her lover . . . on the other hand . . . she implies that husbands make their wives seem foolish . . . Marson's own philosophy, unformed at this point, may have been emerging.
>
> (Smilowitz 1984: 25)

I am not arguing that feminist theory was a blunt instrument to take to Marson's poetry. Indeed, this contradiction of what constitutes woman's desire may have been very fruitfully explored alongside Rachel Blau DuPlessis's feminist meditation on the pressures that govern women's experience, 'For the Etruscans' (1980), that culminates in the deceptively simple question 'How to be? How to be-have?'. Rather I want to locate the way in which Smilowitz seems motivated to reclaim only part of Marson's archive in order to avoid the complex collocations of gender and cultural identity, as well as gender and race politics that Marson's work maps in both an explicit and implicit manner.

Honor Ford-Smith's article 'Una Marson: black nationalist and feminist writer' (1985), the only other article of length to investigate Marson's poetry in the 1980s, is very valuable for its contextualisation of Marson's work within women's organisations and race associations of her time, and is also of great significance in its exploration of Marson's work as a playwright, an aspect of her work which has been almost completely neglected (mainly due to the fact that the plays have survived only in manuscript form). Although Ford-Smith explores Marson's involvement in countering racial oppression, she is also attentive to Marson's gender politics. However, whereas Smilowitz had pursued the 'feminine' identification established by the early male critics, highlighting the icon of the 'lonely, frustrated woman', Honor Ford-Smith's focus is on 'the feminist'. Ford Smith's article does not discuss the early material which Smilowitz concentrates on and this selection enables her to disengage from the devotional sonnets and lyrics that may appear to militate against a clear feminist reading that is premised on oppositional and resistant politics. Certainly the sentimental, self-sacrificial love sonnets found in *Tropic Reveries* disrupt the securing boundaries which late twentieth-century feminism has constructed around our notion of the postcolonial female subject, and consequently we might trace Ford Smith's discussion of the politics of Marson's poetry as being informed by a desire to reassert identity-based politics through an identification of the points at which resistance seemed most startling. However, there is a danger that the poetic work of a figure like Marson, who was clearly involved in the struggle against female oppression, can become misrepresented as uniformly harmonious with an agenda of contemporary feminism and consequently denied a substantive reading which is sensitive to the particular complexities of her own work, complexities that speak very meaningfully to the contradictions and tensions of her own critical moment.

In her 2002 study, *Contemporary Caribbean Women's Poetry: Making Style*, deCaires Narain focuses on Marson and Phyllis Shand Allfrey, a white Dominican, as her foundational literary figures. Neither has been easily accommodated into Caribbean poetic traditions to date and deCaires Narain offers a detailed account of both poets' works that positions them consciously at the beginning of an alternative genealogy of women poets.

> I would suggest that considering Marson and Allfrey *provisionally* as foundational literary figures is a productive way to begin a discussion of contemporary Caribbean women poets, for it allows sustained attention to be given to work which has, historically, been considered marginal to 'mainstream' literary activity.
>
> (deCaires Narain 2002b: 1)

In the present critical moment, more interested in and accustomed to ambivalence, mimicry and hybridity as signs of postcolonial writing, DeCaires Narain is particularly interested in Marson's textual construction of a black woman poet and attentive to the 'contradictory nature of Marson's poetic oeuvre and some of the more nuanced strands of colonial cultural exchanges between Britain and the West Indies' (deCaires Narain 2002b: 17). deCaires Narain foregrounds 'the unevenness of the poems and the very partiality of their "success" as poems, . . . as . . . an index of the transitional moment at which Marson was writing' (deCaires Narain 2002b: 29).

Writing for resistance and the double agent: the poetry of Una Marson

Having examined the ways in which Marson has been constructed in previous literary histories, I now want to test her status as a literary 'double agent' and discuss how her work contests the mutually exclusive categorising of the two poetic modes that have dominated her literary profile as a woman writer – the sentimental and the polemical, the feminine and the feminist. Drawing on the concept of double agency enables me to read the way in which Marson works both with and against the binaries of submission and resistance, collusion and contestation onto which the competing models of womanhood have been mapped and thereby to locate a mode of resistance and a structure of agency that has been less visible to date. Although Carolyn Cooper's ground-breaking study, *Noises in the Blood*, examines the operations of 'double agency' within popular cultural forms, her framing of 'the bloodline of this heritage of transgressive innocence' through the works of Louise Bennett, Jean Breeze, Mikey Smith and Sistren may also be useful to a reading of Marson's high poetic diction, which although generically very different might also be seen to deploy the Caribbean strategy 'play fool fi ketch wise' and to 'write and perform a script of cultural resistance to the hegemony of anglocentrism' (Cooper 1993: 9).

My reading returns the critical gaze to the unstable territory of Marson's first volume of poetry, *Tropic Reveries*, published in 1930. It is this volume that has received absolutely minimal critical attention to date and, not coincidentally, it is also this volume that is seemingly most reliant on a model of devotion to both European poetic models and patriarchal versions of female subjectivity. In this work a startling and somewhat disturbing sonnet sequence, in which the Elizabethan language of imperialism denotes the romance saga in classical terms, is set alongside parodies of Shakespeare and Kipling which boldly redress tradition with the aim of giving language the power of woman's experience. By reading examples from these two genres side by side, I hope to explore Donna St Hill's argument that

> An absolute opposition of the terms 'victimhood' and 'agency' is an oversimplification and does not take into account the true complexity of women's experience of subordination and their continuous negotiation of what Kandiyoti (1988) terms 'patriarchal bargains'. A feminist consciousness not only involves the realization of gender-specific injury, but it is the very mechanism by which urgency, dedication, and empathy become engaged with the utopian project of contemplating its transformation.
>
> (St Hill 2003: 62)

I wish to begin with 'In Vain' because it disrupts the assumption that a poem written in a form as conventional as a sonnet will be proportionately reliant on that structure's eurocentrically gendered system of signification. This poem also raises the issue of mimicry as colonial crime, as it holds many echoes of Elizabethan and courtly love poetry but is crucially different to that genre.

In vain I build me stately mansions fair,
And set thee as my king upon the throne,
And place a lowly stool beside thee there,
Thus, as thy slave to come into my own.

In vain I deck the halls with roses sweet
And strew the paths with petals rich and rare,
And list with throbbing heart sounds of thy feet,
The welcome voice that tells me thou art near.

In vain I watch the dawn break in the sky
And hope that thou wilt come with coming day:
Alas, Diana calmly sails on high,
But thou, king of my heart, art far away.

In vain one boon from life's great store I crave,
No more the king comes to his waiting slave.
                                    (Marson 1930: 27)

The language and imagery of imperialism, which surfaces in a number of Marson's 'love poems' in *Tropic Reveries* with such disturbing and shocking effect, could be traced to the Elizabethan sonneteers. Both offer the same classical framework, in which the lover is apotheosised with the characteristic blurring of religious and amatory imagery. The frustration of fulfilment (all is 'in vain') could also be seen as mere convention, the portrayal of necessary cruelty and indifference on the part of the lover.

However, Marson presents an inverted imitation of the paradigm of courtly love; the man is unattainable, placed on a throne rather than a pedestal, and the woman is actively, and inevitably unsuccessfully, wooing. By inverting the gender roles, Marson brings new meaning to the genre. The adoration of woman and her fictive ability to wield power through indifference and abstinence within male courtly love poetry is revealed as playful and even derisory, since the real power structures of society frustrate any such notion of female power. The politics of such poetry exist then in the space between art and life, whereas in Marson's poem it is the relation between the art and life of a black woman which makes the 'slave image' such a disturbing, difficult and fascinating one. While this poem obviously provokes consideration of the power relations that govern heterosexual, patriarchal, colonial societies, I would suggest that it takes us beyond a simple illustration of what has elsewhere been termed 'the pornography of Empire'.

As I have already stated, criticism to date has attempted to either suppress or dismiss sonnets such as this one, which is part of an eight-poem sonnet sequence.[6] These approaches are strongly suggestive of the fact that such poetry is considered to be a saccharine subgenre of gendered verse and embarrassingly colonial. Within the Jamaican context 'A Lover's

Discourse' is not only 'unwarranted' (to quote Barthes 1978). The sentimental and sacrificial proves a particularly treacherous territory for the postcolonial feminist critic for whom such poems occasion a fighting back both of charges of emotional excess and of literary dependency.

However, locating the double agency of 'In Vain', I want to argue that this poem offers us a point from which to resist these negative evaluations. The proposition of the first stanza that submission and servitude represent an opportunity 'to come into my own' undermines any static notion of feminine self-sacrifice or cultural masochism. At the point of submission the slave should be owned; it is a moment which traditionally signifies the denial of subjectivity and agency, not the acquisition of it. By calling the issues of ownership and self-determination into question, Marson's poem allows us to glimpse the figure of the double agent in the strange (strained) agency of the oppressed woman. Indeed, we might wish to extend this principle to a consideration of Marson's poetics here and suggest that by consciously crafting a poem in which subordination is undermined, any relationship of 'In Vain' to the European sonnet tradition is similarly subverted. Thus by rehearsing a position of servitude – to poetic convention as well as to the lover/master figure – this poem is able to articulate a space in which the subject can position itself even within the structure of slavery, which might be seen as a place of no resistance. By operating within convention, the poem explores but does not endorse the surrender of self that might be seen as the traditional destiny of the female and colonial subject. It also makes visible the unseen figure of resistance in both an epistemological and an ontological history.

Certainly the figure desiring mastery is not the only trope of woman to undergo revision in this volume. Interestingly, it is in *Tropic Reveries*, the volume most densely populated by these seemingly self-sacrificial love poems, that we also find the most acerbic attacks on matrimony – the socially enforced conclusion of heterosexual romance. In this volume Marson remodels two of the 'sacred' speeches of English Literature (Kipling's 'If' and Hamlet's soliloquy 'To be or not to be . . .') playfully shifting the poetic axis from a discussion of 'man's condition' to an exploration of woman's. In Marson's 'If', although much of the text in terms of language and form is taken directly from Kipling, the effect of the poem as a whole is far from mimetic. Reconstruction on the levels of diction and form facilitates deconstruction on the level of ideas. It is clear that the Jamaican woman poet is not bidding to be a pale imitation of a brilliant predecessor, but is rather playfully engaging with received models to elucidate her own ideas and express a state of consciousness and a social role which has been left uninterrogated by patriarchy and colonialism.

The parody of Kipling's grand recipe for manhood has an interesting subtext with reference to him as colonial writer, but I want to concentrate here on gender politics. While Kipling's poem inscribes the ethos of imperial masculinity *par excellence*, Marson's parody appropriates this framework with daring and decorum in order to communicate the consciously anti-heroic role of a 'wife worthwhile'.

> If you can keep him true when all about you
> The girls are making eyes and being kind,
> If you can make him spend the evenings with you
> When fifty Jims and Jacks are on his mind;
> If you can wait and not be tired by waiting,
> Or when he comes at one, be calm and sleep,
> And do not oversleep, but early waking
> Smile o'er the tea cups, and ne'er think to weep.
>
> If you can hear bright tales and quit them faster,
> And, for your peace of mind, think him no knave;
> If you can bear to hear the truth you tell him
> Twisted around to make you seem a fool,
> Or see the Capstan on your bureau burning
> And move the noxious weed, and still keep cool.
>
> If you can make one heap of all he gives you
> And try to budget so that it's enough,
> And add, subtract and multiply the issue,
> So that the Grocer will not cut up rough;
> If you can force your dress, and hat, and stocking
> To serve their turn long after they are worn,
> And pass the 'sales,' and do not think it shocking
> To wear a garment that has once been torn:
>
> If you can walk when he takes out the Ford
> And teaches girls to drive before you learn,
> And list to tales of tyres without a wry word,
> And let him feel you're glad for his return:
> If you can fill the unforgiving minute
> With sixty seconds work and prayer and smile,
> Yours is the world and everything that's in it,
> And what is more you'll be a wife worth while.
>   (*With apologies to Kipling*)
>   (Marson 1930: 83–4)

The trials which mark a boy's rite of passage into manhood are travestied by the domestic obstacle course which faces a prospective bride. In the poem, the initiation into matrimony is revealed to be an exercise requiring practical skills, dissimulation and self-delusion. Indeed, although Kipling writes of maturity and Marson of matrimony the ultimate subject of both poems is significantly the same, in terms of a discussion of masculine fulfil-ment, and yet crucially different. The fact that the high proportion of unmarried women in Jamaica would become a focus of the colonial authority's anxiety attack after the 1937 unrest and prompt a mass social-isation campaign into matrimony clearly speaks to the conjoined politics of colonial patriarch governance.

Marson's poem effectively redefines and realigns the status of this 'achievement', again raising a question mark over established notions of value. The references within the third stanza point to the very real prob-lems of budgeting in what was a period of acute economic distress in Jamaica, but they also suggest that to be contented and worthwhile a wife must learn to play with the concept of value. The manipulation of figures which the wife must learn stand figuratively for the creative accounting with her own happiness which she must perform in order negotiate 'patri-archal bargains'. In this poem, Marson acknowledges and 'plays off' the primary text with critical awareness, thus making the ideological inflec-tions of the intertextuality far more explicit. To undervalue parody as either a sign of the writer's inability to escape received models or of a penchant for apolitical play would be to miss the radical relationship which these poems establish between different models of experience and different participants within an established discourse. As Linda Hutcheon points out, parody 'establishes difference at the heart of similarity. No integra-tion into a new context can avoid altering meaning, and perhaps even value' (Hutcheon 1985: 8). Indeed, it is crucial that the transcontextual act becomes transvaluative as the issue of sexual difference is written into Marson's versions.

Rhonda Cobham-Sander has described Marson's parodies as 'of slight literary merit . . . probably written while Marson was still at school for the entertainment of school friends' (Cobham-Sander 1981: 218). Although this suggestion of commonplace schoolgirl activity is purely speculative it might be interesting to pursue. Rather than indicating the lesser value of these poems (the implication is that they are somehow inconsequential and aesthetically immature), the idea that these poems were produced in the context of and as a direct response to the colonial educational system serves to highlight their inherently subversive quality. The pedagogic imperative for repetition which was instilled by this system is radically revised here through parodies of high literary discourses. By choosing to travesty such well-established texts, Marson is able to demonstrate her knowledge of tradition, whilst asserting a counter-discourse via the substi-tution of woman's experience. The apology to Kipling at the end of the parody does not signal the filial relationship with indifference. Marson deliberately foregrounds the 'original creator' and text and thus ironically references the consciously disobedient nature of this poem through a gesture of mock-humility. Her feigned reverence offers another glimpse of the double agent.

While Cobham-Sander seeks to give agency to the education system, with Marson simply in the role of reactor, my reading seeks to highlight how this poem actually reclaims agency from an institution founded on a belief in the hierarchy of discourses in order to communicate a consciously non- (if not anti-) élitist perspective. Far from being any incidental act of verbal play, this parody presents ideological rivalry, offering Marson an opportunity to radically dislocate tradition from authority and to question the gender politics of the patriarchal script. Rather than reading this parody as an insignificant experiment with form or as a 'miscellaneous' work unrelated to the volume as a whole, I wish to propose that Marson's parody be read as a paradigmatic text for an analysis of the tensions between imitation and creation within much of her work where inter-textuality operates more subtly. With its possibility for split signification, parody works both within and against the colonial imperative to mimic, making a double demand on meaning that I would suggest is also operating in her devotional 'love poems' on a less explicit level.

Although these works from Marson's first volume are far less obviously feminist in orientation than those of her 1937 volume, *The Moth and The Star*, they provide an archive that remains as challenging in our critical moment as it was in its own time. Moreover, these works seem to confirm Natasha Barnes' observation that 'women's relationship to feminism is often a layered and unruly process' (Barnes 1999: 38). As my reading of Marson's poetry has revealed, Caribbean female subjectivity in her work can usefully be approached through the figure of the 'double agent', as agency is often achieved through 'doubling', masking, subverting or otherwise playing with the operations of power in which women find themselves situated.[7] Indeed, it is as a double agent that Marson seems to confirm Lou Bennett's now celebrated affirmation

> An long before Oman lib bruck out
> Over foreign lan
> Jamaica female wasa work
> Her liberated plan!
>   (Bennett 1982: 22)

Bridging the gaps in history: Indian-Caribbean women's writing

Despite the fact that much writing on the subject of feminism has foregrounded the importance of bringing ethnicity into the orbit of gender politics, very little attention was paid to Indian-Caribbean women's writing before the late 1990s. It would seem that just as period, location and gender have delineated and limited, at different moments, what can be considered properly Caribbean within critical discourses, so too ethnicity has functioned as a separation boundary in women's literary and critical histories. Indian-Caribbean writing has very clearly remained on the margins of a Caribbean women's canon, with even contemporary works receiving sparse critical attention. However, this is not to say that there have not been Indian-Caribbean women writers of note, although it is very hard to locate works written in the first half of the twentieth century. In Trinidad, Agnes Ramcharan, editor and writer on the radical *Spectator* magazine, published a number of pieces in the late 1940s but her work has only come to light in 2002 with the publication of Kris Rampersad's comprehensive study *Finding a Place: Indo Trinidadian Literature*.[8] Even Rajkumari Singh's 1960 collection of short stories, *A Garland of Stories*, is seldom critically attended to and is located only in the context of her own life and as testimony to her struggle to publish as the mother of five young children.

The first known novel by an Indian-Caribbean woman writer was Lakshmi Persaud's *Butterfly in the Wind*, published in 1990. As Persaud's work has received a good deal of critical attention, it is perhaps only important to note here that this text offers a series of vignettes through which the secure family and community life of a Hindu household in Pasea village, rural Trinidad, is fondly rendered.[9] The book does clearly address the gendered injustices, prohibitions and morally invested religious stories that form the core of female education in this village culture, but the narrative as a whole is imbued with a tender backward glance. Its historical and personal chronicle centres on 'the quiet revolution taking place amongst the East Indian population' (Persaud 1990: 155) that brings accelerated changes in women's possibilities of being during the second half of the twentieth century. At the end of the narrative Kamala's 'achieve-ment' of a life beyond the village is described in terms of success but also of loss: 'Never before had a female, either on my mother's or my father's side of the family, had the opportunity to go to university – furthermore a university four thousand miles away where there was neither family nor friend' (Persaud 1990: 191).

Narmala Shewcharan's 1994 novel, *Tomorrow is Another Day*, offers a far more unforgiving and politically charged portrait of postcolonial Guyana, dominated by the PNC régime of Forbes Burnham.[10] In the time-frame of this novel – the 1960s to 1980s – the utopian ideal of cooperative socialism in Guyana became a vile reality in which political expediency, corruption, racial intimidation, and violence (mainly) against Indian-Caribbean men and women, thrived. At one level, the novel charts a familiar, even dominant, political narrative through its central figure of Jagru Persaud. In a desperate and deteriorating Guyana, Jagru is persuaded by the increasingly visible demands of 'realpolitik' to change political allegiance and take up a post with the ruling party, a thinly veiled People's National Congress (PNC). Persaud makes the decision in good faith, 'He thought of the many good things that he could do with such authority . . . He would work his way through. He would make things happen' (Shewcharan 1994: 15). However, in this novel, set during the crisis years of the Guyanese state, Shewcharan shows how the anticipated nationalist models of public power and masculine agency are no longer functioning in the service of egalitarian anti-colonialism. The inefficiency, corruption and many scandals of the state simply negate the possibility of transformative politics that Jagru initially invests in.

It is against the failed grand narrative of political Independence and shared empowerment that Shewcharan writes in other real power struggles of this era – the daily struggles of women to feed and clothe children and to protect the values of honesty and friendship. As the narrative unfolds we are increasingly encouraged to read Chandi Panday, and her survival narrative, as the focalising politics of the novel. Writing both within and against the grand narrative of this era of Caribbean history, Shewcharan displaces the already over-determined discourses of party politics in favour of the overtly gendered issue of domestic politics and, in particular, Chandi's enduring struggle to raise her five children alone. Effectively abandoned by her husband, Lal Panday, who leaves to embed himself in the political campaigns of the Workers Party, Shewcharan makes clear the different stakes of political struggle in the public and the private spheres.

As Lal affirms his understanding of the sacrifice of political commitment, the gendered irony of his statement is clear to the reader. Lal's credibility as a leader among his 'brothers' is dependent on the suffering of his family.

> My job gave me shelter over my head. It gave my children bread in their mouths. But the day came when I had to stand back and take stock. I left my job. How could I continue? How could I allow for myself to be fed and housed and to be a cog in system that was allowing so many others to starve? . . . I stand before you, brothers, an unemployed man. I have no house, no job, no bread. My children live in a shack. Sometimes they get to eat. Sometimes they don't . . . I have forgotten my own tomorrows and those of my children.
>
> (Shewcharan 1994: 72)

The novel makes it clear that Chandi, who does not have the luxury of standing back, must pay the price for Lal's amnesia of the everyday, as she must work even harder to survive in the face of her husband's 'sacrifice'.

Just as Shewcharan disrupts the expectations of a dominant political and national narrative in this text, she also complicates the representation of lines of alliance and hostility. The normative narrative of this period is that of racial suspicion and intimidation (as promoted by the PNC). Shewcharan does not deny this very real and serious abuse. The racial and sexual violence that has dominated most accounts of Indian women's lives in this time and place is figured through the allusion to anonymous victims, 'They killed her afterwards. The police find her with her hands tied. She had marks all over her body' (Shewcharan 1994: 25). All the same, the rape of Indian women by African men that stands as testimony to the most extreme acts of racial and gendered violence perpetrated in Guyana during this period is arguably written over in this text by Lal's rape of Chandi, the rape of a wife by a husband. This disturbing act that violates the assumed sacred and threatened bonds of Indian family and marriage is accepted by Chandi as a displacement of the suspicion, desperation and brutality of that moment onto her body, but her forced understanding is undertaken at the cost of her own emotional survival: 'She would not open the Pandora's box of feelings to think about the violence he had forced on her body' (Shewcharan 1994: 198–199). Through this representation of rape, Shewcharan importantly broadens the agenda of women's rights within her scripted moment and enacts an important unsilencing of domestic violence within Indian-Caribbean communities, addressing one of the aspects that Ramabai Espinet also represents as 'Barred' in her 1991 story of that name set in Trinidad (see Puri 1999: 261).

In her bold focus on the exchanges and hostilities that govern domestic politics, it is perhaps interesting that Shewcharan does not represent a comforting version of Indian sisterhood. Rather, she examines the fractures within ethnic and gender communities. Radika (Jagru's wife) is Chandi's schoolgirl friend but her swift rejection of Chandi is clearly figured as one based on class shame. There is however an alliance between Kunti (Jagru's mother) and Chandi based on their shared history of toil and suffering. While Chandi's 'lined face was showing every second of her thirty-eight years' (Shewcharan 1994: 35), Kunti's body is marked not only by the toils of reproductive labour but also by those of cane-cutting, 'Her back still ached with the constant bending she had done in the canefields and her hands were scarred from handling the long stalks' (Shewcharan 1994: 25). The alliance between these two women is represented directly as a recognition of shared suffering and survival, 'she had grown to like Chandi, to admire the way she faced up to things and to realise that they were alike' (Shewcharan 1994: 144).

Although Shewcharan does not represent an easy kinship between women or among Indians, perhaps more strategically significant in her narration of this historical moment, characterised by the mobilisation of antagonist racial discourses, is the friendship between Chandi and Aunt Adee, an African Guyanese market woman. Adee helps Chandi to locate her agency within a crumbling economy and thereby to secure the needs of her family for a short time. However, in a text that captures the anti-utopian moment of a dream gone so wrong for so many, the failures of this political moment inevitably determine the finite conditions of empowerment for these women too. Chandi commits suicide so that her family can benefit from the insurance money. Her real act of sacrifice stands as a powerful reminder of her genuine commitment to the care of others that Lal had so passionately preached.

'She children going to be all right, now,' Aunt Adee said. 'The big boy, the one who go way to sea. He back. He going to college. Artie going back to school too.' She cackled: 'The insurance company going to pay up. They na can prove anything'.

(Shewcharan 1994: 233)

In *Tomorrow is Another Day*, Chandi is represented as a woman unable to write her own history, both metaphorically and literally. When Lal first abandons the family Chandi takes out her diary, an act that symbolises her effort to take back control over the framing of her subjectivity. However, her sense of herself as a subject emptied of historical promise that confronts her as she begins to write creates a bare testimonial of her being – an unadorned statement of despair – that is the hidden history of this moment.

She rummaged in a barrel, seizing a little tin box. This contained her diary, one she had cherished when she was still a schoolgirl, dreaming of attending college and going on to a glorious career. Brushing away the dust, she flicked the pages open and stared at them for a long time. Who was that girl who had written those girlish things so long ago? There were still some empty pages, but what could this person she had become write now? She had moved so quickly from student to wife to mother that the diary, along with the fripperies of her youth, had been flung side. Now she felt an overwhelming need to put into words the despair thrust upon her since her husband had gone into hospital.

She sat still for a moment, then began: 'I don't know what to do. I just don't. I have no one to help me. No one.' She paused.

(Shewcharan 1994: 18)

The problematic relationship between Indian-Caribbean women and acts of representation was clearly outlined by Ramabai Espinet in her 1989 essay, 'The Invisible Woman in West Indian Fiction'. Published before many Indian-Caribbean women had begun circulating literary works that offered up complex and conflictual subject positions, Espinet declaims the limitations of Indian-Caribbean women as represented in male literary works.

She is a fleeting, unseen creature, functioning unambiguously within the constraints of the tight familial structure. The world outside is not her domain: still protected by the veil, she exists in that area of the Indian sensibility which is private, unrevealed even to one's self, and about which exploration is tentative.

(Espinet 1989: 120)

However, Espinet is not just interested in cataloguing the contours of a literary history in this piece. She links the lack of creative representation to the erosion of Indian-Caribbean women's rights and thereby makes a connection, crucial to feminist practice, between the conditions of literary and social visibility.

> This is a sad and critical state of affairs. It is damaging to the health of the society as a whole and to this sub-group in particular. The distance between the real existence of hundreds of women and the images thrown up by the fiction of the region needs to be *bridged*.
>
> (Espinet 1989: 121, emphasis mine)

In her 2003 novel *The Swinging Bridge* Espinet returns to this urgent task as writer rather than critic. In an accomplished and exciting literary work, she re-members the bridges between history and the present and between the imagined subject and the historical subject in such a way as to enable new versions of Indian-Caribbean women's subjectivity to be made visible.[11] The epigraph to the novel, taken from Gabriel Mistral, begins with the lines: 'I enter as one who raises / a cloth from a covered face'. The reference back to her earlier criticism of the false icon of the veiled woman and the 'ohrni-blinkered sensibility' of the male writer that had blocked the recovery and representation of Indian-Caribbean women could hardly be more direct. As writer, Espinet has taken up the task to unveil a different version of Indian-Caribbean female subjectivity, a task which she has already invested with enormous cultural and social value.

The Swinging Bridge is a novel acutely conscious of the demands for historical redress. The prologue that describes the crossing made by Indian women from Calcutta to Trinidad opens with the words 'It is an untold story', and then, without pause, begins the act of telling. The narrative voice speaks with assurance and detail, 'The year is 1879, and the women have been brought by train from Benares to the port city of Calcutta' (Espinet 2003: 3). It speaks of particular dates and makes reference to laws and historical records. Offering a very visual image of the ship and its new passengers, the narrator (a researcher and secret script-writer, as we will soon learn) gradually zooms in to offer an intimate, family portrait, 'my own great grandmother Gainder, crossing the unknown of the kala pani, the black waters that lie between India and the Caribbean' (Espinet 2003: 4). This shifting between the long and short lenses of history occurs throughout this narrative that is involved in the act of telling the history of a people, a family and an acutely self-conscious self.

Mona Singh, the narrator, is a woman obsessed with history and as the narrative proper opens, she is recording her own on January 15, 1995.

> That's me. I live in the eye of the storm. My whole life arches back-wards and forwards according to the speed of the gust around me.

In the centre, near the eye, in the place where I live, it is still. A
small mercy.

(Espinet 2003: 5)

As a single, independent woman working for Films Canadiana, 'a small
innovative outfit', with her friend Carene, at the opening of the novel
Mona has escaped the gusts of family expectation and the confines of
the Indian Trinidadian familial domain. She is also keen to explain that
she actively resists her boyfriend Roddy's proposal of shared domestic
arrangements: 'Living together would just tie me up in knots from which
I would have to break loose' (Espinet 2003: 12). However, it is not surprising that Espinet's much anticipated inscription of Indian-Caribbean
woman's liberation is not as simple or transparent as this.

Disturbed by a phone call in the middle of her musings about her almost
vertiginous and certainly precarious position as a subject haunted by a
language that is 'beckoning [her] into the past', Mona hears her mother
Muddie's voice and feels a bridge coming down – 'my brother Kello lying
in a hospital bed, his lanky figure stretched between us like a hammock'
(Espinet 2003: 5). Her dying brother's body becomes a bridge that will
return her to the heart of her family, but also one that will launch her
across continents and back centuries in order to recover the distant as well
as the near past of her ancestors. Kello's illness does not only disrupt
Mona's writing of consciousness. His request drives an urgent reconnection to that past that Mona, the perpetual historian and compulsive
voyeur, had until then displaced through her work.

In collaboration with Carene, Mona had been researching and editing
a film about Haitian women in Montreal but, unlike Carene, Mona could
not reconcile herself to a narrative that disconnected these women's
contemporary lives from their revolutionary history.

These Haitian mothers and grandmothers spoke to us freely, full of
story, full of history, full of proverbs and riddles of *libète*, the liberty
they continued to pursue, the liberty that had brought them here to
the shore of Montreal.

(Espinet 2003: 10)

The idea of women as bearers of narratives that need to be restored to
the status of history is not a casual observation on Mona's behalf. Most
of all, she wanted to restore 'the part played by a priestess, a *manbo* named
Cecile Fatman, in the Bois Caiman ritual, which Haitians acknowledge
as the act that launched the revolution' (Espinet 2003: 10). Her concern
with women 'edited out of history', confirms her role as feminist histori-
ographer. Yet despite her passion, Mona is not leading this project and
she does not have control over the final cut of the film. As she leaves to
visit her family in Toronto, Mona is agitated about leaving Cecile Fatiman

in the hands of Carene. At this stage, she does not know that this journey across Canada will be one stage in a much more ambitious crossing that will finally take her back not only to Trinidad and a new engagement with her familial history there, but finally to India and the history embodied in the ancestor figure of Gainder on the swinging bridge in 1879.

When Mona visits Kello in hospital he asks her to return to Trinidad in order to secure the family's old land on Manahambre Road in Princes Town that he had planned to buy, '"You can do it better than I can, you always researching Trini ting, you're the best one to go. Do this for me, Mon. I want this land, Pappy's land"' (Espinet 2003: 52). Mona is charged with a very specific burden of history by her dying brother. She must purchase that land that will reconnect him to the paternal inheritance his own father had disowned. Kello's plan is in defiance of his father who had sold the family land passed on to him by Pappy, his own father, in order to fund a move into the modern urban environment of San Fernando. Kello sees the land as emblematic of Pappy's strength and endurance in the face of a hostile culture, 'they survived and they kept the land. And that land will be ours again, Mona. All is not lost' (Espinet 2003: 58). For Kello, dying of AIDS, it is not the end of life that signals absolute loss but the disconnection from history.

In his desire to reclaim his paternal, even patriarchal, inheritance of the land, Kello may be seen to assert an identity at odds with his queer subjectivity, but in this narrative the bridges between the present and the past are crucial to the preservation of memory, story and identity that Kello, as a dying man, is clearly preoccupied with. In as much as Mona has retained her connection to the Caribbean through her work, his decision to ask her to act as his advocate is entirely appropriate. However, Mona is quite explicitly a feminist historian and although she is increasingly engaged in the task of recovery that Kello initiated, her own reconnection with Trinidad and the past is less one of possession than repossession.

> As for Kello, all his talk was about my going to Trinidad as his proxy for the land deal. He was bent on buying, but I couldn't help trying to tell him how ownership meant nothing to me.
>
> (Espinet 2003: 55)

Nevertheless, as Mona agrees to Kello's request she begins her own process of historical recovery and volunteering to clean the attic at her parent's house, she 'found [her]self approaching the job with interest, wanting to handle the evidence of our passage – the mementos, the letters and prizes from a past time' (Espinet 2003: 59).

The letters and documents that Mona discovers again explicitly foreground this novel's engagement with history. Her recovery of forgotten texts establishes a historical and textual presence for Indian Trinidadians and makes it plain that history at the level of family and nation is a narrative act based on inclusions and exclusions that are always motivated by the politics of both culture and gender. Among the discarded, Mona rediscovers Etwaria, Pappy's 'bamboo wife', who had been displaced by 'Mama . . . a fine young Christian girl' and whom Mona imagines 'died alone in her tapia hut' (Espinet 2003: 64).

However, Mona's realisation that she is not simply the spectator and archivist of the past is also central to this narrative. Mona discovers that she is also a historical subject, shaped by the very forces that had governed the lives of her forgotten foremothers.[12] Diverting her attention back to the demands of the present, Kello forces Mona's reconnection with her own historical trauma in order to bring reparation between Mona and Da-Da.

> 'You tried to kill Mona because she had a Creole boyfriend. Ask Mona to forgive you. You have to do it. The last thing I'm asking you for, you must do it Da-Da.' . . .
>
> Kello had said the unsayable. Da-Da has never directly punished me about Bree. The kneeling on the gravel, the burning of the shift dress, all of it was about Bree, we both knew that, Da-Da and I, but we had remained locked in silent conspiracy. Kello had smashed open that locked box.
>
> (Espinet 2003: 207)

As her father explains his fears for her, his 'own-way' daughter, in a Trinidadian society in which the Indian daughter's purity was still a potent marker of the family's cultural integrity and pride, he arrives at his own moment of 'righting' history.

> If I could turn back the clock, so help my living God I would turn it back. Mona I am so sorry, you have to believe me, you have to believe how sorry I feel. I can't change what happened then, but we must cross that bridge.
>
> (Espinet 2003: 209)

Mona's humiliation is not a history that can be replayed, but the image of crossing a bridge is a clear signal within the novel of the demands for reconciliation.

For Mona, this is a process that takes her back in order to move forward. Her recourse to history connects her to Grandma Lil, with whom she shares the clear prohibition from marrying the boy that she loved because of racial prejudice, but it also takes her to Gainder, the ancestor figure, whose songs were 'barred' from the house and whose links to India are not the guarantee of her passivity but rather the very site of her resistance and creativity. The history of wrongs against women that Mona traces back through each generation finally takes her back to the silencing of Gainder, the lost and disavowed woman whose life Mona is able to piece together from the fragments of her grandmother's 'shop books'. After the death of her father, Gainder had braved the *kala pani* at the age of thirteen to escape an unwanted marriage. She had worked and saved and sang and danced, and her reputation brought her the attentions of a 'good' husband, Joshua, who, after their marriage, told her 'that she must never sing or dance in public again. Her heart turns to stone when she hears these words' (Espinet 2003: 249). Her courage and strength and voice were finally lost through her incorporation into family and domestic life – and history.

The link between textual and historical recovery is very strong in this text. In one of her diary entries that open the narrative, Mona writes that 'words are ghosts, ancestors on this side' (Espinet 2003: 5). By the end of the narrative Mona has constructed a representational bridge across which Gainder can walk back into the world of the reader, and Espinet has narrated two powerful figures (Mona and Gainder), both bearing the history of Indian-Caribbean women's resistance as well as resilience – a history and a subjectivity that is just now being acknowledged and recovered by feminist historians and theorists. Finally then, in this novel, liberation is not simply the freedom to escape the history that has been laid before you but more importantly the freedom to engage with that history, to know its traumas, to celebrate its triumphs and to negotiate its telling.

As Mona suspects, Carene does not include Cecile Fatiman in the final cut of the film and while she laments Cecile's erasure, she recovers her own unacknowledged female revolutionary and is able to restore her to both the familial and national narratives from which she had been edited. Recovering Gainder's songs and their link to female empowerment through matikor, an all female ritual, Mona, finds her hidden family treasure, 'these songs were my bounty, swinging open a doorway into another world' (Espinet 2003: 293). As the book ends, Mona both claims and represents her recovered inheritance as she plans her film on this other rebel woman who initiated a quiet, ongoing revolution through her assertion of agency and creativity.

Textual and sexual recovery: celebrating matikor

Although it explores a very different relationship between Indian-Caribbean women's historical lives and the issue of writing, one important recent publication is Verene Shepherd's (2002b) fascinating work *Maharani's Misery: Narratives of a Passage from India to the Caribbean*. This text is an account of the evidence relating to the rape and death of Maharani, a bonded woman who sailed from Calcutta on the *Allanshaw* in 1885 but who never made it to walk the swinging bridge onto Guyanese soil. Seventeen bonded servants died on this passage, but Maharani's death alone caused controversy and sparked an investigation as it was widely believed that the sexual violence perpetrated against her led to her death. There are several interesting issues that arise from this incident and the investigation that help locate the central debates that continue to govern the issue of Indian women's subjectivity, and in particular sexual subjectivity, in our critical moment. What does this incident tell us about the differently constituted representation of Indian women's identity as opposed to that of African women who had been routinely sexually abused on the slave ships of the Middle Passage? How has this differentiation inflected their relations to colonial culture and to each other? Related to this is the fact that the African man accused of taking part in the rape denied his part and claimed to have been framed for the crime, while the Englishman also accused was never even investigated. How does the figure of the Indian women mobilise different ethnically-inflected versions of masculinity?

At the moment of their arrival in the Caribbean, and possibly even beforehand, Indian women were already framed by the overlapping discourses of race and sex that determined ideas of the Other woman within the colonial matrix. Given that a relatively high number of the women who crossed the ocean were single, it is perhaps not surprising that their sexual morality was immediately put under suspicion within the discourses of colonial history. As Kamala Kempadoo concludes from her reading of Reddock's, Mangru's and Shepherd's research,

> British colonial officials held that many of the female immigrants were prostitutes, social outcasts and women who had abandoned marriage and domesticity, all of whom were considered to 'have gone astray', to be 'prone to immoral conduct', to exercise a 'corrupting influence' on 'respectable' women . . . In the eyes of officialdom then, the women were highly sexual, of dubious character and well outside the boundaries of decent colonial womanhood.
>
> (Kempadoo 2003: 171)

Interestingly though, in twentieth-century cultural discourses Indian women have more commonly been represented as docile, loyal and submissive. Feminist scholars have pointed out how this representation is often constructed as oppositional in relation to African-Caribbean women. Rhoda Reddock discusses how

> The new 'East Indians' . . . were defined in opposition to their labouring predecessors both internally and externally as they sought also to define themselves . . . 'East Indians' were constructed as hardworking and thrifty, common characteristics of immigrants anywhere . . . These analyses, however, could be taken much further, for nowhere is the differential construction as clear as in relation to women. Indian

women have been defined in opposition to African women. 'She' is everything the African woman is not. Through a combination of male violence and state legislation, a localised 'East Indian woman' was constructed in many ways as an essentialised and orientalised Indian woman.

(Reddock 2002: 116)

Sheila Rampersad's comprehensive examination of the 'gendered representational matrix, in which Indian women are chaste and pure; African women are vulgar and promiscuous' (Rampersad 2000: 53) that has been mobilised within both the political and the popular cultural sphere in Trinidad since the 1930s leads her to conclude that

The Indian woman is presumed to be voiceless, without agency and reduced to functioning as a commodity to be exchanged or not exchanged between Indian and African men . . . the Indian women [is] pulled on one hand by the Indian community which extrapolated its cultural integrity from her racial endogamy, and on the other by the African community which utilises her as a final test of the depth of the Indian community's wish to be truly Trinidadian, that is, creole. In this model, she is reduced to her sexuality and the battle between Indians and Africans takes place on her body. The real question posed by this face-off . . . is not whether the Indian woman should be exploited or not, but **who** has the **right** to exploit her.

(Rampersad 2000: 61, bold in the original)

As Rampersad's research highlights, Indian women have continued to be given social meaning in Trinidadian society only on the terms of their sexuality, but it has been a meaning always negotiated on male terms and on the assumption of female silence and consent.

The work of Patricia Mohammed has examined the ways in which this icon of femininity was also mobilised from within the Indian community and in relation to its own cultural inheritance, 'Through the retention of a Brahminic ideal Indian women were expected to mirror themselves after the image of Sita, the virtuous, long-suffering and faithful bride of Rama' (Mohammed 1998a: 13). However, while women were under historical pressure to be obedient, subservient and compliant in line with the Hindu mythological precedent of Sita, whom Mohammed argues 'embodies femininity, the ideal of female love and devotion and a lesson to all women on how they should behave in their daily lives' (Mohammed 1998b: 395), there is also evidence that they became double agents in their dealings with this history.

Rather than being traced to an unbroken line of Indian femininity that guaranteed passivity, subservience and loyalty to patriarchal structures, Mohammed argues that the route through which women of Indian descent in Trinidad connected to Indian women on the subcontinent was also constructed through feminist politics. As she points out, the 'tradition of an anti-colonial female militancy in India was conveyed to Trinidad through the medium of newspapers in a section entitled 'Indian News and Views' regularly featured in the Trinidad *Guardian* on Thursday and Sunday' (Mohammed 1998b: 13). In this sense, Indian-Caribbean women's subjectivity may be regarded as oppositional, not only in relation to that of African Caribbean women, but also in its structuring of oppositional agency.

As these critical interventions demonstrate, a serious challenge to the naturalised image of the docile and enduring Indian woman is currently underway and it is interesting that this challenge is often informed by the 'other' earlier version of their identity that links their crossing of the *kala pani* with their abandonment of proscribed femininity. This alternative history of female subjectivity and sexuality has recently been recovered by feminist historians and critics in a wave of both literary and critical publications that I want to suggest can be read as a recent and ascendant critical moment in Caribbean literary history.

In one of the essays in the groundbreaking collection *Matikor: The Politics of Identity for Indo-Caribbean Women*, edited by Rosanne Kanhai, Nesha Haniff describes Indian women as Caribbean historical subjects in such a way as to completely explode the stereotypes that have dominated twentieth century cultural circuits.

> This early history of Indo-Caribbean women is diametrically opposed to the current perception of them as docile and submissive . . . These early indentured women were not only free to live with whomsoever they wished, but worked for their own money as well . . . These early indentured women knew that they would pay with their lives for doing as they pleased and yet they continued, undeterred . . . Today . . . like their early indentured mothers, they are reasserting their sexual freedom.
>
> (Haniff 1999: 21)

Historians have not achieved anything like an easy consensus on the issues around indentured women's freedoms, but research on their position as wage earners on the estates, their participation in strikes and demonstrations, their possible polyandry and their cultural capital as 'bride price' (because of the relative scarcity of women compared to men) does need to be accounted for alongside the acute suffering and deprivations that also shaped women's experience during this period (Angrosino 1976; Reddock 1986; Shepherd 1995). What is particularly interesting in relation to my study is the way in which Haniff's narrative implies a conjecture between the indentureship period and the contemporary period in terms of Indian-Caribbean women's freedom, in particular their sexual freedom.[13]

I want to work from Haniff's point of conjecture to explore the strategic foregrounding of sexuality in the discourses of both representations and rights as they pertain to Indian-Caribbean women in the present, critical moment at the beginning of the twenty-first century. I will discuss Caribbean sexuality as a transgressive and liberatory politics of identity in more detail in the following chapter, but it cannot go unmentioned here that Indian-Caribbean women, who have consistently had their identities defined in relation to the norms and transgressions of sexual conduct as represented variously by colonial, African-Caribbean, Hindu and Muslim edicts (among others) have seemingly elected to frame their own stories and critical interventions around this issue as they come to both literary and critical visibility. I do not wish to argue that these works are acts of 'writing back' to twentieth-century Indian-Caribbean female identity; rather, I want to read them as acts of 'writing forward' and also, crucially, of 'writing sideways' too, and therefore as acts that establish a new archive of creative identities which enables both an emancipatory and a transformative poetics of representation and relation.

My focus is not intended to discredit the very important studies of Indian-Caribbean women's critical invisibility during the twentieth century, such as Ramabai Espinet's important early essay 'The Invisible Woman in West Indian literature' (1989) or Jeremy Poynting's survey work that sought to account for the relative silence, as well as tentative voicing, of an Indian-Caribbean female literary tradition in the 1980's.

> The domestic, educational, occupational and social disadvantages suffered by Indo-Caribbean women are reason enough not to be surprised at the small quantity of imaginative writing they have produced. To date some forty individuals have contributed poems and stories to local journals; one collection of short stories and a dozen slim volumes of poetry have been published; as yet no novel has appeared.
>
> (Poynting, 1985)

These essays helped to offer an explanatory narrative for the low profile of Indian-Caribbean women writers in the last century. They have also attended to important early works and it is only through a recognition and reading of these that we can avoid another mistaken narrative of spontaneous genesis.

However, for the purpose of plotting an important moment in contemporary Caribbean literary history, I want rather to follow the critical direction established in Rosanne Kanhai's essay, 'The Masala Stone Sings: Poetry, Performance and Film by Indo-Caribbean Women'. Like Kanhai, 'My concern here is less with the perceived silence than with the coming to voice' (Kanhai 1999: 211). In this essay Kanhai begins to plot, through her reading of selected works in the *Creation Fire* poetry anthology and Michelle Mohabeer's film, *Coconut/Cane and Cutlass*, a new critical moment in which Indian-Caribbean women's cultural production is beginning to achieve critical prominence and acclaim and to assert its own representational terrain. In a bold and provocative move, she draws on *matikor* as a cultural locale from which to imagine this terrain.

> Matikor – a pre-wedding fertility performance in traditional Hindu weddings where women get together to sing and perform sexually suggestive dances and to indulge in good-natured ribaldry in a safe, closed space.
>
> (Kanhai 1999: 226)

There are two aspects of *matikor* that need to be addressed in relation to my construction of double agents and the relevance of this identity category to Indian-Caribbean women. First, that Kanhai deliberately chooses a Hindu (Indian) cultural practice through which to stage the assertion of sexual agency and therefore foregrounds the way in which Indian-Caribbean women have been able to structure resistance and rebellion within, as well as against, the licence of dominant cultural imperatives. Second, that it is the arena of the erotic that is invoked as transformative and liberatory for women.

> This erotic is a meeting place of history and experience, of the material, the carnal and the spiritual. It is that distinctly female space from which Indo-Caribbean women transform, yet maintain, themselves as they make art. From here feminism can begin.
>
> (Kanhai 1999: 234)

Mobilising the very discourse that has sought to define and confine Indian-Caribbean women within the social and cultural spheres, Kanhai offers the site of oppression as that of emancipation and Indian-Caribbean women are figured almost as sexual double agents.

My aim here is to draw attention to the specific critical paradigm that Indian-Caribbean women scholars have constructed in recent years in order to enable new readings of historical subjectivities, as well as important literary and cultural texts. I will continue my discussion of Indian-Caribbean women's fiction in relation to this subject in the following chapter with a reading of Oona Kempadoo's novel *Buxton Spice*, which is explicit in its depiction of female sexual awakening, and a discussion of Shani Mootoo's playful and disturbing representations of Indian women's sexuality in her texts *Out on Main Street* and *Cereus Blooms as Night*, respectively.

It is nevertheless important to acknowledge that *matikor*, although tremendously important as a marker of critical history, has remained something of a marginal study within recent analyses of Caribbean women's writing and that both the excellent essays that comprise the volume and the radical act of imagining which positions the Hindu ritual of *matikor* as a site of liberation and feminism have not as yet had much response from critics working from a Black Atlantic or African-Caribbean paradigm. In many ways the two paradigms operate without reaching into each other's domain, and this is potentially limiting in terms of an engagement with a tradition of women's regional writing across all ethnic groups. Nevertheless, as I am keen to point out, this is very much a recent development and as the work of scholars such as Espinet, Kanhai, Puri, Rampersad and others comes into wider circulation, the possibilities of the *matikor* paradigm can be developed further.

As my reading of these creative and critical texts highlights, in this critical moment Indian-Caribbean women are powerfully reclaiming their sexual subjectivity as a site of agency, creativity and integrity. By translating the erotic power of *matikor* into intellectual and literary representations, Indian-Caribbean's women's writing and critical voices become visible on their own terms. More than this however, the opening up of new terms on which their rights and representations can be discussed also provides the opportunity for a new conversation between Caribbean women to take place concerning the agendas of feminist practice. It is in order to address this possibility that I want to conclude this chapter with a discussion of dougla poetics as an indigenous feminist theory that both contests and deconstructs those dominant political and theoretical discourses that frame Caribbean women's alliances as always inevitably fractured along ethnic divides, and their interests and enfranchisement as set in competition with each other.

Indigenous feminist theorising and a dougla poetics

The strong emergence of literary and critical discourses by Indian-Caribbean women has been a crucial recent development within Caribbean literary history. Kanhai's deployment of *matikor* as an identity performance through which Indian-Caribbean women can assert their presence, difference and agency is useful to the act of imagining ground from which Indian-Caribbean women writers and critics can engage in a conversation with each other. Yet while *matikor* implies an empowering space shared by women from a particular ethnic group (although not restricted to this), dougla poetics very clearly refuses the idea of any discourse that privileges ethnic or racial origins.

In the first critical voicing of this idea, Shalini Puri is deliberately qualified in her framing of the ethical possibilities of the term 'dougla poetics'.

> I am making a relatively circumscribed claim that elaborations of a dougla poetics and the figure of the dougla could provide the vocabulary for figuring disallowed Indian identities; furthermore, they

could offer ways of reframing the problematic of black-Indian party politics, race and gender relations.

(Puri 1997: 161)

Nevertheless, the modesty of her approach does not obscure the ambition of this proposal for a transformative model through which the historically embedded oppositional identities of African-Caribbean and Indian-Caribbean can be invested with new cultural and social meanings. Against the reiteration of the dougla as a figure of regression and contamination within the purist rhetoric of extreme cultural nationalist groups, and against a history of continuing antagonistic relations between Indians and Africans in both Trinidad and Guyana, Puri chooses the figure of 'interracial contact' as the figure of ethical potential and of hope. Again the re-routing of Indian women's sexual history and power is implicit in this concept.

> Keeping in mind, then, that the original meaning of the word 'dougla' was 'bastard', or 'illegitimate', I suggest that one might think of a dougla poetics as a means for articulating potentially progressive cultural identities de-legitimized by both the dominant culture and the Mother Culture.
>
> (Puri 1997: 161)

In a later, expanded version of her argument, Puri claims that 'the very anxiety surrounding the figure of the dougla is a measure of its radical possibilities' (Puri 2004: 220). In this framing, the dougla becomes a double agent through which the discourses of cultural hostility and mutual suspicion are transformed into an emancipatory rhetoric of relationality.

In her own work on the debates and issues concerning relations between Africans and Indians within Trinidadian society and the way in which these relate to cultural as well as political discourses, Sheila Rampersad has added her own inflection on this concept that she terms 'dougla feminism'.

> In my understanding, a dougla feminism does not seek to replace dominant Afro-centric perspectives with Indo-centric perspectives and indeed must guard against overemphasising what Guyanese feminist, Kamala Kempadoo . . . calls 'a politics of separate identity'. Instead it privileges inter-racial Indian/African concerns . . . and concentrates . . . on how an inter-racial space that pays equal attention to both groups, can be forged.
>
> (Rampersad 2000: 164)

In a later piece, Rampersad moves on from this elaboration to a definition that enables douglarisation to be recognised as a process in which

African-Caribbean women are also engaged. This creative engagement with Puri's conceptualisation itself offers an important model of feminist scholarly exchange and, at the same time, makes a very valuable contribution to the establishment of a feminist model of horizontal exchange between women of different ethnic groups. Through a reading of Merle Hodge's *Crick Crack, Monkey* and *For the Life of Laetitia*, Rampersad argues that

> The dougla poetics in her creative expressions announces itself not only in the magnanimity and intimacy with which she treats Indian figures, but in the deliberate yet delicate evolution of her novels' capacity to reach into the Indian community in Trinidad in the configuring of 'folk' community.
>
> (Rampersad 2002:150)

There is already evidence that dougla poetics is the starting point for a new conversation between Caribbean women (see Kanhai 1999; Reddock 1994b). As both a feminist epistemology and a feminist politics that is indigenous to the Caribbean, dougla poetics is a timely theoretical intervention that privileges both inclusivity and horizontality.

My purpose in this chapter has been to signal the dominant critical positions and agendas through which discussions of Caribbean women's writing and a feminist poetics came to be both configured and contested in the early 1990s and the critical moment of Black Atlantic and postcolonial feminism critique. I have sought to restore a very small portion of a complex and diverse women's (literary) history still to be recovered and to put the ideas of double colonisation and invisible women, both of which were crucial to the momentum of early feminist research, under scrutiny for their value in the present critical moment when both historical and marginal texts and writers are achieving more attention. My focus on the recent scholarly interventions by Indian-Caribbean women writers and scholars that offer new and promising critical paradigms through which Caribbean feminism and its discontents can be re-imagined and re-grounded is both a deliberate realignment of the marginal as central and an acknowledgement of all those Caribbean double agents who have operated so powerfully and creatively under the 'veils' of historical, poetic, mythological and social orthodoxies throughout the twentieth century.

Notes

1 See for example, *Women and Change in the Caribbean* (1993) edited by Janet Momsen and Rhoda Reddock's (1994a) *Women, Labour and Politics in Trinidad and Tobago: A History*. Christine Barrow's 1998 edited collection, *Caribbean Portraits: Essays on Gender Ideologies and Identities*, brings together multidisciplinary feminist scholarship.

2 Scholars interested in the recovery of Indian Trinidadian women's voices will find many fascinating peep-holes that can be developed in Kris Rampersad's inspirational 2002 study.

3 See also Marson 1937a and 1937b.

4 Anthony Boxhill, 'The beginnings to 1929', in King 1979: 41.

5 The phrase 'the personal is political' was first coined by Carol Hanisch in 1970. Works such as Adrienne Rich's 'When We Dead Awaken: Writing as Revision' (1979) and Elaine Showalter's essay 'Towards a Feminist Poetics' (1982) worked this concept in relation to women's writing.

6 For a reading of this sequence see Donnell (1997).

7 For a reading of double agency within Kincaid's *Lucy* and in particular her resistance to the dominant theoretical paradigms deployed to read Caribbean women's writing, see Donnell 1992.

8 See Rampersad 2002: 224–225 for more details.

9 See Brinda J. Mehta 1999 and 2000.

10 Lakshmi Persaud's 2003 novel, *For the Love of My Name*, also chronicles the history of Guyana during the Forbes Burnham era through an allegorical tale in the fictional location of Maya. I find this the least engaging and rewarding of Persaud's novels as the wonderful but simple details of recovered experience that characterise her previous works are ideologically over-determined and divested of literary power.

11 Her inscription of a queer Indian-Caribbean male identity is clearly also part of the book's radical agenda. Indeed, there is so much more that can be said about this wonderful novel than my strategic discussion here can allow. Its interest in sexuality, in violence, in food, in the creole, the visual and the genealogical all merit detailed discussion.

12 In this narrative that cannot go forward without going back, Mona is quite literally depicted as occupying the realm of spying and espionage that I earlier related to the figure of the double agent. As a child she is initially disappointed on Christmas morning when her greatly awaited camera turns out to be a pair of field glasses her father has won on a racing trip. However, she soon realises that 'everything looked clearer and bigger when I looked through the field glasses, and I liked that' (Espinet 2003: 32). She freely admits to spying on Miss Lady and the way in which her vision has been shaped by her visual code-switching from the long view to the zoom lens is integral to the novel's exploration of Indian-Caribbean woman as historical subjects. Mona also confesses to spying through the rotting floorboard at Grandma Lil's house, 'Lying down there, I was completely invisible, completely happy' (Espinet 2003: 35).

13 For an account of women's lives and gender relations in Trinidad during the post-indentureship period see Mohammed 1995 and Shepherd 1995.

4 Sexing the subject

Writing and the politics of Caribbean sexual identity

It was a while before we came to realize that our place was the very house of difference, rather than the security of any one particular difference.

(Audre Lorde)

Gayness is not generally seen as a human rights issue, and where it is, it is felt that it runs second to issues such as violence and the underperformance of the economy. The tendency to deem gay rights as secondary to other more compelling issues discloses a lack of understanding of the interconnection of rights.

('Lawson Williams')

The demands on Caribbean literary criticism have clearly changed over the decades and it has been a central project of this book both to map and to theorise those changes, as well as to offer alternatives to the pathways cut through these writings by the dominant political–critical coordinates of the past. However, this chapter, more than others, ventures off the map of established Caribbean literary histories to suggest a new and urgent demand that critics should address in their theorisations of difference, as well as an exciting body of writing that is just beginning to be documented and analysed. It focuses on a recent and important development in Anglocreole Caribbean literature – namely the articulation and inscription of diverse sexual identities within a body of creative writing.

I wish to argue that, taken collectively, writing on this subject can be seen to have called into question the dominant matrix of race, ethnicity, gender, class and nation through which Caribbean literary forms and cultural identities have been discussed for the past decade, both locating a significant absence within models of identification and supplementing this model by writing sexual identities onto the Caribbean matrix. In order to make this argument, this chapter will offer an overview of writings dealing with this subject, drawing some broad conclusions about the different dimensions of the debates relating to sexuality in the region, as well as a detailed discussion of several texts that I regard to be crucial to this new articulation. One of the aims of this chapter is to position the period from the 1990s to the present day as a new critical moment and one that has, to date, received very little attention.

The conservative Anglican Christianity that dominates most Anglocreole Caribbean societies makes the discussion of sex and sexuality a sensitive issue, although often this conservative attitude sits uncomfortably alongside sexual overstatements to create 'the contradictory picture of a Caribbean sexual landscape in which attitudes to sex and sexuality veer between both poles – of "decency/decorum" and "slackness/crudity"' (de Caires Narain 2002b: 112). All the same, the voices of Anglican authority, as well as those of orthodox Rastafarian, Hindu and Muslim positions held in various islands, create a less complex picture with regards to same-sex loving and discussions of homosexuality are consistently socially explosive. It is perhaps no surprise that against this landscape the vast majority of Caribbean narratives have been 'innocent', avoiding any direct or explicit discussions of sexuality. Both the genre of national epics (Vic Reid's *New Day* (1949), Earl Lovelace's *Salt* (1996) and Walcott's *Omeros* (1990) come to mind) and the focus on childhood experience in many of the region's canonical narratives have created distinct sexual silences.[1]

It would certainly be hard to dispute that one of the overriding tropes of canonical Caribbean writing from the 1950s onwards by both men and women has been the focus on childhood and the perspective of the child narrator. From Lamming's G in *In the Castle of My Skin* (1953) to Hodge's Tee in *Crick, Crack, Monkey* (1970), Caribbean fiction has worked with the child's experience and through the child's eye to very powerful effect, allowing the complex power structures of colonial institutions and ideologies to be exposed at their most basic level through the child's encounter with the school, the church, the cinema and the people of the communities in which they live. Whilst the diverse critical possibilities offered by these texts have now been explored far beyond the crude interpretations of the Jamesian framework of national allegories (with the growth of the nation mirroring that of the protagonist), I would argue that this core of child-hood narratives has nevertheless limited the critical response to Caribbean literature in one important way: it has arrested the discussion of sexuality. When Lamming, Hodge and Kincaid leave G, Tee and Annie at the beginning of their journey away from their countries of birth, they also leave them on the threshold of adolescence. These texts focus on the growth of political, cultural and even gender awareness at the expense of that other kind of transition, the development of a sexual identity, which is what actually marks the crossing from child to adult world.[2] Indeed, it may be possible to argue that their sexual identities remained a literary unspoken for almost twenty years.

By focusing on texts that have spoken into this silence and opened up discussions and representations of sexuality, this chapter seeks to bring sexuality to the fore, alongside race, gender, and class, in order to argue that all these identificatory categories are mutually affective, and that our understanding of all would be poorer if we chose to ignore or suppress one, as would the possibilities for a politics of social change that has remained so central to both the projects of writing and of criticism in the Caribbean. In recent years, the urgent and highly-charged public and political debates over sexual identity within the region have created what I take to be a critical moment in redefining the boundaries of national and cultural identity. To date it has been popular cultural forms that have been at the centre of these debates, with the 1992 Buju Banton 'battyman' affair at the very eye of the storm.[3] I want to demonstrate that during this same period Caribbean writers, significantly based outside the region, have begun publishing texts that address issues concerning sexual self-determination and sexual diversity.

This chapter seeks to offer readings of these texts that alert us to the way in which the issues and debates concerning sexuality in the critical moment of the twenty-first century often demand representation and awareness of the deeply embedded historical processes that have determined the social and cultural meanings of sexuality in the Caribbean alongside and in articulation with those of race, gender and class. To my mind, these texts enable a discussion of the way in which sexual difference has been shaped by and incorporated into both colonial societies and postcolonial Caribbean nations, as well as the various discourses and practices – social, legal, cultural – through which these societies have produced legitimate sexual subjects. In one sense my argument is that certain of these texts historicise the present, often through the presentation of strategic issues (such as the sexual relations between Indian women and African men) that operate in the overlapping registers of both current and historical cultural anxiety. In another sense, these texts revisit the past, which is also a literary past, in order to make visible the politics that operate around sexuality by demonstrating how specific cultural practices play into wider relations of power. I also want to position some of these writings alongside recent political, legal and cultural developments concerning the governance of sexuality in the Caribbean region in order to assess to what extent they present interventions in the representation and understanding of sexual self-determination.

However, although I have argued that sexual silences were prevalent in the majority of Caribbean writings until the 1990s, this is not to suggest that representations of sex were absent from earlier publications, but rather that sexual identity was not put forward for critical scrutiny or debate in the same way as national, ethnic or even gender identity. It is true that Selvon's novels of West Indians in London, *The Lonely Londoners* and *Moses Ascending*, published in 1956 and 1975 respectively, acknowledged the sexual tension that played into other relational orders (of race, class, gender), but the sexist jokes and affectionately comical stereotypes of Caribbean masculinity that can be found in Moses and his comrades do not raise particularly interesting or serious questions about sexuality beyond the awareness that although men talk about (white) women as sexual objects their relations with them are far from empowering or satisfactory.[4] In the community of Earl Lovelace's *The Dragon Can't Dance* (1979), sex is not ignored: 'they rested themselves before they gathered themselves for the dancing and drinking and fucking and joking and masquerading of Carnival' (116). As this quotation demonstrates, having sex is just one of the things that people do in this wonderfully synthetic and tightly-woven story of a Trinidadian town. However, although the novel is attentive to the power that Sylvia gains through her beauty and her body, the question of sexuality and particularly of women's sexuality – a commodity that most women must learn to trade in – is only addressed from a normatively masculine perspective. I want to argue that textual discussions of sexuality are now taking a more direct and more sophisticated approach. This chapter is concerned to demonstrate how recent writings can be read as participating in the struggle for the recognition of diverse sexualities within the terms of national and regional identity.

It is a central objective of this chapter to bring writers and writings that represent same-sex relations into the tradition of Anglocreole Caribbean literature. However, the terms through which to enact this reconfiguration remain problematic at the level of language, as well as of cultural politics. Caribbean writers do not adopt the terminology of the West – queer, homosexual, gay, lesbian – in order to name this experience or desire. Their writings are rather characterised by an un-naming of this desire and sexual practice. In my own analysis I do refer to homosexuality, although I am aware that to deploy this term is possibly to fix sexual binaries and therefore close off the possibilities of more fluid and plural sexual attachments and behaviours that are often rendered in the literature. Indeed, while the silencing of queer subjects may appear to be a consequence of a recalcitrant subjectivity seeking to survive in a homophobic context in some instances, it is also important to acknowledge that any gesture of naming may in fact make the positions and choices with regard to sexuality more limited and closed rather than more open and visible. Not identifying with the term homosexuality may also be a choice to opt out of a particular (western) issue-based politics, as well as to deny a radically normative sexuality. The way in which the vocabularies of self-imagination influence the possibilities for self-understanding should not be underestimated and I remain open to the idea that 'imported' western terminologies may actually have enacted epistemic violence to the possibilities of articulating a culturally specific vocabulary of sexual relations. Nevertheless in the absence of any affirmative term for this order of relations with the text, at times I have resorted to the labels queer, homosexual and homoerotic.

Sex and the plantation

From important early work such as *Black Skins, White Masks* by Frantz Fanon (1986, first published in 1952), that linked the project of anti-colonialism to an understanding of psychoanalysis, to Kumkum Sangari's groundbreaking work *Politics of the Possible: Essays on Gender, History, Narratives, Colonial English* (1999) and Anne McClintock's *Imperial Leather: Race Gender and Sexuality in the Colonial Contest* (1995) which also introduced feminist criticism into this connected orbit, postcolonial theorists and critics have outlined the ways in which the fundamental inequalities sponsored by imperialism (from slavery and colonialism through to tourism) mapped themselves onto the axes of sexual, as well as economic and political, power. It is nothing new to point out that the distorting and damaging entwining of racial and sexual preferences that licensed the exploitation of black bodies and the idealisation of white (particularly female) bodies was bequeathed by slavery and perpetuated by colonial plantocracies. The study of this history is not my interest here, but nevertheless it seems important to signal, albeit briefly, the way in which the dynamics of sexual representation were established in relation to the Caribbean.

In *Colonial Desire: Hybridity in Theory, Culture and Race*, Robert Young discusses Edward Long's notorious *History of Jamaica* (1774) and the way in which Long's 'racism constantly teeters into what has now become the familiar structure of sexual attraction and repulsion' (Young 1995: 150). As Young points out, Long writes both luridly and disapprovingly of 'African' women who are, to him, as 'libidinous and shameless as monkies, or baboons' and cites their essential difference from white women in terms of sexual desire as explanation for the troubling preference that white men demonstrated for attachments to black women at this time (Young 1995: 150).[5] However, while it is Young's project to examine the way in which the cultural construction of race has been negotiated alongside ideas of sexual desire and difference, my own interest here lies in examining how Long's colonial discourse constructs sexual identity as always already determined by those structures and vocabularies governing the difference of race. It is not surprising, given the ongoing inequalities and tensions operating around race and ethnicity in the Caribbean, that an examination of the way in which race and sexuality operate as articulated categories is still the focus of most Caribbean writings that approach the subject of sex at all. Indeed, although many contemporary women writers and poets have worked quite explicitly to address and redress the sexual objectification of the black woman normalised within colonial discourse, there is a persistent and often disturbing reciprocity between the difficult issues of race and sexuality in Caribbean writings. The colonial matrix of desire, fantasy and violence often returns in a postcolonial context. My purpose in looking back to Long and the tradition of colonial inscription that he stands within is not to suggest a straightforward textual continuity in the representations of Caribbean sexuality that needs to be addressed, but rather to situate the link between historical circumstance, the operations of power and the representational strategies that charge the issue of sexuality in the Caribbean in particular ways at particular moments. Reading Long helps us to witness how and why the category of African-Caribbean women's sexuality as threatening and divisive came into being. Recent writings by Caribbean authors, I would argue, help us to understand that the political, economic and legal sanctions under which sexual oppression operated historically remain relevant to discussions of sexual oppression and exploitation today.

Although a body of writing that shows a primary engagement with the subject of sexuality has only emerged in the last decade, it is significant to note that it has returned to what we might construct as the primal scene of colonisation – the plantation. Although, as Rosamond King points out, as far back as 1917, A. R. F. Webber's novel *Those That Be in Bondage*, set on a Guyanese sugar estate, described the plantation as a place 'where the whole atmosphere reeks of sex and its trying complications', there is no detailed engagement with this dimension of the struggle for power or even existence within the work itself.[6] David Dabydeen's first collection of poetry, *Slave Song* (1984), has since given a powerful voice, importantly in Guyanese creole, to the way in which the sexual energetics of the plantation were governed by obscene racial fantasies about potency and purity. 'Largely concerned with an exploration of the erotic energies of the colonial experience, ranging from corrosive to a lyrical sexuality' (Dabydeen 1984: 10), this collection succeeded in rendering the sordid and distorting imaginings through which desire finds articulation in an environment of exploitation, fear and hatred: an environment which experiences a 'norm of pain' (Dabydeen 1984: 15).

Dabydeen's title may suggest one historical moment, but in fact this collection of poems spans the centuries from slavery to the 1970s, and its ambitious chronology speaks directly to the fact that the operations of racism are an issue to which Caribbean writers must return in order to begin the reinvention of both community and sexuality. The impeccable scholarly notes that supplement these poems, tell us that 'For Mala' is concerned with 'the main heritage of the Colonial Era, which is racial conflict' (Dabydeen 1984: 46). This poem documents the discovery in a river of the body of a young girl who had been raped and murdered during the Wismar Riots, the culmination of the 1964 racial clashes between those of African and East Indian descent in Guyana, during which the whole village's Indian population was made homeless by fire attacks, and violent and sexual assaults took place on a terrifying scale. The poem moves from the stark description of the assault Mala suffered, 'When deh bin done wid she, deh shove bruk –|Top bottle up she front jess fo fun, fo see she squirm', to the dream of a peaceful and racially united society, 'An sitar and steelband go sound wheh gunfire bin a deh'. The violence enacted against Mala also connects this poem back to a history of violence and subjection articulated in a number of other lyrics in this collection in which male slaves fantasise about raping the white mistress. In this way, the collection establishes how, during slavery and even today, sexual difference was powerfully, sometimes fatally, mapped onto other orders of difference established by the colonial process. The collection documents therefore how the humiliations of physical intimacy, the degradations of sexual fantasies, and the enactments of sexual violence become historically embedded in an unequal culture dominated by the operations of racism from the era of slavery right through to the late twentieth century. These poems, along with V. S. Naipaul's notorious *Guerrillas*, may be seen to initiate a discussion of the 'pornography of Empire' within Caribbean writing that Clem Maharaj develops in his short plantation novel, *The Dispossessed* (1992).

Like Dabydeen, Maharaj grew up on sugar estates and draws on this environment in his novel set on a sugar estate in the 1950s, although it is significant that Maharaj's narrative is set in Trinidad rather than Guyana, where racial clashes have been more fierce and sustained. *The Dispossessed* is centrally concerned with how the power dynamics operating between people of European/Indian/African and mixed descent on a bankrupt plantation come to crisis regarding negotiations over sexual availability. In terms of its structure and characterisation, the novel sits comfortably alongside much earlier works by Earl Lovelace and George Lamming, with each chapter taking the name and examining the preoccupation of one character, and the communal identity of the estate emerging as the novel's central motif. What is distinctive about Maharaj's work and what marks it out as emerging at this critical moment is the explicit discussion of the sexual dimensions of power within a plantation economy. Maharaj may be seen to be revisiting something of a literary past when, as in Lamming's *In the Castle of My Skin* and Lovelace's *The Dragon Can't Dance*, community is depicted as strong and worthwhile even though inevitably fractured by the powerplay of race. However, I want to argue that his strategic concentration on issues of sexual exploitation and trans-racial consensual relations enables Maharaj to connect his own moment at the end of the twentieth century to an almost continuous history of complex sexual dynamics rooted in the plantation since the seventeenth century. By staging specific connections between the social meanings attributed to sexual behaviours across this historical reach, Maharaj constructs representational terrain on which some of the sexual silences of the twenty-first century Caribbean can be heard.

Although it is bankruptcy that provides the central metaphor for this text, it is through the operations and abuse of sexual power that the moral bankruptcy of the characters and their emotional ruin is revealed. The strain placed on every member of the community by the financial collapse of the estate has led to the breakdown of kinship bonds and all other bonds of loyalty, responsibility and protection towards others. As the narrative declares, 'Love and respect were absent in this world' (Maharaj 1992: 38). It is a world where mothers and fathers abandon their children; spouses and lovers betray each other; religious men succumb to lust; and the strong prey on the weak. The most crude manipulation of sexual power arises when Goddard, the white overseer put in to manage the remaining labour tasks on the estate, starts to trade sexual favours from individual women in return for a week's employment for the group. Although Maharaj figures this racialised dimension of sexual power in the 1950s, the trading of sexual favours and women's bodies for capital gain clearly has strong historical roots in the Caribbean, as Kamala Kempadoo, drawing on the work of Beckles and Reddock, discusses.

> In times of economic slump on plantations (particularly in British colonies), when blacks, both men and women, were expected to provide for themselves or to bring in wages through work outside the plantation, 'the number of slave women placed on the urban market as prostitutes by sugar planters would rapidly increase' and in towns 'masters and mistresses would frequently send out female slaves as prostitutes for ships' crew' (Beckles 1989: 142–3). Reddock reports that in Trinidad, 'For the most part women were hired out as domestic slaves, field labourers, as concubines, to temporary male European settlers, or were made to work as petty traders or prostitutes.'
>
> (Kempadoo 2003: 167–8)

In Maharaj's novel unpaid sexual labour is the gateway to paid employment and the income flow of all the women is dependent on the acquiescence of each. Hitler, the leader of the women's gang, tells Sadwine, 'What ah asking yh to do is foh all ah we survival . . . me and yuh is one' (Maharaj 1992: 26).

These women are not able to turn 'their weakness into strength by capitalizing upon white men's sexual desire for them' (Kerr 1995: 210).[7] Indeed, the women are not only disempowered within the conventional labour market by their sexual contract with Goddard, but their forced sexual relations with him endanger their consensual relations with fellow workers. For Sadwine, the estate beauty, whose marriage to the holy man Sadhu was against her wishes and in payment for her sister's dowry, her affair with Harry is an escape and a rebellion. Although the fact that they meet in the latrine, 'the stench of shit permeating every illicit meeting' (Maharaj 1992: 21), graphically depicts the denial of any space for romance in this fictional world, their meetings are genuinely joyful and moments of meaningful contact for both. However, when Harry finds out that Sadwine too had to succumb to Goddard's sexual bribery he rejects her and commits suicide.

In his head, he knew what made her visit Goddard, but in his heart, where it hurt the most, he felt she had betrayed not only him, but all men of East Indian origin. She was now stained for life and her status in the village would be destroyed. An Indian woman in appearance only was fair game for anyone of any race.

(Maharaj 1992: 94)

Harry's reproach of Sadwine marks one of several moments in the novel when Maharaj seems to raise the historical stakes of the narrative. This reflection connects Harry's personal hurt to the collective humiliation of East Indian men – a humiliation inflicted by the indenture and plantation systems; the lack of attachment to land; the pressures placed on traditional family structures and gender identities by the demands of the labour market; the residual doubts about the morality of many Indian women who came to the Caribbean as indentured labourers (only one third were married women who travelled with their husbands) and the general powerlessness over their economic and social conditions. More interestingly to my mind, Harry's comment that Sadwine is now marked as sexually available to 'anyone of any race' points to the issue of sexual relations between ethnic groups that remains highly charged in Trinidad today. Within the narrative, when the news of Sadwine's 'strategic prostitution' reaches the community, she is taken as being sexually available to others. Raped, she dies a lonely death at the roadside. The ramifications of both colonial forms of sexual exploitation and sexual violence against women legitimated by racialised interests are, as in Dabydeen's depiction, fatal.[8]

As Shalini Puri has pointed out:

It is one of the great ironies of decolonisation in Trinidad that racial tensions have taken the form of lateral hostility between blacks and Indians . . . rather than vertical hostility directed by blacks and Indians together against the French Creole elite, the white plantocracy, or transnational capital.

(Puri 2004: 172)

Yet, while the violence done to women across racial divides that is found both in this text and in Dabydeen's 'Mala', are important representations of this lateral hostility, the issue of consenting sexual relations between these two groups is much more fraught and far less commonly discussed. I want to argue that in its depiction of Indian women who choose to take African men as partners, the narrative enacts a kind of doubling of the historical reference zone in which the racialised relations of sexual power signify as both past and present anxiety.

Given that statistics suggest that very few unions between African men and Indian women did take place on the plantation, Maharaj's novel appears to represent a strategically disproportionate amount of women seeking to break this 'ultimate taboo'.[9] In the relatively small East Indian cane-cutting community of the Highlands Estate, Eddie and Vernon's mothers, Sankar's first wife and Mona, Sonny Boy's wife, all choose African partners. When Mona declares her ethnic migration to Sonny Boy – 'Ah turn Creole now, no more slaving and sweating foh me, ah tired being a coolie ooman, ah want to enjoy meself' (Maharaj 1992: 112) – she is clearly rejecting the traditionally constructed Indian model of womanhood and the gender politics that govern her life. However, her gesture immediately after speaking – 'she kissed the tall, strong-looking man nearest to her' (Maharaj 1992: 112) – confirms that is through sexual 'betrayal' that this rejection is made most dramatically and finally.

Sankar, the protagonist, reflects on this same 'betrayal' when he thinks about his first wife who ran off with an African man:

> He did not blame his wife for running away; the life on an estate was a hard one and few outsiders felt able to endure it. But for her to run away with a person of a different race, that was the bit he could hardly face. He felt totally ashamed and humiliated. His wife not only let him down but his whole race. She had broken the ultimate taboo and he took the burden of guilt and remorse for what she had done.
>
> (Maharaj 1992: 53)

This sensitive issue of electing sexual partners across the Indian-African divide is taken seriously by this novel, as is the violence against women who make this choice, including rape, which seems to have cultural sanction.

From our critical moment, it is not insignificant that Maharaj repeatedly focuses on the figure of the vulnerable or racially contaminated woman and the fear of sexual unions – whether forced or consensual – between African men and Indian women. This issue has been central to the arguments about threats to ethnic 'purity' and claims for an ethnically distinct power base being put forward by elements of the orthodox Hindu Sanatan Dharma Maha Sabha organisation in contemporary Trinidad.[10] Sheila Rampersad's important work in this area has drawn attention to the way in which 'ethnic animosity and control of female sexuality became one and the same in conservative discourses and that Indian/African antagonisms are played out on the bodies of Indian women' (Rampersad 2000: 165–6).[11] In this critical moment, then, Maharaj's representations of Indian women as electing to take African men as sexual partners appear very destabilising to those claims, as well as to the notions of ethnic separatism and hostility that such claims support.

Another resonant figuration that crosses into the concerns of this critical moment with regard to issues of sexuality can be found in the depiction of same-sex relations between men. In contrast to the brutality of Goddard, the novel depicts the acute emotional and sexual vulnerability of Donald, the white man who formerly owned the Highlands Estate. It could be argued that following the collapse of his estate Donald is no different from the other men on the bankrupt piece of land in that, like them, 'he resorted to drinking and lovemaking to ease the pain of failure' (Maharaj 1992: 67). Notably, it is the fact that he craves comfort, love and sexual intimacy with another man, his employee Blue Jean, that marks him out more than his whiteness. Although the co-dependency that exists between master and servant has long been acknowledged and analysed, the sexual dimension portrayed here is particularly engaging as Donald's tenderness towards Blue Jean, 'My love, come here and give me a cuddle' (Maharaj 1992: 35), reveals a horizontal reaching out across hierarchies of race and class which is made both more possible by his own loss of economic power, and also less possible as he now lacks the means and status to guarantee sexual favours. It is also significant that, against his own emotional inclinations, Blue Jean rejects his lovemaking with Donald as 'white men an dere dirty habits' (Maharaj 1992: 36) and chooses not to leave Highlands Estate with Donald but to stay and publicly declare his wish to marry and have a family. This declaration marks a clear affirmation of the discourse of normative Indian-Caribbean masculinity. Blue Jean's assertion of his conjugal desire is clearly framed within a culture (of both the plantation and contemporary Trinidad) in which the queer subject must deny or erase his sexuality in order to preserve his ethnic and gendered coordinates on the Caribbean identity matrix.[12]

The repression of same-sex desire is also represented in the novel through the figure of Madan, who taunts Blue Jean for his relationship with Donald and yet who also 'tried to stifle the fear that he too might discover that the sort of sex Blue Jean practised might appeal to him' (Maharaj 1992: 38). Indeed, although the novel presents at least three men who express some form of homosexual desire, the prohibitions against homosexuality are strongly in evidence and Madan also tries to conform to the dominant attitude of intolerance and thereby of masculinity 'by conjuring up revulsion, the traditional method of dealing with that sort of sexuality' (Maharaj 1992: 38). No character is able to find fulfilment in a homosexual partnership: Donald leaves the estate isolated and bereft, Blue Jean fades into the background of estate life and Madan commits suicide.

I want to argue that Maharaj's *The Dispossessed* can be read therefore as engaging with the complex interactions between constructions of ethnicity and sexuality that are still prominent in Trinidad and Guyana, where the populations of people of East Indian descent equal those of African descent. Maharaj chooses to return to the critical, if not foundational, moment of the breakdown of the plantation system in the novel. However, his interest in tackling many of the cultural sore spots of contemporary Trinidad – violence against women and between ethnic groups; cross-cultural partnerships; sexual exploitation; homosexuality and homophobia – also locates his text in this present critical moment, a moment in which the issue of sexual power is being explored and discussed in new ways. Although the narrative structure and characterisation are in many ways familiar to readers of canonical Caribbean literature, the novel does not simply offer a backward glance. *The Dispossessed* represents sexual practices and beliefs from the accepted ideological ground of the 1950s in such a way as to bring them to particular attention in the contested grounds of the contemporary. Moreover, if the novel helps to locate the historical practices of sexual control and transaction that have informed the contemporary pathologies governing sexual restraint and taboo within certain groups and communities operating in Trinidad today, it also rehearses the dismal and fatal consequences of those practices.

Sexual openness and the liberation of women's pain

The sexual objectification of the black woman was central to the pornography of Empire and remained central to those modes of sexual exploitation that developed during the era of slavery and beyond. Its operations were perhaps most glaringly and disturbingly exemplified in the treatment of Saartje Baartman, the 'Hottentot Venus', whose body, and in particular buttocks and genitalia, were not only used as a 'live spectacle' of sexual difference and curiosity but also, after her death in 1815 and the dissection of her body by George Cuvier, as scientific 'proof' of African women's sexual lasciviousness.[13] This construction of a racialised trait had already been powerfully inscribed in colonial narratives such as Long's infamous *History of Jamaica*. The powerful matrix of epistemological and actual violence enacted upon the body of Saartje Baartman continued to exert pressure on black female bodies into the twentieth century, as the narrator in H. Nigel Thomas' *Spirits in the Dark* declares:

> For centuries White men had simply ordered Black women to sleep with them. His mother was a product of that, and his grandmother had been a broken woman because of it. All around him were people of all ages who were the results of such demand sex. *Drop yo' drawers – if you could afford them – or starve.*
>
> (Thomas 1993: 107)

Many texts by Caribbean writers address these dimensions of power and abuse as they figure in contemporary cultures and societies. Sexual violence against black women is explicitly dealt with in Dionne Brand's *Sans Souci* and also in Joan Riley's *The Unbelonging*. Both of these texts are concerned to document the operations of racism and sexism that continue to position black women as disempowered.

Indeed, given the historical context, the textual precedents and the contemporary cultural milieu of the Anglocreole Caribbean, it is perhaps not surprising that many of the texts recently published do not offer representations of a comfortable or liberating sexuality. Certainly, there have been several texts that bring sex into the Caribbean literary corpus, but it is possible to argue that what is distinctive about many of the recent writings that look at the question of sexual identity, and in particular of women's sexual identity, is the absence of sensuality and pleasure.

Evelyn O'Callaghan's important 1998 article, 'Compulsory Heterosexuality and Textual/Sexual Alternatives in Selected Texts by West Indian Women Writers', which offers a crucial early survey of the issues around sexuality in women's writing, concludes that

> Female sexuality in the work of West Indian prose writers is either shrouded in secrecy and shame, or a matter of casual and unfeeling acquiescence to male pressure. In most cases, it has negative consequences for the woman's economic, social and psychological well-being ... sex is rarely described with any degree of explicitness and certainly without ... joyful eroticism.
>
> (O'Callaghan 1998: 297)

Two texts which may help to map out the relations between the presence of shame and the absences of feeling and of joy and the wider fields of power in which sex and sexuality come into play for Caribbean women are Edwidge Danticat's *Breath, Eyes, Memory* (1994) and Jamaica Kincaid's *Lucy* (1990). Both texts have received a great deal of critical attention, but they nevertheless merit some discussion in the context of women's rewriting of Caribbean sexual histories, particularly the way in which these histories demand the release of historical trauma and pain.

Issues of sexuality are very powerfully addressed in Danticat's *Breath, Eyes, Memory* (1994), which although written in English is a text by a Haitian woman set in both Haiti and the US. While the practice of gaining distance in order to speak out is common to many of the texts which discuss sexuality, this crossing into a different language represents another dimension of the process that Miriam Chancy identifies as 'searching for safe spaces' in her book of that name.[14] My interest in the narrative lies in the intersection that it stages between the intimate relations that exist between women, especially between mothers and daughters, and the political and cultural pressures that govern these intimacies. Sophie Cacao, raised in Haiti by her grandmother and Tante Atie, is sent for by her mother, Martine, who has settled in the US after Sophie's birth in order to put distance between herself and the trauma of her rape at sixteen by a Tonton Macoute. Sophie's birth, as a result of this rape, situates her whole life in a matrix of sexual and political violence that the book explores in its different dimensions.

Perhaps the most crucial scene in which the overlapping context of cultural, familial and gendered violence can be witnessed is Martine's 'testing' of Sophie, a physical testing of the intactness of the hymen that, despite being carried out by mothers on daughters, is a patriarchal method of governing women's sexuality that preserves the security of the male conjugal sphere. As her grandmother tells her, 'From the time a girl begins to menstruate to the time you turn her over to her husband, the mother is responsible for her purity' (Danticat 1994: 156). However, it is not just the simple but all too familiar twist of the mother acting as patriarch that makes this scene troubling, but also the fact that Martine chooses these sessions as appropriate moments to tell her daughter folktales. The opening of this pathway of cultural transmission that is valued within oral cultures as a way of preserving community knowledge and values is traditionally seen as a strategy for female empowerment. This unauthorised language and knowledge informs the complex constitution of female (post-) colonial subjectivity, and often provides an important site of resistance and of shared knowledge beyond official, public (male) culture. The different texture and value of this linguistic tradition is emphasised in Trinh T. Minh-Ha's eulogy of matrilineal transmission.

> The world's earliest archives or libraries were the memories of women. Patiently transmitted from mouth to ear, body to body, hand to hand ... The speech is seen, heard, smelled, tasted and touched ... Every woman partakes in the chain of guardianship and of transmission. In Africa it is said that every griotte who dies is a whole library that burns down.
>
> (Minh-Ha 1989: 121–122)

In *Breath, Eyes, Memory* the scene in which the transmission of embodied knowledge, memory and strength passes from woman to woman, is also marked and marred by the transmission of that other intimate Haitian history – sexual 'testing'.

> I closed my eyes upon the image of my mother slipping her hand under the sheets and poking her pinky at a void, hoping that it would go no further than the length of her fingernail. / Like Tante Atie, she has told me stories while she was doing it, weaving elaborate tales to keep my mind off the finger, which I knew would one day slip into me and condemn me.
>
> (Danticat 1994: 155)

The link between the oral tradition and embodied knowledge in Jamaica that has been brought to light with great affirmative power by Carolyn Cooper in her 1993 study *Noises in the Blood* may provoke a shared 'echo in the bone or a noise in the blood', but for Haitian women here it is the echo of historical violence and the noise of continuous trauma.[15]

The consequences of this sexual violence and its continued 'noises' in the body finally prove to be fatal for Martine (as for Mala and Sadwine) and she kills both herself and the child she was carrying in a terrible and stylised scene of self-violation: 'She stabbed her stomach with an old rusty knife. I counted, and they counted again in the hospital. Seventeen times' (Danticat 1994: 224). Sophie too has earlier styled a violent act of self-mutilation, breaking her own hymen with a pestle in order to end the testing: 'My flesh ripped apart . . . I could see the blood slowly dripping onto the bed sheet.' (Danticat 1994: 88). It should not go unnoticed that, through these terrible acts, both Martine and Sophie deny the sexual history that their mothers tried to secure for them through acts of violent governance. The bloodstained sheets of the virgin bride are rehearsed *in extremis* in two horrifyingly violent spectacles. Yet, while Martine seems trapped within a performance of violence in which she repeats, with a fatal difference, the various acts of sexual violation to which she has been subjected, Sophie's self-mutilation can be read as enactment for liberation, as she claims sexual self-determination. Although Sophie's shame and pain are acutely realised in this scene, her actions remove her from the constant anticipation, memory and experience of violation that her mother cannot escape, and for Sophie the consequences are scarring but not fatal.

These horrifying scenes of sexual violence enacted upon women by each other and themselves foreground the hidden history of female relations in Haiti and bring new meaning to Sophie's declaration that 'My mother-line was always with me . . . No matter what happens. Blood made us one' (Danticat 1994: 207). The political dimension of the hidden histories of sexual violence in *Breath, Eyes, Memory* is given extensive and careful analysis in Donnette Francis' article, 'Silences too horrific to disturb: writing sexual histories in Edwidge Danticat's *Breath, Eyes, Memory*' (2004), in which she connects the sexual violence in the narrative to the particular operations of the Duvalier régime in Haiti during the second half of the twentieth century.

> The Duvalierist state (1957–1986), however, ushered in a shift in the reigning paternalistic construction of women as 'political innocents' to women as 'enemies of the state'. Under this administration, when women voiced their political opinions in support of women's rights or the opposition party, they were defined as 'subversive, unpatriotic and unnatural'. As such, they were deserving of punishment, which often took the form of sexual torture. In 1959, for example, Duvalier instated Tonton Macoutes, a rural militia group, to gain control of the rural countryside. Within a two-year time span, Duvalier's rural militia wielded more power than the Haitian Army and their own brand of 'political rape' was a notorious method of maintaining their power. Trained by the US-sponsored National Guard, it is not coincidental

that this militarism created a hyper-machismo, enacted upon women's bodies, and characteristic of Duvalier's government.

(Francis 2004: 78)

In addition to the violent consequences of this state-sponsored régime of sexual punishment, what Francis also, importantly, draws attention to is the way in which these sexual atrocities were part of the campaign to keep women silent and, furthermore, how this silence was maintained by state-generated discourses that kept crimes against women out of official histories during the Duvalier régime.

> Under the Duvalierist regime, women emerged as a specific category subject to surveillance, discipline and punishment. Yet, their narratives of sexual violations were rendered invisible as the state exercised its power to obscure violations against women by dismissing their testimonies as nonsensical or inconsequential to the political life of Haitian society. When, for example, The Commission on Human Rights examined incidents of sexual violations committed against Haitian women, local state administrators flattened sexual violence to 'the general violence affecting women' and further attributed it to 'a culture of repression of those who are vulnerable or inferior'. Here a deferral to class is meant to account for and simultaneously dismiss sexual violence against women. Such instances of the state's refusal to acknowledge political rapes relegates this real trauma to a silence too horrific to disturb, while further reifying the notion of black female sexuality in which rape is unimaginable.
>
> (Francis 2004: 79)

As Francis' work demonstrates, *Breath, Eyes, Memory* uncovers a history of sexual subjection that is effectively silenced and erased from other sources. Martine's ordeal is perpetrated by the 'invisible' enemy – the Tonton Macoute – and Sophie's by the intimate enemy (to borrow Ashish Nandy's term) – her own mother. Like *The Dispossessed*, this novel can be read productively, although not transparently, as making a textual intervention in debates around the management of female sexuality in Caribbean societies by uncovering stories of sexual subjection and self-determination that have overlapping concerns in different historical moments.

In Kincaid's *Lucy*, the examination of the dynamics of sexual power is linked to Lucy's own unconventional attitude to sex. Although the same issue of needing to move away from the mother's internalised systems of patriarchal control that demands our attention in *Breath, Eyes, Memory* also informs *Lucy*, here the protagonist travels to the US in order to leave behind, rather than to find, her mother. Her main motivation for leaving is to be free from her mother's low expectations for her future and high hopes for her sexual 'morality'; free, that is, from the conventional scripting of Antiguan femininity. If Lucy's painful refusal of her mother is one way of distancing herself from what is revealed to be a patriarchal version of her future, then her participation in sexual activities at her pleasure and for her pleasure is another such method.

Her willing embrace of the identity that her mother most feared for her, that of the 'slut', is an important part of Lucy's freedom – a freedom which is consistently undercut in the text by her awareness of herself as still inhabiting a land equally scarred by the legacy of colonisation, oppression and injustice. Lucy is seemingly empowered by her very ability to withdraw emotionally and analyse her sexual activities with a 'cold heart', as well as by her sense of being in control. As Evelyn O'Callaghan observes, 'significantly, all these experiences are depicted as Lucy's sexual *conquests*, for issues of power and control predominate in every relationship' (O'Callaghan 1998: 295). Her narration of her first sexual experience is a good example:

> There was Tanner, and he was the first boy with whom I did everything possible you can do with a boy. The very first time we did everything we wanted to do, he spread a towel on the floor of his room for me to lie down on, because the old springs in his bed made too much noise; it was a white towel, and when I got up it was stained with blood. When he saw it, he first froze with fear and then he smiled and said, 'Oh,' a note too triumphant in his voice, and I don't know how but I found the presence of mind to say, 'It's just my period coming on.' I did not care about being a virgin and had long looked forward to the day when I could rid myself of that status, but when I saw how much it mattered to him to be the first boy I had been with, I could not give him such a hold over me.
>
> (Kincaid 1991: 82–83)

Although it is clear that Lucy denies Tanner the power of sexual conquest in this scene, I want to argue that it is vital that Lucy is only *seemingly* empowered by her sexual encounters. The fact that she is entirely open with her American employer/surrogate mother, Mariah, about her sexual relationships might be taken as a sign of her liberation, but throughout the text there is a strong sense of Lucy rehearsing and staging strategically defiant and oppositional identities, what Antonia MacDonald-Smythe has called 'a nonpenitent and contrary consciousness' (MacDonald-Smythe 1999: 96). Lucy is acutely aware of and takes pleasure in the shock value of her narratives and her self-staged 'slut' act; moreover, the fact that her stories are uncomfortably reminiscent of the boasts that men make about their sexual exploits – lies and inflations that are usually rooted in insecurity and inexperience, and seldom to be believed – should not be overlooked.

> Except for eating, all the time we spent together was devoted to sex.
> I told her what everything felt like, how surprised I was to be thrilled
> by the violence of it ... what an adventure this part of my life had
> become, and how much I looked forward to it.
>
> (Kincaid 1991: 113)

Lucy may be able to use the power dynamic that operates in sexual
relations in order to hold her complex relationships with her mother, her
homeland and her history at bay, but she is not able to arrive at any
lasting or meaningful sense of fulfilment through her chosen forms of sexual
contact. Lucy's sexual empowerment can be read as a form of subversive
resistance within the broad social and political context of the Caribbean
in which the sexual subjection of women to men remains normative. It is
clear that Lucy's satisfaction is not emotional or physical as much as historical, it is about evening up the odds between men and women, Americans
and West Indians, mothers and daughters – as Kincaid herself has said,
'the powerful and the powerless'.

These two novels by women writers offer important portals to the main
issues concerning the conditions regulating the expression and constitution
of women's sexual identity in the Caribbean. Yet both texts also confirm
O'Callaghan's observation about the absence of joy, and neither represents mutually empowering sexual encounters between men and women.
Oona Kempadoo's *Buxton Spice* (1998) and Robert Antoni's *My Grandmother's
Erotic Folktales* (2000) are two texts that have begun the process of relating
sexual experience and sexual identity as a pleasurable, vital and natural
part of human experience. Antoni's collection of stories, told by a 97 year-
old grandmother, are lewd and ludicrous. They draw upon a strong
vernacular tradition of comic and bawdy storytelling. Interestingly, this
form of sexual narration has not found a successful transition into literary
works despite the fact that recuperation of the folk and oral narratives was
central to agendas of indigeneity in the 1960s and 1970s. The stories represent a new form of literary articulation in as much as they represent sex
as powerful, strange and funny, and the wrongs enacted through sexual
infidelities as not necessarily historical, deeply-felt or indelible.

Buxton Spice, perhaps more than any other Caribbean fictional work,
focuses explicitly on the effects of adolescence upon both the psychology
and the body of its narrator.[16] As Wyck Williams comments in his review
of the book, 'As an erotic coming of age book it goes where Guyanese
writers from an earlier, more ruminative time chose not to tread.'[17] For
Lula, the twelve-year-old mixed African-Indian (dougla) narrator of the
story and her close girlfriends, sex, its secrets and its joys are very much
at the fore of their lives. The book is vivid in its descriptions of the self-
absorption, fascination and confusion that puberty brings and equally
detailed and lively in its portrayal of the fiery enthusiasm for the physical
experiences associated with the awakening of sexuality. In many ways this

text breaks the silence of a positive sexuality by narrating the girls' sexual pleasure and freedom, as well as their celebration of other sexually empowered women, such as Bullet, a local prostitute who 'had that same thickset way of walking and bouncing her bubbies. The bouncing said to everybody "I like sex. So what?"' (Kempadoo 1998: 69). However, while there is no denying that the book offers a wonderful description of adolescence, as its political narrative unfolds the free space of sexual experimentation and pure sensation rubs up against the fixed matrix of racial and gender configurations where sexuality is again implicated in conflicts over ethnic identity.

Significantly, the loss of innocence that inevitably accompanies encroaching maturity does not come as the result of sexual experience. It is not the casual encounters with boys, the masturbation, voyeurism, role-playing or experimental same-sex encounters that all play a part in Lula's erotic passage into adulthood that occasion this loss. Initiation into the adult world is painful, not because sex itself is difficult or traumatic, but because sex inevitably becomes political in divided societies. At times the book is set in the most private and recognisable all-female spaces where intimate exchanges of knowledge and pleasure take place behind drawn curtains. All the same, the public world of 1970s Guyana ruled over by Forbes Burnham and his People's National Congress, divided by race conflict and weakened by the economic consequences of his centralised economic structure, increasingly encroaches on Lula's consciousness and the novel itself.

Tamarind Grove where the novel is located is a 'black village' although a handful of 'Putagee' families and Lula's Indian father remain there. Lula has heard the stories about violence and race riots under Burnham's rule: 'He make black people hate Indians. He take everyt'ing de Indians had an say is government own. He put big fat black people to run de sugar an rice factories. You must'e see all dat' (Kempadoo 1998: 53). Yet, as the narrative draws to a close, her world is to be torn open by the realities of such racial hatred within her own community when Mrs DeAbro accuses her white daughter, Judy, of having sex with the young black man, André. Not only does Emelda DeAbro verbally abuse her daughter for breaking the script of her sexual destiny on two counts, '"In de bus shed like a whoa! *Black* Man!"' (Kempadoo 1998: 167), but she subjects her to the humiliation and violation of being 'checked' for the physical signs of sexual activity. The privacy and intimacy of Judy's sexual life is destroyed by the public scrutiny of her body and the policing of racial, as well as sexual, contamination.

As in *The Dispossessed*, literature becomes a space in which socially silenced stories relating to consensual trans-racial relations can be heard. Judy's public 'testing' demonstrates how she is socially dismembered and confirms that her sexual parts belong to the women who caretake feminine and racial propriety: Agnes's head was down, shaking. Ann-Marie looking from on top. Emelda pushed her head closer, fixing her glasses. '*Red!* Why your crease red? *Red!*' (Kempadoo 1998: 168). In this one critical moment, the innocence of budding sexuality and the promise of physical pleasure which all the girls had shared are spoiled as the adult world, with its rules, its language and its power to hurt, comes rushing into their view. Although much of the novel endorses a positive model of sexuality for women, as its interests in sexual politics and the politics of a racist régime merge, it does not evade the issue of sexual power being used against women. Finally though, *Buxton Spice* does tell the 'secret' story of adolescent sexual experimentation and of trans-racial desire and it is arguably in these private stories that the deconstruction of the public regulation of sexual behaviour can be best imagined.

As I have discussed, the emergence of critical works devoted to women's writing as a tradition in its own right in the 1980s and 1990s, and the attendant consolidation of Caribbean women's writing as an almost separate area of study, has generated lively and divergent critical approaches to issues of gender difference, although questions of sexuality still usually remain marginal. More marginal still, however, is criticism that seeks to foreground the representation of queer identities and relationships. It may be possible to argue that the feminist critical agenda with its focus on women's writing and women's sexual subjectivities has promoted the focus on women's sexual autonomy in critical writings to date and thereby generated the normalisation of heterosexuality within discussions of sexual politics. Denise deCaires Narain has offered a subtle reading of the way in which sex 'as a bold assertion of acceptance of woman's individuality and her embodiment, the first step to self-validation in a hostile and conformist Caribbean', 'stands in the way of love' in Kincaid's woman-centred narratives (deCaires Narain 2002a: 356). Her focus on the issue of women's empowerment in a culture where structural inequalities weigh against women, encourages her to make the claim that

> Attitudes to sexuality shuttle between a frank and raucous explicitness about sex and an almost Victorian prudery and decorousness. Clearly class is a deciding factor in the location one can occupy in this continuum; but across all classes, men unquestionably have a greater degree of sexual mobility and agency.
>
> (deCaires Narain 2002: 336)

There are few grounds on which this claim can be disputed with reference to heterosexual men and women, but the issue of agency is far more fraught and difficult in relation to non-heterosexual men. Indeed, it is through a discussion of the persistent and extreme subjection, both representational and actual, that queer subjects have suffered in the region that we can locate an allied archive of writings that also engage with the issues of hidden histories, of pain, and of liberation. Unlike women's writing, this archive is still struggling to find a critical presence and in order to do so it must both encounter and undo the heteronormativity of cultural and critical vocabularies as they relate to discussions of sexuality.

Same-sex freedom struggles

Before offering a reading of Caribbean literary forms in relation to the issue of same-sex loving, I wish to look briefly at the wider picture of post-colonial scholarship on this issue as this helps to frame, as well as to differentiate, the Caribbean experience. It is important to point out, in the first place, that homophobia exists in every society, as the 2001 Amnesty International report, 'Crimes of hate, conspiracy of silence: torture and ill-treatment based on sexual identity', makes clear:

> In virtually every part of the globe, LGBT [lesbian, gay, bisexual and transgender] lives are constrained by a web of laws and social prac-tices that deny them an equal right to life, liberty and physical security, as well as other fundamental rights such as freedom of association, freedom of expression and rights to private life, employment, educa-tion and health care. While the degree to which discrimination is institutionalized varies from country to country, almost nowhere are LGBT people treated as fully equal before the law.
>
> (Amnesty International 2001: 6)

While the causes of equality and freedom so central to gay rights campaigns may encourage us to have higher expectations of postcolonial societies whose own political struggles have long been engaged in fighting discrimin-ation and injustice, in fact, except for pockets of South East Asia, North Africa and Latin America, there is a generally intolerant attitude towards homosexuality in postcolonial nations and a widespread belief that it is a European export or contamination – a belief which is now increasingly contested by histories of diverse sexual practices and sexual identities within Africa and Asia.[18] Although it is not my interest here to find explanations for the dominance of homophobia in certain postcolonial cultures, it is interesting to consider to what extent the models of heterosexual identities historically demanded in these societies have impacted on the repression and oppression of queer subjects. The argument that Caribbean hetero-sexual identities are rooted in constructions of reproductive sexuality bequeathed by slavery and deployed post-emancipation by both men and women as a way of claiming social entitlements is made persuasively by Makeda Silvera:

> To be male was to be the stud, the procreator; to be female was to be fecund, and one's femininity was measured by the ability to attract and hold a man, and to bear children. In this way, slavery and the

post-emancipated colonial order defined the structures of patriarchy and heterosexuality as necessary for social mobility and acceptance.

(Silvera 1992: 23)

Moreover, Silvera's framing of a historically specific 'heterosexual matrix', to use Judith Butler's term, helps to identify the particular shape and hold of the matrix's coordinates in a Caribbean context.[19]

From a distance, the two fields of postcolonial studies and gay and lesbian studies look like promising allies in intellectual and political terms – they share attention to marginal voices, social identities, silences and silencing, as well as self-representation and the theorisation of difference. The fact that they both operate from an albeit increasingly nuanced and complex identity-based politics may seem like a good basis for mutually informing and challenging scholarship – such as that between postcolonial and feminist research. Moreover, freedom struggles and rights movements have been the political foundation of postcolonial studies from its very beginnings. Redefinitions of the politics of identity and the rights to self-definition and self-representation in both the political and the cultural spheres have been its touchstones. Nevertheless, the campaign for gay rights is perhaps the one major international liberation or civil rights movement that has not been attached to the wider anti-imperial struggle in postcolonial accounts.

Over the last decade, there have been quite a few significant publications that look at gay postcolonial culture such as *Defiant Desire: Gay and Lesbian Lives in South Africa* edited by Mark Gevisser and Edwin Cameron (1995), *The Development of Gay Latino Identity* (Garcia 1999), the critical collection *Postcolonial, Queer: Theoretical Intersections* edited by John Hawley (2001) and Ian Lumsden's *Machos, Maricones, and Gays: Cuba and Homosexuality* (1997) that gives an account of how male homosexuality and AIDS has been managed by post-Revolution Cuban society.[20] Some have been text-specific, such as the special issue of *Ariel* edited by Terrie Goldie in 1999. However, the dates of these publications reveal how very recently this critical voice has emerged; they also confirm Cecil Gutzmore's observation that scholarly intervention on the issue of Caribbean homophobia, and I would suggest postcolonial homophobia, remains a process 'carried out largely in the geographically distant and socially remote pages of academic journals, far-off published newspapers, in radio programmes and in films usually unheard and unseen by the majority in Jamaica' or other postcolonial locations (Gutzmore 2004: 120).[21] Moreover, in a Caribbean context, these distant academic critiques of homophobia exist in contrast to many local pronouncements and events that seem to highlight continued and embedded prejudice within the societies themselves.

Tension in relations between the state and queers has been raised considerably in the recent past in the Caribbean region in connection to two situations. First, the urgent need to address the AIDS epidemic in the

Caribbean, which is second only to that in sub-Saharan Africa, an issue that I shall discuss later. Second, the imposed decriminalisation of male homosexual acts, through the abandonment of the sodomy laws, in January 2001, as part of the 'White Paper' new agreement for British Dependent Territories Overseas (Anguilla, the Cayman Islands, the British Virgin Islands, Montserrat and the Turks and Caicos). Objections from these territories on the grounds of Christian religious belief were disregarded and the decision, in line with international treaties on human rights, was seen locally as a contemporary colonial imposition. When Montserrat and the Cayman Islands among others protested against this legal imposition they generated a rare and uncomfortable moment in postcolonial history, a moment in which the colonial power stood on the side of freedom struggles and moved against practices instituting inequality and towards the legalisation of self-definition. However, an impassioned defence of the sodomy laws is not confined to British Dependent Territories Overseas.

In relation to the independent Anglocreole Caribbean where the buggery laws remain intact throughout with the exception of Bermuda and Antigua, homosexuality and homophobia have been discussed in a variety of public contexts, and the tension and heat that these discussions generate is often both extreme and notorious. In August 1997 riots broke out in St Catherine's District Prison and Kingston's General Penitentiary in Jamaica after the Commissioner of Corrections announced the distribution of condoms and therefore made acknowledgement of homosexual intercourse. Prisoners took the opportunity to target those known or believed to be gay – sixteen prisoners were killed and forty others were injured. In 1998, the Minister of Tourism and Transport for the Cayman Islands refused to allow a cruise ship with 900 gay men on board to dock in Grand Cayman for even seven hours. His comments about not being able to rely on these passengers to behave appropriately confirmed the widely held belief that homosexuality is a Western 'contamination' and that gay behaviour is generally unacceptable.

Several other events have also occasioned a level of debate and a sense of impassioned contention indicative of an urgent and serious dispute over rights and the politics of sexual identity in recent years. The founding of J-Flag (an organisation for Jamaica's 'All-sexuals') in 1988 and its submission to the Joint Select Committee on the Charter of Rights Bill which sought to amend the non-discrimination clause of the Constitution of Jamaica to include 'Sexual Orientation' marked a critical moment of coming out of the national closet. The now infamous Buju Banton 'battyman' affair which brought Jamaica's homophobia to international scrutiny, and more recent cases of gay Jamaicans being granted asylum in the United Kingdom on the grounds that it would endanger their lives to return, have both been central in making the secret history of acute homophobia both known and contested on an international scale.[22] The work of various NGO groups on HIV projects during the last decade or so has helped to raise awareness of both safe sexual practices and the reality of sexual diversity within the region. However, despite such shifts in profile and practice, what differentiates the Caribbean is that discrimination against queer people is not only inscribed in the law but that recent events have shown that some Caribbean governments are intent on protecting and even strengthening legal measures to criminalise same-sex acts.

Trinidad and Tobago's repeal of the Sexual Offence's Bill in 1986 effectively made lesbian sex a crime for the first time, as well as re-inscribing the illegality of and harsh punishment for male same-sex relations. In 1989, the Bahamas Sexual Offences and Domestic Violence Act criminalised 'non-productive' sex with prostitutes, as well as homosexual sex. In January 2001, despite being unanimously passed by the National Assembly in Guyana, a bill banning discrimination against persons based on their sexual orientation was denied assent by the President. Furthermore, the fact that buggery carries punishments equivalent to those for crimes such as rape and incest within these legal frameworks confirms its status in state definitions as morally reprehensible, deviant and an act of violation. This seemingly widespread concept of homosexuality as one marker point on a continuum of sexual depravity and deviancy is made explicit in the words of the chairperson of the Guyana Council of Churches, Bishop Juan Edghilt, who is quoted as saying that the proposed legislation to ban discrimination on the grounds of sexual orientation would, 'open the door to homosexuality, bestiality, child abuse and every form of sexual perversion being enshrined in the highest law of this land'.[23]

However, despite such public and state-sponsored statements of homophobia, and the very real risks of abuse, violence and prosecution, it is acknowledged that there are spaces in which homosexual relations take place within all Caribbean communities. Indeed, perhaps the most revealing demand that was levelled at J-Flag was that it should be 'quiet'. An article in the *Daily Observer* also plainly stated this imperative to stay out of national discourses and spaces: 'None of us want them to take their song and dance routine to the National Arena or to Jamaica House.'[24] A similar response was levelled at GEATT (The Gay Enhancement Advocates of Trinidad and Tobago) and UGLAAB (United Gays and Lesbians Against AIDS in Barbados) whose claims to social visibility and voice are similarly regarded with contempt. As both *Buxton Spice* and *Breath, Eyes, Memory* make clear, sexual politics is often the nexus at which pressure from the private and the public spheres of the national build up to a crisis point and create a fracture in constructions of the national. In our current critical moment, demands for this false separation of public and private worlds are clearly demands for the repression of any claim to public rights or social entitlements on the behalf of queer subjects. In his analysis of current entitlements, Cecil Gutzmore argues that class position is also a crucial factor in determining levels of tolerance. While middle-class homosexuals are afforded some tolerance because of their economic capital and the kinds of social spaces in which they meet, working-class homosexuals are 'unprotected ... by favourable class and race connections'.[25] Yet even if there is a tolerance of homosexual communities as long as they remain hidden and silent, what is striking is the lack of advocacy for gay rights within the Caribbean region itself, even from movements with aligned interests.

In her paper 'When the Closet is a Region: Homophobia, Heterosexism and Nationalism in the Commonwealth Caribbean' (2001), Tara Atluri demands recognition of the connection between sexist attitudes towards women and homophobic attitudes, 'based on a discriminatory nationalism that uses both religious conformity and conformity to capitalist patriarchy as a basis for inclusion' (Atluri 2001: 4). Atluri notes the 'overwhelming lack of Caribbean feminist scholarship which attempts to address issues of sexuality' (2001: 5) and draws on the work of Hopkins and Rubin to demonstrate the link between the binary heterosexist definitions of masculine and feminine identities and homophobia which is understood as 'an effort to maintain and reproduce strict categories of gender, in which women are inferiors of the male-female pair'. (Atluri 2001: 9) Connected to Atluri's observations, although not emerging from a Caribbean context, is Hollibaugh and Moraga's work on sexual silences in feminism which, they argue, have allowed heteronormativity to persist:

> Feminism has never directly addressed women's sexuality except in its most oppressive aspects in relation to men (e.g. marriage, the nuclear family, wife battering, rape, etc.). Heterosexuality is both an actual sexual interaction *and* a system. No matter how we play ourselves out sexually, we are all affected by the system inasmuch as our sexual values are filtered through a society where heterosexuality is considered the norm ... We all suffer from heterosexism every single day (whether we're conscious of it or not).
>
> (Hollibaugh and Moraga 1981: 58)

This work connecting the challenges to sexism and heterosexism is significant in its efforts to collocate systems of subordination and locate potential common ground between groups or movements that have previously not sought to link to each other, but as yet it is a call without response. Instead, Jacqui Alexander's question 'On what terms will women and "wives" of different sexualities express a mutual solidarity and define their own subjectivities?' (Alexander 1991: 147) would appear to remain unanswered.

Un/popular alternatives and literary power

Most of the debates about homophobia in the Caribbean have focused on popular culture, and in particular the dancehall, and Atluri gives a very clear explanation for this emphasis.

> Silence and shame guard Caribbean homosexuality. Therefore, I
> have found few avenues upon which to form an analysis of hetero-
> sexism and homophobia in the region. Popular culture, in the form
> of dancehall and reggae seems to be some of the only concrete cultural
> discourses in which attitudes towards homosexuality are expressed
> outright. While dancehall and reggae lyrics have come under fire for
> their crude portrayal of sexual politics, they offer an opening. They
> are explicit. And while they may be explicitly prejudiced, they do what
> respectable silences do not. They start the conversation.
>
> (Atluri 2001: 14)

The fact that homophobia is an attitude embedded in, and arguably
normalised through, Jamaica's popular cultural forms is almost impossible
to contest. It is difficult to imagine an argument that could fully recuperate the lyrics of Capleton, Shabba Ranks, Anthony B, Beenie Man, Bountie
Killa and others, many of whom do make direct condemnations of homosexuality and incite violence against homosexuals. Indeed, although Buju
Banton's 'Boom Bye Bye' may have been the eye of the storm, a decade
later the clouds are still gathering. It is not my intention to engage in
these debates within this current work. Scholarly interest in this area is
lively and a range of discussions about the contested power of the dancehall can be found in recent special issues of *Small Axe* and *Interventions*.[26]
However, the range of critical responses to this debate is important
to acknowledge in a discussion connected to the search for a liberatory
politics, as it is precisely the dancehall that is being championed by key
critics within the region as a space of cultural possibility and even of
political hope for a Jamaica still suffering from the adverse effects of
the IMF structural adjustment programme of the 1970s and the US
Caribbean Basin Initiative of the 1980s, with the continuing devaluation
of the Jamaican dollar, the extreme strain on public services and the
alarming rise in drug-related killings.[27] To these critics, dancehall culture
is countercultural in important, if not predictable or orthodox, ways.

Carolyn Cooper's groundbreaking 1993 study *Noises in the Blood* was
central in clearing an academic space for the study of popular culture and
instrumental in breaking down the established hierarchies between official
and folk culture, as well as oral and scribal discourses. Her essay 'Slackness
hiding from culture: erotic play in the dancehall' (1990) was the first
scholarly work to read dancehall culture as a radical confrontation with
the values of middle-class Jamaica and it set the benchmark high for subsequent scholars interrogating the issues of sexuality, gender and race, and
the democratisation of identity.

In the final chapter of David Scott's book, *Refashioning Futures: Criticism
After Postcoloniality*, he posits the popular cultural arena as a very enticing
ethical-political alternative to 'integration into the available forms of middle-
class identification offered by the postcolonial state' (Scott 1999: 215).

It is the figure of the *ruud bwai* (rude boy) to whom Scott turns in seeking to remap the possibilities of a postcolonial Jamaica. The *ruud bwai*, he claims, 'disrupts the dominant régime of cultural-political truth that bodies are to be educated into a particular raced/classed régime of sensibility, breeding, and conduct' (Scott 1999: 214). Scott's work is extremely useful and instructive in its elucidation of how dancehall and other popular cultural forms have given both shape and voice to the changing cultural and political terrain of the contemporary Caribbean, with the clearing of unorthodox pathways to empowerment for those previously termed the underclass. Bringing his scrutiny of popular culture within the orbit of post-colonial theory, Scott demonstrates how class struggle, social transformation and cultural resistance can be found in the dancehall.

Scott may be pointing to a genuine form of liberation in his observation that

> dancehall pluralizes the political field, both by interrupting the normalized middle-class nationalist-modern whose 'out of many, one' creole universalism has sought either to exclude, assimilate, or contain, and by asserting, projecting, or cultivating other raced and gendered identities that require cultural space in which to grow.
>
> (1999: 218)

However, he does not mention the Caribbean identity that is not granted any space in which to grow – the queer. By setting up the dancehall and postcolonial middle-class Jamaica as oppositional social orders, one representing the potential breakdown of the other, Scott fails to discuss what is shared by both – homophobia. Indeed, with respect to queerness the popular actually colludes with the very agents of middle-class socialisation that it has sought to challenge – the Church, the family, the school. I would argue that it is on the issue of sexual self-determination that the popular fails to offer us an adequate emancipatory voice and despite a consistent focus on the popular within discussions of Caribbean sexuality, I want to argue that it is actually to the literary that we must turn in order to find inscriptions of meaningful liberation in relation to sexual self-determination.

In his 1997 article '"Bullers" and "Battymen": Contesting Homophobia in Black Popular Culture and Contemporary Caribbean literature', Timothy Chin states that 'Caribbean literary production has traditionally maintained a conspicuous silence around issues of gay and lesbian sexuality' (Chin 1997: 128–129). There is undoubtedly a culture of containment and repression within the Caribbean that has both stifled and hidden literary as well as other forms of public declarations and representations. This is not to suggest that queers have not had an active role in the construction of that history but rather that Caribbean historiography, in particular literary historiography that is the issue of this book, has not yet acknowledged that role. It speaks of the degree and history of Jamaican homophobia that Claude McKay, commonly termed the father of Jamaican poetry, was barely able to come out in his writing, even after years in the US. Indeed, many critics still do not acknowledge McKay's sexuality and it is only in very recent years that work attending to this has been published.[28] As my readings will demonstrate, those Caribbean writers representing queer subjects live outside the region and remain, it would seem, outside of national and literary histories.[29] Indeed, while the majority of survey texts of Caribbean literature now have at least the obligatory chapter on women writers, there is not even a footnote on writings that represent same-sex relationships. In terms of existing scholarship in relation to Caribbean writing directly, there have been no more than a handful or so of articles and book chapters. The most important publication to date is a special issue of the Caribbean journal *Small Axe* on 'Genders and Sexualities' edited by Faith Smith which collects together pieces of legal, literary and popular cultural analysis in a collective attempt to calibrate and evaluate the ways in which, as Smith says, 'homosexuality marks the nation's ethical limit' (Smith 2000: vi). In some ways, my aim in the remaining section of this chapter is to supplement this project, by drawing attention to those writings that have tested that limit and those that have sought to reconfigure it.

It is also my argument that literary works may, in less obvious ways than the work of J-Flag or other organisations, negotiate with the state regulation of sexuality and in particular with the silencing of homosexual subjects. I want to offer readings of various works as being involved in the same struggle for the recognition of sexual diversity within definitions of national subjectivity. Moreover I shall argue that these works enable a new Caribbean representational matrix onto which the intersecting identifications of ethnicity, nationality, gender and now sexuality too may be mapped. I want to designate these interventions as 'unpopular alternatives' in order to signal two factors. First, the fact that they extend the range of cultural forms engaged in this debate beyond the hardcore popular cultural forms of the dancehall to the arena of literary inscription and second, the fact that these writings do not sit comfortably within the contemporary cultural and literary milieu of most Caribbean nation states.

Homoerotics

While the texts that I have discussed above demonstrate a clear engagement with the issues of sexual politics, and more specifically the politics of sexual identities within Caribbean societies, there is almost a diagnostic quality to the writing, an airing of prejudices, traditions, and social practices that disempower through the policing of rigid sexual and racialised identities. These texts often highlight the trauma, damage and loss that are caused by the denial of sexual self-determination and by the violent enforcement of female purity. They recover the absent stories and repressed dimensions of violence and violation – both physical and epistemic – that have received little attention within dominant analyses of colonial power. Against this recovery of pain, what is notable is that there are very few Caribbean texts to date which may be seen to sit comfortably within a literary homoerotics; by this I mean to indicate writings in which same-sex relations is not a subject up for debate but the very structure of feeling from which the narrative proceeds. In relation to homoerotic writing, most notably there is the work of Audre Lorde (1982) and her engagement with legendary history of lesbian love in Carriacou, Dionne Brand, Makeda Silvera and Shani Mootoo (who, I am sure not coincidentally, are all based in Canada), as well as the British-based Lawrence Scott.[30]

Scott's *Aelred's Sin* (1998), a complex narrative about love and sexual desire between men that I want to read as initiating a tradition of Caribbean male homoerotics, is explicit in its treatment of both sexual prejudice and sexual encounter. Within a Caribbean context, the religious nature of this book is also interesting for its challenging representation of homosexuality within scriptural works, most notably those of St Aelred of Rievaulx (1110–1167) and his *Treatise on Friendship* which teaches the way to Christ through the love of fellow men.[31] Given that Biblical authority is commonly cited as a primary rationale for homophobic attitudes in the Caribbean, this presentation of Christian philosophy is particularly relevant to the region's belief-system, and perhaps even more so in the present critical moment which is marked by the division of the Christian Church along continental fault-lines on this very issue.[32] The way in which Biblical and religious authority is directed towards homophobic ends in Caribbean culture has been discussed in some detail by Cecil Gutzmore, but in the context of Scott's exploration of the deep anguish, struggle and pain associated with the expression of same-sex love and desire, it is important to acknowledge that as recently as 2000 Anthony Pantin, Archbishop of Trinidad and Tobago, Scott's home island, complained that 'They [homosexuals] refuse to accept that there is anything wrong with them: "That's the way God made me and I have a right to enjoy myself as much as other people"' (Pantin 2000: 20).[33] In terms of literary representation Pantin would find very little to support such an accusation. Very few texts to date have claimed the rights to self-representation. In fact, it is the long and very turbulent struggle to achieve a sense of their own right to recognition and self-determination that marks the majority of Caribbean narratives depicting loving same-sex relationships in a context of repeated condemnation.

Three aspects of *Aelred's Sin* are important to my discussions of homoerotics here. First, the very graphic and emotionally charged way in which scenes of sexual love between men are depicted. Second, the way in which the book works towards and gives voice to the heterosexual man's understanding of and sensitising to homosexuality. Third, the way in which the experience of sexual and racial oppression are mapped onto each other in a challenging model of empathetic identification. Let me begin by stating that *Aelred's Sin* offers the boldest portrayal of homosexual love that I have encountered within Caribbean writing. The novel does not shy away from the brutal homophobia that its protagonist, Jean Marc, later to become Brother Aelred, experienced as an adolescent growing up in the Caribbean. From washroom graffiti and classroom taunts to a brutal gang-rape, this homophobia literally destroys Ted, Jean Marc's first love and first lover. It drives Jean Marc to take refuge in a Benedictine monastery in England in order to escape the stigma of his 'sin', the scorn of his family and the break in his heart. However, the narrative does not allow this homophobia to silence Jean Marc's sexual passion. His sexual feelings for other men are presented as an organic part of his identity, as the sexual experimentation of his adolesence confirms:

> It seemed as if it was as far back as he could remember that he and Ted used to play games which were to do with touching and other things. They used to undress together.
> 'Rub my totee.' He heard their boyhood word.
> 'Suck me now.'
> 'Yes.'
> 'Put it in.'
> 'Where?'
> 'In my bottom.'
> 'My finger?'
> 'No.'
> 'Come. Come. Push it in. Push it in.'
> He remembered when their first orgasms started.
>
> (Scott 1998: 83)

The way in which the physical act of lovemaking is rendered in such plain and neutral, if explicit, terms, simply representing the encounter between these boys as part of the natural and often inept process of sexual discovery, is almost unique within the Caribbean literary tradition. Kempadoo's *Buxton Spice* and parts of Kincaid's texts offer the female version of this experimentation. Yet, if the narrative's attention to the physical contact through which men seek to realise their desires for each other is very distinctive, so too is the complex exploration of the characters' emotional lives: *'Ted and I placed questions in the hearts of each other. We placed them in our wrestling young bodies, like athletes in an arena we did not understand the rules of'* (Scott 1998: 173, italics original). It is through the narrative's insistence on a detailed, precise and sustained representation of both the physical and emotional dimensions of homosexual desire and love that it is able to create such a powerful and expressive portrait of both, as well as of the social forces that threaten and destroy its transformative power.

Interestingly though, despite its focus on homosexual love, the book is structured around a heterosexual man's realisation and gradual acceptance of his brother's homosexuality and as such offers a metacritical frame in which the homophobic response to its own literary homoerotics is already contained and significantly, overcome. When Robert de la Borde travels to England from Les Deux Isles – a fictionalised location very reminiscent of Scott's own two-island home, Trinidad and Tobago – after his brother's death in the 1980s, he enters into the complex and contesting worlds of the cloister and the closet, the love of God and the love of men, that his brother had occupied during his life. Robert reads Aelred's journals and talks with the monks at Ashton Park Monastery, which his brother had joined as a Benedictine novice, as well as with Joe and Miriam, the friends with whom he lived after he left the order. He begins to comprehend not just who Aelred was but also the genuinely perplexing, compelling and often agonising emotional states through which he had struggled to bring himself into being. Aelred's inability to calibrate his emotional life to the scales of morality and physical expression enforced by both the Caribbean society he had left and the monastic order he had joined is wonderfully realised. In both situations, the strength and integrity of his feelings can find no recognition: 'There appeared to be nothing more beautiful than what Aelred felt for Benedict, his love for him. That too was a sin, Aelred's sin' (Scott 1998: 123). It is through Robert that Aelred's emotional life is given a context and through him that his silent sufferings, both in the boarding school and in the monastery, are able to be communicated and given acknowledgement.

Robert only comes to understand his brother through his writings, and after his death from AIDS, but the reconciliation that the novel offers is important not only because it frames the possibility of coming to awareness and empathy, a crucial model for the region facing the challenge of recognising homosexuals as equal citizens, but also because it offers writing as a form through which empathetic engagements can be positively channelled, thereby implicitly positioning Caribbean narrative itself as another space from which tolerant identification can be achieved.[34] As Robert moves into the worlds that Aelred had inhabited and connects with those who had been meaningful in his life he also begins to revisit his own part in Aelred's early life, especially in the taunting of J. M. and Ted that had led to their brutal gang rape and finally to Ted's death and J. M.'s exile from the island. His own passage through trauma, guilt and regret brings him to connect with Aelred, Ted and Benedict and, almost as if in a classical tragedy, to come to his moment of realisation and acceptance too late for all their sakes, but not for us as readers who can witness and empathise with his predicament, as well as with Aelred's.

Significantly, Robert's efforts at reparation become linked to those of textual recovery. He connects Aelred's journal to the writings of the medieval monk and re-evaluates both as writings of love rather than obscenity:

> I feel sad and lonely. I wanted to take care of them now. I wanted the details of their love to be named. Aelred of Rievaulx had tried to name his sin, writing to his sister. This is a hagiographic tale, not a pornographic story. It is of the passion of those whose young love was inspired by saints and who were wrestling with their nature. His words lead me ... I look out on his world. It falls under his gaze, now my gaze.
>
> (Scott 1998: 221)

Certainly, this factoring in of empathy marks a distinctive move in terms of Caribbean writing on the subject of homosexuality which virtually without exception documents the abuse, dispossession and violence which faces same-sex relations without representing the processes of recognition or reconciliation. However, what is particularly significant to this book's model of compassion and empathetic engagement is that it extends to both sexual and racial divides. In Robert's journey of coming to consciousness he describes how, like Aelred, he keeps 'coming back to these two things, sorting out in my mind my brother's love for a man and his guilt about race. These are the two things that I have to sort out myself' (Scott 1998: 106). Although initially Robert cannot appreciate why his brother was so acutely sensitised to issues of race, as he begins to see his own past through his brother's eyes, he also begins to witness the racial dynamics that had allowed him to be blind to his own involvement in the recent history of his brother's homophobic persecution, as well as the history of slavery and black oppression that informs his life as a plantation owner.

Aelred's own figuring of himself within this history is far more intimate and transgressive. His persistent awareness of himself as always differently different (as pale in Trinidad, but dark-skinned in England, as making different kinds of friendship with men, as seeking out different spiritual guides) and often as isolated, leads him to make an identification with a slave boy, whom he names Jordan, and whom he 'discovers' in a painting and more literally in a grave at Ashton Park. Aelred's dream in which Ted is buried in Jordan's grave makes clear the implied shared persecution of slave and homosexual, as does his own vision of being hunted along with runaway slaves as he wanders through Ashton Park having just confessed the truth of his love for Edward, another novice, to the Abbot.

Interestingly, this moment of identification is most fully realised in aesthetic terms when Aelred sees himself in the slave's portrait: 'His face was superimposed upon that of the boy whose face shone from beneath, so that the black face seemed to be his own' (Scott 1998: 78–79). In many senses this is a highly transgressive identification, one that crosses an almost originary divide in Caribbean societies between those whose ancestors were slaves and those whose were slave-owners. It is also a bizarrely inverted representation of Fanon's *Black Skin, White Masks* (1952) which similarly marks the desire to be in two places, even two identities at once, that Fanon analyses as a condition of the colonial subject. Significantly, in this text, sexual otherness figures as the psychic projection through which he can occupy the space of the other although it is still the representational vocabulary of race that structures the scene.

In one sense, the way in which Aelred sees himself as Jordan through the painting stands alongside the blurring of Robert's gaze with that of his 'brother' Aelred, as well as that of Aelred of Rievaulx which is achieved through his study of their writings and works. Moreover, these two recognitions of self as other are affirmations of the significance that empathetic identification may hold in terms of transgressing the boundaries policed by both national and sexual identity politics and may be read as metonymic of Scott's text which also rests on the hope that, as Joe tells Robert, 'Human compassion can confound us' (Scott 1998: 271). In another sense this imaginative, empathetic link between a slave and a descendent of slave-owners maps the enormity of the political, emotional and cultural divide that must be bridged in Caribbean societies in order to overcome the entrenched bias of heteronormativity. In this reading, the transgressive identification that Aelred makes with Jordan brings into ideological visibility the parallel journey across seemingly unbridgeable divides which Robert must make in order to identify with his brother, Aelred. Both instances of empathetic mobility represent the radical possibility of symmetrical reflection on a Caribbean identity matrix along the lines of both racial and sexual orientation. This possibility of experiencing the elsewhereness of marginal identities, and the difference that sexual difference makes within the matrix of cultural crossings, opens up the possibility of a range of positions that we may occupy although without the guarantee of permanent residency.

In terms of a literary historiography, it cannot go unmentioned that in this scene Scott's book makes an important intervention in seeking to bridge that Sargasso Sea of white/black experiential terrain that Brathwaite mapped out as essentially divisive and unbridgeable in his now notorious dismissal of Jean Rhys' *Wide Sargasso Sea* as a West Indian text in his *Contradictory Omens* back in 1974. For Brathwaite, the friendship between the white Antoinette and black Tia was not a credible or useful model of cross-cultural interaction in his moment of 1970s Jamaica in which African culture was devalued and the race politics of the newly independent Caribbean were keenly debated. Yet Brathwaite's remarks, as I have already argued, are located very specifically to that time and place:

White Creoles in the English and French West Indies have separated themselves by too wide a gulf, and have contributed too little cultur- ally, as a group, to give credence to the notion that they can, *given the present structure*, meaningfully identify or be identified with the spiritual world on this side of the Sargasso Sea.

(Brathwaite 1974: 38, italics mine)

Perhaps gesturing to the demands of a new structure for the present time in its opening up of emotional routes through which this sea can be bridged, *Aelred's Sin* not only offers an exceptional portrayal of same-sex love but also a model of compassion and openness that may be important to reconcile some of the divides and no man's lands that still exist in dominant literary histories.[35] The way in which the text deliberately stages this collocation of racial and sexual otherness as imaginable and empathetic rather than essentalised identifications can possibly be read as a provoca- tion that demands an understanding of the way in which the regimes of power and objects of oppression are historically variable. Perhaps more than this, it may suggest that the sexual liberation of Caribbean citizens may actually be dependent upon the renegotiation of dominant post-1970s nationalist politics and claims to authentic cultural identities that plotted particular configurations of masculinity and femininity onto the Caribbean identity matrix that have actually strengthened homophobia in the region.

More silent still: writing lesbian experience and identity

In both the wider cultural discourse on homophobia and the small body of Caribbean-specific writing and criticism to date, the exclusion of lesbians and transsexuals has created a no (wo)man's land. Atluri, who spent a year researching at the Centre for Gender and Development Studies at the University of the West Indies, Cave Hill, Barbados, reported in her paper: 'The absence of material dealing specifically with lesbianism in the Caribbean context . . . the silence is indicative of one of the largest gaps in information I have found' (Atluri 2001: 14–15). Even the Caribbean nation states' fierce governance of sexuality seems to take less interest in lesbian experience which is commonly marginalised, even unrecognised, within the legal framework of many territories. Same-sex acts between women are only criminalised in Trinidad, Barbados and St Lucia. How- ever, the absence of legal reproach does not indicate tolerance or acceptance of same-sex relations. Although by no means as prominent as declarations of anti-male homosexuality, the Jamaican dancehall scene has staged some anti-lesbian sentiment, gesturing to wider social intolerance.[36]

Within a literary tradition, lesbianism seems to occupy a more hidden space still. O'Callaghan examines the fact that in writings by Michelle Cliff and Patricia Powell, although 'homosexuality is dealt with frankly

and with varying degrees of explicitness, it is *male* homosexuality'
(O'Callaghan 1998: 310). Moreover, few literary representations of same-
sex loving between women are located on Caribbean territory, although
Antonia MacDonald-Smythe's theory of the 'macocotte' relationship which
draws on a vernacular term used in St Lucia and Dominica to describe
'unusually intense same-sex friendships' between adolescent girls which
often include sexual experimentation enables the intimacy of same-sex
adolescent relationships found in the works of Jamaica Kincaid and
Oonya Kempadoo to be reconsidered.[37] MacDonald-Smythe argues that
macocotte is a different identification to zami (the vernacular term for
lesbian) and that it is not necessarily an indicator of homosexual desire in
adult life. As MacDonald-Smythe's important intervention makes clear,
the emergence of a vernacular vocabulary with which to name and explore
culturally-specific sexual identities and practices will continue to enrich the
understanding and acknowledgement of diverse and complex Caribbean
sexualities beyond the limited theorisation across a homo/heterosexual
binary.

In Dionne Brand's novel, *In Another Place, Not Here* (1996), the search to
find a place in which Caribbean lesbians and their right to humanity,
kinship and love can exist forms the central subject and motif of the
narrative which tracks the journeying of Verlia and Elizete between the
Caribbean and Canada. In her reading, Heather Smyth asserts that this
'novel draws together erotic and political utopias by connecting the two
women's love with the revolutionary's love for "the people"' (Smyth 1999:
156–7). Certainly through the character of Verlia, who is committed to
Caribbean revolutionary politics and writings (reading Che Guevara and
C. L. R James), Brand's narrative captures the colossal energy stirred
by the promise of revolutionary change. The novel is set in Grenada
during the rule of Maurice Bishop (who is figured as Clive in the narrative) and the People's Revolutionary Government which held power from
1979. The final section of the narrative culminates with the overthrow
and murder of Bishop and his pregnant partner and fellow revolutionary,
Jacqueline Creft, as well as many of his ministers and supporters orchestrated by another estranged minister Bernard Coard, at Fort St George.
The book places Verlia at this event in October 1983, as one of several
people who threw themselves over the cliffs to escape the gunfire. For a
book so embedded in a particular critical moment of Caribbean history
that is itself so powerfully associated with the possibility of new social
contracts and egalitarian politics, Verlia's death for the revolution is
figured as an escape from struggle: 'She's in some other place already,
less tortuous, less fleshy' (Brand 1996: 247). Yet the celebratory prose
of this final belonging does not help me to locate an erotic utopia in
this narrative. Indeed, I would argue that we must attend to the fact that
Brand's representation of the lesbian attachment between these two
women is very alert to the fractures of class difference.

In a novel which lays out the conditions of oppression in the barest prose, 'They were Third World people going to the white man country. That in itself lowered them in their own estimation, they could not hope to look forward to being treated right' (Brand 1996: 60); the powerlessness of Caribbean women to heal even each other is one of the most poignant and discomforting issues that the book addresses. Elizete cannot bear for Verlia to kiss the scars on her body because 'It was too easy, too light. She knows that there is no kiss deep enough for that' (Brand 1996: 55), and Verlia too admits her own limited conditions of loving:

> 'I am not a man,' she had said, 'I cannot take care of you like that; a man can promise things that will never happen not because he is lying but because they are within his possibilities in the world.'
>
> (Brand 1996: 72)

The reality of the relationship between these women is, as Elizete repeats, 'Not simple'. Brand's narrative is in no way tempted to fill in the representational blank with simple, easy or celebratory depictions of women who love women, and Elizete's evaluation of her relationship with Verlia is a fitting description of the narrative's own terms 'Nothing simple about it. All that opening like breaking bones' (Brand 1996: 78).

However, amidst the litany of indignities, sexual violations, deprivations and humiliations that the women must endure in order to survive, including the fake rituals of compulsory heterosexuality, there are glimpses of lyrical prose in which same-sex loving is given both tender expression and emotional credence:

> She'd never thought of men like that. Her breasts in the curve of a woman's is how she'd imagined it. Some of the women with whom she'd sat later in her room in Toronto drinking beer, she'd thought of in the crook of her arm, in the curve of her back, in the slope between her legs. But to appear normal she had slept with men at first. Slept with was hardly the phrase, certainly not fucked. Sex. Yes, she had sex with men until one day she couldn't have it any more, just couldn't and returned to the thought of her breasts in the curve of a woman's, her legs wide to her tongue, her lips warm to her face, the fat of her belly, her hands searching her back, easing her muscles, watering her thighs. She's thought of the brush and ease of the skin, the melt into the soft and swell of the body.
>
> (Brand 1996: 204)

All the same, given their limited conditions of possibility in both the Caribbean and Canada, for these women lesbian identity remains both an unspoken revolutionary text and an identity on the run: 'She has too much to tell. That's the answer, too much she holds and no place to put it down that would be safe' (Brand 1996: 61–2). The narrative's depiction of unsafe places and deferred moments of being gives powerful expression to the anguish of poor and powerless migrants but it does not finally bring Elizete, Verlia or the reader to a safe place where lesbian experience can rest or unfold. In a sense the text represents the deferral of a critical moment in which the homecoming can take place and, as in Kempadoo's text, the bitter failure of a political project with colossal promise in terms of new models of indentification reveals the way in which state failings are registered through individual pain and loss.

Shani Mootoo's collection of short stories, *Out on Main Street* (1993), is one of the few texts by a Caribbean woman writer to depict same-sex loving between women with range, humour and confidence.[38] Lesbian desire and lifestyle figure in four of the nine stories in this collection; in the remainder heterosexual relationships are consistently depicted as unfulfilling and mismatched, or even damaging and violent arrangements that only service male pride and power. None of the stories represent heterosexual relationships as equal, fulfilling or even contented and, somewhat problematically, it is against this backdrop and its intimations of marital abuse, neglect and male violence that the depictions of lesbian love take shape. In 'Lemon Scent', the only story in the collection seemingly set in Trinidad, Kamini, a young trophy wife snatches passionate and exciting moments with Anita, her female lover, despite her husband's warning that he will kill them both if he finds out that they have slept together. The story makes their sexual enjoyment in each other clear, although not explicit, but their possibilities for happiness are nevertheless pitched against Kamini's sense of duty and fear which forces her to maintain sexual relations with her husband and Anita's anger and jealousy at having to share her lover. Although the story ends with a portrait of the physical and emotional intimacy between these women that is confirmed as 'natural' within the narrative by its closing gesture of pathetic fallacy, 'The blue of the sky has turned warm yellowish white', the spectre of the violent and menacing husband still haunts their snatched moment.

In 'Out on Main Street', it is not the problems of marital but of cultural status that threaten to disrupt any open lesbian identification. In many ways a humorous story about a failed attempt at social masquerade, this narrative connects the straight performance that the narrator and her lover, Janet, enact for the Indian sweet sellers in Main Street with their masking of Trinidadian identity. Indeed, in order to 'pass' for 'grade A Indians' (Mootoo 1993: 45) both their sexuality and their ethnicity must be hidden. The latter, however, slips off the narrator's tongue as she tries to order the sweets that they both crave and that entice them into this dangerous territory of cultural authenticity. Her misnaming of these delicacies reveals their cultural vulnerability, 'all a we in Trinidad is cultural bastards' (Mootoo 1993: 52), but when Sandy and Lise enter the shop 'all cover get blown' (Mootoo 1993: 57). Unlike Janet and the narrator, Sandy and Lise are indeed 'out' on Main Street, 'it have no place in dey life for man vibes', and the overt disapproval shown to them by both shop-keepers and customers is extended to the narrator and Janet, whom they embrace. The couple's reluctant 'outing' by Canadian lesbians in the pres-ence of Indian heterosexuals also makes ironic comment on the assumed freedom of migration given that Janet had left Trinidad 'in two twos . . . so she could live without people shoo-shooing behind her back' (Mootoo 1993: 46–7).

Although in many ways a light-hearted snapshot of the heterosexual masquerade that is required within homophobic societies, the way in which being culturally and sexually 'inauthentic' are mapped onto each other in the context of an Indian enclave of Canada does initiate a discussion of the particular tensions of a lesbian tricontinental identity (Indian Trinidadian Canadian) in which being a 'cultural bastard' and 'look[ing] like a gender dey forget to classify' (Mootoo 1993: 48) are somehow connected states of unbelonging within all national frameworks. This association of the Caribbean (and India) with a necessary denial of lesbian identity and even of (s)exile is strong in *Out on Main Street* and it is Canada that gives a social context, albeit fraught with problems concerning cultural and ethnic identification, for an expression of same-sex affection and sexual desire. As Rosanne Kanhai concludes in 'The masala stone sings', her own survey of CAFRA's *Creation Fire* anthology, the song performance called Chutney and Michelle Mohabeer's film *Coconut/Can and Cutlass*: 'It is certainly no coincidence that lesbian creative expression featured in this essay comes from a woman based in North America. There is little space for the Indo-Caribbean lesbian in the closely guarded Indo-Caribbean community' (Kanhai 1999: 230).

The tensions which play into and even threaten the possibilities of lesbian relationships across cultures are further explored in 'The Upside-downness of the World as it Unfolds'. This long, short story traces the turns, divisions and reversals of cultural capital that have shaped the narrator's life as an Indian Trinidadian Canadian lesbian from her childhood dismissal of her Indian grandmother and indoctrination by an English tutor, to her introduction to a Hare Krishna temple by two 'good-looking white dykes' (Mootoo 1993: 118). The issue of misrecognition centres both the humour and the cultural criticism of the tale but the relations of denial, rejection and false worship that she accrues across a lifetime create an empty space between the layers of others' expectations in which the narrator's sense of self fails to find anchorage. Her repeated awareness of her ethnic and sexual subjectivity as being misplaced is clearly connected to her 'migra-tions of the subject', to borrow Carole Boyce Davies' term, but rather than effecting any homecoming these migrations leave the narrator stranded in a space in which the actual conditions of her being cannot be legitimated.

While the narrator is sexually attracted to Meghan, whom she encoun-ters in a music store, and sees their arrangement to meet at an 'Indian' restaurant as a date, Meghan (though 'family') is attracted to the narrator, her brown skin and assumed authenticity, on cultural grounds. Her ironic status as 'Indian' other is not lost on the narrator who actually knows far less about Indian culture, food or language than Meghan and her white partner, Virginia, who both embrace all things Indian with studious intent. However, the humour associated with the narrator's mistaken identity in the present is undercut by the story's depiction of her history that tells of both the cultural neglect and discrimination that such pigmentation fetish has left in its wake.

> So now that I want to know about India, Ahji has died, and I can't afford to go there. And White friends, unlike my White childhood tutor, no longer want to whiten me but rather they want to be brown and sugary like me.
>
> (Mootoo 1993: 112)

Finally, it is their divided experience of history rather than their shared sexuality that the story communicates as the bond of 'family' breaks down when Meghan and Virginia take the narrator to a Hare Krishna temple. Her anger rises as she witnesses 'His Holiness, a white man in orange . . . sat on a throne surrounded by his entourage . . . The Brown women [falling] into their places at the very back, against the wall' (Mootoo 1993: 120–1). Sensing her anger and oblivious to the fact that they had in part provoked it, Meghan and Virginia assume that she shares their misgivings on the ground of gender politics and try to bring her into their perspective with the remark, 'Pretty sexist, eh! That's a problem for us too' (Mootoo 1993: 121). At the climax of the story, however, the narrator feels the fracture of race that runs through both sisterhood and family. She returns to her awareness of difference over sameness, of her painful vision in their blind spot of cultural power dynamics, and it is an insight made all the more acute given the bond of actual kinship that the narrator had to break in order to claim her sexual kinship:

> When my mother found out (a story in itself) that I preferred the company of women, she said that I had put a knife in her heart, but when she heard that the object of this preference was Muslim, she said that I had shoved the knife deeper and twisted it in her Hindu heart.
>
> (Mootoo 1993: 113)

Indeed, while *Out on Main Street* deploys humour in order to illuminate and navigate the perils of postcolonial identity politics in the global marketplace where cultural value is continuously being re-evaluated, these stories also make it clear that being a lesbian makes the rules all the more fraught and the stakes even higher.

Dying not to speak: Caribbean AIDS narratives

There is no doubt that the infection rate of HIV/AIDS in the Caribbean region is a very serious problem, but the way in which the management of this pandemic intersects with the interests, rights and representations of homosexuals within the region has been less clear. One might want to argue that the HIV situation has at least demanded a discussion of queer identities and practices. The 10th Annual International Conference for People Living with HIV/AIDS was held in Trinidad and Tobago in November 2001 to draw both regional and international attention to the AIDS problem in the Caribbean. However, this creation of a platform has not been synonymous with any acknowledgement of rights. Rather, the criminalisation of homosexuality has actually been defended on the grounds that it reduces the HIV/AIDS epidemic. Not only is such a link inaccurate and damaging to public health awareness, but it implies that AIDS is a homosexual disease and by implication that homosexuals are diseased.[39]

If denunciation and criminalisation are identifiable responses to the link between AIDS and homosexuality, it is a startling fact that in January 2004 no government website dealing with the spread of HIV and the public health measures needed to contain and curtail that threat makes reference to the gay community. Recently though, the state's desire for a quiet, invisible version of homosexuality seems to be increasingly under threat. In 2001 the Caribbean Conference of Churches' (CCC) conference on 'Human Sexuality and HIV/AIDS in the Caribbean – a Theological Approach' addressed the urgent need to promote understanding and compassion towards those suffering with HIV and AIDS. Luis Valerio challenged church leaders to 'become part of the solution instead of the problem', arguing for nothing less than a reframing of Anglican doctrine that has previously lent weight to condemnations of same-sex relations and practices.[40] There have also been calls for the decriminalisation of male homosexual acts in Jamaica, specifically in connection with campaigns to control the spread of HIV/AIDS and the social stigma associated with this illness. In April 2001, Dr Peter Figueroa, Jamaica's senior medical officer, argued obliquely for decriminalisation and the need to 'combat homophobia' throughout the Caribbean:

> In order to raise the level of response [to the HIV/AIDS epidemic], Caribbean countries need to develop appropriate social and legal frameworks ... Social stigma and discrimination made the epidemic worse by driving the epidemic underground ... We must strengthen the legal and ethical framework and actively combat all instances of discrimination and stigma.[41]

A similar intervention, and in similarly coded language, came in 2003 from Barbados's Attorney-General Mia Mottley. According to an article in *The Nation* newspaper, 'She is determined to remove the "cancer of discrimination" that is preventing "highly at risk" segments of the population from benefiting from HIV/AIDS prevention' (Dear 2003). An almost exceptional collaboration between government and the gay community in Barbados was earlier demonstrated through the founding of UGLAAB (United Gays and Lesbians Against AIDS in Barbados), an organisation launched on World AIDS Day in December 2001 in collaboration with the Ministry of Health, the National HIV-AIDS Commission and the NGO, AIDS Society of Barbados.[42] It has also been reported that Damian Greaves, Health Minister for St Lucia, is pressing for a review of the country's criminal code in order to make more positive moves towards tackling the AIDS crisis. However, such proposals remain unpopular and even Caricom, the organisation responsible for coordinating Health Care and AIDS prevention in the Caribbean Region, recommends imprisonment for five years for consenting sex between two members of the same sex in its 'model legislation for sexual offenses'.

In the acutely homophobic culture of the Caribbean to identify as HIV positive is to risk being identified as gay and all that threatens. Likewise, to identify as gay (or Haitian) is almost equivalent to identifying as HIV positive. There is therefore a total impasse in terms of claiming a positive space for self-identification and literary texts that represent AIDS seem to have difficulty negotiating this. Given that AIDS is the issue around which legal, ethical and theological questions concerning the governance of sexuality are now being opened up for debate in the Caribbean region, the fact that AIDS remains almost a literary unspoken, even in texts concerned with the struggle for sexual self-determination, is arguably perplexing. Indeed, HIV/AIDS seems to mark the limit of literary works in terms of the structuring of representational agency, possibly even to mark a discursive crisis at the present moment in the Caribbean – a region which is seemingly still dying not to speak about AIDS.

Undoubtedly, the chronic prejudice that queer people in the Caribbean face on a daily basis makes the articulation of HIV status painful and difficult. As Godfrey Sealey, the Trinidadian playwright, who is openly gay and HIV positive, comments in his article 'We are our own worst enemies':

> In recent years I have seen what this silence, denial and fear have done to friends. I watched as people denied their sexuality. I witnessed many friends who were dying of HIV-related illnesses refuse to acknowledge that they had the disease and refuse offers of support and assistance.[43]

Although Godfrey's call for a more supportive, open and caring homosexual community in Trinidad is a very positive intervention that resonates with his own work, including the first Caribbean play about AIDS, *One of Our Sons is Missing*, other narratives that explore the issues are less optimistic.

Ramabai Espinet's 2003 novel, *The Swinging Bridge*, addresses the complex issues that inform both the naming and the silencing of AIDS. With the narrator, Mona, this narrative swings from Toronto to Trinidad and back, but there is little attention to the wider social attitudes to AIDS in this family saga. When Mona first discovers that her brother, Kello, is dying from AIDS she refuses to see why his illness has to remain secret.

> Why would he want to keep it secret? Muddie and Da-Da were not ignorant people – they were forward-thinking and they deserved to know the truth. And how did he get AIDS? Promiscuous sex? Needles? Was Kello gay? So what if he had AIDS? Surely we weren't such creeping, crawling hypocrites, inching along, looking over our shoulders every second for fear of what people would say?
>
> (Espinet 2003: 47)

However, as her musings return to her brother's private life and to the shame of sex, they begin to unravel even her own normative assumptions: 'I had never thought of myself as homophobic and found my inability to take in Kello's unknown life somewhat surprising' (Espinet 2003: 50).

In her naming of Kello's illness as AIDS and her acknowledgement of his loving as equal to hers, Mona confirms her refusal to live according to the imperatives of shame and secrecy that govern Indian-Caribbean sexuality, the history of which her own bridging of two centuries, as well as two continents, recovers. Importantly, what challenges her desire to unearth Kello's buried history, along with those of various other dis-avowed figures within Indian-Caribbean histories – the bamboo wife, the indentured woman, is Kello's own silence.

> I wanted to tell Kello that I knew something about love, that I too had risked much to understand it. I knew that loving brought us fully to life, forced us to risk ourselves, and I was happy for him and Matthew . . . But Kello only stared at me in silence . . . He was intent on shutting me out.
>
> (Espinet 2003: 156)

Finally, there is no bridging of this intimate story of love in the familial and national narratives that Mona restores. For Kello, silence is a vital protection of that which cannot be named in positive terms, his love for another man. For Mona, it brings a recognition that unspoken histories still inform family ties, 'In our own separate ways, I suppose, we all stayed in that place of silence about Kello's illness' (Espinet 2003: 15).

Even Lawrence Scott's novel *Aelred's Sin*, set in the West of England, which I have argued delivers a narrative journey through which both heterosexual and homosexual men come to terms with their own sexuality and to an acceptance of each others', ends with the silent destruction of

AIDS. Although Aelred's death is the catalyst for the journeys and journals that constitute the narrative, the narration of his death and that of his lover Edward are withheld until the final pages. Aelred's letter to Benedict that details Edward's death in 1983 from a mystery illness, identifiable as AIDS from its physical symptoms, provokes a shift in tone and direction. In this narrative which has been centrally concerned with the intimate bonds and kinships between men and the coming to tolerance, openness and empathy, Edward's death forces the reader to look outwards, both widening and sharpening the novel's context to account for the homophobic structures of society against which gay men sought to find places of contact:

> You know a little of how Edward and I eventually parted, how that love we risked so much for could not hold, had little to hold it up at first, no community to give it recognition, no traditions, no laws, no rules. They allowed us nothing but secrecy and anonymity ... It seemed that the one thing, the pleasure that men can have together in each other's bodies, being so denied, so outlawed by church and state, made it the narrow quest of so many of us. They allowed us places outside the city, those places where those of us who died of the plague are buried. They allowed us dark places in the city. Alleyways, dives, seedy cinemas, public lavatories where we scratch our messages of desire.
>
> (Scott 1996: 437)

The novel's closing gesture of examining the enforced underworld of gay life in such a way as to link the repression of homosexuality with the emergence of the then anonymous disease, returns the reader to the reality of homophobia and sexual secrecy, this time in 1980s Britain. In *Aelred's Sin*, AIDS figures almost as a trope of silence, fear and disconnection and although its impact is profound, it is figured within the novel's discussion of a symptomatics of oppression and slides into the discursive openings made by the issues of persecution, silencing and denial. AIDS is realistically present in this narrative, but its social meanings are not explored in any depth.

Aelred's Sin performs the important task of writing in new metaphors for same-sex desire, love and acceptance within the repressive culture of Caribbean homophobia – metaphors that strike at the heart of established politics of identity in order to establish new and radical horizons of kinship. However, if this text teaches us how to read for reconciliation then we must also learn from its internal silence that there is another still to which we must reconcile the demands of our reading within the present structure and time.

> How could we say that the question of AIDS is not also a question of who gets represented and who does not? AIDS is the site at which

the advance of sexual politics is being rolled back. It's a site at which not only people will die, but desire and pleasure will also die if certain metaphors do not survive, or survive in the wrong way.

(Hall 1992: 285)

The internal tensions and silences that cannot be ignored within this text around the issue of representing AIDS are amplified in other recent works.

I want now to discuss three texts that deal with the subject of AIDS within a Caribbean context, all of which present the dilemmas of sexual identification and the unspeakable nature of this illness, particularly in its connections to homosexual sex: Jamaica Kincaid's *My Brother*, published in 1997, a narrative account of her brother's death from AIDS in 1996; Patricia Powell's novel, *A Small Gathering of Bones*, published in 1994, concerning the spread of AIDS through the Jamaican homosexual community in 1978; and *The Final Truth*, a play written and directed by Thom Cross, produced by Cecily Spencer-Cross and staged in Barbados at the Frank Collymore Hall in November 2001, with a special World AIDS day performance on 1 December, 2001.

Kincaid's *My Brother* is important as one of the first texts to explicitly broach the subject of homosexuality. However, I will argue that ultimately the text is a confirmation of a heterosexual self that actually participates in the process of othering her brother in terms of his sexuality. In this disturbing and frank narrative of her brother's death from AIDS, Kincaid demonstrates the reality of homophobia in Antigua by working through the fact that she had no idea that her brother had homosexual relationships until after his death, but she also voices the disgust, reproach and fear of contamination that the reconnection to her brother after twenty years provokes. In a society in which, as Sealey points out, 'The ill and dying are faceless: we do not know who they are, and society really does not seem to care' (Sealey 1995), it is perhaps ironic that Kincaid's conflicted auto/biography, that takes the step to name her brother, Devon, his life, his death and the disease that killed him, is ultimately more preoccupied with the threats to her own existence than to his. In interview with Marilyn Snell in 1997, Kincaid commented that 'I also suspect that my interest in him [Devon] was because I thought if circumstances had been different that might have been my own life' (Snell 1997). This persistent awareness of Devon as someone she might have become encourages me to read *My Brother* not as a biography, but rather as an auto/biographical work, as defined by Liz Stanley; a work that draws our attention to the way in which 'accounts of other lives influence how we see and understand our own and that our understanding of our own lives will impact upon how we interpret other lives' (Stanley, 1994: i). However in this text, unlike *The Autobiography of My Mother* (which Kincaid was writing during the period when her brother was diagnosed and died), it is a resistance to the reciprocal constitution of self and other that emerges, as Kincaid's account of her brother's life brings her to see herself in old rather than new ways.[44]

As she observes her brother on his deathbed Kincaid figures herself as occupying his space; it is not the affective structure of empathy that constructs this relation but rather the individualised mediation of fear.

> When I was looking at him through the louvered windows, I was not thinking of myself in the sense of how it came to be that he was lying there dying and I was standing there looking at him. I was thinking about my past and how it frightened me to think that I might have continued to live in a certain way, though, I am convinced, not for very long, I would have died at about this age, thirty-three years, or I would have gone insane.
>
> (Kincaid 1997: 90)

Throughout the narrative Kincaid packages Devon, alongside Antigua and her mother, as a threat to all that she has achieved, a kind of atavistic presence that must be managed appropriately. Ostensibly, she achieves this: she arranges her brother's retroviral drugs which are not available in Antigua, she pays for these drugs, for his new bed, and for her travel between him and 'her family' in Vermont, but she is always alert to her need to keep a distance. When someone suggests that she takes her brother back to America with her for treatment she is clear in her negative response and reflects honestly: 'What I really meant was, no, I can't do what you are suggesting – take this strange, careless person into the hard-earned order of my life: my life of children and husband' (Kincaid 1997: 49).

This absence of empathy and of identification is marked in the text by a repeated assertion of her difference via her family, her 'American Cinderella story' life, her work, her voice and, most interestingly in its naturalisation of heterosexuality, her own sex life that she claims 'can be described as a monument to boring conventionality' (Kincaid 1997: 41). Finding herself in a force-field of memory and history that is not only personal, but also political, Kincaid consolidates her identity around that which is different and elsewhere from her brother. While Robert, in *Aelred's Sin*, develops sufficient openness and compassion to be able to see himself in J. M.'s place across a horizon of kinship, for Kincaid there is a residual fear of regression that haunts her relation with Devon. Her denial of empathy is connected to her inability to differentiate Devon's illness from the rest of his existence that displaced her in her mother's affections, to differentiate his life from her mother's, and both of them from Antigua and the refusal that she must repeatedly make of all that this may mean to her. For just one moment after his death, when she seemingly discovers 'his homosexuality', this guard breaks down.

A great sadness overcame me, and the source of the sadness was the deep feeling I had always had about him: that he had died without ever understanding or knowing, or being able to let the world in which he lived know, who he was; that who he really was – not a single sense of identity but all the complexities of who he was – he could not express fully: his fear of being laughed at, his fear of meeting with the scorn of the people he knew best were overwhelming and he could not live with all of it openly. His homosexuality is one thing, and my becoming a writer is another altogether, but this truth is not lost to me: I could not have become a writer while living among the people I knew best.

(Kincaid 1997: 162)

Even in this moment, the horizontal reaching across to an understanding of the impossible conditions of her brother's life becomes a downward gaze at what she has escaped in order to make her own life possible and the centred 'I' returns. As a book about 'the effort engaged by the speaking subject to distill her personal experience in order to make sense of death,' (Covi 2003: 111) *My Brother* is compelling, but in our critical moment, its representations of homosexuality and AIDS cannot be overlooked.[45]

Sealey's observation that 'too often fear of public disclosure is more frightening than the disease itself' (Sealey 1995) finds a poignant echo in Devon's defiant and troubling attempts to re-identify as heterosexual. His persistent need to flirt with women and to frame his hopes within a hetero-sexual matrix is the central pathos of this book: 'In his daydreams he became a famous singer, and women removed their clothes when they heard him sing' (Kincaid 1997: 60). Since Devon never names himself sexually in the narrative and Kincaid gives less than a page to the one woman who could have told a different story of Devon's life, *My Brother* finally abandons Devon to the confined and unspoken spaces of the closet and the AIDS ward, her writing no longer enough to save anyone's life but her own.

Arguably the most interesting aspect of this work are the uneasy points of crossing between Kincaid's description of the intolerance shown towards homosexuals and people with AIDS in Antigua and her own engagement with the discourses of prejudice. Despite the fact that Kincaid does not narrate her encounter in a Chicago bookstore with a lesbian from Antigua who tells her that Devon was homosexual until the last section of the book, a deferral of knowledge that curiously makes her own understanding of him appear more limited than that of the reader, clearly as writer her awareness of his sexuality informs the narrative as a whole. Early on in the book she acknowledges that

This disease, in Antigua, produces all the prejudices in people that it produces elsewhere, and like so many other places, the people afflicted with him and their families are ashamed to make their suffering known.

(Kincaid 1997: 30)

She even seemingly makes Devon's suffering known through her writing and yet it is in this task that her sustained textual project to bridge the spaces between intimate strangers with crafted words comes to something of a crisis. She exposes the sores on his penis, the 'stream of yellow pus [that] flowed out of his anus constantly; the inside of his mouth and all around his lips ... covered with a white glistening substance, thrush' (Kincaid 1997: 138). However, his bodily exposure is unbalanced by the marginalisation of his own voice – his speech appears only in parentheses. Further, this distancing not only appears to be motivated by the fact that Kincaid does not want to speak for him but also by her distrust of his words. Within the narrative Devon is described as regretting his wasted life and as intending to redeem it, mistakenly believing himself to have the opportunity:

> How sorry he was that he had let things go like that, he had wasted his life, he was going to look for a job as soon as he was able ... he wanted to settle down and start a family. He would say that again and again.
>
> (Kincaid 1997: 57)

Although it is not made explicit, the implication that AIDS is a social disease, even a punishment, is obvious here, as is the corrective measure of normative and socially directed heterosexuality. Kincaid makes no intervention to challenge this conservative perspective, but rather is keen herself to point out his culpability, 'how his ... carelessness with his own life might have led to such an early death' (Kincaid 1997: 195). She even questions her tears for him when she considers that 'if by some miracle Devon could be cured of his disease he would not change his ways; he would not become industrious ... he would not become faithful to one women or one man' (Kincaid 1997: 195), as if without such reparation he barely has a life to grieve for.

His absence or withdrawal from her idea of what constitutes life is most crucially revealed at an early point in the text when Kincaid claims: 'Nothing came from him; not work, not children, not love for someone else' (Kincaid 1997: 13). Even if she is in a position to judge the first two she cannot know the third. The way in which she labels Devon as unproductive figures him as metonymic of the ruin of Antigua via an *ad personam* ventriloquising of the colonial version of the Caribbean that, as Jennifer Rahim points out, Kincaid's alter-ego, V. S. Naipaul, infamously articulated in his statement that 'nothing was created in the West Indies' (Naipaul 1962: 29).[46] Moreover, this particular accusation also connects Kincaid directly with conservative, homophobic constructions of queers as 'unproductive'.[47] Kincaid does not finally express any clear acceptance of her brother's homosexuality and her serious accusation that her brother had, during remission, had unprotected sex with a number of women remains in place. Ultimately, it seems that Kincaid's narrative is not as interested in the ethics of sexuality as in the possibility of escaping the island past in which she fears she may finally recognise herself.

The field of terror and rejection that asserts itself around Devon in *My Brother* (1997) becomes a murderous force in Patricia Powell's *A Small Gathering of Bones*. Set in Jamaica in 1978, this novel depicts the effect of AIDS (then an unidentified illness) upon a group of homosexual men. What is significant about this text is its depiction of the diverse everyday lives of gay men, of their domestic arrangements, their quarrels, jealousies, moments of anguish and moments of passion. The novel makes Jamaican homosexual lives quotidian, recognisable and meaningful. As the writer Thomas Glave points out in his introduction to the 2003 edition, the novel represents Kingston as 'one of the few places at the time where same-gender-interested communities could have existed in significant numbers, as they do today, without constantly incurring too much of the wrath of neighbours, police and others' (Glave 2003: viii). However, this is not to suggest that the book presents an easy reality of either homosexual consciousness or of homosexual relationships in a homophobic society. Indeed, two debilitating spectres are cast over the daily lives of these men: the first emerging from without – the heterosexual imperative and homo-phobia – and the other from within – AIDS. The focus on the lives of a small group of men in Kingston from February to November 1978 high-lights the narrative's strategy of local chronicle, and the way in which our entry into this community is mediated through the central character, Dale, a young gay man, generates a sense of inside, participatory narration, as opposed to the spectator mode generated by the defiantly heterosexual narrator of *My Brother*. The novel is particularly strong in its depiction of the uneasy, often isolated and precarious, status of being 'inside', a status that is in part connected with the struggle to claim a gay identity at a time when both homophobia and AIDS were further limiting the condi-tions of possibility, and in part about the experience of enforced separation and social, familial (s)exile.

At the start of the novel Dale still shares a house with his older ex-lover, Nevin, and occupies a bridging point between Nevin's world of gay clubs, Nevin's mother's world of the Church and his own romantic and affectionate attachments to other men – one of whom, Ian Kaysen, also Nevin's ex-lover, he nurses through his illness. The narrative's com-mitment to reflect the range of Dale's same-sex attachments from casual and fleeting physical encounters, his sexual and intellectual attraction to the married Alexander, the long-term and high-valency emotional attach-ment between himself and Nevin, to the nurturing, tender and filial bond he develops with Ian is clearly crucial in terms of establishing a range of gay lifestyles and attachments and thus preventing the reductive collapse of sexuality, morality and death. However, although the novel depicts Dale's attachment to Ian as asexual, 'Dale did tidy-up and clean Ian's apartment the time, wash his clothes and bring him food, for him take after his mother that way; can't stand to see bad things happen to people' (Powell 1994: 3–4), it does not shy away from a description of the arid, almost wilfully detached sex that Scott glosses, though does not describe, at the end of *Aelred's Sin*. Dale's encounter with the unknown, unseen man in the park is in part a wilful escape from the social responsibilities that his emotional bonds have induced:

> all of a sudden, Dale didn't care about anything. Not about God or Deacon Roache, Ian's disease or Bill's hypocrisy or Miss Kaysen's craziness. Him didn't care about Nevin, about Loxley, about Mrs Morgan and Rose's pending marriage. All him wanted was this man, this burly brute with callous hands and acrid breath.
>
> (Powell 1984: 113)

Furthermore, the narrative directly challenges the link between a 'homosexual lifestyle' and AIDS in its depiction of Loxley with whom Dale lives briefly, and who we are told had had a ten-year relationship with a policeman, maintained a loving and close relationship with his parents and had a successsful career as a lawyer. For, although 'him [Dale] didn't even stop for a minute to contemplate that this might be the same disease plaguing Ian' (Powell 1994: 96), Loxley also develops the cough and then the lesions that are symptomatic of AIDS. The narrative's discussion of AIDS though centres on Ian Kaysen. In this novel, the missing son of Sealey's play is actually willed out of existence by his own mother. Mrs Kaysen's complete rejection of her son represents the most extreme and disturbing instance of homophobia. From the moment that Ian 'comes out' to his mother, a process of double insinuation through which he merely suggests his own orientation via his uncle's also unspoken 'strangeness' ('You know how him funny that way' . . . 'I'm that way too'), she enacts a total disavowal of him.

> 'I am not your mother.' . . .
>
> 'I never did like you from the beginning. Miss Iris couldn't get you out . . . They did have to force cow-itch tea down me throat to get you to budge. Even then you were no damn good. Should've followed me heart and put a blasted end to you, then.'
>
> (Powell 1994: 21–22)

Drawing a clear line placing Ian outside of family, society and God, Mrs Kaysen will not accept visits, letters or gifts from him. At an advanced stage in his illness and under the influence of his nurse, Miss Dimple, and his friend Bill, who has now 'given up' his own homosexual relationships, Ian decides to join the church and be baptised. Powell uses Bill to voice the theory of AIDS as a divine retribution designed to sanction homosexuals, 'Him need to give up this nonsense, this man-loving shit. You too.' . . . 'God punishing him, making him poorly. It's happening all over, abroad, everywhere' (Powell 1994: 106). However, the childish word 'poorly' indicates the naïvety of this perspective, and the narrative makes clear that Ian's turn to religion as a form of absolution and his desperate attempt to be re-identified as heterosexual are informed only by his pressing need to be accepted by his mother again.

> His mission to *straighten* out things once and for all with his mother. Him would show her the picture of Bill's sister him have in his wallet. She was a nice-looking light-skinned girl with good hair. Her nose wasn't too broad . . . and her lips weren't too wide.
>
> (Powell 1984: 128, my italics)

Ian's attempt to straighten himself out – in both senses – is clearly identifiable as a common, if troubling, survival strategy to Sealey.

> People are so insecure about their sexual orientation that they will go to absurd lengths to prove that they are not what others think they are, regardless of whether it is true or not. They are constantly hiding behind a mask, trying to fit into a society that abhors homosexuality. They lie to themselves and believe that by working doubly hard, by overcompensating, they will be loved and respected just like any other members of society.
>
> (Sealey 1995)

Also, as Ian's choice of 'girl' demonstrates, his mother's homophobia is part of a package of social prejudice that she is unwilling to unwrap even for the love of her son. In the final scene of the narrative when Ian goes to his mother on his birthday and demands that she see him by banging on her bedroom door, she pushes him down the stairs and it is this act of violent denial that finally kills him. Crucially then, *A Small Gathering of Bones* does not finally confirm the link between homosexuality and death as much as that between acute social intolerance and its fatal consequences, and we are also told of Nevin's mother, Mrs Morgan, who aborts her unborn grandchildren because she cannot tolerate the thought of a Rastafarian inheritance 'inside' her family.

This emphasis upon the way in which gay identity tests the limits of familial bonds is common to all the narratives that I have discussed so far. *Aelred's Sin* and *My Brother* are centrally concerned with the way in which an acknowledgement of sexual orientation both strains and strengthens the filial bond, although both are structured as journeys of self-discovery and weighted more towards a narration of the processes involved in recognition and possible reparation than towards a representation or discussion of a queer Caribbean subjectivity. Although more speculative, if we read Powell's novel as at least partially a narration of her gay elder brother's life, then perhaps we could argue that her own experience of queerness enables a more genuinely filial affiliation in the sense that her narrative gives voice to homosexuals as selves rather than as others.[48] In *The Final Truth*, the homosexual interrupts the conjugal rather than consanguinal bond and it is the act of betrayal between husband and wife (the socially normative unit that both colonialism and the postcolonial state have enforced) that frames the particular moral purchase of this text.

The Final Truth is the only one of these texts to declare its purpose in relation to raising awareness of the AIDS pandemic and to name the illness. The programme for this play carries a statement by Dr Carol Jacobs, Chairman of the National HIV/AIDS Commission in Barbados which is clearly an endorsement of the play as an AIDS education exercise: 'I know that this will be yet another step in our journey which we make together as a nation, in raising our consciousness about the complex issues which surround HIV/AIDS' (programme, 14). This text and the stage production both name HIV/AIDS and therefore break its status as a unspoken illness in the texts that I have discussed previously. However, the play's content – the consequences of a gay extramarital, transracial affair upon a devoted Bajan wife – is not referred to directly in the programme and the dynamics of same-sex relations remain marginal to the performance, as the 'cost' of homosexuality is brought centre stage.

The play is structured by a series of front-of-stage acted scenes which open with the courtship of a heterosexual couple, Shannah and Sean, followed by their marriage, and later flashbacks to Sean Osbourne's affair with the charismatic white Jewish American professor, Daniel Bernstein. Daniel's admission to Sean that he is suffering from AIDS is acted out, as are those scenes in which we witness Sean's inability to tell his wife of his infidelity or his HIV status. These acted scenes are juxtaposed with large screen projections of the video dairy of Shannah Osbourne, the wronged wife, filmed from the hospital bed in which she lies dying of AIDS in 2001. Significantly, the images of the wronged and ailing wife take centre stage. The message is structured within a politically conservative scenario in which the innocent heterosexual wife is wronged by her husband, and by implication the homosexual world through which her husband contracted AIDS. It is also framed by a worrying cultural politics which suggests that AIDS is a foreign illness.[49] Berstein is clearly the origin of the disease and the fact that he is white, based in the US and older than Sean makes for a very problematic representation that allows for the disease and the root of same-sex desire to be displaced outside of the

Caribbean.[50] Ultimately, this play does not address the problem of AIDS as a Caribbean reality, nor does it address the issue of consenting sexual relations between Caribbean men. Although the Jewish professor is arguably the moral anchor of the piece, informing his lover of his HIV status, procuring the necessary drugs for him and advising him to tell his wife and also pass the drugs to her, the overall presentation of AIDS as a dishonourable contamination that destroys the heterosexual family does not favour this reading, but rather points to an attempt 'to manage sexuality through morality' (Alexander 1991: 133) that similarly characterises the state's illiberal attempts to govern sexuality in the region.

Sexual offences and sexual difference – towards a new ontology of desire

I want now to addresses the question of ethical limits and sexual subjectivity specifically in relation to Shani Mootoo's *Cereus Blooms at Night*. Published in 1998, this novel intertexts with its literary precursors and with the legal and ethical issues relating to Caribbean sexuality in disturbing and yet productive ways. Mootoo's text issues a roll call to some of the most sensitive issues around sexuality in the Caribbean – same-sex loving, transgender identities, incest and rape – many of which I have already discussed. However, I want to argue that this novel not only raises some particularly interesting and troubling questions about sexual identities and attitudes towards sexual orientation which resonate for the Caribbean region, but that it also helps to position a new ontology of desire that redrafts the ethical limits and boundaries of Caribbean subjectivity. If it is a general precept of postcolonial literary criticism that reading literature can bring us to an understanding of the conditions of being in such a way as to increase the possibility of positively reshaping those conditions, then I would want to position my reading of *Cereus Blooms at Night* within this critical model and within the present critical moment when issues of sexuality so urgently demand our attention. Although I take this novel to be marginal to dominant constructions of Caribbean Literature that consistently avoid discussions of sexuality, it would be wrong to give the impression that this is a marginal text. *Cereus Blooms at Night* has been a great international success – on the long shortlist for the Mann Booker Prize, nominated for the Giller Prize, on Barnes and Noble's 'discovery list', this is not a hidden narrative and yet there has been very little response to it within the terms of Caribbean criticism.[51]

As I wish to offer a sustained and detailed reading of this novel that is complex in both its narrative structure and its formal arrangements, unfolding and intertwining by layers, I shall begin with a summary.[52] *Cereus Blooms at Night* is a tale told by Tyler, a nurse in the alms house in Paradise, a town on the fictional Caribbean island of Lantanacamara, who is only given the task of nursing an old lady because she is as socially marginal and stigmatised as him. This old lady, Mala Ramchandin, is discovered in the overgrown ruins of her childhood house and taken to the alms house as a frail, emaciated but physically restrained body – an accused murderer and a town myth taking bodily form. As Tyler devotes himself to Mala's care, she begins to eat just a little and make noises – not language, but birdsong and insect calls – and along with him we become intimate with her sensual world and eventually her past.

But the narrative structure ensures that we hear her father's, Chandin Ramchandin's, story before we hear Mala's, this time from the lips of Tyler's grandmother and in response to his question 'Nana, can your Pappy be your Pappy and your Grandpappy at the same time?' From Nana we discover the sad and belittling life of Mala's father. Chandin had been taken from his East Indian parents by a white missionary family, the Thoroughlys, with the promise of a home, an education away from the cane fields and a career with the church and he sees this as an opportunity to escape his designated identity. In fact, Chandin, despite his willingness and aptitude to transform himself into a 'mimic man', is never accommodated within the family. His awareness of himself as an outsider in terms of race is most painfully experienced by Reverend Thoroughly's cruel dismissal of his romantic intentions towards his daughter Lavinia, as well as by Lavinia's own rejection of him which later is revealed to be one based on sexual rather than racial preference. Chandin instead marries Sarah, an Indian girl educated within the mission, as he 'wanted nothing more than to collapse in the security of a woman, a woman from his background and Sarah was the most likely possibility' (Mootoo 1998: 45), and they have two daughters – Mala and Asha. However, when Lavinia returns from Canada, having broken her engagement to a promising suitor, she becomes increasingly attached to the Ramchandin family, much to Chandin's delight and excitement until he eventually realises that Lavinia and his wife Sarah are lovers. Chandin ruins their plans to escape the island with the girls, and the two sisters are left behind with their distraught and destructive father.

The way in which the narrative is constructed means that as we discover that the aged Mala is accused of killing her father, so too we discover that, as the narrative expresses it, after her mother's desertion, her father had 'mistaken Mala for his wife' and had been sexually and physically abusing her for years, if not decades.[53] As the narrative of Mala's life emerges, we come to realise that she has taken on the role of wife and mother to a disturbing degree, mainly in order to protect her sister, Asha, whose escape she plans but whose sisterhood she misses desperately. With Asha and her mother both gone, Mala is heartened by the return of Ambrose, her rather cowardly childhood friend who had gone to the 'Shivering Northern Wetlands' to study. Mala and Ambrose begin a romance that is both tender and loving, although this is not how the respectable citizens of the village perceive it:

Ambrose E Mohanty returned from study abroad to become the most eligible young man in Paradise, a foreign-educated fop with the airs and speech of a Shivering Northern Wetlansman lord. It seemed a waste to the townspeople that such a catch would be so preoccupied with *a woman whose father had obviously mistaken her for his wife, and whose mother had obviously mistaken another woman for her husband.*

(Mootoo 1998: 109, emphasis mine)

Nevertheless, the relationship blossoms and eventually they make love in a scene of great emotional charge for us as readers, who know the trials of Mala's other sexual experiences and also the high price to be paid if they are discovered. This is indeed what happens, and after a violent scuffle Ambrose leaves the house and Mala to her father's rage. Ambrose is in shock, not just at the events of that moment, but in response to the terrible realisation of the nature of Mala's life with her father which dawns in a moment of anguish from which he takes decades to recover. In disturbingly graphic and physical prose, Mala's multiple rape and attack by her father is related. Mala attacks back, taking her father's body down into the basement room. So traumatised is she by Ambrose's desertion (he does go back but she has transformed and cannot recognise him) and her father's attack that she disassociates from her adult self, caring for herself as the Poh Poh of her girlhood. She begins to withdraw, not only from society which had already withdrawn from her, but from language – the basic link to the social world – embedding herself more deeply and securely in a natural world populated by insects, animals and plants and dominated by often bizarre and painful rituals that are difficult to analyse from a point within the rational.

In the phase before Mala stopped using words, lexically shaped thoughts would sprawl across her mind, fractured here and there. The cracks would be filled with images. Soon the inverse happened . . . Eventually Mala all but rid herself of words . . . Mala's companions were the garden's birds, insects, snails and reptiles. She and they and the abundant foliage gossiped among themselves.

(Mootoo 1998: 126–127)

It is the discovery of Mala by Otoh, Ambrose's child, on one of his monthly 'food runs' decades later, that brings us back to the beginning of the story and Mala's transportation by stretcher, in restraints, to the almshouse at Paradise. Although Ambrose has remarried and had Ambrosia (who later transforms into Otoh), he only copes with his abandonment of Mala by sleeping for the whole of each month and waking simply to assemble food parcels for her. But this is not the end of the story, although the circle is in a sense complete, for the liberation of Mala and her story and the liberation of Tyler and Otoh are intimately entwined.

As Tyler tells us at the beginning of the narrative, 'I and the eye of the scandal happened upon Paradise on the same day' (Mootoo 1998: 5). Tyler is the only man to nurse on the island and his presence anchors an explicit intertextuality to Michelle Cliff's *No Telephone to Heaven* (1987) and the figure of Harry/Harriet, a homosexual transsexual who lives as a woman and works as a nurse. However, it is not only Tyler's choice of profession that casts doubts on his masculinity. Tyler, although not openly transvestite, is 'the figure that disrupts' in his unsettling of the binary categories of male and female.[54] He is labelled a pansy and taunted for the clothes he wears and the sexuality they imply. But as the alliance between Mala and Tyler grows stronger, based on a recognition of their 'shared queerness' (Mootoo 1998: 53), both grow in confidence. While Tyler nurses Mala, she begins to tend to his broken identity too. She steals a nurse's uniform from the washing line and presents it to him both as a gift and as a call to be himself, the self that she can perceive but that is not openly stated: 'But she had stolen a dress for me. No one had ever done anything like that before. She knows what I am, was all I could think. She knows my nature' (Mootoo 1998: 76).

When Ambrose and Otoh begin to visit Mala in the almshouse – a process of reparation for all – they help Tyler to piece together her life and join in the narration of her story, but there is another kind of attraction emerging between Tyler and Otoh: 'On visiting days . . . I practically hover above the ground with excitement' (Mootoo 1998: 247) and this new relationship becomes an important dimension of the novel's ethical closure. Yet throughout his narration Tyler has struggled to come to terms with the fact that Asha left her sister and he makes all possible efforts to contact her, thinking of Mala's sister as the last link to her recovery and his orchestration of reparation. Finally, Ambrose prompts the judge, who had taunted Mala as a child, to make amends too and he locates a dusty bundle of Asha's letters in the post office. In a clear reference to Alice Walker's 1983 novel of paternal abuse, *The Color Purple*, we learn from these letters that Asha had been searching for their mother and seeking to bring Mala to her. However, in *Cereus Blooms at Night* the centre does not hold and neither Asha nor the mother is restored. Unlike *The Color Purple*, *Cereus* is not a fable and women who love other women are 'forced to lose their families, their communities, or their lives' (Smith 1991: 121).

It might seem curious that a harrowingly lyrical and sensual novel that is ostensibly about an abused recluse, a repressed transvestite and a masked transsexual and which is set mainly within an almshouse, a derelict house and a house of sleep, and that is clearly autobiographically informed, is perhaps the first piece of literature to address the very public debate about the acute intolerance of sexual diversity in Caribbean societies in such a sustained and complex way. However, the fact that this is a narrative interested in the question of sexual identities is made very explicit. Tyler declares:

Over the years I pondered the gender and sex roles that seemed available to people, and the rules that went with them. After much reflection I have come to discern that my desire to leave the shores of Lantanacamara had much to do with wanting to study abroad, but far more with wanting to be somewhere where my 'perversion,' which I tried diligently as I could to shake, might be either invisible or of no consequence.

(Mootoo 1998: 47)

This impossibility of reconciling the two identities, queer and Caribbean, is spoken by Tyler in very direct terms: 'How many of us, feeling unsafe and unprotected, either end up running far away from everything we know and love, or staying and simply going mad' (Mootoo 1998: 90). Tyler persistently narrates his consciousness of difference and his inability to find a way to articulate his identity in his Caribbean home. His emotions are both reminiscent of Michelle Cliff's (1980) 'killing ambivalence' and Judith Butler's idea of 'a domain of abject beings, those who are not yet "subjects", but who form the constitutive outside to the domain of the subject' (Butler, 1993: 3). He never names himself sexually and when he quotes what others call him, he sees no match between what he knows himself to be and the identities on offer to him:

Nana had accepted me and my girlish ways but she was the only person who had ever truly done so. Thoughts of her suddenly lost their power. Try as I might, I was unable to stand tall. I wondered for the umpteenth time if Nana would have been able to accept and love the adult Tyler, who was neither properly man nor woman but some in-between, unnamed thing.

(Mootoo 1998: 71)

Tyler's awareness of his identity as being in-between and unnamed does not, however, situate him within the matrix of a celebratory postcolonial identity that is hybrid, fractured and mobile, in enabling ways. Indeed, differences in sexual orientation have no place as yet on the identity map of multiple and intersecting models of difference that has epitomised theorisations of Caribbeanness, and arguably of postcoloniality in its contemporary fashioning. Despite the fact that in theoretical terms there are strong persuasions towards reading in-betweenness as fashionable and difference as strengthening, creolised sexualities is not a term that we hear being used. Tyler's is a difference that removes him from that very map, he is outside of social definition and approval, even – he wonders – beyond emotional kinship. His sexuality, like that of Boy Boy in H. Nigel Thomas' *Spirits in the Dark*, 'was a constant point of reference for what society would not accept' (Thomas 1993: 94).[55]

This whole issue of naming sexual identity and practice is also crucial in this novel as the lack of a vocabulary of self-identification for queer subjects means that 'other' sexual acts are flattened out onto a continuum of deviance when calibrated against heterosexual norms. The linguistic negotiation of what Chandin does *to* Mala and what Sarah does *with* Lavinia implies an equivalence between incestuous abuse and a lesbian relationship: 'a woman whose father had obviously mistaken her for his wife, and whose mother had obviously mistaken another woman for her husband' (Mootoo 1998: 109). The formulation of sexual substitution in both cases seems to present these acts as equally transgressive misrecognitions rather than to differentiate between abusive and consenting relations. A crucial differentiation that I want to argue *Cereus Blooms at Night* demands us to consider.

For Otoh, whose story of sexual re-identification is somewhat different, somewhere between Virginia Woolf's version of gender transformation staged in her 1928 work *Orlando: A Biography* and Judith Butler's theories on gender performativity and the relationship between naming and belonging enables him to claim a social identity:

> By the time Ambrosia was five, her parents were embroiled in their marital problems to the exclusion of all else, including their child. They hardly noticed that their daughter was transforming herself into their son. Ambrose slept right through the month, undisturbed until the first Saturday of the next, and Elsie, hungry for a male in the house, went along with his (her) strong belief that he (she) was really and truly meant to be a boy. Elsie fully expected that he (she) would outgrow the foolishness soon enough. But the child walked and ran and dressed and talked and tumbled and all but relieved himself so much like an authentic boy that Elsie soon apparently forgot she had ever given birth to a girl. And the father, in his few waking episodes, seemed not to remember that he had once fathered one.
>
> The transformation was flawless. Hours of mind-dulling exercise streamlined Ambrosia into an angular, hard-bodied creature and tampered with the flow of whatever hormonal juices defined him. So flawless was the transformation that even the nurse and doctor who attended his birth, on seeing him later, marvelled at their carelessness in having declared him a girl.
>
> (Mootoo 1998: 110)

The linguistic flow from her to he (she) to he and the emphasis on the flawlessness of his tranformation is interesting because what it relies on is the absence of biological sexual difference as a guarantee of gender identity. Otoh is almost the perfect example of Judith Butler's argument that gender is always a doing, though not a doing by a subject who might be said to pre-exist the deed ... There is no gender identity behind the expressions of gender; that identity is performatively constituted by the very 'expressions' that are said to be its results.

(Butler 1990, 25)

Otoh's re-gendered self is precisely 'structured by repeated acts that seek to approximate the ideal of a substantial ground of identity' (Butler 1990: 141). Ambrosia's ability to become Otoh betrays the fact that sexual identities are actually social contracts between individuals and their societies, contracts that can seemingly only be negotiated around heterosexual and gender normative imperatives in the Caribbean.

As Otoh, Ambrosia takes on a new seemingly essential, fully realised sexual identity that guarantees him the social acceptance that Tyler, who is visibly ambivalent, 'not a man and never able to be a woman' (Mootoo 1998: 77), cannot expect.[56] It is, therefore, almost something of a shock given this acceptance of Otoh, and the fact that he behaves and indeed is treated by the whole community as a man, when his mother turns to him and declares:

> 'She know you don't have anything between those two stick legs of yours? Don't watch me so. You think because I never say anything that I forget what you are? You are my child, child. I just want to know if she know. She know?'
>
> 'Ma!' was all Otoh, thoroughly embarrassed, could utter.
>
> 'What you ma-ing me for? You think I am stupid or what? Now the fact of the matter is that you are not the first or the only one of your kind in this place. You grow up here and you don't realize almost everybody in this place wish they could be somebody or something else?'
>
> (Mootoo 1998: 237–8)

Two points here are interesting. First the fact that Otoh's mother articulates her understanding that identities in general are never natural, stable or self-present in the context of a novel in which sexual identity is only acknowledged socially as natural, stable or self-present. Nevertheless, her implication that Otoh's difference or imaginative reconstruction of himself is somehow equivalent to others' is not confirmed by the social world the characters inhabit. The second point concerns the social organisation of sexual behaviour and identities. Otoh can identify as a man because although he is not a man, man is a stable socially assigned sexual identity offering an apparently essential guarantee of the natural through which he can be accommodated. In fact, Otoh needs to identify as a man (he has to hide the obvious flaw of his transformation) because what he cannot be, because there is no name, no tolerance and no place for them, is that in-between, unnamed thing that Tyler knows himself to be – a transsexual or a transvestite.

This cultural imperative towards socially sanctioned sexual identities is also confirmed through other incidents in the story. The description of other queer figures does not affirm a potential community to which Tyler and Otoh might belong, but rather the prohibitions and tensions around queer identities and the need to make strongly normative re-identifications. At one point in the narrative Otoh is propositioned by a stranger offering him a lift:

> 'Who is this lucky friend you dress up nice-nice so, goin' to see? Tell me, na? Why she – is a she you going to see or is a he? Don't mind me asking, you know. Why she so lucky and not me? A nice fella like you need a friend to show you the ropes. Let me give you a ride, na?'
>
> (Mootoo 1998: 148)

But when Otoh finally declines, although he admits to enjoying the flirting, by saying that he is courting a woman, the man feels exposed, vulnerable and retreats to his normative identity signalled not only by his wife, but also his children who figure as witness to his productive sexuality:

> 'Oh, you courting her. You? You courting a woman! I see. Is a lady you courting, eh. Uhuh. Well, I better not keep you back, because I have to go and meet my wife to take she to matinee. And my children coming with us too. What I was asking you was to come to the pictures with my family. You understand, na.'
>
> (Mootoo 1998: 149)

Even this casual and anonymous exchange is a danger zone in which identities have to be brought back into socially acceptable categories. When Mr. Hector, the gardener at the alms house, confides in Tyler about his brother, Randolph who had been sent away because he was 'funny', the stakes involved in speaking such stories are registered in Tyler's extraordinary reaction:

> 'He was kind of funny. He was like you. The fellas in the village used to threaten to beat him up. People used to heckle he and mock his walk and the way he used to do his hands when he was talking.'
>
> That he was brave enough to say it suddenly lifted a veil between us. Unexpectedly, I felt relief it was voiced and out in the open. I had never before known such a feeling of ordinariness.
>
> (Mootoo 1998: 73)

This recognition of sameness in a life lived in an acute awareness of difference is comforting to Tyler, who is more clearly marked by ambivalence and difference than Otoh, but it is not a sustaining comfort, for Randolph could not stay and he is no longer occupying the same position as Tyler.

In many ways then, this text seems to represent the way in which sexually transgressive identities need to be contained in order to preserve social citizenship. Sarah and Lavinia are exiled as soon as they come out, Tyler is isolated before he finds Otoh and all other queers in the text are either in denial or in the US. Accordingly, perhaps one of the most urgent questions that we need to ask of this text is whether it actually participates in that act of containment by representing a romance between an anatomically heterosexual couple at its centre? The question of whether Tyler and Otoh's relationship is a structure which brings difference back to sameness, the transgressive into the normative, is vexing but significant to the debate about Caribbean sexualities. Does this coupling of a man who desires men and a biological woman who has the social identity of a man enable a kind of anatomical normalisation to take place that is reassuring to a homophobic society?

In order to answer this question I want to read Otoh and Tyler's relationship alongside the history of sexuality as publicly controlled in Trinidad and Tobago, where Mootoo grew up. In her article 'Redrafting Morality: the Postcolonial State and the Sexual Offences Bill of Trinidad and Tobago', M. Jacqui Alexander examines the consequences and effects of the legal status of sexual practices in Trinidad and Tobago. She centres her discussion on the controversy over the Sexual Offences Bill (1986) which in Clause 4 of its first draft decriminalised buggery committed in private between consenting adults. However, after great public outrage, the whole of parliament reconvened to redraft the Bill and the resultant legislative document not only recriminalised homosexuality but in addition 'lesbian sex became punishable under a new offence called "serious indecency" if "committed on or towards a person sixteen years of age or more"' (Alexander 1991: 136). As Alexander points out, the government used the fact that Trinidad and Tobago had the highest incidence of AIDS within the Caribbean as its extra-judicial rationale for criminalising homosexuality but it also declared that the new legislation was designed to restore the moral fabric of society and it is presumably under this moral rubric that lesbian sex was banned (although it still carried half the penalty of male homosexual intercourse – five years as opposed to ten).

Reading *Cereus* in this context a new possibility emerges for the coupling of Otoh and Tyler to represent a more radical category of experience and alliance than that offered by a representation of loving homosexuality. Their relationship suggests a sexual continuum which destabilises the oppositional construction of homo- and heterosexuality through which sexual identities are taken to be constituted, represented and governed.

It enacts 'resistance to the normativity which demands the binary proposition, hetero/homo' (Hawley 2001: 3). Indeed, the union between Tyler and Otoh is radical precisely because it is anatomically normative but socially queer; it represents a sexuality that is neither criminalized nor legalised, a sexuality which the state does not have the will to condone nor the legal power to punish. Moreover, I would want to argue, it helps us to think about desire and sexual relations outside the discourse of the state by desegregating ideas of the 'natural' and those of sexual identity.

Other aspects of the text are similarly brought into focus alongside Alexander's discussion. She examines the way in which the legal measures made the newly defined crime of rape within marriage difficult to prosecute and her detailed analysis of the Bill and its social contexts and contestations concludes that the political aim of this legal redefinition of normative sexuality was to conflate 'morality with heterosexuality' and to '[reassert] the conjugal bed' (Alexander 1991: 147). Both the reassertion of the conjugal bed and the issue of non-normative sexuality are taken up in *Cereus Blooms at Night*. In this text the conjugal bed is reasserted through a terrible and violent substitution of daughter for wife. It is a bed that represents violence, crime, corruption and death, for it is on this bed that Chandin rapes his two daughters and also on this bed that Mala deposits her father's body and where his rotten remains are discovered decades later. It seems reasonable to conclude that in concordance with Alexander's analysis, Mootoo's writing points to the damage done by imposing the centrality of so-called natural relations between husband and wife as the only available paradigm for sexual relations.

The discussion of lesbian identity is not prominent in the novel, but rather operates as an unspoken relation. The intimacy between Sarah and Lavinia is first observed by Mala who has 'no words to describe what she suddenly realised was their secret' (Mootoo 1998: 56). Outside of the social order and even the social imagination, lesbian relations can exist as unspoken secrets. However, when Chandin recognises the intimacy between his wife and Lavinia the two women are forced to plan for an alternative future together. No longer secret, their relationship cannot exist in Lantanacamara, '"We have no choice but to make a decision." There was a pause and then Aunt Lavinia said, "Don't worry. Please don't worry about that. I have known that at some time in my life I would have to face it"' (Mootoo 1998: 59). The exchange goes on to focus on the children, '"They are every bit a part of our lives. I too want them with us, no less than you. We will *never* be parted from the children. I promise you that"' (Mootoo 1998: 59). And eventually on the promise of a life together not caught in secret snatches: '"We will be able to be together within the next few days. We can sleep at night and hold each other and ...."' (Mootoo 1998: 59). The ellipses that follow, although suggestive of the sexual desire as well as the deep emotional bond that binds these women, repeat the refusal to give words to same-sex loving between women. Indeed, this refusal to give representation to queer sexual encounters is notable within the narrative and can be theorised as a careful omission. As Dionne Brand has argued, 'in a world where black women's bodies are so sexualised, avoiding the body as sexual is a strategy' (Brand 1994: 27), and perhaps one that is even more urgent for queers for whom in the eyes of the state, as Alexander says, 'sex is what we do and consequently the slippage, sex is what we are' (Alexander 1994: 9).

In terms of non-representation, it also seems strategic that Sarah's words are not heard beyond the faint 'Yes yes . . . as long as the children can be with us' (Mootoo 1998: 59). Throughout she is a backgrounded figure. If her role as a mother had been elaborated in the novel it would make her decision not to return for the children even harder to accept. All the same, the abandonment of the children is a problem within the narrative. She does not intend to abandon them, so it is not that the narrative is challenging that it is unnatural for a mother to leave her children. Indeed, what is missing from this text is what is so central, what we have perhaps come to see as the anchor theme of Caribbean women's writing – the mother–daughter relationship. Sarah is one figure who cannot be integrated (Asha, her sister, is recuperated at the end through her letters, but part of what they relate is that she does not find her mother). The lesbian still has no place.

Perhaps most crucial to my reading of *Cereus Blooms at Night* is Alexander's proposition that through the 1986 Bill the state created of a broad category of criminalised sex in which buggery, bestiality and serious indecency 'occupy contiguous spaces in the unnatural world of the legal text' (Alexander 1991: 141) and receive equal punishment. Her slightly later piece further details this consolidation of illegal and unnatural sex as she draws attention to the way in which both the Trinidadian and Bahamian Sexual Offences Acts 'conflated buggery, bestiality and criminality' (Alexander 1994: 8) as well as 'violent heterosexual domination, such as rape and incest, with same sex relations' (Alexander 1994: 10). Although Alexander's analysis is more interested in the implications that this categorisation has upon marginalised woman and their agency (not only lesbians but women who endure rape and violence within marriage), I wish to foreground the fact that under the 1996 Bill incest carried the same penalty as male homosexual sex and the fact that there was no legal distinction between male homosexual consensual relations and male homosexual rape.[57] It is against these aspects of the Bill that I read *Cereus* as making an intervention in our understanding of the current debates through which sexuality is represented and managed in Caribbean societies.

Ostensibly it may appear anomalous that in a novel all about desire and the conventions, restraints and channels through it which it is guided and policed, the central narrative spectacle is the act of incestuous rape – an act that has nothing at all do with desire. I would argue that the effect of having the rape of a daughter by her father at the centre of a narrative that is occupied by characters with diverse sexualities is to break open what is commonly represented as a flattened continuum of sexual deviance in the Caribbean, running from homosexuality to incest, encompassing rape, bestiality and other acts of non-consensual sex. In its place *Cereus* works to realign sexual identities around issues of individual consent and desire on the one hand and socially sanctioned power and violence on the other.[58] In other words, perhaps the climate of gross intolerance and prejudice towards queer sexual practices that exists in the Caribbean means that it is necessary to stage the violence of incestuous rape in order to enable a differentiation between sexual practices which are harmful and those which are expressions of reciprocated desire.

I want to read *Cereus* therefore as a text that historicises the present through its discussion of sexual identity and social intolerance. Not only does the novel demonstrate the consequences of a belief system that places the queer as beyond, outside and other to the social subject that post-colonial Caribbean governments have obliged their citizens to become, but it also offers a way of reading this intolerance as an historically implicated operation implicitly aligned to the systems of racial classification, gender socialisation and moral rectitude naturalised by colonial domination. Read in this way, Mootoo's novel testifies to the fact that the space of articulation is still not owned by those who need to make self-representation, and reveals the painful and troubling consequences of the heterosexual imperatives which operate in the Caribbean. Importantly, it also offers us the terms of a new social contract through which sexual difference can be mapped onto the identity matrix of Caribbeanness through a shift in the terms on which the debates about sexual identifications are both being framed and contested. I am not seeking to position *Cereus Blooms at Night* as a literary response to this Bill but rather to read it as a text located in this particular historical and political moment that opens up a new discursive space in which to rethink the debates around the demands currently placed on Caribbean subjects in terms of their sexual conduct and sexual identification. Reading *Cereus* also helps me to locate what I would want to define as a 'critical moment' now, in which we can connect literature to new political struggles that must continue to shape Caribbean criticism as a socially engaged form of scholarship, and reconnect these works to the long tradition of Caribbean Anglocreole writing involved in the political–theoretical project towards social justice.

In 1999, The Sexual Offences (Amendment) (No. 2) Bill was passed in Trinidad and Tobago. Attorney General Ramesh Maharaj argued that the existing legal framework was not adequate to protect citizens: 'If ever there was a crying need for (the) legislature to act in a matter, it is for this matter.' About the proposed amendments, he declared, 'I make no apologies for this Bill if it is considered to be ferocious. Laws, at times, have to be ferocious because we are not living in a society of yesteryears.'[59] The amendment made provision for men to be convicted of rape and sexual assault against their wives, although the penalties are less than for raping strangers. Incest now carries a penalty of life imprisonment and there is a compulsion by law to report violence against children. There is a differentiation in the penalties for incest and buggery, although the latter now carries twenty-five years imprisonment. Certain objections to the amended bill indicate that many of the problems identified in response to the 1986 Act remain. Senator Dr Eric St Cyr argued that the Bill would actually increase antagonist relations between men and women, that it is anti-men and 'that the logical consequences of the proposed legislation would be to drive men into homosexuality'. The Leader of Opposition Business in the Upper House, Nafeesa Mohammed, expressed concerns over the provision for husbands to be charged with raping their wives, 'And you have the other side of the coin, that in some situation if a woman is perturbed in her marriage, that her husband is involved with somebody else or there is some problem, she could easily cry rape too.'[60] Both the Act itself and these responses clearly indicate that the politics of sexuality remain an urgent area of contestation and struggle.

Liberatory criticism in the twenty-first century

Caribbean writers have been absolutely central in the project of imagining and representing new Caribbean subjects – national subjects, ethnic subjects and gendered subjects. Likewise, Caribbean critical practice has an inspiring tradition of engaged, combative and revolutionary writings. As I hope to have shown through this study, writers and critics have both initiated and negotiated the changing demands and orientations of rights-bearing discourses across the twentieth century, offering distinctive and differentiated versions of nationalism, feminism, class politics and ethnic solidarity in such as way as to speak to and for the complexities of Caribbean history and place. Literature has offered new terms for the social understandings of race, gender and class, and criticism has been animated and committed in its attention to these. Sexuality is perhaps the one politics of identity and of difference that has not been addressed on a significant scale until now and I want to affirm Timothy Chin's insistence that the challenge to homophobia, both within the popular and the literary spheres, is 'an integral component of what we might call a decolonised Caribbean discourse' (Chin 1999: 18).

The issue of Caribbean sexualities offers a timely and urgent opportunity to link the energies of liberatory writings with those of liberatory criticism. I have already drawn attention to the ways in which Caribbean writings that represent diverse sexual identities refuse to trade in (or off) the vocabulary and identity politics of what Joseph Massad, in his work on Arab states, has termed 'the gay international', a particular Western-owned model of sexual orientation that Massad argues is 'heterosexualizing a world that is being forced to be fixed by a Western binary' (Massad 2002: 370). While this eschewing of a Western and normalising model may have its rewards, it also has its risks. In the present critical moment, writers are offering new social understandings of sexuality and asserting the much-cherished right to define Caribbean subjectivity in their own terms, but without a critical discourse to bring these issues and debates forward, the un-naming of sexual subjectivity that characterises these works may not be recognised as a crucial demand for and imagining of new kinds of rights-bearing discourses.

As I complete this work, the rights to sexual self-determination within the Caribbean are seemingly being fought for by US- and UK-based 'Stop Murder Music' campaigns and pressure groups such as OutRage!, who have set their own Western-based discourse of freedom and rights against the explicit homophobia of the dancehall artists (Beenie Man, Capleton and Bounty Killer, among others), and the embedded homophobia of Caribbean legal and state apparatus. Organisations like J-Flag are struggling to find a space within the clashes of these globalised discourses in which to speak of the lived experiences of Caribbean citizens under threat. The presentation of a 'them and us' struggle in which culturally and politically regressive Caribbean nations are being enlightened by US and UK human rights' interest groups has not gone unnoticed in the global media and it cannot go unchallenged. Against the present tide of media frenzy and the noise of White Atlantic interventions, I want to argue that the most engaging debates about rights, political ethics and cultural integrity in relation to sexual self-determination are actually being played out in the quieter revolution of the literary. The literary works that I have discussed in this chapter offer new possibilities of self-imagination to Caribbean subjects in terms of sexual identity that are both more radical and more open than those affirmed by the spokespeople on either side of the current battle lines. As I complete this study, I am confident that the long tradition of Caribbean liberatory poetics will again be mobilised to address the demands of this and future critical moments with the same commitment and energy that has characterised its efforts over the last one hundred years.

Working across an archive of twentieth-century critical and creative writings has been an inspiring and daunting task. I am aware that my exploration of critical moments in the literary history of the Anglocreole Caribbean is inevitably limited and flawed by the blindspots of my own position as critic and those of my theoretical enterprise. Nevertheless, this study is intended as tribute to a body of writing and scholarship that has challenged, nurtured and shaped my development as a critic. It is also an extended prologue to a conversation on Caribbean writing that I hope to continue to share and to enjoy.

Notes

1 For sociological information on attitudes to sex and the lack of knowledge about sex see Olive Senior (1991: 69–76).

2 The novels that I refer to here are *In the Castle of My Skin* by George Lamming (1953), *Crick, Crack, Monkey* by Merle Hodge (1970) and *Annie John* by Jamaica Kincaid (1985).

3 The affair was provoked by the response of the gay community in the US to the release of Banton's song 'Boom bye, bye', that allegedly condoned the killing of homosexuals.

4 The sexual politics of Selvon's novels did receive lively, if belated, attention in the 1980s when feminist critics reread canonical works with an interest in their sexual politics. For a recent discussion of the stereotyped rendition of Caribbean masculinity in fiction, see Michael Bucknor (2004).

5 It is also significant to this study to note that Long saw white Creole women as vulnerable to assimilation into African-Caribbean women's culture and advocated that they should maintain contact with other whites in order to retain culturally, and by implication sexually, appropriate behaviours.

6 Webber (1917: 6), cited in King 2002.

7 As recently as 2000, a report by the Caribbean Centre for Development Administration found that 'Many female employees in the timber industry [in Guyana] live in fear that resistance or protest can lead to dismissal or victimisation, there are "widespread incidents of sexual abuse, demands of sexual favours, harassment or subtle pressures to comply"' (*Guyana Chronicle* March 2000).

8 For more optimistic and positive portrayals of contact between African and Indian communities in Trinidad see Samuel Selvon's *A Brighter Sun* (1952), Ismith Khan's *The Obeah Man* (1964), Earl Lovelace's *The Dragon Can't Dance* (1979) and Merle Hodge's *Crick Crack, Monkey* (1970).

9 See Shepherd (1999: 129–140).

10 See Shalini Puri's (1997) 'Race, rape and representation: Indo-Caribbean women and cultural nationalism' for a fascinating discussion of how this discourse of purity is mobilised against the calypsonian Drupatee Ramgoonai.

11 See also Rampersad's online 1998 article, 'Jahaaji Behen? Feminist literary theory and the Indian presence in the Caribbean', http://www.uohyd.ernet.in/sss/cinddiaspora/occ2.html.

12 This idea of homosexuality as foreign contamination is common in discussions of queerness in the region and will be taken up later in this chapter.

13 For a detailed discussion see Sander Gilman (1985) 'Black bodies: toward an iconography of female sexuality in late nineteenth century art, medicine, and literature'.

14 See Chancy 1997.

15 This quotation from Vic Reid's *Nanny Town* (1983) gives the title to Cooper's groundbreaking study.

16 It could be argued that Erna Brodber's 1980 novel, *Jane and Louisa Will Soon Come Home*, is an earlier work that focuses directly on the adolescent struggle, but for the protagonist of this work, Nellie, acceptance and understanding of her own sexuality is far more fraught, obliquely realised and interwoven with feelings of guilt, disgust and self-reproach.

17 http://www.guyanacaribbeanpolitics.com/books/buxton-spice.html.

18 See Delroy Constantine-Simms (ed.) (2001) *The Greatest Taboo: Homosexuality in Black Communities.*

19 M. Jaqui Alexander's 1994 article, 'Not Just (Any) *Body* Can Be a Citizen: The Politics of Law, Sexuality and Postcoloniality in Trinidad and Tobago and the Bahamas', also offers a useful discussion of the influence of colonial history on the normalization of sexual identities that informed Caribbean nationalist projects.

20 See also earlier work by Lourdes Arguelles and B. Ruby Rich (1984).
21 Ian Smith's 1999 article, 'Critics in the Dark', is an exception.
22 See Tony Thompson (2002) for material relating to asylum claims.
23 Richard Stern (2003).
24 Mark Wignall, quoted in Lawson Williams (2000) 'Homophobia and Gay Rights Activism in Jamaica', *Small Axe* 7: 108. A similar argument is aired in the Radio 4 programme by Ricky Beagle-Blair, *The Roots of Homophobia*, 21 August 2001.
25 Gutzmore (2004: 124) and Carr, Robert (2003) On 'Judgements': Poverty, Sexuality-based Violence and Human Rights in 21st-century Jamaica' in *The Caribbean Journal of Social Work*, 2, 71–87 also examine the particular vulnerability of working-class Jamaican men to homophobic attacks. Carr is director of the NGO Jamaica AIDS Support. See also Sealey (1995) for a discussion of class differentiation in terms of homosexual identifications and alliances.
26 See *Small Axe* 13 (March 2003) and *Interventions: International Journal of Postcolonial Studies* 6, 2 (2004).
27 Isaac Julien's 1993 film for BBC2's *Arena* programme, *The Darker Side of Black*, that examines the homophobia of Jamaica's dancehall culture, in particular 'the Buju Banton affair', from a black British queer perspective, has been criticised by Paige Schilts for its construction of Banton as 'childish, inarticulate and brutish' (Schilts 2001: 172). This is one example of the ideological and cultural contestations that this field provokes.
28 See Chin (1999), Hathaway (1999), Somerville (2000), Christa Schwarz (2003), Woods (1994) and Maiwald (2002).
29 Jennifer Rahim's forthcoming work on lesbian relationships in Alfred Mendes' 1934 novel *Black Fauns* is an important exception to this rule.
30 See also Chancy (1997: 153–7) for a reading of Rosa Guy's *Ruby*.
31 See Boswell (1980).
32 The ordination of Canon Gene Robinson, who is openly homosexual, as Bishop in the Diocese of New Hampshire in the US in 2003 sparked much controversy and debate within the church on a worldwide scale.
33 This quotation came to my attention in Atluri (2001). See Gutzmore 2004: 124–126.
34 The way in which empathy and understanding are factored into this narrative may also be significant to its Caribbean reception. As Stewart Brown has documented, the Trinidadian Press predicted a hostile reception on its launch in Trinidad: 'Had Scott known that the *Trinidad and Tobago Independent* would liken to him to a local version of Salman Rushdie, he might have felt a little more nervous about his own fatwa. "All the important communities will line up to lynch him," predicted the newspaper cheerfully.' In fact, Scott felt that most reviewers responded to the text positively and did not focus merely on its homosexual content. Stewart Brown, 'The worlds of Lawrence Scott' http://www.caribvoice.org/Profiles/scott.html. The novel also won the Caribbean and Canada regional Best Book Award for the Commonwealth Writer's Prize for 1999.
35 For an important account of one such no man's land see Sean Lokaisingh-Meighoo's (2000) article 'Jahaji Bhai: Notes on the Masculine Subject and Homoerotic Subtext of Indo-Caribbean Identity', which observes that 'It seems that between the queer Caribbean subject and the queer South Asian subject, there is no space for the queer Indo-Caribbean subject to stand' (Lokaisingh-Meighoo 2000: 90).
36 For example, see Simpleton 'See it deh' on *Heaven Me Reach*, World Records, WRCD005, 1993: track 9.
37 Antonia MacDonald-Smythe, 'Macocotte – female friendship by another name: an exploration of same-sex friendships in *Buxton Spice* and *Annie John*', Paper

Presented at the 23rd Annual Conference of West Indian Literature, Grenada, March 2004.

38 While it is part of the critical approach inherent in this chapter to subordinate the categories of class, ethnicity and gender to that of sexuality it still seems important to note that many of the more radical representations have come from Indian-Caribbean writers and that this runs almost directly against the grain of cultural stereotyping through which we are not only encouraged to see Indian-Caribbean women as slower to come to writing, but also as more bound by traditional roles, as I discussed in Chapter 2.

39 This contamination theory is already freely expounded on the dancehall. For example see Anthony B 'Repentance Time', *Real Revolutionary* (Greensleeves, GRELCD 230, 1996, track 16).

40 The conference was held at the Costa Caribe Hotel, Juan Dolio in the Dominican Republic, 13–17 November 2001. The objectives of the conference were:

1   To contribute to and deepen the theological understanding of and ethical debate on human sexuality in the Caribbean.
2   To facilitate a more comprehensive understanding of the issue of human sexuality and to explore its relationship to the HIV/AIDS epidemic in the region.
3   To make available to CCC member churches the most up to date information on HIV/AIDS in the region.
4   To assist member churches in developing policies which would inform pastoral programmes as a compassionate response to persons living with HIV/AIDS and their families.

41 http://www.jamaicaobserver.com/news/html/20010426t.

42 See Dr Funmilayo Jones, *The Barbados Advocate* December 20 2001: 9. I am grateful to Evelyn O'Callaghan for sending me relevant newspaper cuttings from Barbados.

43 Sealey, Godfrey (1995).

44 For a reading of *The Autobiography of My Mother* see Donnell (1999). For a more positive reading of relational identities in *My Brother* see Giovanna Covi (2003: 111–116).

45 Within a US context, Kincaid may be seen to be deliberately and characteristically refusing the sentimental portrait of the family, but my focus here is on the status of *My Brother* as a Caribbean narrative. For a fascinating reading of Kincaid's text as a displaced family romance in which 'Kincaid reaches across gaps in time, class, gender, language and cultural situatedness to heal the emotional and physical wounds that have fed her alienation since Devon [her brother] was born in 1962 when she was thirteen' see Sandra Pouchet Paquet (2002: 249), 'Death and sexuality: Jamaica Kincaid's *My Brother*'. The issues around homosexuality are not discussed in any detail.

46 Rahim, 'No place to go: homosexual space and the discourse of unspeakable contents in Mendes' *Black Fauns* and Kincaid's *My Brother*', paper given at the 23rd conference of the University of the West Indies on Caribbean Literature, Grenada, 2004 (forthcoming in *Small Axe*).

47 In its conflation of HIV status and death, *My Brother* further conforms to conservative AIDS narratives, such as those defined by Steven Kruger in his study, *AIDS Narratives: Gender and Sexuality, Fiction and Science* (1996).

48 See Goldstein (1998) for Powell's 'coming out' story.

49 A reversal of this displacement can be seen in Danticat's *Breath, Eyes, Memory*. 'Many of the American kids even accused Haitians of having AIDS because they had heard on television that only the "Four Hs" got AIDS – Heroin addicts, Hemophiliacs, Homosexuals, and Haitians' (Danticat 1994: 51).

50 Chin is keen to point out the fact that in Michelle Cliff's *No Telephone to Heaven*, 'the discursive positioning of homosexuality as a "foreign contamination", that I would argue *The Final Truth* colludes with, is refuted by de-allegorizing the rape by a British officer of Harry/Harriet when he/she was a child' (Chin 1999: 29). However, the theory that homosexuality is a white, Western contamination remains widespread. In contradiction to this theory, but also a damaging racialised idea, is the suggestion that AIDS is an African disease. See Cherimutuua and Cherimutuua, 1987 for a discussion of how AIDS has functioned as a major site of scientific racism.

51 See Phillips Casteel (2003) and Smyth (1999).

52 Mootoo was born in Ireland, grew up in Trinidad and moved to Canada at the age of 19. Sexually abused as a child, she confided in her grandmother and was told never to say the words again – this prohibition actually occasioned a withdrawal from language and a move towards the visual and she has worked successfully as an artist and film-maker.

53 One reading of Chandin's incestuous abuse of Mala might be that it is in fact a displacement of the incest taboo that Reverend Thoroughly had invoked to prevent Chandin from establishing relations with Lavinia. Chandin knows it to be racial prohibition and that the real taboo which cannot be broken is miscegenation.

54 This figure is identified by Marjorie Garber in her pioneering book on cross-dressing, *Vested Interests: Cross-Dressing and Cultural Authority* (1992).

55 It is also important to note that in *Cereus* Sarah is also taken off the map, as there is no space on the matrix for the lesbian mother.

56 His name Otoh comes from his nickname Otohboto 'one the one hand but on the other' which seems to confirm the radical undecidability that his gender and sexual identity perform in the text.

57 Most critical analysis of the 1986 Bill has centred on the issues of rape and lesbianism. See Atluri (2001) and Robinson (2000).

58 For an astute discussion of the way in which the state co-opts the right of consent in the service of its own moral agenda see Alexander (1991: 141–142). Narmala Shewcharan's 1994 novel, *Tomorrow is Another Day*, which connects the corruption of Guyanese party politics to male sexual misadventure, seemingly confirms this category of deviancy in its description of a homosexual who threatens rape compared to a husband who actually does rape his wife; the former is described as essentially depraved 'like animals … perverted and sadistic' (Shewcharan 1994: 222), while the latter is depicted as a victim of circumstance: 'the ragged, driven man who had almost become a stranger to her' (Shewcharan 1994: 197).

59 Peter Richards, 'Coming Down Hard on Sex Offences' http://www.ips.org/rights/news/nup251299_02.htm. As I have discussed in Chapter 3, going back to the case of Maharani in 1885, sexual violence against women has been a recurring issue in Trinidadian society.

60 Ibid.

References

Agrosino, M. V. (1976) 'Sexual Politics in the East Indian Family in Trinidad', *Caribbean Studies*, 16(1), 44–66.

Aiyejina, Funso (ed.) (2003) *Earl Lovelace, Growing in the Dark (Selected Essays)* (Lexicon Trinidad Ltd: San Juan, Trinidad).

Alexander, M. Jaqui (1991) 'Redrafting Morality: the Postcolonial State and the Sexual Offences Bill of Trinidad and Tobago' in Chandra Talpada Mohanty, Ann Russo, Lourdes Torres (eds) *Third World Women and the Politics of Feminism* (Bloomington, IN: Indiana University Press), 133–152.

Alexander, M. Jaqui (1994) 'Not Just (Any) *Body* Can Be a Citizen: The Politics of Law, Sexuality and Postcoloniality in Trinidad and Tobago and the Bahamas', *Feminist Review* 48, 5–23.

Allfrey, Phyllis Shand (1953) *The Orchid House* (London: Constable).

Allis, Jeanette B. (1990) 'The Decade of the Critic: West Indian Literary Criticism in the 1970s' in Edward Baugh and Mervyn Morris (eds) *Progressions: West Indian Literature in the 1970s* (Kingston, Jamaica: Department of English UWI Mona).

Amnesty International (2001) 'Crimes of hate, conspiracy of silence: torture and ill-treatment based on sexual identity' (London: AI Publications).

Anderson, Benedict (1983) *Imagined Communities: Reflections on the Origin and Spread of Nationalism* (revised edn 1991) (New York: Verso).

Anim-Addo, Joan (ed.) (2002) *Centre of Remembrance: Memory and Caribbean Women's Literature* (London: Mango Publishing).

Antoni, Robert (2000) *My Grandmother's Erotic Folktales* (London: Faber and Faber).

Appadurai, Arjun (1996) *Modernity at Large: Cultural Dimensions of Globalization* (Public Worlds Volume 1. Minneapolis, MN: University of Minnesota Press).

Arguelles, Lourdes and B. Ruby Rich (1984) 'Homosexuality, Homophobia, and Revolution: Notes Toward an Understanding of the Cuban Lesbian and Gay Male Experience, Part I *Signs* 9(4) (Summer), 683–399.

Ashcroft, Bill (2001) *Post-Colonial Transformation* (London: Routledge).

Ashcroft, B., Griffiths, Tiffin (eds) (2002) *The Empire Writers Back*, 2nd edn (London: Routledge).

Atluri, Tara L. (2001) 'When the Closet is a Region. Homophobia, Heterosexism and Nationalism in the Commonwealth Caribbean'. Working Paper Series (Cave Hill) 5 (Centre for Gender and Development Studies, University of West Indies).

Bailey, Amy (1937) 'Women and Politics?' *Public Opinion* 6 March, 10.

Bailey, Amy (1939) *Daily Gleaner*, 23 February 1939.

Bailey, B. (1966) *Jamaican Creole Syntax* (Cambridge: Cambridge University Press).

Baksh-Soodeen, Rawwida (1998) 'Issues of Difference in Contemporary Caribbean Feminism' in Patricia Mohammed (ed.) *Rethinking Caribbean Difference, Special Issue on the Caribbean, Feminist Review* 59 (June), 74–85.

Balutansky, Kathleen and Marie-Agnes Sourieau (eds) (1998) *Caribbean Creolization: Reflections on the Cultural Dynamics of Language, Literature, and Identity* (Miami, FL: University Press of Florida and Kingston, Jamaica: University of the West Indies Press).

Barnes, Natasha (1999) 'Reluctant Matriarch: Sylvia Wynter and the Problematic of Caribbean Feminism', *Small Axe* 5 (March), 34–47.

Barriteau, Eudine (2003) *Confronting Power, Theorizing Gender: Interdisciplinary Perspectives in the Caribbean* (Jamaica: University of the West Indies Press).

Barrow, Christine (ed.) (1998) *Caribbean Portraits: Essays on Gender Ideologies and Identities* (Kingston, Jamaica: Ian Randle Publishers).

Barthes, Roland (1978) *A Lover's Discourse* (New York: Hill and Wang).

Baugh, Edward (1968) 'Towards a West Indian Criticism', *Caribbean Quarterly* 14.1 and 2 (March–June), 140–1.

Baugh, Edward (1971) *West Indian Poetry; 1900–1970; A Study in Cultural Decolonisation* (Kingston, Jamaica: Savacou).

Baugh, Edward (1978) 'Introduction' in *Critics on Caribbean Literature: Readings in Literary Criticism* (London: Allen and Unwin), 11–15.

Beagle-Blair, Ricky (2001) *The Roots of Homophobia*, All Out Production for BBC Radio 4, 21 August.

Beckles, Hilary (1989) *Natural Rebels: A Social History of Enslaved Black Women in Barbados* (London: Zed Books).

Bell, Vera (1948) 'Ancestor on the Auction Block', *Focus*, 187.

Benitez-Rojo, Antonio (1992) *The Repeating Island: the Caribbean and the Postmodern Perspective* (trans. James E. Maraniss) (Durham, NC: Duke University Press).

Bennett, Louise (1957) *Anancy Stories and Dialect Verse* (Kingston, Jamaica: Pioneer Press).

Bennett, Louise (1982) *Selected Poems* (Kingston, Jamaica: Sangster Ltd).

Bennett, Wycliffe (1948) 'Poets Play Part in Jamaica's Life', *The Sunday Gleaner*, 17 October, 6.

Berry, James (ed.) (1976) *BlueFoot Traveller – An Anthology of West Indian Poets in Britain* (London: Limestone Publications).

Bhabha, Homi (1994) *The Location of Culture* (London: Routledge).

Binder, Wolfgang (1991) 'An Interview with Lorna Goodison', *Commonwealth Essays and Studies*, 13(2) (Spring), 49–59.

Birbalsingh, Frank (ed.) (1996) *Frontiers of Caribbean Literature in English* (London and Basingstoke: Macmillan Educational Ltd).

Boehmer, Elleke (1995) *Colonial and Postcolonial Literature: Migrant Metaphors* (Oxford: Oxford University Press).

Bogues, Anthony (2002) 'Politics, Nation and Postcolony: Caribbean Inflections', *Small Axe*, 11, 1–30.

Bongie, Chris (1998) *Islands and Exiles: The Creole Identities of Post-colonial Literature* (Stanford: Stanford University Press).

Booker, M. Keith and Dubravka Jur?~a (2001) *The Caribbean Novel in English* (Heinemann, Portsmouth).

Boswell, John (1980) *Christianity, Social Tolerance, and Homosexuality: Gay People in Western Europe from the Beginning of the Christian Era to the Fourteenth Century* (Chicago, IL: University of Chicago Press).

Boxhill, Anthony (1979) 'The Beginnings to 1929' in Bruce King (ed.) *West Indian Literature* (London: Macmillan Press Ltd), 30–44.

Boyce Davies, Carole and Savory Fido, Elaine (eds) (1990) *Out of the Kumbla: Caribbean Women and Literature* (Trenton, NJ: Africa World Press).

Boyce Davies, Carole (1994) *Black Women, Writing and Identity: Migrations of the Subject* (London and New York: Routledge).

Brah, Avtar (1996) *Cartographies of Diaspora: Contesting Identities* (London: Routledge).

Brand, Dionne (1989) *Sans Souci* (Toronto: Firebrand Books).

Brand, Dionne (1994) *Bread out of Stone: Recollections, Sex, Recognitions, Race, Dreaming, Politics* (Toronto: Coach House).

Brand, Dionne (1996) *In Another Place, Not Here* (London: The Women's Press).

Brathwaite, E. K. (1957) 'Sir Galahad and the Islands', *Bim* 25, 8–16.

Brathwaite, E. K. (1967) *Rights of Passage* (London: Oxford University Press).

Brathwaite, E. K. (1967a) 'Jazz and the West Indian novel – I', *Bim* 12(44), 275–84.

Brathwaite, E. K. (1967b) 'Jazz and the West Indian novel – II', *Bim* 12(45), 39–51.

Brathwaite, E. K. (1968) *Masks* (London: Oxford University Press).

Brathwaite, E. K. (1968–9) 'Jazz and the West Indian novel – III', *Bim* 12(46), 115–26.

Brathwaite, E. K. (1969) *Islands* (London: Oxford University Press).

Brathwaite, E. K. (1970) 'Timehri', *Savacou* 235–44.

Brathwaite, E. K. (1974) *Contradictory Omens: Cultural Diversity and Integration in the Caribbean* (Mona, Jamaica: Savacou Publications).

Brathwaite, E. K. (1977) The Love Axe: Developing a Caribbean Aesthetic 1962–1974 – I, *Bim* 16(61), 53–65.

Brathwaite, E. K. (1984) *History of the Voice* (London: New Beacon Books).

Brathwaite E. K. (1993) 'Caribbean Critics' in *Roots* (Ann Arbor, MI: University of Michigan Press), 111–126. First published in 1969.

Brathwaite, E. K. (1993) (first published in *Bim* 1963) 'Roots' in *Roots* (Ann Arbor, MI: University of Michigan Press), 28–54.

Brathwaite, E. K. (1993) *Roots* (Ann Arbor, MI: University of Michigan Press).

Brathwaite, E. K. (1994) *Barabajan Poems* (New York: Savacou North).

Brathwaite, E. K. (1995) 'A Post-Cautionary Tale of the Helen of our Wars', *Wasafiri*, 22 (Autumn), 69–78.

Breiner, Laurence A. (1993) 'How to behave on paper: the *Savacou* debate', *Journal of West Indian Literature* 6(1) (July), 1–10.

Breiner, Laurence A. (1998) *An Introduction to West Indian Poetry* (Cambridge: Cambridge University Press).

Brennan, Timothy (1997) *At Home in the World: Cosmopolitanism Today* (London: Harvard University Press).

Brodber, Erna (1988) *Myal* (London: New Beacon Books).

Brodber, Erna (1994) *Louisiana* (London: New Beacon Books).

Brodber, Erna (1998) 'Where Are All the Others?' in Kathleen Balutansky and Marie-Agnes Sourieau (eds) *Caribbean Creolization: Reflections on the Cultural Dynamics of Language, Literature, and Identity* (Miami, FL: University Press of Florida and Jamaica: University of the West Indies Press), 68–75.

Brodber, Erna (1999) *The People of My Jamaican Village, 1817–1948* (Jamaica: Blackspace).

Brown, Lloyd (1978) *West Indian Poetry* (New York: Twayne).

Brown, Stewart (2003) 'The Bright Berries of an Island: Jamaican Poetry Now', *Wasafiri* 83 (Spring), 61–2.

Bucknor, Michael (2004) 'Staging Seduction: Masculine Performance or the Art of Sex in Colin Channer's Reggae Romance *Waiting in Vain?*', *Interventions* 6(1), 67–81.

Burgess, Jacquie, Hodge, M., McDonald, D., Mutota, F. and Rampersad, S. (1998) "Time for Women to Fix Race Relations", *Sunday Guardian*, 8 March, 1–4.

Burnett, Paula (1999) "Where else to row, but backward?: Addressing Caribbean Futures through Re-visions of the Past", *A Review of International English Literature* 30(1) (January), 11–37.

Bush, Barbara (1990) *Slave Women in Caribbean Society 1650–1838* (London: James Currey).

Butler, Judith (1990) *Gender Trouble: Feminism and the Subversion of Identity* (London: Routledge).

Butler, Judith (1993) *Bodies That Matter: On the Discursive Limits of 'Sex'* (London: Routledge).

Carew, Jan (1961) *The Last Barbarians* (London: Secker & Warburg).

Carr, Robert (2003) 'On "Judgements": Poverty, Sexuality-based Violence and Human Rights in 21st century Jamaica', *The Caribbean Journal of Social Work*, 2 (July), 71–87.

Cassidy, F. G. (1961) *Jamaica Talk: Three Hundred Years of the English Language in Jamaica* (London: Macmillan).

Cassidy, F. G. and Le Page, R. B. (1967) *Dictionary of Jamaican English* (Cambridge: Cambridge University Press).

Castañeda, Digna (1995) 'The Female Slave in Cuba during the first half of the Nineteenth Century' in Verene Shepherd, Bridget Brereton and Barbara Bailey (eds) (1995) *Engendering History: Caribbean Women in Historical Perspective* (London: James Currey), 141–154.

Chambers, Ian (1994) *Migrancy, Culture, Identity* (London: Routledge).

Chancy, Myriam J. A. (1997) *Searching for Safe Spaces: Afro-Caribbean Women Writers in Exile* (Philadelphia, PA: Temple University Press).

Cherimutuua, Richard C. and Cherimutuua, Rosalind J. (1987) *Aids, Africa and Racism* (London: Free Association Books).

Chin, Timothy S. (1997) '"Bullers" and "Battymen": Contesting Homophobia in Black Popular Contemporary Caribbean Literature', *Callaloo* 20(1), 127–141.

Chin, Timothy S. (1999) 'Jamaican Popular Culture, Caribbean Literature, and Representation of Gay and Lesbian Sexuality in the Discourses of Race and Nation', *Small Axe* 5, 14–33.

Chrisman, Laura (2003) *Postcolonial Contraventions: Cultural Readings of Race, Imperialism and Transnationalism* (Manchester: Manchester University Press).

Cliff, Michelle (1980) *Claiming An Identity They Taught Me To Despise* (Watertown, MA: Persephone Press).

Cliff, Michelle (1987) *No Telephone to Heaven* (New York: Dutton).

Clifford, James (1988) *The Predicament of Culture: Twentieth-Century Ethnography, Literature, and Art*, (Cambridge, Mass: Harvard University Press).

Clifford, James (1992) 'Traveling cultures', in Lawrence Grossberg, Cary Nelson, and Paula Treichler (eds) *Cultural Studies* (New York: Routledge), 96–116.

Clifford, James (1994) 'Diasporas', *Cultural Anthropology* 9(3), 302–338.

Clifford, James (1997) *Routes: Travel and Translation in the Late Twentieth Century* (Cambridge, MA: Harvard University Press).

Cobham, Rhonda and Merle Collins (eds) (1987) *Watchers and Seekers: Creative Writing by Black Women in Britain* (London: The Women's Press).

Cobham-Sander, Rhonda (1981) 'The Creative Artist and West Indian Society, Jamaica 1900–1950' (unpublished Ph.D. dissertation, University of St Andrews).

Cohen, R. (ed.) (1995) *The Cambridge Survey of World Migration* (Cambridge, MA: Harvard University Press).

Cohen, Robin (1998) *Global Diasporas: An Introduction* (Washington: University of Washington Press).

Collymore, A. F. (1955) *Glossary of Words and Phrases of Barbadian Dialect*, 5th edn (Bridgetown, Barbados: Barbados National Trust).

Constantine-Simms, Delroy (ed.) (2001) *The Greatest Taboo: Homosexuality in Black Communities* (California, Alyson Books).

Cooper, Carolyn (1990) 'Slackness Hiding from Culture: Erotic Play in the Dancehall', *Jamaica Journal* 23(1), 44–51.

Cooper, Carolyn (1993) *Noises in the Blood: Orality, Gender and the 'Vulgar' Body of Jamaican Popular Culture* (London: Macmillan Caribbean).

Cooper, Carolyn (2004) 'Branding Jamaica: popular culture in "postcolonial" context', *Interventions: International Journal of Postcolonial Studies* 6(1), 1–9.

Cooper, Wayne F. (1987) *Rebel Sojourner in the Harlem Renaissance* (New York: Schocken).

Coulthard, G. R. (1961) 'The Literature of the West Indies' in A. L. McLeod (ed.) *The Commonwealth Pen: an Introduction to the Literature of the British Commonwealth* (Ithaca: Cornell University Press), 185–202.

Coulthard, G. R. (ed.) (1966) *Caribbean Literature: An Anthology* (London: University of London Press).

Covi, Giovanna (2003) *Jamaica Kincaid's Prismatic Subjects: Making Sense of Being in the World* (London: Mango Season).

Cudjoe, Selwyn (ed.) (1990) *Caribbean Women Writers: Essays from the First International Conference* (Wellesley, MA: Calaloux).

Cumber Dance, Daryl (1992) *New World Adams: Conversations with Contemporary West Indian Writers* (Leeds: Peepal Tree Press).

Cumper, George (1957) 'Literary Period Piece', *Public Opinion*, 26 January, 7.

Dabydeen, David (1984) *Slave Song* (Mundelstrup, Denmark: Dangaroo Press).

Dakers, Andrew (1953) 'Interview with Roger Mais', *John O'London Weekly*, 1 May.

Danticat, Edwidge (1991) *Krik? Krak!* (New York: Soho Press).

Danticat, Edwidge (1994) *Breath, Eyes, Memory* (London: Abacus).

Das, Mahadai (1977) *I Want to be a Poetess of My People* (Guyana: Guyana National Service Publishing Centre).

Das, Mahadai (1982) *My Finer Steel Will Grow* (Vermont: Samisdat).

Das, Mahadai (1987) 'They Came in Ships' in David Dabydeen and Brinsley Samaroo (eds) *India in the Caribbean* (London: Hansib), 288–9.

Das, Mahadai (1988) *Bones* (Leeds: Peepal Tree Press).

Dash, J. Michael (1998) *The Other America: Caribbean Literature in a New World Context* (Charlottesville, VA: University Press of Virginia).

Dathorne, O. R. (ed.) (1966) *Caribbean Narrative: An Anthology of West Indian Writing* (London: Heinemann Educational Books Ltd).

Dathorne, O. R. (ed.) (1967) *Caribbean Verse: An Anthology* (London: Heinemann Educational Books Ltd).

Dear, Karen (2003) 'Time for Change', *The Nation*, October 12.

deCaires Narain, Denise (2002a) 'Standing in the Place of Love: Sex, Love and Loss in Jamaica Kincaid's Writing' in Patricia Mohammed (ed.) *Gendered Realities: Essays in Caribbean Feminist Thought* (Kingston, Jamaica: University of the West Indies Press), 334–360.

deCaires Narain, Denise (2002b) *Contemporary Caribbean Women's Poetry: Making Style* (London: Routledge).

deCaires Narain, Denise (2003) 'The Politics and Poetics of Belonging in Caribbean Women's Poetry', *Wasafiri* 38, 13–19.

DeLisser, H. G. (1913) *Twentieth Century Jamaica* (Kingston, Jamaica: Jamaica Times Ltd).

DeLisser, H. G. (1914) *Jane's Career* (London: Methuen).

DeLisser, H. G. (1929) *The White Witch of Rosehall* (Kingston, Jamaica: Jamaica Times).

Dirlik, Arif (1997) *The Postcolonial Aura* (Boulder, CO: Westview Press).

Donnell, Alison (1992) 'Dreaming of Daffodils: Cultural Resistance in the Narratives of Theory', *Kunapipi*, XIV 45–52.

Donnell, Alison (1997) 'Sentimental Subversion: the poetics and politics of devotion in the work of Una Marson' in V. Bertram (ed.) *Kicking Daffodils* (Edinburgh: Edinburgh University Press), 113–124.

Donnell, Alison (1999) 'When Writing the Other is Being True to the Self: Jamaica Kincaid's *The Autobiography of My Mother*' in Pauline Polkey (ed.) *Women's Lives into Print* (Basingstoke, Macmillan), 123–136.

Döring, Tobias (2002) *Caribbean-English Passages: Intertextuality in a Postcolonial Tradition* (London: Routledge).

Drayton, Arthur D. (1970a) 'West Indian Consciousness in West Indian Verse', *Journal of Commonwealth Literature*, 9, 66–88.

Drayton, Arthur D. (1970b) 'The European Factor in West Indian Literature', *Literary Half-Yearly*, 11, 71–95.

Du Bois, W. E. (1903) 'Of Our Spiritual Strivings' in *The Souls of Black Folk* (Chicago, IL: A. C. McClurg).

Edmondson, Belinda (1999) *Making Men: Gender, Literary Authority, and Women's Writing in Caribbean Narrative* (Durham, NC: Duke University Press).

Ellis Russell, Nadia (2001) 'Interview with Erna Brodber' http://www.inthefray.com/200105/imagine/brodber2/brodber2.html.

Espinet, Ramabai (1989) 'The Invisible Woman in West Indian Literature', *World Literature Written in English*, 29.2, 116–126.

Espinet, Ramabai (1991) 'Barred: Trinidad 1987' in Carmen C. Estevez and Lizabeth Paravisini Gebert (eds) *Green Cane and Juicy Flotsam: Short Stories by Caribbean Women* (New Jersey: Rutgers University Press), 80–85.

Espinet, Ramabai (2003) *The Swinging Bridge* (Toronto: HarperCollins).

Fanon, Frantz (1986) *Black Skins, White Masks* (London: Pluto Press). First published 1952.

Figueroa, John (1986) 'Review', *Caribbean Quarterly*, 32(1) and 2(59).

Figueroa, John (ed.) (1966) *Caribbean Voices: An Anthology of West Indian Poetry* (London: Evans Brothers Ltd).

Ford-Smith, Honor (1985) 'Una Marson: Black Nationalist and Feminist Writer', Research Project: Women and Development, Institute of Social Studies, The Hague.

Ford-Smith, Honor (2004) 'Unruly Virtues of the Spectacular: Performing Engendered Nationalism in the UNIA in Jamaica, *Interventions: International Journal of Postcolonial Studies* 6(1), 18–44.

Francis, Donnette (2004) 'Silences Too Horrific to Disturb: Writing Sexual Histories in Edwidge Danticat's *Breath, Eyes, Memory*', *Research in African Literatures*, 35(2) (Summer), 75–90.

Garber, Marjorie (1992) *Vested Interests: Cross-Dressing and Cultural Authority* (New York: Routledge).

Garcia, Bernado (1999) *The Development of Gay Latino Identity* (New York and London: Garland).

Gevisser, Mark and Edwin Cameron (eds) (1995) *Defiant Desire: Gay and Lesbian Lives in South Africa* (New York: Routledge).

Gikandi, Simon (1992) *Writing in Limbo: Modernism and Caribbean Literature* (Ithaca and London: Cornell University Press).

Gilkes, Michael (1981) *The West Indian Novel* (Boston, MA: Twayne Publishers).

Gilkes, Michael (1986) 'Creative schizophrenia: the Caribbean cultural challenge' (Coventry: Centre for Caribbean Studies).

Gilman, Sander (1985) 'Black Bodies: Toward an Iconography of Female Sexuality in Late Nineteenth Century Art, Medicine, and Literature', *Critical Inquiry* 12(1) (Autumn), 204–242.

Gilroy, Paul (1993) *The Black Atlantic: Modernity and Double Consciousness* (London: Verso).

Glave, Thomas (2003) 'Introduction' to Patricia Powell, *A Small Gathering of Bones* (Oxford: Heinemann Educational Publishers) vii–x.

Glissant, Edouard (1989) *Caribbean Discourse: Selected Essays* (Charlottesville, VA: University of Virginia Press).

Goldie, Terry (ed.) (1999) 'Postcolonial and Queer Theory and Praxis'. Special issue of *Ariel* 30.2.

Gomes, Albert (1974) *Through A Maze of Colour* (Trinidad: Key Caribbean Publications).

Gourevitch, Philip (1994) 'Naipaul's World', *Commentary* 98(2) (August), 27–31.

Goveia, Elsa (1970) 'The Social Framework', *Savacou* 2, 7–15.

Greig, Beatrice (1932) 'Mahatma Gandhi', *The Beacon* II(4) (August).

Griffiths, Glyne A. (1996) *Deconstruction, Imperialism and the West Indian Novel* (Kingston, Jamaica: The Press University of the West Indies).

Griffiths, Glyne A. (2003) '"This is London Calling the West Indies": the BBC's *Caribbean Voices*' in Bill Schwarz (ed.) *West Indian Intellectuals in Britain* (Manchester: Manchester University Press), 196–208.

Gutzmore, Cecil (2004) 'Casting the First Stone: Policing of Homo/sexuality in Jamaican Popular Culture', *Interventions: International Journal of Postcolonial Studies*, 6(1), 118–134.

Guyana Chronicle (2000) 'Human Services Minister to probe sexual abuse report', *Guyana Chronicle* 30 March (http://www.landofsixpeoples.com/gynewsjs.htm)

Hall, Stuart (1990) 'Cultural Identity and Diaspora' in Jonathan Rutherford (ed.) *Identity, Community, Culture, Difference* (London: Lawrence and Wishart), 222–237.

Hall, Stuart (1992) 'Cultural Studies and its Theoretical Legacies' in L. Grossberg, C. Nelson and P. Treichler (eds) *Cultural Studies* (New York: Routledge), 277–294.

Hall, Stuart (1996) 'Minimal Selves' in Houston A. Baker, Jr, Manthia Diawara, Ruth H. Lindeborg (eds), *Black British Cultural Studies: A Reader* (London: University of Chicago Press), 114–119.

Haniff, Nesha (1999) 'My grandmother worked in the field: Stereotypes regarding East Indian women in the Caribbean: Honorable Mention' in Rosanne Kanhai (ed.) *Matikor: The Politics of Identity for Indo-Caribbean Women* (St Augustine, Trinidad: School of Continuing Studies, University of the West Indies), 18–31.

Hanisch, Carol (1970) 'The Personal is Political' in *Notes from the Second Year* (New York: Radical Feminism), 76–78.

Harney, Stefano (1996) *Nationalism and Identity: Culture and the Imagination in a Caribbean Diaspora* (London: Zed Books).

Harris, Wilson (1967) *The Waiting Room* (London: Faber and Faber).

Harris, Wilson (1967) *Tradition, the Writer and Society: Critical Essays* (London: New Beacon Books).

Hathaway, Heather (1997) 'Claude McKay' in William L. Andrews, Frances Smith Foster and Trudier Harris (eds) *The Oxford Companion to African-American Literature* (Oxford: Oxford University Press), 489–90.

Hathaway, Heather (1999) *Caribbean Waves: Relocating Claude McKay and Paule Marshall* (Bloomington, IN: University of Indiana Press).

Hawley, John (ed.) (2001) *Postcolonial, Queer: Theoretical Intersections* (Albany, NY: State University of New York Press).

Hayes Edwards, Brent (2003) *The Practice of Diaspora: Literature, Translation and the Rise of Black Internationalism* (Cambridge, MA: Harvard University Press).

Hazel, Vivian (1956) *Poems* (Devon: Arthur H. Stockwell).

Hearne, John (1950) 'Barren Treasury', *Public Opinion*, 11 November, 6 and 8.

Hendricks, A. L. and Lindo, Cedric (eds) (1962) *Independence Anthology of Jamaican Literature*.

Henry, Paget (2000) *Caliban's Reason: Introducing Afro-Caribbean Philosophy* (New York and London: Routledge).

Hodge, Merle (1970) *Crick Crack, Monkey* (London: Andre Deutsch).

Hodge, Merle (1993) *For the Life of Laetitia* (New York: Farrah, Straus and Giroux).

Hollar, Constance (1941) *Flaming June* (Kingston: New Dawn Press).

Hollar, Constance (ed.) (1932) *Songs of Empire* (Kingston, Jamaica: Gleaner).

Hollibaugh, Amber and Moraga, Cherrie (1981) 'What We're Rollin Around in Bed With: Sexual Silences in Feminism: A Conversation Toward Ending Them', *Heresies* 12, 58–62.

Holst Petersen, Kirsten and Rutherford, Anna (eds) (1986) *A Double Colonization: Colonial and Post-Colonial Women's Writing* (Oxford: Dangaroo Press).

hooks, bell (1994) *Outlaw Culture: Resisting Representations* (London: Routledge).

Howe, Barbara (ed.) (1966) *From the Green Antilles: Writings of the Caribbean* (London: Panther Books Ltd).

Hutcheon, Linda (1985) *A Theory of Parody: The Teachings of Twentieth-Century Art Forms* (London: Routledge).

Hutton, Albinia (1930) *Life in Jamaica* (London: Arthur H. Stockwell).

Hutton, Albinia (1932) *Hill Songs and Wayside Verses* (Kingston).

James, C. L. R. (1963) *Beyond A Boundary* (London: Hutchinson).

James, C. L. R. (1967) 'Introduction to Tradition and The West Indian Novel' in Wilson Harris, *Tradition, the Writer and Society: Critical Essays* (London: New Beacon Books).

James, C. L. R. (1969) 'Discovering Literature in Trinidad: the 1930s', *Journal of Commonwealth Literature* 7, 73–80.

James, Louis (1968) *The Islands in Between: Essays on West Indian Literature* (Oxford: Oxford University Press).

James, Louis (1999) *Caribbean Literature in English* (Harlow, Essex: Longman).

James, Louis (2003) 'The Caribbean Artists Movement' in Bill Schwartz (ed.) *West Indian Intellectuals in Britain* (Manchester, Manchester University Press).

Jarrett-Macauley, Delia (1998) *The Life of Una Marson, 1905–65* (Manchester: Manchester University Press).

Jones, Funmilayo (2001) 'Unite in Fight Against AIDS', *The Barbados Advocate*, December 20, 9.

Jones, Stephanie (2000) 'The Politics and Poetics of Diaspora in V. S. Naipaul's *A Way in the World*', *Journal of Commonwealth Literature* 35(1) (Spring), 87–97.

Juneja, Renu (1995) 'Contemporary Women Writers' in Bruce King (ed.) *West Indian Literature*, 2nd edn (London and Basingstoke: Macmillan Educational).

Juneja, Renu (1996) *Caribbean Transactions: West Indian Culture in Literature* (London and Basingstoke: Macmillan Educational).

Kanhai, Rosanne (1999) 'The Masala Stone Sings: Poetry, Performance and Film by Indo-Caribbean Women' in *Matikor: The Politics of Identity for Indo-Caribbean Women* (St. Augustine, Trinidad: School of Continuing Studies, University of the West Indies), 209–237.

Kanhai, Rosanne (1999) (ed.) *Matikor: The Politics of Identity for Indo-Caribbean Women* (St. Augustine, Trinidad: School of Continuing Studies, University of the West Indies).

Kaplan, C. (1996) *Questions of Travel: Postmodern Discourses of Displacement* (Durham, NC: Duke University Press).

Kempadoo, Kamala (2003) 'Theorizing Sexual Relations in the Caribbean: Prostitution and the Problem of the "Exotic"' in Eudine Barriteau (ed.) *Confronting Power, Theorizing Gender: Interdisciplinary Perspectives in the Caribbean* (Jamaica: University of the West Indies Press).

Kempadoo, Oona (1998) *Buxton Spice* (London: Phoenix House).

Kerr, Paullette A. (1995) 'Victims or Strategists?: Female Lodging-house Keepers in Jamaica' in Verene Shepherd, Bridget Brereton and Barbara Bailey (eds) *Engendering History: Caribbean Women in Historical Perspective* (Kingston, Jamaica: Ian Randle), 197–212.

Khan, Ismith (1964) *The Obeah Man* (London: Hutchinson and Co).

Kincaid, Jamaica (1985) *Annie John* (London: Pan Books Ltd).

Kincaid, Jamaica (1991) *Lucy* (London: Jonathan Cape).

Kincaid, Jamaica (1997) *My Brother* (New York: The Noonday Press).

King, Bruce (ed.) (1979) *West Indian Literature* (London: Macmillan Press Ltd).

King, Bruce (ed.) (1995) *West Indian Literature*, 2nd edn (London and Basingstoke: Macmillan Educational).

King, Lettuce Ada (Tropica) *The Island of Sunshine* (New York, 1904).

King, Rosamund (2002) 'Sex and Sexuality in the English Caribbean Novels – Survey from 1950', *Journal of West Indian Literature* 11(1), 24–38.

Kirshenblatt-Gimblett, Barbara (1994) 'Spaces of Dispersal', *Cultural Anthropology*, 9(3), 339–344.

Kruger, Steven (1996) *AIDS Narratives: Gender and Sexuality, Fiction and Science* (New York and London: Garland).

La Rose, John (1974) 'A West Indian in Wales', *Savacou* 9/10 (Kingston and London: Caribbean Artists Movement).

Lamming, George (1953) *In the Castle of My Skin* (London: Michael Joseph).

Lamming, George (1960) 'The Occasion for Speaking' in G. Lamming *The Pleasures of Exile* (London: Michael Joseph), 23–50.

Lazarus, Neil (1999) *Nationalism and Cultural Practice in the Postcolonial World* (Cambridge: Cambridge UP).

Le Page, R. B. (1960) *Jamaican Creole: An Historical Introduction to Jamaican Creole* (New York: St Martin's Press).

Le Page, R. B. (1969) 'Dialect in West Indian Literature', *Journal of Commonwealth Literature*, 7 (July), 1–7.

Lindo, Archie, (ed.) (1940) *Year Book of the Poetry League of Jamaica, 1940* (Kingston, Jamaica: New Dawn Press).

Lindo, Archie (ed.) (1941) *Year Book of the Poetry League of Jamaica, 1941* (Kingston, Jamaica: New Dawn Press).

Lindo, Archie (ed.) (1942) *Year Book of the Poetry League of Jamaica, 1942* (Kingston, Jamaica: New Dawn Press).

Lindo, Archie (1948) 'Poet's Corner', *The Sunday Gleaner*, 19 September, 19.

Lokaisingh-Meighoo, Sean (2000) 'Jahaji Bhai: Notes on the Masculine Subject and Homoerotic Subtext of Indo-Caribbean Identity', *Small Axe* 7, 77–92.

Long, Edward (1774) *History of Jamaica. Or General Survey of the Antient and Modern State of that Island; with Reflextions on its Situation, Settlements, Inhabitants, Climate, products, Commerce, Laws, And Government, 3 vols* (London: Lowndes).

Lorde, Audrey (1982) *Zami: a New Spelling of my Name* (Watertown, MA: Persephone Press).

Lovelace, Earl (1968) 'Creating Communities' in F. Aiyejina (ed.) *Growing in the Dark (Selected Essays)*, San Juan, Trinidad: Lexicon Trinadad Ltd).

Lovelace, Earl (1968a) 'The Arts, the Critics and A New Society', *Express*, 9 June, 16 reprinted in Funso Aiyejina (ed.) *Growing in the Dark (Selected Essays)* (Lexicon Trinidad Ltd (San Juan, Trinidad, 2003), 63–64.

Lovelace, Earl (1968b) 'Watch, Your Freedom is in Jeopardy' *Express*, 30 January, 16 reprinted in Funso Aiyejina (ed.) *Growing in the Dark (Selected Essays)* (Lexicon Trinidad Ltd: San Juan, Trinidad, 2003), 65–67.

Lovelace, Earl (1979) *The Dragon Can't Dance* (London: André Deutsch).

Lovelace, Earl (1983) 'Rhythm and Meaning' in F. Aiyejina (ed.) *Growing in the Dark (Selected Essays)*, San Juan, Trinidad: Lexicon Trinadad Ltd).

Lovelace, Earl (1992) 'Artists as Agents of Unity' in F. Aiyejina (ed.) *Growing in the Dark (Selected Essays)*, San Juan, Trinidad: Lexicon Trinadad Ltd).

Lovelace, Earl (1996) *Salt* (London: Faber and Faber).

Lowenthal, David (1972) *West Indian Societies* (London: Oxford University Press).

Lumsden, Ian (1997) *Machos, Maricones, and Gays: Cuba and Homosexuality* (London: Latin American Bureau).

MacDonald-Smythe, Antonia (1999) 'Authorizing the slut in Jamaica Kincaid's *At the Bottom of the River*, in *MaComère* (Harrisonburg, James Maddison University), 96–113.

MacKay, Albinina Catherine (1912) *Poems by Albinia Catherine MacKay* (Jamaica: Kingston).

Mahabir, Thora (1944) 'Readers' Forum', *The Observer* [Trinidad], June, 10 in Rampersad, Kris (2002) *Finding a Place: IndoTrinidadian Literature* (Kingston, Jamaica: Ian Randle Publishers), 217.

Maharaj, Clem (1992) *The Dispossessed* (Oxford: Heinemann Educational Books).

Mais, Roger (1940) 'Where the Roots Lie', *Public Opinion*, 9 March, 12.

Mais, Roger (1942) *And Most of All Man Stories* (Mona, Jamaica: Mais Collection, University of the West Indies Library).

Mais, Roger (1944) 'Now We Know', *Public Opinion*, 11 July, 10.

Mais, Roger (1946) *Face and Other Stories* (Kingston, Jamaica: Universal Printery).

Mais, Roger (1953) *The Hills Were Joyful Together* (London: Jonathan Cape).

Mais, Roger (1954) *Brother Man* (London: Jonathan Cape).

Mais, Roger (1955) *Black Lightning* (London: Jonathan Cape).

Maiwald, Michael (2002) 'Race, Capitalism, and the Third-sex Ideal: Claude McKay's Home to Harlem and the Legacy of Edward Carpenter', *Modern Fiction Studies* 48(4), 825–857.

Mangru, Basdeo (1987) 'The Sex Ratio Disparity and its Consequences Under the Indenture in British Guiana', in D. Dabydeen and B. Samaroo (eds) *Indian in the Caribbean* (London: Hansib), 211–230.

Manley, Edna (1943) 'Foreword', *Focus*.

Manley, Edna (1960) 'Foreword', *Focus*.

Markham, E. A. (1989) *Hinterland: Caribbean Poetry from the West Indies and Britain* (Newcastle upon Tyne: Bloodaxe Books).

Marson, Una (1930) *Tropic Reveries* (Kingston, Jamaica).

Marson, Una (1931) *Heights and Depths* (Kingston, Jamaica).

Marson, Una (1933) 'Nigger', *The Keys*, July, 8–9.

Marson, Una (1937) *The Moth and the Star* (Kingston, Jamaica).

Marson, Una (1937a) 'Some Things Women Politicians Can Do?' *Public Opinion* 27 February, 10.

Marson, Una (1937b) 'Women – Work and Wages' *Public Opinion* 6 March, 10.

Marson, Una (1937c) 'Feminism' *Public Opinion* 10 April, 10.

Marson, Una (1937d) 'Wanted: Writers and Publishers' *Public Opinion* 12 June, 6.

Marson, Una (1945) *Towards the Stars* (London: University of London Press).

Marson, Una (ed.) (1950) *14 Jamaican Short Stories* (Kingston, Jamaica: Pioneer Press).

Massad, Joseph (2002) 'Re-Orienting Desire: The Gay International and the Arab World', *Public Culture* 14 (Spring), 361–85.

McClean and Bishop (2003) 'Of Hearts Revealed: an interview with Olive Senior', *Calabash: A Journal of Caribbean Arts and Letters* 2(3) (Summer/Fall), 3–13.

McClintock, Anne (1995) *Imperial Leather: Race Gender and Sexuality in the Colonial Contest* (London: Routledge).

McFarlane, J. E. C. (1929) (ed.) *Voices From The Summerland: An Anthology of Jamaican Poetry* (London: Fowler Wright Ltd).

McFarlane, J. E. C. (1945) 'On the Nature of Poetry' in *The Challenge of Our Time* (Kingston, Jamaica: New Dawn Press).

McFarlane, J. E. C. (ed.) (1949) *A Treasury of Jamaican Poetry* (London: University of London Press).

McFarlane, J. E. C. (1953) 'The Prospect of West Indian Poetry', *Kyk-Over-Al*, 5.

McFarlane, J. E. C. (1956) *A Literature in the Making* (Kingston, Jamaica: Pioneer Press).

McKay, Claude (1912) *Constab Ballads* (London: Watt & Co.).

McKay, Claude (1912) *Songs of Jamaica* (Kingston, Jamaica: A. W. Gardner & Co.).

McLeod, A. L. (ed.) (2002) 'Introduction' to *Wings of the Evening: Selected Poems of Vivian Virtue* (Kingston, Jamaica: Ian Randle Publishers), 1–43.

McLeod, A. L. (ed.) (2002) *Wings of the Evening: Selected Poems of Vivian Virtue* (Kingston, Jamaica: Ian Randle Publishers).

Meeks, Brian (1996) *Radical Caribbean: From Black Power to Abu Bakr* (Kingston, Jamaica: The Press University of the West Indies).

Mehta, Brinda J. (1999) 'Cultural Hegemony and the Stranglehold of Brahminic Patriarchy in an Indo-Caribbean Context', *Journal of Commonwealth Literature*, 6(1), 125–152.

Mehta, Brinda J. (2000) 'The Colonial Curriculum and the Construction of the "Coolie-ness" in Lakshmi Persaud's *Sastra* and *Butterfly in the Wind* and Jan Shinebourne's *The Last English Plantation*', *Journal of Caribbean Literatures* 3(1), 132–148.

Minh-Ha, Trinh T. (1989) *Woman, Native, Other: Writing Postcoloniality and Feminism* (Bloomington, IN: Indiana University Press).

Mitchell, David M. (1929) 'Introduction', *Voices From The Summerland: An Anthology of Jamaican Poetry*, J. E. C. McFarlane, ed. (London: Fowler Wright Ltd).

Mohammed, Patricia (1995) 'Writing Gender into History: The Negotiation of Gender Relations among Indian Men and Women in Post-Indenture Trinidad Society, 1917–47' in Verene Shepherd, Bridget Brereton and Barbara Bailey (eds) (1995) *Engendering History: Caribbean Women in Historical Perspective* (London: James Currey).

Mohammed, Patricia (1998a) 'Towards Indigenous Feminist Theorizing in the Caribbean' in Patricia Mohammed (ed.) *Rethinking Caribbean Difference, Special Issue on the Caribbean, Feminist Review* 59 (June), 6–33.

Mohammed, Patricia (1998b) 'The Reconstitution of Gender Identities among Indians in Trinidad through Mythology' in Christine Barrow (ed.) *Caribbean Portraits: Essays on Gender Ideologies and Identities* (Kingston, Jamaica: Ian Randle Publishers), 391–413.

Mohammed, Patricia (2002b) 'The "Creolisation" of Indian women in Trinidad' in Verene Shepherd and Glen Richards (eds) *Questioning Creole: Creolisation Discourses in Caribbean Culture* (Kingston: Ian Randle Publishers), 130–147.

Mohammed, Patricia (2003) 'A Symbiotic Visiting Relationship: Caribbean Feminist Historiography and Caribbean Feminist Theory' in Eudine Barriteau (ed.) *Confronting Power, Theorizing Gender: Interdisciplinary Perspectives in the Caribbean* (Kingston, Jamaica: University of the West Indies Press).

Mohammed, Patricia (ed.) (2002a) *Gendered Realities: Essays in Caribbean Feminist Thought* (Kingston, Jamaica: University of the West Indies Press).

Momsen, Janet (ed.) (1993) *Women and Change in the Caribbean* (London: James Currey).

Mootoo, Shani (1993) *Out on Main Street* (Vancouver: Press Gang Publishers).

Mootoo, Shani (1998) *Cereus Blooms at Night* (London: Granta).

Mordecai, Pamela and Betty Wilson (1989) *Her True-True Name: An Anthology of Women's Writing from the Caribbean* (Oxford: Heinemann International).

Morris, Mervyn (1967a) 'On Reading Louise Bennett, Seriously', *Jamaica Journal* 1(1), 69–74.

Morris, Mervyn (1967b) 'Some West Indian Problems of Audience', *English* 16.

Morrison, William (1931) 'Introduction' to Una Marson *Heights and Depths* (Kingston, Jamaica: Gleaner).

Morrison, William (1932) 'Foreword' to Constance Hollar (ed.) *Songs of Empire* (Kingston, Jamaica: Gleaner).

Naipaul, V. S. (1962) *The Middle Passage: Impressions of Five Societies* (London: André Deutsch).

Naipaul, V. S. (1994) *A Way in the World: A Sequence* (London: Random House).

Nanton, Philip (2004) 'London Calling', *Caribbean Beat* 63 (January–February).

Nasta, Susheila (ed.) (1991) *Motherlands: Black Women's Writing from Africa, the Caribbean and South Asia* (London: The Women's Press).

Nasta, Susheila and Rutherford, Anna (eds) (1995) *Tiger's Triumph: Celebrating Sam Selvon* (Hebden Bridge, West Yorkshire: Dangaroo Press).

Nettleford, Rex M. (1978) *Caribbean Cultural Identity: The Case of Jamaica* (Kingston, Jamaica: Institute of Jamaica).

O'Callaghan, Evelyn (1993) *Woman Version: Theoretical Approaches to West Indian Fiction by Women* (London and Basingstoke: The Macmillan Press Ltd).

O'Callaghan, Evelyn (1998) 'Compulsory Heterosexuality and Textual/Sexual Alternatives in Selected Texts by West Indian Women Writers' in Christine Barrow (ed.) *Caribbean Portraits: Essays on Gender Ideologies and Identities* (Kingston: Ian Randle Publishers), 294–319.

O'Callaghan, Evelyn (2003) *Women Writing the West Indies, 1804–1939* (London: Routledge).

Oakley, Leo (1970) 'Ideas of Patriotism and National Dignity in Some Jamaican Writings', *Jamaica Journal*, 4, 16–21.

Olson, Nellie France Ackerman (1956) *Pondered Poems* (Kingston, Jamaica: The Gleaner Co).

Owens, R. J. (1961) 'West Indian Poetry', *Caribbean Quarterly*, 7, 120–127.

Pantin, Anthony (2000) 'Church condemns homosexual acts,' *Trinidad Guardian* (Port of Spain) 8 January, 20.

Patterson, Orlando (1969) 'The Ritual of Cricket,' *Jamaica Journal* 3 (March), 23–25.

Persaud, Lakshmi (1990) *Butterfly in the Wind* (Leeds: Peepal Tree Press).

Persaud, Lakshmi (1993) *Sastra* (Leeds: Peepal Tree Press).

Persaud, Lakshmi (2003) *For the Love of My Name* (Leeds: Peepal Tree Press).

Pheng Cheah and Bruce Robbins (eds) (1998) *Cosmopolitics: Thinking and Feeling Beyond the Nation* (University of Minnesota Press).

Phillips Casteel, Sarah (2003) 'New World Pastoral: the Caribbean garden and Emplacement in Gisèle Pineau and Shani Mootoo', *Interventions: International Journal of Postcolonial Studies*, 5(1), 12–28.

Phillips, Caryl (1994) 'The Voyage in a Way in the World', *The New Republic* 210(24) (13 June), 40–45.

Pouchet Paquet, Sandra (1979) 'The Fifties' in Bruce King (ed.) *West Indian Literature* (London: Macmillan Press Ltd), 63–77.

Pouchet Paquet, Sandra (1997) 'Documents of West Indian History: Telling a West Indian Story', *Callaloo* 20(4) (Fall), 764–776.

Pouchet Paquet, Sandra (2002) *Caribbean Autobiography: Cultural Identity and Self-Representation* (Madison, WI: University of Wisconsin Press).

Powell, Patricia (1994) *A Small Gathering of Bones* (Oxford: Heinemann Educational Publishers).

Poynting, Jeremy (1985) 'Literature and Cultural Pluralism: East Indians in the Caribbean', unpublished dissertation, University of Leeds.

Procter, James (2003) *Dwelling Places: Postwar Black British Writing* (Manchester: Manchester University Press).

Puri, Shalini (1997) 'Race, Rape, and Representation: Indo-Caribbean Women and Cultural Nationalism', *Cultural Critique* (Spring), 119–163. Also reprinted (1999) in Rosanne Kanhai (ed.) *Matikor: The Politics of Identity for Indo-Caribbean Women* (St Augustine, Trinidad and Tobago: The University of the West Indies School of Continuing Education).

Puri, Shalini (ed.) (2003a) *Marginal Migrations: The Circulation of Cultures within the Caribbean* (Oxford: Macmillan Caribbean).

Puri, Shalini (2003b) 'Beyond Resistance: Notes Towards a New Caribbean Cultural Studies,' *Small Axe* 14 (September), 23–38.

Puri, Shalini (2004) *The Caribbean Postcolonial: Social Equality, Post-Nationalism, and Cultural Hybridity* (New York: Palgrave Macmillan).

Rahim, Jennifer (1999) 'The "Limbo Imagination" and New World Reformation in Earl Lovelace's *Salt*' *Small Axe* 5 (March), 151–160.

Ramchand, Kenneth (1970) *The West Indian Novel and Its Background* (London: Heinemann).

Ramchand, Kenneth (ed.) (1992) Eric Roach, *The Flowering Rock: Collected Poems 1938–1974* (Leeds: Peepal Tree Press).

Ramchand, Kenneth (1968) 'Dialect in West Indian Fiction', *Caribbean Quarterly* 14(1/2).

Ramchand, Kenneth (1980) 'Introduction' in *West Indian Narrative: An Introductory Anthology*, revised edn (Walton-on-Thames, Surrey: Thomas Nelson and Sons Ltd), i–x.

Ramchand, Kenneth (1993) 'Introduction' to Sam Selvon, *An Island Is a World* (Toronto, Canada: Tsar Publications), v–xxv.

Rampersad, Kris (2002) *Finding a Place: IndoTrinidadian Literature* (Kingston, Jamaica: Ian Randle Publishers).

Rampersad, Sheila (1998) 'Jahaaji Behen? Feminist Literary Theory and the Indian Presence in the Caribbean' http://www.uohyd.ernet.in/sss/cinddiaspora/occ2. html

Rampersad, Sheila (2000) 'Douglarisation and the Politics of Indian/African Relations in Trinidad Writing' (unpublished Ph.D. dissertation, Nottingham Trent University).

Rampersad, Sheila (2002) 'Merle Hodge's Revolutionary Dougla Poetics' in Joan Anim-Addo (ed.) *Centre of Remembrance: Memory and Caribbean Women's Literature* (London: Mango Publishing).

Reddock, Rhoda (1985) 'Freedom Denied: Indian Women and Indentureship in Trinidad and Tobago, 1845–1917', *Economic and Political Weekly*, 20.43.

Reddock, Rhoda (1994a) *Women, Labour and Politics in Trinidad and Tobago: A History* (London: Zed Books).

Reddock, Rhoda (1994b) 'Douglarisation and the Politics of Gender Relations in Contemporary Trinidad and Tobago: A Preliminary Exploration' in R. Deosaran, R. Reddock and N. Mustapha (eds) *Contemporary Issues in Social Science: a Caribbean Perspective* (St Augustine, Trinidad: Ansa McAl Psychological Research Centre, University of the West Indies), 98–127.

Reddock, Rhoda (1998a) 'Women's Organizations and Movements in the Commonwealth Caribbean' in Patricia Mohammed (ed.) *Rethinking Caribbean Difference, Special Issue on the Caribbean, Feminist Review* 59 (June), 57–73.

Reddock, Rhoda (1998b) 'Contestations over National Culture in Trinidad and Tobago: Considerations of Ethnicity, Class and Gender' in Christine Barrow (ed.) *Caribbean Portraits: Essays on Gender Ideologies and Identities* (Kingston, Jamaica: Ian Randle Publishers), 414–435.

Reddock, Rhoda (2002) 'Contestations over Culture, Class, Gender and Identity in Trinidad and Tobago: "The Little Tradition"' in Verene Shepherd and Glen Richards (eds) *Questioning Creole: Creolisation Discourses in Caribbean Culture* (Kingston, Jamaica: Ian Randle Publishers), 111–129.

Reid, V. S. (1949) *New Day* (New York: Alfred A. Knopf).

Reid, V. S. (1978) 'The Cultural Revolution in Jamaica after 1938'. Address delivered at the Institute of Jamaica.

Reid, V. S. (1983) *Nanny Town* (Kingston: Jamaica Publishing House).

Rhys, Jean (1966) *Wide Sargasso Sea* (London: André Deutsch).

Rice, Alan (2003) *Radical Narratives of the Black Atlantic* (London and New York: Continuum).

Rich, Adrienne (1979) '"When We Dead Awaken": Writing as Revision' in *"On Lies Secrets and Silence": Selected Prose 1996–1978* (Norton).

Rich, Adrienne (1980) 'Compulsory Heterosexuality and Lesbian Existence', *Signs* 5. Reprinted in H. Abelove, M. A. Barale and D. M. Halperin (eds) *The Lesbian and Gay Studies Reader* (New York: Routledge, 1993), 227–254.

Richards, Peter 'Coming Down Hard on Sex Offences' http://www.ips.org/rights/news/nup251299_02.htm.

Roach, E. M. (1952) 'Letter to Lamming in London', *Bim* 17, 36–37.

Roach, Eric (1952) 'Homestead', *Caribbean Quarterly* 2.3, 54.

Roach, E. M. (1991) *The Flowering Rock: Collected Poems 1938–74*, edited by Kenneth Ramchand (Leeds: Peepal Tree Press).

Robbins, Bruce (1998) *Cosmopolitics: Thinking and Feeling Beyond the Nation* (Minneapolis, MN: University of Minnesota Press).

Robinson, Tracy (2000) 'Fictions of Citizenship: Bodies Without Sex and the Effacement of Gender in Law', *Small Axe* 7 (March), 1–27.

Rodney, Walter (1969) *Groundings With My Brothers* (London).

Rohlehr, Gordon (1970) 'Sparrow and the Language of Calypso', *Savacou* 2, 87–99.

Rohlehr, Gordon (1977) 'Poetry, Politics and the February Revolution', *Trinidad and Tobago Review* 12(4) (December).

Rowell, Charles (1988) 'An interview with Olive Senior', *Callaloo*, 11(3), 480–90.

Said, Edward (1993) *Culture and Imperialism* (London: Chatto & Windus).

Salkey, Andrew (ed.) (1960a) *West Indian Stories* (London: Faber and Faber).

Salkey, Andrew (1960b) *Escape to an Autumn Pavement* (London: Hutchinson).

Salkey, Andrew (ed.) (1965) *Stories from the Caribbean* (London: Paul Elek Books Ltd).

Salkey, Andrew (ed.) (1967) *Caribbean Prose* (London: Evans Bros).

Sander, Reinhard (ed.) (1978) *From Trinidad: An Anthology of early West Indian Writing* (London: Hodder and Stoughton).

Sander, Reinhard W. (1979) 'The Thirties and Forties' in Bruce King (ed.) *West Indian Literature* (London: Macmillan Press Ltd), 45–62.

Sangari, Kumkum (1999) *Politics of the Possible: Essays on Gender, History, Narratives, Colonial English* (London: Anthem Press).

Sangari, Kumkum and Sudesh Vaid (eds) (1989) *Recasting Women: Essays in Indian Colonial History* (Delhi: Kali for Women).

Savory Fido, Elaine (1990) 'Textures of Third World Reality in the Poetry of Four African-Caribbean Women' in Boyce Davies, Carole and Savory Fido, Elaine (eds) *Out of the Kumbla: Caribbean Women and Literature* (Trenton, NJ: Africa World Press), 29–44.

Schilts, Paige (2001) 'Queering Lord Clark: Diasporic Formations and Travelling Homophobia in Isaac Julien's *The Darker Side of Black*,' in J. C. Hawley (ed.) *Post-Colonial Queer: Theoretical Intersections* (New York: State University of New York) 165–184.

Schwarz, A. B. Christa (2003) *Gay Voices of the Harlem Renaissance* (Bloomington, IN: Indiana University Press).

Schwarz, Bill (ed.) (2003) *West Indian Intellectuals in Britain* (Manchester: Manchester University Press).

Scott, David (1999) *Refashioning Futures: Criticism after Postcoloniality* (Princeton, NJ: Princeton University Press).

Scott, Lawrence (1996) *Aelred's Sin* (London: Allison & Busby Ltd).

Sealey, Godfrey (1995) 'We are our own worst enemies' in Elizabeth Reid (ed.) *HIV and AIDS: The Global Interconnection* (Kumarian Press) http://www.undp.org/hiv/publications/book/bkchap11.htm downloaded 28 Jan 2004.

Sealey, Godfrey *One of Our Sons is Missing*.

Selvon, Sam (1952) *A Brighter Sun* (London: Allan Wingate).

Selvon, Sam (1956) *The Lonely Londoners* (London: Allan Wingate).

Selvon, Sam (1958) *Turn Again Tiger* (London: MacGibbon and Kee).

Selvon, Sam (1975) *Moses Ascending* (London: Davis Poynter).

Selvon, Sam (1993) *An Island Is a World* (London: Allan Wingate). First published 1955.

Senior, Olive (1985) *Talking of Trees* (Kingston, Jamaica: Calabash).

Senior, Olive (1986) *Summer Lightning* (London: Longman).

Senior, Olive (1989) *Arrival of the Snake Woman* (London: Longman).

Senior, Olive (1991) *Working Miracles: Women's Lives in the English Speaking Caribbean* (London: James Currey).

Senior, Olive (1994) *Gardening in the Tropics* (Toronto: McClelland and Stewart).

Senior, Olive (1995) *Discerner of Hearts* (Toronto: McClelland and Stewart).

Senior, Olive (2004) *Encyclopedia of Jamaican Heritage* (Kingston, Jamaica: Twin Guinep Publishers Ltd).

Seymour, A. J. (ed.) (1950) 'Poetry in the West Indies', *Kyk-Over-Al* (Special Issue, 'The Literary Adventure of the West Indies'), 2.

Seymour, A. J. (ed.) (1972) *New Writing in the Caribbean* (Guyana: Guyana Lithographic Co. Ltd).

Shapiro, Stephen (2001) 'Reconfiguring American Studies?: The Paradoxes of Post-nationalism' in *Dislocations: Transatlantic Perspectives on Postnational American Studies, 49th Parallel Interdisciplinary Journal of North American Studies*, E Journal http://www.49thparallel.bham.ac.uk Issue 8 http://www.49thparallel.bham.ac.uk/back/issue8/shapiro.htm

Sheller, Mimi (2003) *Consuming the Caribbean: From Arawaks to Zombies* (London: Routledge).

Shepherd, Verene (1995) 'Gender, Migration and Settlement: the Indentureship and Post-Indentureship Experience of Indian Females in Jamaica 1845–1943' in Verene Shepherd, Bridget Brereton and Barbara Bailey (eds) (1995) *Engendering History: Caribbean Women in Historical Perspective* (London: James Currey).

Shepherd, Verene (1999) *Women in Caribbean History* (Kingston: Ian Randle Publishers).

Shepherd, Verene (2002) *Maharani's Misery: Narratives of a Passage from India to the Caribbean* (University of the West Indies Press).

Shepherd, Verene and Richards, Glen (eds) (2002) *Questioning Creole: Creolisation Discourses in Caribbean Culture* (Kingston, Jamaica: Ian Randle Publishers).

Shepherd, Verene, Brereton, Bridget and Bailey, Barbara (eds) (1995) *Engendering History: Caribbean Women in Historical Perspective* (London: James Currey).

Sherlock, Philip (1937) 'Introduction' to Una Marson *The Moth And The Star* (Kingston, Jamaica).

Shewcharan, Narmala (1994) *Tomorrow is Another Day* (Leeds: Peepal Tree Press).

Shiw Parsad, Basmat (1999) 'Marital Violence within East Indian Households in Guyana: A Cultural Explanation' in Rosanne Kanhai (ed.) *Matikor: The Politics of Identity for Indo-Caribbean Women* (St Augustine, Trinidad: School of Continuing Studies, University of the West Indies).

Showalter, Elaine (1979) 'Towards a Feminist Poetics' in M. Jacobus (ed.) *Women Writing and Writing About Women* (London: Croom Helm).

Showalter, Elaine (1982) *A Literature of Their Own*, revised edn (London: Virago).

Silvera, Makeda (1992) 'Man Royals and Sodomites: Some Thoughts on the Invisibility of Afro-Caribbean Lesbians' in Makeda Silvera (ed.) *Piece of My Heart: A Lesbian of Colour Anthology* (Toronto: Sister Vision).

Singh, Rajkumari (1960) *A Garland of Stories* (Ilfracombe, UK: Arthur J. Stockwell & Co).

Smilowitz, Erica (1991) 'Interview with Kamau Brathwaite', *The Caribbean Writer* 5, 73–78; also available at http://www.thecaribbeanwriter.com/volume5/brathwaite. html

Smilowitz, Erika (1983) 'Una Marson: Woman Before Her Time', *Jamaica Journal*, 16.2, 62–68.

Smilowitz, Erika (1984) '"Weary of Life and All My Heart's Dull Pain": The Poetry of Una Marson', in Erika Smilowitz and Roberta Knowles (eds) *Critical Issues In West Indian Literature* (Iowa: Caribbean Books), 19–32.

Smith, Barbara (1991) 'The Truth that Never Hurts: Black Lesbians in Fiction in the 1980s' in Chandra Talpada Mohanty, Ann Russo and Lourdes Torres (eds) *Third World Women and the Politics of Feminism* (Bloomington, IN: Indiana University Press), 101–129.

Smith, Faith (ed.) (2000) *Small Axe: a journal of criticism* Special Issue on Sexualities, 7 (March).

Smith, Ian (1999) 'Critics in the Dark' *Journal of West Indian Literature* 8(2), 2–9.

Smyth, Heather (1999) 'Sexual citizenship and Caribbean-Canadian fiction: Dionne Brand's *In Another Place, Not Here* and Shani Mootoo's *Cereus Blooms at Night*', *Ariel, a Review of International English Literature* 30.2, 141–160.

Snell, Marilyn (1997) 'Jamaica Kincaid Hates Happy Endings', *Mother Jones* (September/October) accessed at http://www.motherjones.com/news/qa/1997/09/snell.html

Somerville, Siobhan B. (2000) *Queering the Color Line: Race and the Invention of Homosexuality in American Culture* (Durham, NC: Duke University Press).

St Hill, Donna (2003) 'Women and Difference in Caribbean Gender Theory: Notes Towards a Strategic Universalist Feminism' in Eudine Barriteau, *Confronting Power, Theorizing Gender: Interdisciplinary Perspectives in the Caribbean* (Kingston, Jamaica: University of the West Indies Press), 46–74.

St. John, Omar (1950) 'On Jamaican Poetry', *The West Indian Review* 2(15) (August), 12, 17.

Stanley, Liz (ed.) (1994) *Lives and Works: Auto/biographical Occasions* (double issue) 3(1), 3(2), i–ii.

Stern, Richard (2003) 'Caribbean AIDS Outreach Efforts Hampered by Homophobic Violence', *St Lucia Star*, 31 July.

Sunder Rajan, Rajeswari (2000) 'Righting Wrongs, Rewriting History?', *Interventions: International Journal of Postcolonial Studies* 2(2), 159–170.

Thomas, H. Nigel (1993) *Spirits in the Dark* (Oxford: Heinemann Educational Books).

Thompson, Tony (2002) 'Jamaican Gays Flee to Save Their Lives', *Sunday Observer*, 20 October.

Tropica (real name Wolcott, Mary Adella) (1904) *The Island of Sunshine* (New York: Knickerbocker Press).

Trouillot, Michel-Rolph (2000) 'Abortive Rituals: Historical Apologies in the Global Era', *Interventions: International Journal of Postcolonial Studies* 2(2), 171–186.

Vaz, Noel (1960) 'Creative Potential at Home', *Focus* 143–148.

Walcott, Derek (1970) 'What the Twilight Says: An Overture' in *Dream on Monkey Mountain and Other Plays* (New York: Farrar, Straus & Giroux), 3–40.

Walcott, Derek (1977) *The Star-Apple Kingdom* (New York: Farrar, Straus & Giroux).

Walcott, Derek (1990) *Omeros* (London: Faber and Faber).

Walcott, Derek (1992) *The Antilles: Fragments of Epic Memory* (The Nobel Lecture), (London: The Nobel Foundation and Faber and Faber).

Walcott, Derek (2000) 'A Frosty Fragrance', *The New York Review* 15 June, 61.

Walker, Alice (1983) *The Color Purple* (London: The Women's Press).

Walmsley, Anne (1968) *The Sun's Eye* (Harlow, Essex: Longman Group).

Walmsley, Anne (1995) 'Sam Selvon: Gifts' in Susheila Nasta and Anna Rutherford (eds), *Tiger's Triumph: Celebrating Sam Selvon* (Hebden Bridge, West Yorkshire: Dangaroo Press), 76–77.

Waters, Erica J. (1999) 'Music of Language: An Interview with George Lamming', *The Caribbean Writer*, 13, 190–201.

Webber, A. R. F. (1917) *Those That Be In Bondage – A Tale of Indentures and Sunlit Western Waters* (Georgetown, Guyana: The Daily Chronicle Printing Press).

Wilkinson, Sue and Celia Kitzinger (eds) (1996) *Representing the Other: A Feminism & Psychology Reader* (London: Sage Publications).

Williams, Denis (1963) *Other Leopards* (London: Heinemann).

Williams, Lawson (2000) 'Homophobia and Gay Rights Activism in Jamaica', *Small Axe* 7, 106–111.

Wilson-Tagoe, Nana (1998) *Historical Thought and Literary Representation in West Indian Literature* (Oxford: James Currey).

Wood, Marcus (2000) *Blind Memory: Visual Representations of Slavery in England and America* (Manchester; Manchester University Press).

Woods, Gregory (1993) 'Gay re-readings of the Harlem Renaissance poets', *Journal of Homosexuality* 26(2–3), 127–43.

Woolf, Virginia (1928) *Orlando: A Biography* (London: Hogarth Press).

Wright, Richard (1953) *The Outsider* (New York: Harper Row).

Wynter, Sylvia (1968) 'We Must Learn to Sit Down Together and Talk About a Little Culture: Reflections on West Indian Writing and Criticism I', *Jamaican Journal*, 2(4), 23–32.

Wynter, Sylvia (1969) 'Reflections on West Indian Writing and Criticism II', *Jamaican Journal*, 3(1), 27–42.

Wynter, Sylvia (1971) 'Novel and History, Plot and Plantation', *Savacou* 5, 95–102.

Wynter, Sylvia (1972) 'One Love – Rhetoric or Reality? – Aspects of Afro-Jamaicanism', *Caribbean Studies* 12, 64–97.

Wynter, Sylvia (1973) 'Creole Criticism: A Critique', *New World Quarterly*, 5.4, 12–36.

Wynter, Sylvia (1990) 'Beyond Miranda's Meanings: Un/silencing the "Demonic Ground" of Caliban's "Woman"' in Boyce Davies, Carol and Savory Fido, Elaine (eds) *Out of the Kumbla: Caribbean Women and Literature* (Trenton, NJ: Africa World Press), 355–370.

Young, Robert (1995) *Colonial Desire: Hybridity in Theory, Culture and Race* (London: Routledge).

Index

THE CYBERNETICS
OF PREJUDICES
IN THE PRACTICE
OF PSYCHOTHERAPY

in alphabetical order
Gianfranco Cecchin
Gerry Lane
Wendel A. Ray

Foreword by
Bradford P. Keeney

Systemic Thinking and Practice Series

Series Editors
David Campbell & Ros Draper

London
KARNAC BOOKS

This edition first published in 1994 by
H. Karnac (Books) Ltd.
58 Gloucester Road
London SW7 4QY

British Library Cataloguing in Publication Data

A CIP catalogue record for this book is available from the British Library.

ISBN: 1 85575 056 2

Printed in Great Britain by BPC Wheatons Ltd, Exeter